DATE DUE

American University Studies

Series X
Political Science

Vol. 39

PETER LANG
New York • San Francisco • Bern • Baltimore
Frankfurt am Main • Berlin • Wien • Paris

William D. Pederson and
Norman W. Provizer, Editors

Great Justices of the U.S. Supreme Court

Ratings and Case Studies

PETER LANG
New York • San Francisco • Bern • Baltimore
Frankfurt am Main • Berlin • Wien • Paris

Library of Congress Cataloging-in-Publication Data

Great justices of the U.S. Supreme Court : ratings and case studies / William
   D. Pederson and Norman W. Provizer, editors.
     p. cm. — (American university studies. Series X, Political science ;
vol. 39)
   Based on conference held in Louisiana State University in Shreveport,
Nov. 15-16, 1990.
   Includes bibliographical references and index.
   1. Judges—United States—Rating of—Congresses.   2. United States.
Supreme Court—History—Congresses. I. Pederson, William D.
II. Provizer, Norman W.   III. Series.
[347.3073534] KF8744.G74   347.73'2634—dc20   92-40142
ISBN 0-8204-2066-2   CIP
ISSN 0740-0470

Cover Design by Geraldine Spellissy

The paper in this book meets the guidelines for permanence and
durability of the Committee on Production Guidelines for
Book Longevity of the Council on Library Resources.

© 1993, 1994 Peter Lang Publishing, Inc.

Printed in the United States of America.

Second Printing.

For

Norman and Peggy Kinsey

and

Samuel and Marion Fishman

Acknowledgments

The editors wish to express heartfelt thanks to the patient contributors—in particular to Henry J. Abraham, the keynote speaker at our conference on Great Justices of the U.S. Supreme Court. Each of us was a fellowship recipient from the American Political Science Association and the National Endowment for the Humanities. These fellowships enabled us to attend some of his exceptional seminars, so we can claim to have experienced a master teacher at work, in addition to reading his classics on the judiciary. Our special appreciation goes to Brenda J. Cox of Noel Memorial Library at LSU in Shreveport, who went far beyond the call of duty.

The Conference was made possible through the generosity of Norman and Peggy Kinsey, the founders of the American Studies program at Louisiana State University in Shreveport. Peggy Kinsey was the driving force behind Shreveport's leading role in observing the bicentennial of the U.S. Constitution from 1987 to 1991.

Table of Contents

Foreword

Louisiana State University in Shreveport was the first public institution of higher education in the state to be designated a bicentennial campus by the Louisiana Commission on the Bicentennial of the U.S. Constitution. It also produced the first written record designed to link the U.S. Constitution to the local level (Norman W. Provizer and William D. Pederson, eds., *Grassroots Constitutionalism: Shreveport, the South and the Supreme Law of the Land*, Lanham, MD: University Press of America, 1988).

Another primary activity of the LSUS campus has been to use its American Studies Fall Forum for dialogues on dimensions of American constitutionalism during the national 55-month commemoration (1987-1991) to observe the U.S. Constitution. Indeed, the nature of the annual Forums was slowly transformed during these years from a Thursday evening lecture series, to a two-day program with several speakers and, finally, evolving into the first national conference sponsored on the LSUS campus.

In 1989, the two-day program dealt with the Congress during its bicentennial anniversary. The focus was on congressional and presidential relations after 200 years, relations which some observers believe have resulted in the phenomenon of "divided government" that began in the South in the early 1950s. The proceedings from this conference were later published (William D. Pederson, ed., *Congressional-Presidential Relations: Governmental Gridlock*, Lewiston, NY: Edwin Mellen Press, 1991).

The present volume grew out of the first national conference held on the LSUS campus. It took place on November 15-16, 1990, and dealt with the issue of greatness on the U.S. Supreme Court. The presentations ranged from poll findings that tried to identify and confirm the greatest justices on the

U.S. Supreme Court, to case studies that explored the lives of individual justices. Except for Felix Frankfurter and perhaps Harlan Fiske Stone, the justices who typically rank as "greats" are covered in ten case studies. "Near greats" William Howard Taft and William O. Douglas are also included, as well as William Brennan and Lewis Powell whose places in history are still uncertain. Charles Evans Hughes receives treatment in two chapters because he has also been found to be among the "greats" of twentieth-century governors, as well as secretaries of state. In fact, he is the only American politician to receive these high ratings for the various positions that he held during his career.[1] The link between justices and presidents receives emphasis in the two Taft chapters and the chapter on Ronald Reagan's appointments to the Court.

Though the Conference did not try to reach a consensus on the nature of greatness on the Court, it furnished a local and national foundation to explore the continuing relevance of quality in judicial nominees. The material presented is a legacy of that effort.

William D. Pederson
Norman W. Provizer

---

1   William D. Pederson and Ann M. McLaurin, eds., *The Rating Game in American Politics*. (New York: Irvington Publishers, 1987).

Contributors

HENRY J. ABRAHAM was born in Germany in 1921. He received his Ph.D. in political science from the University of Pennsylvania in 1952. As the James Hart Professor of Government and Foreign Affairs at the University of Virginia since 1978, he has been named by the Commonwealth of Virginia as outstanding teacher in the social sciences and won the University's coveted Thomas Jefferson Award. Among his books are *Justices and Presidents* (1985), *The Judicial Process* (1986), *Freedom and the Court* (1988), and *The Judiciary* (1991). He acts as a consultant to the U.S. Senate Committee on the Judiciary and is a member of the Virginia Commission on the U.S. Bicentennial. Department of Government and Foreign Affairs, University of Virginia, Charlottesville, VA 22901.

WILLIAM D. BADER was born in Connecticut in 1952. A 1974 Phi Beta Kappa graduate of Vassar College, he pursued graduate studies in social psychology at Cornell University and in 1979, received his Juris Doctor degree from the Hofstra University School of Law, and now practices in the area of constitutional law. Between 1988 and 1990 he served as Attorney-Editor at West Publishing Company and was a major contributor to *Corpus Juris Secundum*, among other West publications, as well as guest lecturing extensively on constitutional issues at various law schools and medical schools. He has authored papers on constitutional history and jurisprudence and is currently working on a study of Justice Levi Woodbury with Prof. Henry Abraham.

ROBERT C. BRADLEY was born in Canton, Ohio in 1953. He received his Ph.D. in political science from the University of Kentucky in 1988, and has taught at Illinois

State University since 1982. His work has appeared in the *Justice System Journal* (1985), *Southern Illinois Law Journal* (1980), and *Courts, Corrections and the Constitution* (1990). Department of Political Science, Illinois State University, Normal, IL 61761-6901.

ROGER W. CORLEY was born in Brooklyn, New York in 1934. He received his Ph.D. in history from the University of Kansas in 1973, and has taught at Northwest Missouri State University since 1966. His research has been presented before the Organization of American Historians (1976), the Missouri Conference on History (1980), the Northwest Missouri State Behavioral Science Conference (1982), and he has received NEH fellowships in 1989 and 1984. Department of History, Northwest Missouri State University, Maryville, MO 64468-6001.

BRENDA J. COX was born in Shreveport, Louisiana in 1948. A Librarian, she received her M.L.I.S. from Louisiana State University in Baton Rouge in 1991. Her work has appeared in the *North Louisiana Historical Association Journal*. Noel Memorial Library, Louisiana State University in Shreveport, 71115-2301.

MICHAEL DUNNE was born in 1941. He received his Doctorate in American Studies from the University of Sussex, where he has taught since 1968. Among his many works are *Brighton on the Rocks* (1983), *The United States and the World Court 1920-1935*, (1988), and *American Foreign Relations Since the Second World War* (1990). School of English and American Studies, University of Sussex, Brighton, BNI 9QN, United Kingdom.

JAMES C. DURAM was born in Muskegon, Michigan in 1939. He received his Ph.D. in history from Wayne State University in 1968. His works include *Norman Thomas* (1974), *Soldier of the Cross* (1979), *A Moderate Among Extremists: Eisenhower and the School Desegregation Crisis* (1981), and *Justice William O. Douglas* (1981). He has taught at

Wichita State University since 1968. Department of History, Wichita State University, Wichita, KS 67208-1595.

SHERMAN G. FINESILVER was born in Denver in 1927. He was appointed to the Federal District Court in Colorado in 1971 and became chief judge on that court in 1982. He holds a J.D. degree from the University of Denver Law School and has been awarded honorary doctorates from several universities, including New York University and the University of Colorado. He is also an adjunct professor of political science at Metropolitan State College, Denver, CO 80217.

PATRICK GARRY was born in Fairmont, New Mexico in 1954. He received his Ph.D. in history from the University of Minnesota in 1986 and J.D. from the University Law School in 1983. His major works include *The American Vision of a Free Press* (1990), and *Rediscovering An American Creed* (1991), as well as articles in the *William Mitchell Law Review, Law and Society Review, Marquette Law Review, Law and Social Inquiry, Hamline Law Review* and the *Journal of Law and Religion.* 4901 Colfax Avenue South, Minneapolis, MN 55409.

RODNEY A. GRUNES was born in 1942 in Brooklyn, New York. A political scientist who received his Ph.D. from Duke University in 1972, he is the author of "Obscenity and the Justices" *Seton Hall Law Review* (1978); "Preferential Treatment and the Burger Court," *Southeastern Political Review* (1982); "Prayer in the Public Schools," *Politics and Policy* (1986); and "Creationism, the Courts, and the First Amendment" *Journal of Church and State* (1989); "Justice Brennan and the Problem of Obscenity" *Seton Hall Law Review* (1992). Department of History and Political Science, Centenary College, Shreveport, Louisiana, 71134-1188.

KENNETH M. HOLLAND was born in Charleston, South Carolina in 1948. He received his Ph.D. in political science from the University of Chicago in 1978. His works include *Writer's Guide: Political Science* (1987), *The Political Role of Law Courts in Modern Democracies* (1990). He has been a member and past chair of the Vermont Advisory Committee to the U.S. Commission on Civil Rights, and has taught since 1980. Department of Political Science, Memphis State University, Memphis, TN 38152.

F. THORNTON MILLER was born in Meridian, Mississippi in 1952. He received his Ph.D. in history from the University of Alabama in 1986. His publications have appeared in the *Virginia Magazine of History and Biography; The Proceedings and Papers of the Georgia Association of Historians*; and the *Encyclopedia of Historic American Court Cases, 1640-1990*. He has taught at Southwest Missouri State University since 1989. Department of History, Southwest Missouri State University, Springfield, MO, 65804-0089.

WILLIAM D. PEDERSON was born in 1946 in Eugene, Oregon. He is a political scientist who received his Ph.D. from the University of Oregon in 1979. He has received fellowships from the National Endowment for the Humanities (1981, 1985), the American Political Science Association (1983, 1989), and the Judicature Society (1984). He has taught international law at Westminister College (1980), and constitutional law at the University of South Dakota (1981). He is the editor of *The "Barberian" Presidency* (1989); *The Rating Game in American Politics* (1987); *Grassroots Constitutionalism* (1988); *Morality and Conviction in American Politics* (1990); *Congressional-Presidential Relations in the U.S.* (1991); the author of a variety of articles in journals (*Presidential Studies Quarterly; Social Science Quarterly*); books (*Dimensions of the Modern Presidency* (1981); *Glimpses of Shreveport* (1985); *Fifty American Political Orators* (1987); and encyclopedias (*Modern Encyclopedia of Russia and Soviet History; World Encyclopedia of Political Systems and Practices; Encyclopedia USA; Political Parties and Elections in the U.S.;* and *Encyclopedia of the U.S.*

Congress). Department of History and Political Science, Louisiana State University in Shreveport, 71115-2301.

BARBARA A. PERRY was born in Louisville, Kentucky in 1956. She received her Ph.D. in government from the University of Virginia in 1986. Her publications include *Unfounded Fears: Myths and Realities of a Constitutional Convention* (1989), as well as articles in the *Journal of Church and State, Journal of Law and Politics,* and *Law and Policy Studies.* She has taught at Sweet Briar College since 1989. Department of Government, Sweet Briar College, Sweet Briar, VA 24595.

MARGUERITE R. PLUMMER was born in 1929 in Center, Texas. A historian, she received her MBA and MA from Louisiana State University in Shreveport in 1987. Presently working on her doctorate at the University of Texas-Dallas, she is the author of articles in *Shreveport Magazine* (1982); *Grassroots Constitutionalism* (1988) and *Glimpses of Shreveport* (1985). Director, Pioneer Heritage Center, Louisiana State University in Shreveport, 71115-2301.

NORMAN W. PROVIZER was born in Boston, Massachusetts in 1944. A political scientist who received his Ph.D. from the University of Pennsylvania in 1974, he has received fellowships from the National Endowment for the Humanities (1976, 1981) and the Fulbright Program (1984). Formerly a research associate at the Foreign Policy Research Institute and a professor of political science at Louisiana State University in Shreveport, he is the editor of *Analyzing the Third World* (1978); *Grassroots Constitutionalism* (1988); the author of a variety of articles in *Tulsa Law Journal* (1977); *Journal of Political Science* (1986); *The Southern Quarterly* (1977); *Comparative Politics* (1979); *Journal of African Studies* (1975); *Multidimensional Terrorism* (1987); *Judicature* (1987); and *The Rating Game in American Politics* (1987). Department of Political Science, Metropolitan State College, Denver, CO 80217.

LINDA C. A. PRZYBYSZEWSKI was born in Evanston, Illinois in 1961. She received her Ph.D. in history from Stanford University in 1989. Her work has appeared in *Western Legal History*. She served as a Fellow at the Institute for Legal Studies at the University of Wisconsin — Madison, where she taught in the Law School. Department of History, University of Cincinnati, Cincinnati, OH 45221-0373.

HENRY B. SIRGO was born in New Orleans, Louisiana in 1951. A political scientist who received his Ph.D. from Florida State University in 1976, he has received a Harry S. Truman Library Grant, 1984; NEH Grants, 1982, 1986; and a NSF Chautauqua Grant, 1978. His articles have appeared in *Presidential Studies Quarterly* (1985); *Journal of Political Science* (1985); *McNeese Review*; and the *Proceedings of the Louisiana Academy of Science* (1977). Department of Social Sciences, McNeese State University, Lake Charles, LA 70609.

JOSEPH D. VIGIL was born in Denver in 1956. He received his MA in political science from the University of Colorado at Denver and is currently in the Ph.D. program at the University of Michigan.

Preface

What constitutes "greatness" in a jurist—or in any professional (or, for that matter, layperson)—is necessarily at least partly subjective. To a degree, the concept, the notion, of "greatness" arguably does lie in the eye of the beholder. Yet it would be a disservice simply to leave it at that: For (a) it *is* possible to identify certainly qualities that, taken together, may well meet the criteria of "greatness;" and (b) knowledgeable students of the Supreme Court have, in a series of ratings or rankings undertaken during the past four or five decades, achieved remarkable agreement as to the dozen or so among the 108 individuals who have served on the Supreme Court to date.

Regarding the latter, those viewed by the experts as "greats" are, in chronological order: John Marshall, Joseph Story, Roger B. Taney, John Marshall Harlan I, Oliver Wendell Holmes, Jr., Charles Evans Hughes, Louis D. Brandeis, Harlan F. Stone, Benjamin N. Cardozo, Hugh L. Black, Felix Frankfurter, and Earl Warren. Obviously, that dozen stars spans the proverbial ideological, jurisprudential, and political spectrum and at least some of them have drawn, and would continue to draw, strong dissent. Yet that dozen has appeared on almost every list authored by those who have made the study of the judicial process, in general, and the Supreme Court of the United States, in particular, their abiding interest and concern. Given their diverse background and personalities, what, then, may the dozen be said to have in common that served to earn their recognition as "great" Justices?

In general, they shared, in varying degree—and certainly not without exceptions—but by and large across the overall spectrum, the following ten components (cited in no particular order of perceived significance):

(1) Demonstrated judicial temperament;
(2) professional expertise and competence, including analytical powers;
(3) absolute personal moral and professional integrity;
(4) an able, agile, lucid mind;
(5) appropriate professional educational background or training;
(6) the ability to communicate clearly, both orally and in writing, and especially the latter—in other words, craftsmanship and technique;
(7) resolute fair-mindedness and impartiality;
(8) a solid understanding of the proper judicial role of judges under our written Constitution;
(9) diligence and industry;
(10) on-Court leadership ability.

To repeat the already-indicated reservation, strong dissents as to the total applicability of the ten criteria in each of the twelve jurists named as "great" are on record and defensible. A good many observers and commentators have challenged the inclusion of some of them; for example, the first Harlan and Earl Warren, because of their "judicial activist" commitment, which would seem to fly into the face of the assumptions underlying the eighth suggested criterion. Nonetheless, even if not all ten criteria are *ipso facto* apposite in each of the twelve instances, enough of them have consistently been perceived to be present by the experts to justify their inclusion in the "greatness" Pantheon.

Whatever one's view of the achievements of the dozen Supreme Court that have been accorded the evaluation and appellation of "greatness", they, along with many—although not all—among the other 96, deserve our regard and admiration. Their numbers testify to the rich mine of giants that have served so remarkably well on the Court in its now two centuries of life. They provide proof positive of promises fulfilled and achievements rendered. Indeed notwithstanding the often tiresome, and not infrequently self-serving—albeit exasperating—sniping that has characterized the Court's existence, sniping that has regrettably although not surprisingly, recently emanated most loudly from prestigious centers of learning located near bodies of water on both the East and West Coasts, it has generally been, in James Madison's hopeful plea, a "bench happily filled." His wish expressed in 1787, has in general stood the test of time admirably.

Henry J. Abraham
Charlottesville, Virginia

Who Are the Great Justices and What Criteria Did They Meet?

Robert C. Bradley

"I am very pleased to announce that I will nominate Judge Clarence Thomas to serve as associate justice of the United States Supreme Court. . . . And I believe he'll be a great justice. He is the best person for this position."

> President Bush
> Presidential News Conference
> July 1, 1991

"I believe that President Bush has nominated a stellar candidate to the Highest Court in the land. . . . There can be no doubt. Judge Souter has the legal acumen and ability to be a great Supreme Court justice."

> Senator Danforth
> Proceedings and Debates
> of the 101st Congress
> October 2, 1990

As the above statements illustrate, support for the Thomas and Souter nominations to the Supreme Court was based partly on the expectation that the nominees possessed the personal attributes and legal abilities to eventually become greats on the Court. Ultimately, legal historians, judicial scholars, interested Court observers, and the general public will determine if Justices Thomas and Souter should be classified as 'greats' and thus belong to a preeminent group of Supreme Court jurists. While preliminary assessments can be made about their Court behavior, it is still much too early to forecast accurately if either Thomas or Souter will fulfill the aspirations of their

Preparation of this chapter was supported in part by the College of Arts and Sciences at Illinois State University. I gratefully acknowledge the assistance of Brian Hamilton, a graduate student at Illinois State University, in the data collection.

supporters and be identified at some time in the future as great justices.

To gauge whether Thomas, Souter, or any of the other recent Court appointees will be regarded as great justices, a frame of reference would be quite useful; that is, a list of Supreme Court greats. While there is no dearth of such lists, the most recent of these lists was drafted in 1983 and it was a synthesis of four prior lists that had been made in the 1960s and 70s. While the author of the 1983 list claimed it was "the definitive list" (Hambleton, p. 464), numerous personnel changes on the Supreme Court in the last two decades plus the renewed concern about the selection process of justices initially generated by the Bork defeat and perpetuated by the Thomas affair make it worthwhile to determine whether this list remains unchanged at the outset of the 1990s.

The purpose of this chapter is to present a new list of great Supreme Court justices, which will be based on the responses to surveys administered to several groups, including judicial scholars, state judges, local attorneys, and prelaw students. In addition to identifying great justices, respondents were asked to establish a rank order among their listed 'greats'. Survey respondents were also asked to discuss the criteria used to identify and rank order a justice on the list of 'greats'.

In addition to providing a current list of Supreme Court greats, this chapter represents the first systematic effort to survey various groups either interested or directly involved with the legal system and discern any similarities or differences in their assessments of who should be classified as great justices. Also, this chapter presents the first survey findings detailing the criteria employed by different groups to make their identifications of great justices. Further, this chapter is the first time that a list of 'greats' has been rank ordered according to some set of criteria rather than just chronologically listed.

As indicated, previous lists of Supreme Court greats have been compiled and published. These have appeared sporadically throughout the Court's history partly because their authors encountered several formidable problems in devising the lists. Partly for the benefit of possible future list-makers, I will discuss some of the difficulties of composing a list of "great" justices, indicate reasons why these difficulties should not stop the process of devising such a list, and review the prior lists in some detail. After accomplishing these tasks, I will detail how the surveys were administered for this project and discuss the findings obtained from those surveys. Finally, I will conclude with some reflections on the survey findings and some general observations about the selection process for Supreme Court justices.

Difficulties of Compiling a List of Court 'Greats'

A significant obstacle to be overcome in making a list of Court 'greats' is the lack of "objective" standards of comparison between the justices. As Justice Felix Frankfurter pointed out, "Greatness in the law is not a standardized quality, nor are the elements that combine to attain it." (1957, p. 784) The quality of greatness on the Supreme Court seems to fall into that category of phenomena, such as obscenity, where a consensus on a definition is virtually impossible, but one knows it after seeing or experiencing it.

While a list of traits or abilities desireable in a justice can be developed, it is extraordinarily difficult to apply that list to specific individuals. Objective indicators with precise measurements for most of the items that would comprise such a list would be quite hard to formulate (Goldman, 1991, pp. 201-202). Or as David O'Brien contends, "any definition of judicial merit is artificial." (1990, p. 64). As a result, subjective evaluation rather than reliance upon agreed standards serves as the basis for distinguishing the 'greats' from their Supreme Court brethren. Both public and scholarly discourse on the subject of Supreme Court greats becomes difficult because individuals are using different subjective criteria to evaluate past and present members of the Court.

In compiling a list of Supreme Court greats, some deliberation has to be given as to whether current members of the Court should be considered. Even if current and recently retired justices are excluded, the composition of such a list means examining at least a century and a half of Supreme Court history. This poses another substantial difficulty in devising lists of Supreme Court greats. The business, functions, and status of the Supreme Court have changed dramatically since its inception (Congressional Quarterly, 1990, pp. 3-59). As Chief Justice Rehnquist recently observed:

> Yet despite its lack of the power of the purse or the sword, and despite its occasional retreat in the face of antagonistic popularly elected branches of government, the Court has grown steadily in prestige and authority throughout the two centuries of its existence. (1987, p. 311).

While this observation should come as no surprise to interested Court observers, it reflects that the duties of Supreme Court justices have also changed profoundly since the Court's opening session on February 1, 1790. It is quite difficult to draw meaningful comparisons between Joseph Story, Benjamin Cardozo, and Hugo Black who served on the Supreme Court at different points in time addressing dissimilar legal controversies under different caseload constraints.

Then, is an attempt at identifying the 'great' Supreme Court justices a fruitless endeavor? Do the difficulties outweigh the value of devising a list of great justices? The answer to both questions is no for at least a couple of reasons. First, the Supreme Court is a powerful force in our nation with the proven capacity to influence the welfare and behavior of the American public with its decisions. The power of the Court can be seen in its ability to override majority will by striking down acts of Congress, which was demonstrated in the recent invalidation of key portions of the Gramm-Rudman balanced-budget legislation, and in reminding all public officials, even the President, that no one is above the law. (Louthan, 1991, pp. 42-43). The Court can also have an impact on society's fundamental values, as reflected in its decisions on abortion, various religious practices and displays, obscenity, and the death penalty, and redistribute political power, as evidenced by its numerous reapportionment decisions. (Louthan, 1991, p. 43).

Oftentimes, the opinions and perspectives of a particular justice set the foundation for some of the Court's most important rulings, such as Marshall's pronouncement in *U.S. v. Burr* (1806) that a president could be subject to a court order,

Holmes' expression of the 'stream of commerce' concept in *Swift & Co. v. United States* (1905), or his 'clear and present danger' standard that was eloquently refined in his dissent in *Abrams v. United States* (1919). These standards, concepts, and tests impact on subsequent Court rulings for decades and are devised by justices, who are oftentimes later considered as Court greats partly on the basis of these immense contributions to the development of constitutional law and the authority of the Supreme Court. More generally in regard to the Court's policy-making process, Lawrence Baum, a noted Court scholar, comments, "the single most important factor shaping the Court's policies at any given time may be the identity of its members." (1992, p. 27).

The policy-making decisions of the Court are partly the product of the interaction between its members. Similarly to other small group decisional situations, members of the Court have opportunities to try to influence their colleagues. The justices differ in their desire to wield influence, and vary in possessing certain qualities and personality traits that help to determine interpersonal influence on the Court (Baum, 1992, p. 161). Presumably, a Supreme Court justice labeled as 'great' is one who possessed a high degree of those qualities and traits that are conducive to exercising influence on the Court.

As such, identifying great justices could contribute to our understanding of why certain issues were addressed by the Court in particular terms. In addition, an identification of Supreme Court greats could provide some insight as to why certain decisions or policies were rendered by the Court. As Baum relates, "a highly skilled justice has relatively great influence on the Court." (1992, p. 40)

Further, identifying the attributes associated with being a 'great' on the Supreme Court should be meaningful for the private and public actors who are involved in the selection of justices. If those who possess power in the nomination and confirmation of justices are interested in merit, then it would be prudent for them to discern the attributes that are perceived to be commonly held by Supreme Court greats (Abraham, 1985, p. 11). Specifically, presidents appear to have strong incentives to select individuals of high competence for

Supreme Court service. A candidate who does not possess a high degree of competence is likely to embarrass the president and may not be confirmed by the Senate (Baum, 1992, p. 40). Also, if a candidate is highly skilled, shares the president's policy goals, and is confirmed to become a member of the Supreme Court, then the president's impact on the Court is enhanced (Baum, 1992, p. 40). In fact, membership change has been identified as probably the most important source of policy change on the Supreme Court (Baum, 1992, p. 155).

A further reason for undertaking the task of identifying Supreme Court greats and their attributes is reflected in the prior efforts to list great justices. While the concept of greatness on the Court may not be subject to empirical standards, an examination of the previous rosters of great justices demonstrates the concept not only has meaning for interested Court observers but also that some consensus is present as to who are the 'greats' and what constitutes greatness (Abraham, 1985, p. 11). As John Frank, a Court scholar and former law clerk for Justice Hugo Black, succinctly pointed out in his book *Marble Palace*:

> "Choosing "great Justices" is a little like choosing pretty girls: there is considerable room for personal taste in the selection.   Nonetheless, there are certain commonly accepted estimates." (1958, p. 43)

It is to these "estimates" that I now turn. In discussing the prior lists of Supreme Court greats, I will indicate their similarities and differences, and indicate why another list is justified.

Prior Lists of Supreme Court Greats

As illustrated in Appendix A, there have been several efforts to list great justices. Over a considerable span of time, various individuals, such as Supreme Court justices, law professors, and court observers, have engaged in the task of developing lists of great American judges. While most of the lists are confined to members of the United States Supreme Court, others include state supreme court justices (Pound, 1938; Schwartz, 1979). Also, most of the lists are developed presumably by examining all the facets of judges' behavior, but there are a few that concentrate on a singular aspect of a judicial career, such as the issuance of dissents (Zobell, 1959; Congressional Quarterly, 1990).

The number of judges included on the lists varies considerably. For those lists that are not focused exclusively on dissent behavior, Justice Hughes compiled the shortest list including eight Supreme Court justices (1928), while Frank has the distinction of drafting the longest list of twenty-three great justices (1958). The average number of judges included in a list of 'greats' is just over thirteen. For lists of Supreme Court greats, the most common number was nine, reflecting an influence, as admitted by several list makers, from lists of great baseball players.

Apart from considerable variation in the size of prior lists, there are perhaps more meaningful distinctions to be made between the lists. For instance, different motives appear to have driven the authors of the lists. While most have indicated reasons for developing their lists, others appear to have no clear motive (Pound, 1938; Asch, 1971).

A motive that appears common to several of the list makers is questioning the value of prior judicial experience as a prerequisite for service on the Supreme Court. In a celebrated address at the University of Pennsylvania Law School, Justice Frankfurter argued that the skills and abilities developed while serving either as a state or lower federal judge are not applicable to the functions and responsibilities performed by Supreme Court justices. Specifically, Frankfurter contended that "the correlation between prior judicial experience and fitness for the functions of the Supreme Court is zero". (1957, p. 795)

To buttress his argument, Frankfurter developed a list of sixteen Supreme Court justices whom he considered to be preeminent. Of those justices, only six came to the Court with any form of prior judicial experience (Frankfurter, 1957, p. 785). From that finding, Frankfurter concluded:

"it would demand complete indifference to the elusive and intractable factors in tracking down causes, in short, it would be capricious, to attribute acknowledged greatness in the Court's history either to the fact that a Justice had had judicial experience or that he had been without it." (1957, p. 784)

In his book *Marble Palace*, John Frank also attempted to dispel the notion that prior judicial experience is an essential qualification for service on the Supreme Court. In attacking President Eisenhower's preference for Court appointees who had previous judicial experience, Frank stated "history proves that the best Supreme Court Justices are likely to be those who have not been judges before." (1958, p. 43)

In a similar fashion to Frankfurter, Frank supported his contention by developing a list of great justices who had served on the Court. In examining his list of 'greats', Frank found that the majority of them had no prior experience as either a state or federal judge (1958, pp. 43-44). Frank went even further by citing that many Court justices who had considerable prior judicial experience were notable failures (1958, p. 44). As final support for his argument, Frank pointed out that a list of eight outstanding justices developed earlier by Charles Evans Hughes included only two who had previous judicial experience (1958, p. 45). From this evidence, Frank concludes, however, that previous judicial experience is not necessarily an insurmountable barrier to greatness on the Court. The careers of Justices Oliver Wendell Holmes and Benjamin Cardozo provide ample proof that outstanding justices can come from lower courts (Frank, 1958, p. 43).

A more recent analysis done by two judicial scholars examined how the first ninety-six Supreme Court justices compared on the basis of their prior judicial experience. The results of that analysis clearly confirmed the notion that holding a prior judgeship had no bearing on the performance of a justice on the Court (Walker and Hulbary, 1978, p. 66). In fact, the justices who had the highest performance scores were those who had no previous judicial experience (Walker and Hulbary, 1978, p. 66). In light of Walker and Hulbary's results, previous judicial experience may have an adverse impact on a justice's Court performance.

A possible negative relationship between prior judicial experience and performance on the Supreme Court was explored in a study that appeared in the *ABA Journal* (Nagel, 1970). The findings of that study showed a much higher percentage of great justices had no prior judicial experience than those who did have that experience (Nagel, 1970, p. 958). A conclusion drawn from these findings stated that if great justices are desired for the Supreme Court then appointees should not be required to have prior judicial experience (Nagel, 1970, p. 959).

It may come as quite a surprise to recent presidents and their advisors, but prior service as a state or federal judge is no guarantee of great success on the Supreme Court. In considering future Court appointees, presidents should heed the message that prior judicial experience is not related, and is possibly an adverse influence, to superior Court performance. Due to the heavy reliance placed on track records established during prior judgeships, the import of this message seems to have been lost during the selection of recent justices. From the perspective of Frankfurter, Frank, and others, this is quite unfortunate for the achievement of greatness on the Supreme Court.

Apart from questioning the link between prior judicial service and Court greatness, lists of great justices have been compiled for a variety of reasons. Some appear to have been motivated primarily by the tradition of list making that exists in this nation (Currie, 1964; Hambleton, 1983). Loftier motives have compelled others. Hughes developed a list of 'greats' to support his argument that influence can be exercised by any member of the Court not just the Chief Justice (1928, pp. 57-58). Bernard Schwartz argued that changes in American law warranted a revision of the list of great American judges produced by Roscoe Pound in 1938 (1979, p. 407).

Another noteworthy difference between the various lists of great justices is the use of different criteria to identify particular justices as outstanding. While most indicated the criteria used for the inclusion of justices on their lists, there are some authors who did not (Pound, 1938; Blaustein and Mersky, 1972; Asch, 1971). When used, the criteria have ranged from the specific, such as frequency of dissent (Nagel, 1970), to the abstract, including prophetic vision (Currie, 1964) and affirmative approach to the judicial role (Schwartz, 1979). Generally, the criteria have emphasized the ability of great justices to distinguish themselves from their brethren due to their opinion writing, creativity, leadership, impact on the law, and intellectual capacities.

Despite the numerous differences between the lists, there are also some shared qualities. Virtually every list has been compiled according to the perceptions and feelings of the author of the list. The two exceptions are Hambleton's list (1983), and Blaustein and Mersky's (1972). To a large extent, Hambleton relied on the efforts of previous list makers to arrive at his list. He developed a roster of all-time 'greats' by choosing those justices who had been included the most frequently on four prior lists of great judges (Hambleton, 1983, p. 464). Unfortunately, Hambleton did not provide any rationale for his choice of these four lists, nor did he account for the fact that two of the lists included state supreme court justices thus reducing the number of Supreme Court justices mentioned on the four lists.

Blaustein and Merksy used the responses from their poll conducted in 1970 of sixty-five law school deans and professors of law, history, and political science to compile a list of twelve "great" justices. The participants in the poll were selected because they were presumed to be experts on the Supreme Court and its decisions (Blaustein and Mersky, 1978). The participants were asked to grade each of the first ninety-six justices as (a) great, (b) near great, (c) average, (d) below average, or (f) failure. Other than the grading instructions and a chronological list of justices, the participants were given no guidance as what criteria to use in grading the justices (Blaustein and Mersky, 1978, p. 37).

While the Blaustein and Mersky study is noteworthy for its use of a survey of experts, it is clearly dated. More than twenty years have passed since the poll was conducted. In addition, Blaustein and Mersky provided no specific indication as to how the poll results were used to compile the list of "great" justices. The study cited that John Marshall was the only justice rated great on all the ballots, that Brandeis and Holmes received sixty-two and sixty-one votes in the "great" category, and that Black was in fourth place with forty-two votes as "great" (Blaustein and Mersky, 1978, p. 40). There is no discussion as to how the other eight justices were included on the list of twelve "greats".

Another common feature of the different lists is the chronological listing of justices. Presumably, even among an elite group of justices substantive differences can be noted. Yet, even when the commentary by the list maker directly indicated that certain justices exhibited more greatness than others, that did not effect the order in which the great justices were listed.

For this study, I wanted to devise a list of great justices that would reflect a rank order according to some criteria of greatness, and not be just another chronological roster. In addition, I wanted to specify my method of including justices on the list so that others, if so inclined, could replicate the study in the future. My efforts to achieve both of these objectives will now be detailed.

Data Analysis

Data Collection

Adopting an approach similar to Blaustein and Mersky's, I decided to use the results from surveys administered to several groups to compile a list of great justices. In constructing the survey, I did not want my feelings and perceptions to possibly influence the responses. So I, as Blaustein and Mersky did in their study, gave no indication of the criteria to be used in the survey. As evident in examining a copy of the survey in Appendix B, the survey instructions told participants to use any criteria that they wished to employ to both identify and rank order great justices.

Intentionally, I designed the survey to be quite short and easy to complete. This was done to maximize the response rate. As such, I asked participants to respond to two questions. First, to list and rank order a maximum of ten great justices, and second, to discuss briefly their criteria used to respond to the first question. I decided on ten as a maximum number partly because of its use in prior lists and due to my feeling that a classification of greatness should be reserved for the top ten percent of a group. In a sense, my selection of ten was verified by the fact that only two respondents expressed any reservations about being limited to listing only ten great justices. Interestingly, a number of respondents in each survey group listed less than ten 'greats', some as few as five.

Instead of administering the survey only to those involved in academic pursuits concerning the Supreme Court, I decided to survey several groups who could be categorized as interested Court observers. In addition to judicial scholars, participants to my survey included state judges, local attorneys, and university undergraduate and graduate students taking law-related courses. I wanted to determine if a consensus existed among various groups as to who were the 'greats' of the Court and what criteria are used to identify the 'greats'.

Students in law-related courses were included primarily as a test group for the initial administration of the survey. In order to gauge the validity of the survey, students were polled in three courses: an undergraduate Honors course that focused on the First Amendment, an undergraduate constitutional law course, and a graduate seminar on judicial politics. The survey was also administered to a student audience of a mock trial that was sponsored by a university law club and a law fraternity. From these four settings, a total of one hundred and seventeen undergraduate and graduate students were surveyed. In addition to the previously discussed two questions, the student surveys included several questions related to students' academic backgrounds.

Satisfied with the face validity of the survey, two changes were made before mailing surveys to the other participants. First, the questions about academic background were deleted as being irrelevant to judges, attorneys, and scholars. Second, a chronological list of Supreme Court justices was attached to the survey. The list included all the justices who have served on the Court except for David Souter and Clarence Thomas. Souter and Thomas were not included on the list since they had not been nominated to the Court by the date of my project.

A total of 493 surveys were mailed to scholars, judges, and lawyers. Surveys were mailed to 221 scholars who were listed in the 1989 *Membership Directory* of the Law, Courts, and Judicial Section of the American Political Science Association. An additional 36 surveys were mailed to scholars listed in the 1988 *Membership Directory* of the Law & Society Association. Since neither the state nor county bar associations were willing to divulge their membership lists, the listing of attorneys in the telephone directory was used to obtain names and addresses of local attorneys for the survey mailing. A total of 115 surveys were mailed to local attorneys. Finally, a 1988 list by the Bureau of National Affairs of Illinois judges and the addresses of their courthouses was used to send surveys to 121 state and local judges. The judges were selected to give representation to the different court levels and geographic jurisdictions in the state.

Findings

Responses were excluded from the following tables when respondents indicated that either they objected or were otherwise unwilling to rank order the justices listed on their surveys. For example, the survey from the respondent who made the following observations was not included in the analysis.

> "I don't really view any justices as "great". Hence, I am unable to provide a list for your study. . . . I do consider some individuals as "great", e.g., Einstein, Beethoven, Bach, Picasso, Freud, etc."

There were a few returned surveys where the respondents claimed a lack of sufficient knowledge of the Court and its history to adequately reply to the survey's questions. Perhaps the most intriguing response on a survey that was excluded from analysis was one where the respondent wrote "Judge (XXX) is deceased. Thank you." To date, I am still trying to fathom what the 'thank you' was meant to imply.

To rank the justices, a simple scoring system was devised. Each justice was awarded points based on their listed position on the survey. For instance, if a justice was listed first, then he/she was given ten points. If the justice was listed second, then he/she was given nine points. This scoring system gave points in descending order through the remaining positions on the list. If a justice was not listed in the ten positions on the survey, then he/she received no points for that survey. The rankings reflected in the tables are based on the cumulative number of points a justice received from the included surveys.

Table 1 shows the results of the responses from 96 scholars. In comparison to the list of twelve 'greats' from Blaustein and Mersky's study, some differences can be observed. While Justices Story, Taney, Hughes, and Stone were included in the roster of 'greats' compiled by Blaustein and Mersky from their survey of scholars, they are not included on the list of great justices compiled from this study's survey results. In addition, Justices Brennan and Douglas appear on the current list of 'greats' in Table 1 while not making the roster in Blaustein and Mersky's study. In both lists, John Marshall emerged as the clear favorite for the top choice as a great justice. Almost eighty percent of the scholar respondents for the present study listed Marshall in the number one position on their surveys. Similarly to Blaustein and Mersky's work, Justices Holmes and Brandeis also do quite well on the surveys. Justice Holmes is the most common choice for both the second and third positions on the list, while Brandeis is the most common choice for both the fourth and sixth positions. Possibly reflecting the passage of time since Blaustein and Mersky's poll, Chief Justice Earl Warren does quite well on the current surveys as does Justice Brennan.

Table 1 The Great Justices According to Scholars

Rank	The Current List	Blaustein and Mersky's 12 'Greats'
1.	John Marshall	John Marshall
2.	Oliver Wendell Holmes	Joseph Story
3.	Earl Warren	Roger B. Taney
4.	Louis Brandeis	John Harlan I
5.	William Brennan	Oliver Wendell Holmes
6.	Hugo Black	Charles E. Hughes
7.	John Harlan I	Louis D. Brandeis
8.	William Douglas	Harlan F. Stone

Table 1 The Great Justices According to Scholars (cont.)

Rank	The Current List	Blaustein and Mersky's 12 'Greats'
9.	Felix Frankfurter	Benjamin Cardozo
10.	Benjamin Cardozo	Hugo Black
		Felix Frankfurter
		Earl Warren

A list of great justices compiled on the results of the surveys from judges is shown in Table 2.

Table 2 The Great Justices According to Judges

Rank	Justice's Name
1.	John Marshall
2.	Oliver Wendell Holmes
3.	Benjamin Cardozo
4.	Louis Brandeis
5.	Earl Warren
6.	Hugo Black
7.	Felix Frankfurter
8.	William Brennan
9.	William Douglas
10.	William Taft

While the response rate for scholars was good at a little more than forty percent for the survey, the response rate for judges was considerably lower. There were only fourteen surveys from judges that are included in the analysis. There were additional judges who returned surveys, but they were not included due to not ranking the justices. In fact, judges more than any other group of respondents were unwilling to rank order the justices on the survey.

As in Table 1, Marshall and Holmes finish first and second in a rank order of great justices according to Illinois state and local judges. After the first two positions, the rank order in Table 2 differs considerably from the Current List in Table 1. Justice Cardozo, who appears in the tenth position as a great justice according to scholars, is listed in the third position

according to judges. In comparing the two tables, there are
other differences of less magnitude in the listed positions of
the justices. For instance, Earl Warren is ranked lower by
judges than by scholars, and Felix Frankfurter is ranked
higher by judges than by scholars. In addition, Chief Justice
Taft was included in the roster of great justices by judges,
while they left out Justice Harlan I who was included in the
list by scholars.

A list of great justices according to local attorneys appears in
Table 3.

Table 3 The Great Justices According to Attorneys

Rank	Justice's Names
1.	John Marshall
1.	Oliver Wendell Holmes
3.	Louis Brandeis
4.	Benjamin Cardozo
5.	Felix Frankfurter
6.	Earl Warren
7.	William Douglas
8.	Hugo Black
9.	Roger Taney
10.	Joseph Story
10.	John Harlan II
10.	William Rehnquist

Examining Table 3 reveals that local attorneys have their
own roster of great justices, which is different than those compiled by either scholars or judges. Fortunately, the response
rate for local attorneys was about twice that of judges. There
were twenty seven surveys returned by attorneys that were
used to compile the list in Table 3. As in Tables 1 and 2, Marshall and Holmes appear at the top of the list in Table 3. In
contrast, however, to the lists devised by scholars and judges,
Chief Justice Marshall is not the clear favorite for the first
position according to local attorneys. Marshall and Holmes tie
for the top position in Table 3. Also, local attorneys included
a number of justices on their list of 'greats' who did not appear

on the lists in Tables 1 and 2, such as Taney, Story, Harlan II, and Rehnquist. The inclusion of Chief Justice Rehnquist marks the first appearance of one of the current members of the Supreme Court on a list of great justices in this study. Interestingly, Justice Brennan, who made it on the lists in Tables 1 and 2, did not make it among the ten great justices according to the survey results from local attorneys.

In regard to the inclusion of current justices on a roster of 'greats', students did this far more often than any other group of respondents.

Table 4 The Great Justices According to Students

Rank	Justice's Name
1.	John Marshall
2.	William Rehnquist
3.	Sandra Day O'Connor
4.	Warren Burger
5.	Earl Warren
6.	William Brennan
7.	Oliver Wendell Holmes
8.	Harry Blackmun
9.	Thurgood Marshall
10.	Hugo Black

The list in Table 4 reflects the results from eighty nine student surveys. For students as well as the other groups of respondents, John Marshall is the choice for the top of the list. After Marshall, the list of 'greats' for students as reflected in Table 4 is quite different than the lists in prior tables. For instance, three members of the current Supreme Court, Chief Justice Rehnquist and Justices O'Connor and Blackmun are included on the list of great justices. With the inclusion of recent retirees, Chief Justice Burger and Justices Brennan and Marshall, the list reflected in Table 4 is dominated by recent justices. Justices Brandeis, Cardozo, and Frankfurter, who were included by scholars, judges, and attorneys on their lists of great justices, do not appear on the list in Table 4. In addition, Justice Holmes, who is listed in either the first or second position in the other tables, is ranked seventh according to the student survey results. Perhaps more than a measure of greatness, the list compiled from student surveys reflects the name recognition of current justices for students.

Table 5 shows a list of great justices that is the product of combining the survey results from the four groups of participants.

Table 5 The Great Justices According to All Respondents

Rank	Justice's Name
1.	John Marshall
2.	Oliver Wendell Holmes
3.	Earl Warren
4.	Louis Brandeis
5.	Hugo Black
6.	William Brennan
7.	Benjamin Cardozo
8.	Felix Frankfurter
9.	William Douglas
10.	William Rehnquist

In comparing the various lists, Table 5 most closely resembles the list of great justices in Table 1, which was based on the results from scholars' surveys. Since scholars constituted the second most numerous group of respondents, this finding is not completely surprising. The impact of the most numerous group, students, is dissipated to some extent because their rankings are much more evenly distributed among the justices than the rankings by scholars. Students included names from a much larger group of justices on their surveys than did other respondents, and more frequently listed justices other than Marshall and Holmes in the top two ranks on the survey.

The justices listed in the first four positions in Tables 1 and 5 are identical. After those four positions, some differences appear in the two tables. The most obvious differences are that John Harlan I, who was listed in Table 1, is not included in Table 5, and Chief Justice Rehnquist, who did not make it among the ten 'greats' according to scholars, is included in

Table 5. More subtle differences appear in some shifting of the rankings of the justices from Table 1 to Table 5; for instance, Justices Black and Brennan switch positions, and Cardozo's position is higher.

The wide range of criteria used by survey respondents to identify a justice as 'great' is shown in Table 6.

Table 6 List of Criteria Mentioned by Respondents

Leadership on Court
Writing Ability
Judicial Restraint
Judicial Activism
Enhance Court's Power
Protection of Individual Rights
Length of Service
Impact on Law
Impact on Society
Intellectual/Legal Ability
Protection of Societal Rights
Dissent Behavior
Personal Attributes

As reflected in Table 6, clearly there is a variety of criteria used to establish a justice as 'great'. Many of the listed criteria are the products of combining specific comments on the surveys. For instance, when respondents discussed specific opinions to illustrate the writing style of a justice, those were incorporated in the criteria of writing ability. When specific comments about a justice, such as first female on the Court or exhibited perserverance, were written, these were incorporated into the criteria of personal attributes.

As might be expected from examining the different lists of great justices presented in the previous tables, the various groups of respondents use different criteria to identify the outstanding justices. Table 7 shows the most frequently cited criterion for each group of respondents which was discussed first on their surveys.

Table 7 Most Frequently Cited First Criterion for Different Respondent Groups

Respondent Group	First Criterion
Attorneys	Writing Ability
Judges	Writing Ability; Intellectual Ability
Scholars	Leadership; Impact on Law
Students	Writing Ability

Examination of Table 7 clearly reveals that writing ability is an important criterion in the selection of great justices. Three of the four groups of respondents listed writing ability most frequently as their first criterion for determining greatness on the Court. Interestingly, scholars did not mention writing ability as their first criterion very frequently. Apparently, scholars were more concerned with leadership and impact on the law as criteria for greatness.

Table 8 reflects that different groups of respondents use essentially dissimilar criteria for identifying great justices.

Table 8 Top Five Criteria for the Respondent Groups by Frequency of Mention

	Attorneys	Judges	Scholars	Students
1.	Writing Ability	Intellectual Ability	Intellectual Ability	Writing Ability
2.	Personal Attributes	Leadership	Writing Ability	Personal Attributes
3.	Protection of Individual Rights	Impact on Law	Leadership	Protection of Individual Rights
4.	Intellectual Ability	Writing Ability	Enhance Court's Power	Intellectual Ability
5.	Impact on Law	Length of Service	Impact on Law	Enhance Court's Power

Examination of Table 8 reveals differences as to how frequently certain criterion are mentioned on the surveys from the different groups of respondents, and whether certain criterion are mentioned at all. While both judges and scholars mention intellectual ability more often than any other criterion, intellectual ability is ranked fourth in regard to frequency of mention for both attorneys and students. Interestingly, the list of criteria in regard to frequency of mention is virtually identical for attorneys and students. The first four criteria most mentioned by attorneys are the same as those listed by students. Also, certain criteria mentioned frequently by both attorneys and students, such as personal attributes and protection of individual rights, are not mentioned frequently by either judges or scholars. In addition, the criterion of leadership, which is listed frequently by judges and scholars, is not mentioned frequently by either attorneys or students. Judges are the only respondents who use length of service very frequently as a criterion of greatness.

Conclusion

This study represents the first scholarly effort to assess whether different groups of interested Supreme Court observers use the same criteria to arrive at comparable lists of great justices. In addition, this study is the first attempt to develop a rank order of the 'greats' who have served on the Court. To achieve its ends, the study used the results from mail surveys to devise rosters of great justices and compile lists of the criteria most commonly used by respondents to identify certain justices as 'great'.

While almost universal agreement seems to exist that greatness has been exhibited on the Supreme Court, consensus is not present as to who are the great justices and what criteria identify greatness. Evidently from examining the preceding tables, greatness on the Supreme Court is in the eye of the beholder. While certain commonalities do exist among the different lists of great justices and the criteria used to determine greatness that were developed from the survey responses, there are also some differences. Clearly, John

Marshall is regarded as a 'great' among great justices. The same can be probably said for Oliver Wendell Holmes, and to a somewhat lesser degree for Louis Brandeis and Earl Warren. But what about Benjamin Cardozo, who is close to the top of the lists for both judges and attorneys, but barely makes it on the list for scholars and is not included on the list for students. Apparently, the identity of the evaluative group makes a difference as to who are selected as great justices.

Much the same can be said for the criteria used most frequently to identify the great justices. While writing and intellectual ability seem to be common criteria for the different groups, protection of individual rights is a criterion used frequently by only two of the groups, attorneys and students. Similarly, leadership appears to be a concern for two of the groups, judges and scholars, while not getting much attention from either attorneys or students.

Based on this project's survey results, what can be concluded about the definitive list of all time, all star, all era Supreme Court "greats" that appeared in 1983 and was essentially based on lists from the 1960s and 70s. The line up seems to have changed. Story, Hughes, and Taney have been sent back to the bench, while Brennan, Frankfurter, and Douglas are now out on the playing field joining the other regulars of Holmes, Marshall, Cardozo, Black, Warren, and Brandeis. If a substitution is necessary, then either John Harlan I or a relative newcomer William Rehnquist will be called for duty.

Finally, what does the future hold for the prospects of greatness on the Court. Unfortunately, the immediate future appears to be somewhat dismal. The Bork affair appears to have imparted a valuable lesson on presidents when they are considering nominees to the Supreme Court. If the nomination is to achieve Senate confirmation, then do not pick an individual who has written to create, refine, or support any concept or theory that is not considered to be in the mainstream of legal thought. In addition, presidents would be well advised to certainly not select someone who has expressed in writing any opinion on a controversial topic, such as abortion. Articles and opinions, especially those that are innovative or appear to be controversial, provide ample fodder for the opposition political party, interest groups, and the media to derail a nominee from selection to the Court.

Given the prevailing combative atmosphere surrounding the selection process for Supreme Court justices, the norm for nominees may be to select 'stealth' candidates about whom little is known or likely to be discovered due to a relative absence of a paper trail. Then how do either the president or the Senate discern the writing and intellectual abilities of these 'stealth' nominees? Nominees who are considered for the Court at least partly because their chances for confirmation are raised considerably by the paucity of their own authored works.

One wonders how some of the great justices in our nation's history would fare now in getting either nominated or confirmed to the Supreme Court. How would a Holmes do with his numerous forthright opinions issued on the Massachusetts Supreme Court? How would a Cardozo do with his numerous opinions issued on the New York Court of Appeals and his many writings commenting on the nature of the legal system? How would a Brandeis do with his record as an attorney of using innovative tactics to support oftentimes controversial positions on pressing social issues? The sad fact is it would be unlikely that any of these preeminent jurists would even be nominated to the Court due to their voluminous paper trails.

If the above scenario is valid, then what will happen to the idea that the Supreme Court is not only the highest court in the land but also constitutes a collection of the best legal minds in the country? Perhaps some substantial changes are in order to increase the focus of attention on Supreme Court nominees' legal skills and capacities rather than their abilities to surpass whatever prevailing litmus test is being promoted at the moment. If such changes are made, then additions will be made to future rosters of great justices. If no changes are forthcoming, then we may question in the future the relevancy of discussing greatness in the context of the Supreme Court.

Appendix A

Prior Lists of Great Judges

Author and Date: Charles Evans Hughes (1928)

John Marshall
Joseph Story
Benjamin R. Curtis
Samuel F. Miller
Stephen J. Field
Joseph P. Bradley
Horace Gray
David J. Brewer

Author and Date: Roscoe Pound (1938)

John Marshall
James Kent
Joseph Story
John Bannister Gibson
Lemuel Shaw
Thomas Ruffin
Thomas McIntyre Cooley
Charles Doe
Oliver Wendell Holmes
Benjamin Nathan Cardozo

Author and Date: Felix Frankfurter (1957)

John Marshall
William Johnson
Joseph Story
Roger Taney

Benjamin Curtis
John Campbell
Samuel Miller
Stephen Field
Joseph P. Bradley
Stanley Matthews
Edward White
Oliver Wendell Holmes
William Moody
Charles Evans Hughes
Louis Brandeis
Benjamin Cardozo

Author and Date: John Frank (1958)

John Marshall
William Johnson
Joseph Story
John McLean
Roger Taney
Benjamin Curtis
John Campbell
Samuel Miller
David Davis
Stephen Field
Joseph P. Bradley
Morrison Waite
John Harlan I
David Brewer
Oliver Wendell Holmes
William Moody
Charles Evans Hughes
Louis Brandeis
William H. Taft
George Sutherland
Pierce Butler
Harlan Stone
Benjamin Cardozo

Author and Date: George Currie (1964)

John Marshall
William Johnson
Joseph Story
Roger B. Taney
Samuel Freeman Miller
Joseph P. Bradley
Oliver Wendell Holmes, Jr.
Louis Dembitz Brandeis
Charles Evans Hughes

Author and Date: Stuart Nagel (1970)

John Marshall
William Johnson
Joseph Story
Roger Taney
Benjamin Curtis
John Campbell
Samuel Miller
Stephen Field
Joseph P. Bradley
John Harlan I
David Brewer
Oliver Wendell Holmes
William Moody
Charles Evans Hughes
Louis Brandeis
Benjamin Cardozo
Hugo Black
Felix Frankfurter
William Douglas
Robert Jackson
Earl Warren

Author and Date: Sidney H. Asch (1971)

John Jay
John Marshall

Roger B. Taney
Samuel Miller
John Harlan I
Oliver Wendell Holmes, Jr.
Louis Brandeis
Charles Evans Hughes
Harlan Fiske Stone
Benjamin N. Cardozo
Felix Frankfurter
Robert H. Jackson
Hugo L. Black
William O. Douglas
Earl Warren

Author and Date: Albert Blaustein and Roy Mersky (1972)

John Marshall
Joseph Story
Roger B. Taney
John Harlan I
Oliver Wendell Holmes, Jr.
Charles E. Hughes
Louis D. Brandeis
Harlan F. Stone
Benjamin Cardozo
Hugo Black
Felix Frankfurter
Earl Warren

Author and Date: Bernard Schwartz (1979)

John Marshall
James Kent
Joseph Story
Lemuel Shaw
Oliver Wendell Holmes
Benjamin Nathan Cardozo
Hugo Lafayette Black
Arthur T. Vanderbilt

Earl Warren
Roger John Traynor

Author and Date: James E. Hambleton (1983)

John Marshall
Joseph Story
Roger B. Taney
Oliver Wendell Holmes, Jr.
Benjamin Nathan Cardozo
Louis Dembitz Brandeis
Charles Evans Hughes
Hugo Black
Earl Warren

Prior Lists of Great Dissenters

Author and Date: Karl Zobell (1959)

William Johnson
Benjamin R. Curits
John Harlan I
Oliver Wendell Holmes

Author and Date: Congressional Quarterly (1990)

William Johnson
Benjamin R. Curits
John Harlan I
Oliver Wendell Holmes
Louis D. Brandeis
Benjamin Cardozo
Harlan Stone
Felix Frankfurter
William Brennan
Thurgood Marshall

Appendix B

Survey for Great Justices Project

Please take a few minutes to complete the survey. Thank you for your time and effort.

1. Using any criteria that you wish to employ and considering all the justices who have sat on the Supreme Court, list and rank order ten Supreme Court justices who you consider as great. You can refer to the attached *Chronological List of Supreme Court Justices*. You do not have to list ten justices but the maximum number of justices that can be listed is ten.

1. _____   6. _____

2. _____   7. _____

3. _____   8. _____

4. _____   9. _____

5. _____   10. _____

2. Please indicate briefly the criteria that you used to consider certain Supreme Court justices as "Great Justices". Also, please indicate the criteria that you used to rank the justices in the order that appears on your list.

References

Abraham, Henry J. (1985). *Justices and Presidents*. New York: Oxford.

Asch, Sidney H. (1971). *The Supreme Court and its Great Justices*. New York: Arco.

Atkinson, David N. (1975). Minor Supreme Court Justices: Their Characteristics and Importance. *Florida State University Law Review, 3*, 348-359.

Baum, Lawrence. (1992). *The Supreme Court* (4th ed.). Washington, D.C.: Congressional Quarterly.

Blaustein, Albert P., & Mersky, Roy M. (1972). Rating Supreme Court Justices. *ABA Journal, 58*, 1183-1189.

_____. (1978). *The First One Hundred Justices*. Hamden, Connecticut: Archon.

Congressional Quarterly. (1990). *The Supreme Court at Work*. Washington, D.C.: Congressional Quarterly.

Currie, George R. (1964). A Judicial All-Star Nine. *Wisconsin Law Review, 1964*, 3-31.

Frank, John P. (1958). *Marble Palace: The Supreme Court in American Life*. New York: Alfred A. Knopf.

Frankfurter, Felix. (1957). The Supreme Court in the Mirror of Justices. *University of Pennsylvania Law Review, 105*, 781-796.

Goldman, Sheldon. (1991). Federal Judicial Recruitment. In *The American Courts: A Critical Assessment*, eds., John B.

Gates and Charles A. Johnson. Washington, D.C.: CQ Press.

Hambleton, James E. (1983). The All-Time All-Star All-Era Supreme Court. *American Bar Association Journal, 69,* 462-464.

Hughes, Charles Evans. (1928). *The Supreme Court of the United States.* New York: Columbia University Press.

Louthan, William C. (1991). *The United States Supreme Court.* Englewood Cliffs, New Jersey: Prentice-Hall.

Nagel, Stuart S. (1970). Characteristics of Supreme Court Greatness. *American Bar Association Journal, 56,* 957-959.

Pound, Roscoe. (1938). *The Formative Era of American Law.* Boston: Little, Brown.

Rehnquist, William H. (1987). *The Supreme Court.* New York: William Morrow.

Schwartz, Bernard. (1979). The Judicial Ten: America's Greatest Judges. *Southern Illinois University Law Journal, 1979,* 405-447.

Walker, Thomas G. & William E. Hulbary. (1978). Selection of Capable Justices. In *The First One Hundred Justices,* eds., Albert P. Blaustein and Roy M. Mersky. Hamden, Connecticut: Archon.

Zobell, Karl A. (1959). Division of Opinion in the Supreme Court: A History of Judicial Disintegration. *Cornell Law Quarterly, 44,* 186-214.

Cases Cited

Abrams v. United States, 250 U.S. 616 (1919)

Swift and Company v. United States, 196 U.S. 375 (1905)

U.S. v. Burr, 25 Fed.Cas. 30 (1806)

John Marshall and the Foundations of Judicial Power

Norman W. Provizer

Primus inter pares is a term often used to convey the role played by the Chief Justice on the United States Supreme Court. But if the Chief Justice is "first among equals" on the Court, one Chief Justice stands out as truly first among the small band of 16 men who, through the course of American history, have occupied the only judicial position mandated by the Constitution. That man is John Marshall. And though he died a century and a half ago in Philadelphia, he is still known as "the great Chief Justice"—his stature undiminished by the passage of time.

Marshall was neither the first Chief Justice of the United States (that honor rests with John Jay) nor a man generally considered to be one of the nation's Founding Fathers. Yet he was one of the critical architects of the American political system as we know it today. "More than any other man, more than Washington or Jefferson or Lincoln," Fred Rodell wrote in his 1955 book, *The Nine Men*, "[Marshall] put flesh on the skeletal structure, the bare bones of the Founding Fathers' Constitution—and put it there to stay. Most of what he did to steer for his own times and chart for the future the main course of the country's development, economically, socially, politically, is with us yet . . . and in this fact lies the real mark and monument of Marshall's greatness."

The circumstances of Marshall's appointment give some indication of the scope of his achievement as Chief Justice. Following the election of 1800, lame-duck President John Adams found himself with a vacancy at the head of the Supreme Court. Oliver Ellsworth had retired, and Adams responded by selecting John Jay again to take up the reins of the Court. Jay, however, declined the appointment noting that the Court could not possibly "obtain the energy, weight, and dignity which were essential to its affording due support to the National government, nor acquire the public confidence and respect which, as the last resort of the justice of the nation, it should possess."

The office was then offered Marshall, the 45-year-old Secretary of State in the outgoing administration. Previously, Marshall had turned down an Associate Justice position on the Court. This time, however, he accepted the nomination and he officially took office on February 4, 1801, exactly one month before the transfer of presidential power to Thomas Jefferson.

Once on the Court, Marshall stayed for more than 34 years until his death on July 5, 1835—two months before his 80th birthday. During those years, Marshall set a course for the Court that moved it from its unsteady and uncertain role in American life to a position of power and prestige. Never again would anyone be able to turn down a seat on the Court arguing that it was an insufficient and insignificant institution on which to serve.

While Marshall succeeded in securing an independent and autonomous national appellate judiciary that could act as a force for the rule of law, he never confused that power and prestige with Court hegemony. He well understood that to be independent and autonomous, the Court had to function within limits, avoiding a direct connection to politics. According to G. Edward White's assessment in *The American Judicial Tradition*, Marshall's efforts in this regard produced "the distinctive blend of independence, sensitivity to political currents, and appearance of impartiality that has since constituted the challenge of excellence in appellate judging in America." He provided, in short, for the very genesis of the nation's judicial tradition.

Marshall was born on September 24, 1755 in what would soon become Fauquier County, Virginia. He was the first of 15 children born to Thomas and Mary Marshall (all of whom survived to adulthood). Thomas had grown up in Westmoreland County, where he was both a friend and neighbor to George Washington. The Marshall family moved to the western Virginia frontier where Thomas served in a variety of positions, including an agent for Lord Fairfax, a surveyor, county sheriff, a justice of the peace and a representative to the Virginia House of Burgesses.

The environment in which John Marshall grew up was one influenced by the church (he was an Episcopalian who developed opinions close to Unitarianism) and by the law. Though John did not receive an extensive formal education, his father (and the teachers he provided) gave the young Marshall a firm base of knowledge in history, literature, and the classics. At the same time, his physical surroundings among the mountains of the Virginia frontier gave him, in the words of Justice Joseph Story, a "robust and vigorous constitution which carried him almost to the close of his life. . . ."

John, like his father, was caught up in the winds of revolutionary war. After fighting against the British as a member of the Virginia militia, the young Marshall became a lieutenant in the Continental army. He served in New Jersey, New York, and Pennsylvania, as well as in Virginia. And during the trials of Valley Forge, he was referred to as the "best tempered man" in the camp.

Marshall soon joined George Washington's command group, and emerged as the deputy judge advocate and a captain. In late 1779, Marshall's enlistment expired and he visited Yorktown as an eligible bachelor. He caught the eye of young Polly Ambler. They were married in 1783 when Marshall was 27 and his bride almost 17. Over the years, the Marshalls would have 10 children and John would remain devoted to Polly until her death in 1831. Before his marriage, Marshall had spent six weeks (in 1780) attending William and Mary College where he studied law under George Wythe. While his notebooks contain a lot of doodlings concerning Polly, his performance during the term was sufficient to gain him entrance into the Phi Beta Kappa Society.

In the summer of 1780, he was admitted to the bar of Fauquier county with a license signed by Governor Thomas Jefferson—a distant relative who would become Marshall's major political and philosophical rival. John and Polly settled in Richmond and he began his development as a successful member of the bar. In 1782, Marshall was elected to the House of Delegates in the Virginia General Assembly (and served on the judicially-oriented Executive Council of that body). The year after he married Polly, he was reelected to the House of Delegates. Marshall was also elected to the Richmond city government and chosen as city recorder in 1785, as well as serving on the Hustings Court. He returned to the state legislature in 1787.

Despite his periodic service in legislatures, including Congress, Marshall was never captivated by the legislative branch of government. If anything, he tended to be disenchanted with the legislative process to which he was exposed. Still, his legislative activity reinforced his stature as an able and influential member of Virginia's elite.

Though Marshall was clearly a member of that elite (and a Mason), his paternalistic orientations remained untinged by aristocratic pretensions. He clothed his six-foot frame quite casually and never lost his amiable and informal personality. This casual attitude sometimes carried over to Marshall's work—much to the dismay of certain clients. If Marshall had tendencies toward disorganization (as well as a hint of laziness, according to the French observer La Rochefoucald-Liancourt), he nevertheless had vast talents that were widely recognized.

The true depth of those talents would soon be apparent as the United States prepared to discard the Articles of Confederation and to replace that document with a Constitution providing for greater national unity. In the Virginia Legislature, Marshall was involved with the structuring of the state ratifying convention that would decide the fate of the 1787 Constitution in Virginia. He was elected as a delegate to the convention from Henrico County which contained Richmond.

At that convention, the 33-year-old Marshall exhibited both the power of his thought and some of the ideas that would mark his tenure as Chief Justice. No matter how casual he might appear, Marshall's piercing eyes (often incorrectly described as being black) transmitted his seriousness of purpose. After Patrick Henry spoke against ratification, Marshall, an advocate of the Constitution, responded. He answered those who saw danger in the proposed national government by referring to the role of the judiciary in the new constitutional system. If the government "were to make a law not warranted by any of the powers enumerated, it would be considered by the judges as an infringement of the constitution which they are to guard. They would declare it void."

In getting the best of the exchanges with the anti-Federalists at the convention, Marshall showed the effectiveness of his analytical approach. Later Thomas Jefferson reportedly remarked that "You must never give (Marshall) an affirmative answer, or you will be forced to grant his conclusion." This backhanded compliment shows how well Marshall used logic and syllogistic reasoning—skills that would come to characterize so many of his court opinions.

After the ratification of the Constitution, there was talk of Marshall running for Congress. But he rejected this idea, just as he would reject appointments to be the U.S. Attorney for Virginia, the Attorney General of the United States and the Minister to France, all offered to him by the new Federalist administration of George Washington. Marshall seemed more interested in building his practice (and speculating in land) to provide security for his family than he was in official positions. He did, however, return to the Virginia Legislature and in 1795 became acting Attorney General for the state (though he had lost an earlier electoral bid for that office). Unlike other positions, these did not unduly interfere with Marshall's private pursuits.

As the leading Federalist in Virginia, Marshall's ongoing involvement in politics continued to build the tension between himself and Jefferson, the dominant anti-Federalist. In fact, Jefferson expressed his desire to be rid of Marshall by saying "I think nothing better could be done than to make him a Judge." That was exactly what would occur before too long, with results quite contrary to Jefferson's view that as a judge Marshall would be effectively silenced.

But before he was to don judicial robes, Marshall entered the vortex of international affairs. His stand on the controversial, pro-British Jay Treaty had been to avoid knee-jerk reactions and to call for an in-depth examination of all of the treaty's implications. A similar attitude would mark his brief tenure as one of a trio of commissioners sent to France by President John Adams. Marshall had earlier refused to be appointed the American Minister to France, though he later had second thoughts about that decision. This time the mission would be a temporary one and it would afford him the chance to be exposed to Paris.

He was 42 years old when he (along with a fellow Federalist, Charles Pinckney, and a Republican, Elbridge Gerry) became directly embroiled in the French connection to American partisan politics. The French (like the Jeffersonian Republicans) were angry over the Jay Treaty, and the purpose of the commission was to normalize relations between the United States and revolutionary France. The negotiations, however, never got very far. The commission soon became embroiled in the XYZ Affair. Three agents of Talleyrand, the French foreign minister, had suggested that amity between the United States and France could be purchased by a loan and bribes. The Americans refused, and only Gerry remained in Paris.

At home, the XYZ Affair produced outrage among Americans who believed the nation's honor had been offended. The outrage turned into war fever among the extreme Federalists who saw an opportunity to tar their Republican opponents with the brush of anti-French sentiment. Marshall, who had been involved in the affair, maintained a moderate stance and counseled against an avoidable war. Reason, not passion nor extreme partisanship, was Marshall's guiding light.

A similar approach was also evident when Marshall finally consented, at the urging of George Washington, to run for Congress in 1799. He was elected to the Sixth Congress by a narrow margin and during the campaign he had to square his Federalist affiliation with the unpopular Alien and Sedition Acts that had been passed by the Federalists to control the criticisms of their Republican opponents. He did this by expressing his opposition to the acts, while, at the same time, downplaying their significance. In reality, Marshall distanced himself from extremist Federalist thought without abandoning a fundamentally Federalist perspective.

In Congress, Marshall voted against his "party" on changes in the Sedition Act. He also rose to defend Adams when the president was under attack from extreme elements within the Federalist camp. In 1800, the president appointed Marshall the Secretary of War. He was confirmed for that post, but never served in that capacity. For three days after the confirmation, Marshall was nominated to be Secretary of State. While Marshall had asked Adams to withdraw his nomination as Secretary of War, he accepted the appointment as Secretary of State.

He served in that position for less than a year—until the end of the Adams administration. During that brief period, he was also nominated and confirmed as Chief Justice. Thus, for several weeks, Marshall was both a cabinet official and Chief Justice (though he did not draw his cabinet salary during that time). During his first 45 years, Marshall had established himself as an actor of some significance on the still-young American political scene. If his career had ended with the Republican victory over the Federalists in the election of 1800, Marshall would have been, at least, a footnote in American political history. That, however, did not happen. He went on for more than 34 years as Chief Justice, establishing the independent judicial power of the Supreme Court and thereby shaping the course of American politics and securing a prominent position in the nation's history.

As Chief Justice, Marshall quickly capitalized on the potential of his position. Recognizing, for example, that the Court's place in the American system of government would be enhanced if it spoke as an institution, he ended the practice of issuing opinions *seriatim*. In other words, instead of the Justices individually offering their views on a case, there would now be an opinion of the Court written by one of its members. Institutional identity was needed if the Court as an institution was to capture its rightful, proper and independent role in the still new system of constitutional government.

Though in no way an advocate of unlimited centralization, Marshall was convinced of the need for federal supremacy in order to have an effective state and an orderly society based on the rule of law. As a soldier at Valley Forge, he had witnessed first hand the costs that accompanied the absence of central authority. As a Federalist, he saw in the Constitution a solid foundation for the establishment of such authority, but that foundation would have to be protected from erosion and rein-forced to withstand attacks. A guardian was required to insure the survival of the Constitution and the rule of law. And logi-cally, that guardian should be the federal judiciary.

The challenge facing Marshall was to translate this vision into a concrete reality. For this task, he was uncommonly well suited. Marshall combined an attractive and engaging per-sona—reflecting modesty as well as self-confidence—with an incisive mind and astute political judgment. This combination enabled him to become the dominant voice on a Court that was not without other prominent members. Of the 1,006 indi-vidually written opinions produced by the Court during Marshall's tenure, the Chief Justice authored 519—and he was in the position of a dissenter in a constitutional matter only once in 1827. There would be dissents from Marshall's hold-ings (notably by Justice William Johnson). Still, the Chief Justice's ability to transform his vision of the Court into a standard to be followed by all of its members was remarkable. While Marshall was not alone on the Court, he was then as he still is today (in the words of James Bradley Thayer's 1901 essay on Marshall) "first with no one second."

The list of Marshall decisions that occupy a critical place in the development of America's constitutional system is exten-sive, including the classic quartet of: *Marbury v. Madison* (clearly establishing the principle of judicial review in 1803); *McCulloch v. Maryland* (emphasizing national supremacy and a broad perspective on congressional power in 1819); *Dartmouth College v. Woodward* (protecting property rights against state actions through the Constitution's contract clause in 1819); and *Gibbons v. Ogden* (providing a comprehensive view of inter-state commerce and the primary role of the national govern-ment as the regulator of that activity in 1824).

In his portrait of Marshall for *The Justices of the United States*, Herbert Johnson refers to *McCulloch* as the Chief Justice's most significant decision (a perspective that is widely shared), while *Marbury* appropriately is labeled his "most artful in terms of political acumen" and *Gibbons* as his most "encyclopedic state-ment of the law." In addition to the classic quartet, there was also *Barron v. Baltimore* (which limited the application of the Bill of Rights to the federal government in 1833), *Cohens v. Virginia* (reaffirming the Supreme Court's power to review judgments by state courts in 1821), *Fletcher v. Peck* (combining the contract clause with the theme of natural rights in 1810) and a host of lesser known but nevertheless important decisions.

This is not to say that Marshall or his judicial opinions are beyond criticism. The surface logic of *Marbury*, for example, covers a leap of faith regarding the role of the judiciary in governing, and its specific conclusion relative to the facts of the case (dicta aside) is unnecessary. Yet the power of Marshall's often repeated words—"It is emphatically the province and duty of the judicial department to say what the law is"— defines a core value in a system operating under rules, rather than whim. In *McCulloch*, the Chief Justice reminds us that ". . . courts are the mere instrument of the law, and can will nothing" and then proceeds to will an expansive view of national power. ("Let the end be legitimate, let it be within the scope of the Constitution, and all means which are appropriate, which are plainly adapted to that end, which are not prohibited, but consistent with the letter and spirit of the Constitution, are constitutional.") The seeming contradiction reconciled, quite properly, by Marshall's insistence that, "we must never forget it is a Constitution we are expounding." To expound is to interpret, and to perform that function the Court, by necessity, must occupy that grey area which is less than pure will, but more than a mechanical instrumentality of the law.

Only by understanding both the imperatives of judicial activism and the requirements of judicial restraint, could Marshall firmly establish the foundations of judicial power. In this sense, Marshall was a master blender, mixing together often conflicting principles with practical considerations—and presenting the results with compelling, if not always impeccable logic.

In *Marbury*, he hit Jefferson's weak flank while avoiding a no win and therefore potentially disastrous confrontation. Marshall not only picked his battles carefully, he also comprehended the importance of distinguishing law from politics if the rule of law were to survive. Right after *Marbury*, Marshall's Court would allow the Jeffersonians to eliminate the separate Court of Appeals judgeships created by the 1801 Judiciary Act. In 1805, Marshall, himself, was a very restrained defense witness during the Senate trial of impeached Justice Samuel Chase. The ardent Federalist Chase was not removed from the Court and another cautious step toward a truly independent judiciary was taken. Two years later, Marshall (as part of his circuit duties) presided over the treason trial of Aaron Burr in Richmond. Again, the Chief Justice exhibited skills so crucial in developing the supremacy of law doctrine. While exercising care in dealing with presidential claims of executive privilege, Marshall did not shy away from issuing rulings and excluding evidence that moved the jury toward its not guilty verdict. Jefferson's response, not surprisingly, was anger aimed at Marshall. Yet, in looking at the Burr trial, it is Marshall's standards linked to the rule of law—and not Jefferson's passion and pursuit of Burr—that are most compelling.

George Haskins, a coauthor of the second volume in the *History of the Supreme Court of the United States* series, points out that, "One reason for the success of the early Marshall Court in proclaiming a rule of law free from the intrusion of politics . . . was that by attending to its business in a lawyer-like fashion the Court began to win the respect of important people in the Republican camp." Marshall was thus the critical architect of the constitutional system not only because of his proclamation of principles, but also due to his abilities in putting those principles into practice. The result of his vision and his talents has been aptly summarized by the concluding comment found in an essay by Charles Curtis in *Supreme Court and Supreme Law*: "What we owe to Marshall is the opportunity he gave us of combining a reign of conscience with a republic."

This is not to deify Marshall. By contemporary standards, the fact that he sat on the *Marbury* case would raise more than a few eyebrows since it was the failure of Secretary of State John Marshall to insure the delivery of Marbury's commission that set the scene for the historic opinion. Even more questionable was Marshall's secretive publication, under pseudonyms, of third-person defenses of his *McCulloch* decision.

Later in his career, Marshall's holding in the Cherokee Nation case of *Worcester v. Georgia* (1832) produced the remark attributed to President Andrew Jackson by Horace Greeley, "John Marshall has made his decision. Let him enforce it." Whatever the ethical merits of the decision, this was the kind of direct confrontation Marshall traditionally tried to avoid. Here he failed. In fact, during his last years in the Court (1831-1835), Marshall's influence declined in general. He began anticipating retirement in 1828, but stayed on convinced that President Jackson (who represented more popular democratic, rather than republican principles) would undermine the grand edifice of the Court and the supremacy of law with Marshall's replacement. In 1831, Marshall underwent surgery in Philadelphia to remove kidney stones. While he apparently recovered from that problem, within three years he developed an enlarged liver that led to his death in 1835.

Marshall's fear that his vision of the rule of law would not survive was unfounded. For just as the Court had captured its Republican members (rather than the other way around) even after they had become the majority in 1811, so too would the firm foundation Marshall established continue to support the ongoing development of an independent judiciary after his passing. What he had created would not die with him.

Though Marshall was a man who enjoyed his leisure time and his annual vacations in the mountains of Virginia, he did manage a few added activities beyond his duties as Chief Justice. From 1805 to 1807, he published a five-volume biography of George Washington that enjoyed some commercial success. This aided Marshall in meeting payments on his Fairfax land speculation. Overall he was unhappy with his effort at biography and the practical problems encountered. Later, Marshall served as a member of the Committee of Vigilance to defend Richmond. In 1823, he became president of the Richmond auxiliary of the American Colonization Society (an organization that dealt with the slavery problem by encouraging a black return to and colonization of Africa). Like his opposition to reforms for increased religious freedom and church-state separation in Virginia and his disinterest in broad universal suffrage, Marshall's ability to live with slavery is a fact that does not add to his reputation for greatness. In the context of the times, however, his were understandable sins. And to Marshall's credit, he did, at least, see the dangers contained within the practice of slavery for the South and the nation.

In 1829, he was elected to serve in the convention convened to revise the Virginia Constitution. A fellow delegate writing on that convention noted Marshall's talent for distilling "an argument down to its essence." Throughout his career, on and off the bench, this talent characterized Marshall's analysis of issues, and helped the cogent and compelling statements for which he was (and still is) known.

The scope of Marshall's abilities led Justice Oliver Wendell Holmes to say "that if American law were to be represented by a single figure, sceptic and worshipper alike would agree without dispute that the figure could only be but one alone, and that one John Marshall." In his extensive, four-volume biography of Marshall published during the second decade of the 20th century, Albert Beveridge found Marshall "so surpassingly great and good" that he almost seemed divorced from mankind. Yet, as Holmes pointed out, admiration for Marshall is not limited to his worshippers. For even the most sceptical of his critics have tended to concede that Marshall, during his tenure (one of the longest in Court history), earned the title of "the great Chief Justice."

Marshall may have lost the only case he argued before the Supreme Court as a lawyer (*Ware v. Hylton* in 1796), but he won a world after he joined that Court. He was a Federalist with an interest in the protection of private-property rights. Yet to concentrate on such labels is to simplify Marshall's contribution, and by so doing distort it beyond recognition. Marshall's vision would never have taken hold, if such simple labels truly captured its essence. John Randolph, who admired Marshall's mind much more than he did the Chief Justice's opinions, once said in frustration over Marshall's reasoning, "wrong, all wrong, but no man in the United States can tell why or wherein." Such was the towering presence of this man who, through principles and practice, carved out a tradition that has endured for the ages. Little wonder, ex-president John Adams, called Marshall's appointment "The proudest act of his life."

Bibliography

Marshall's Writings

Adams, John S. (ed.). *An Autobiographical Sketch by John Marshall* (Ann Arber: University of Michigan, 1937).
Information on Marshall's early years written by Marshall.

Gunther, Gerald (ed.). *John Marshall's Defense of McCulloch v. Maryland* (Stanford: Stanford University Press, 1969).
Contains nine essays that appeared in response to criticisms of McCulloch decision. Written by Marshall under the pseudonyms of A Friend to the Union and A Friend to the Constitution.

Johnson, Herbert A. *The Papers of John Marshall*, Vol. 1 (Chapel Hill: University of North Carolina, 1974).
Covers the period of 1775 to 1788 in terms of Marshall's papers and correspondence.

Marshall, John. *The Life of George Washington* (Philadelphia 1805-1807).
Marshall's multi-volume examination of Washington and the early years of the republic.

Mason, Frances N. (ed.). *My Dearest Polly: Letters of Chief Justice Marshall to His Wife* (Richmond: Garret and Massie, 1961).
Offers insights into Marshall's personal life.

Roche, John P. (ed.). *John Marshall: Major Opinions and Other Writings* (Indianapolis: Bobbs-Merril, 1966).

Books on Marshall

Baker, Leonard. *John Marshall: A Life in Law* (New York: Macmillan, 1974).
A long and informative biography that is nonacademic in tone and style, yet makes extensive use of manuscript sources.

Beveridge, Albert. *The Life of John Marshall* 4 vols. (Boston: Houghton Mifflin, 1916-1919).
The classic Marshall biography with a distinct anti-Jefferson bias. Provides much of the information used by later works, though several of the perspectives offered have been reevaluated and called into question.

Corwin, Edward S. *John Marshall and the Constitution* (New Haven: Yale University Press, 1921).
An overview written by one of America's most noted constitutional authorities.

Faulkner, Robert K. *The Jurisprudence of John Marshall* (Princeton: Princeton University Press, 1968).
Focuses on Marshall as a liberal in the tradition of John Locke.

Haskins, George and Herbert Johnson. *History of the Supreme Court of the United States*, Vol. II, Foundations of Power: John Marshall, 1801-1815 (New York: Macmillan, 1981).
Part of the Holmes devise series. Is especially useful for discussion of the separation of politics from law under Marshall.

Johnson, Herbert A. "John Marshall" in Leon Friedman and Fred Israel (eds.). *The Justices of the United States Supreme Court*, Vol. 1 (New York: Chelsea House, 1969).
Solid profile, with representative opinions by the associate editor of the Marshall papers.

Jones, W. Melville (ed.). *Chief Justice John Marshall: A Reappraisal* (Ithaca: Cornell University Press, 1956).
    A useful collection of 10 interpretive essays that contains several distinguished articles.

Kurland, Philip (series ed.). *John Marshall* (Chicago: Chicago University Press, 1967).
    Contains James Bradley Thayer's 1901 monograph on Marshall, as well as essays by Oliver Wendell Holmes and Felix Frankfurter.

Kutler, Stanley I. (ed.). *John Marshall* (Englewood Cliffs: Prentice-Hall, 1972).
    Brief essays and excerpts by and about Marshall, including a lean autobiographical account of Marshall's pre-court days.

Rhodes, Irwin. *The Papers of John Marshall: A Descriptive Calendar*, 2 vols. (Norman: University of Oklahoma, 1970).
    A valuable guide to Marshall's writings.

Servies, James A. *A Bibliography of John Marshall* (Washington: U.S. Commission for the Celebration of 200th Anniversary of the Birth of John Marshall, 1956).
    Contains a year-by-year listing of Marshall's writings, opinions, and letters and a section listing both historical and more contemporary writings on Marshall.

White, G. Edward. *The American Judicial Tradition* (New York: Oxford University Press, 1976).
    Chapters on Marshall and the genesis of the tradition and on the tradition and the future offer thoughtful perspectives on the great Chief Justice.

Joseph Story's Uniform, Rational Law

F. Thornton Miller

Joseph Story, like John Marshall, was a nationalist who believed that the Constitution and federal government, especially the judiciary, acted as strands that tied the nation together; and he worked to fulfil the powers of the federal judiciary as set out in the Constitution. "Nothing can better tend to promote the harmony of the States, and cement the Union (already too feebly supported) than an exercise of all the powers legitimately confided to the General Government, and the judicial power is that which must always form a strong and stringent link. It is truly surprising and mortifying to know how little effective power now exists in this department." Yet, *Swift* v. *Tyson*, one of Story's most significant judicial opinions, was later overturned by the Court. Did the basic constitutional problem lie in the original opinion or in the *Swift* doctrine that later developed? Louis Brandeis, in his opinion in *Erie Railroad Co.* v. *Tompkins*, which overturned *Swift*, believed the former. It was not the specifics of the case but the legal philosophy behind *Swift* that was suspect.[1] *Swift* revealed the law professor and commentator who preferred a scientific, rational, and uniform law. It revealed the opponent of state sovereignty—most famous for *Martin* v. *Hunter's Lessee*—who found a way to circumvent the barriers to the development of the nation erected by the Jacksonian state righters. It also revealed the Federalist—despite his appointment by James Madison—who believed that, for the American nation, there was an American law. His nationalism was not generally accepted after the Era of Good Feelings, and his national law was later rejected by the Court. In both, he proved to be adverse to the diversity inherent in a vast federal system. What appeared rational to him, and what he reasoned was proper for the law and judiciary of a nation, was not necessarily what the Constitution had authorized.

Story joined a federal judiciary that had, from its conception, been constrained by the Judiciary Act of 1789. The Anti-Federalists had hoped that, if the Constitution was ratified, state courts would have jurisdiction over and could form their own interpretation on questions pertaining to the Constitution. The supremacy clause, Article Three, and the Judiciary Act of 1789 made this possible. If the state courts had jurisdiction over areas that touched upon the Constitution or federal law—despite the recourse of appeal into the federal courts through Section Twenty-Five of the Judiciary Act of 1789—Anti-Federalists believed this would act to check the federal courts, and Story agreed: that was exactly what happened. In fact, nothing infuriated him more than watching litigants have to seek through the state courts matters touching a general concern and coming under the Constitution or federal law. He stated: "No court of the United States has any general delegation of authority 'in all cases in law and equity arising under the Constitution, the laws of the United States, and the treaties made, or to be made, under its authority.'" Even the officers of the federal government had in many instances to move through the state courts to enforce the United States law. Is it not incredible, he asked, "that the United States will submit all their own rights, and those of their officers to the decisions of State tribunals?" Doing so violated the trust, integrity, and dignity of the federal government.[2]

Story, again like Marshall, envisioned America becoming a great nation. The federal government would have to have more power vis a vis the states in order for this to happen. "If we are ever to be a great nation, it must be by giving vital operation to every power confided to the Government, and by strengthening that which mingles most easily and forcibly with the habits of the people. I hold it to be a maxim, which should never be lost sight of by a great statesman, that the Government of the United States is intrinsically too weak, and the powers of the State Governments too strong; that the danger always is much greater of anarchy in the parts, than of tyranny in the head." To achieve his nationalist goals, he argued like the Federalists during the 1790s who defended the power of Congress to incorporate the Bank of the United States as a power inherent in all sovereign governments. Thinking in broad and rational terms, Story not only tried—like Marshall —to use the Constitution to build the nation, he asked what powers the judiciary of a nation should have, by definition, instead of what kind had been prescribed by the Constitution and by Congress.[3] His objectives led to a direct confrontation with the state courts. Along the way, he shared with Marshall some judicial antagonists, such as Spencer Roane of the Virginia Court of Appeals, encountered particularly through the Fairfax litigation.

This litigation involved two sets of land disputes in Virginia involving the British Fairfax family: land confiscated by Virginia and, after the Revolution, land that was being escheated by the state (a process reverting property to the state where no one is entitled to inherit). The confiscated land was sold by the state, setting off a land boom. (One of the purchasers was David Hunter.) The Fairfax family hoped to sell the land that was being escheated, and a syndicate headed by Henry Lee and John and James Marshall were interested in purchasing it. The Marshalls, who were the American attorneys for Denny Martin Fairfax and the British Fairfax family, handled both sides of the land dispute litigation, one challenging the sell of the confiscated Fairfax land and the other defending the claim of the Fairfax family to the land being escheated which the Marshall syndicate wished to purchase. John Marshall, while a member of the Virginia General Assembly, managed to work through a compromise. In an act passed by the state legislature, known as the Compromise of 1796, the Fairfax family deeded to the state the land that had been confiscated and the state ceased the escheat actions against the remaining Fairfax land, allowing the sale to the Marshall syndicate to go through. The deal gave the Fairfax family 20,000 pounds sterling, cleared the titles of all the Fairfax land the state had sold, (including David Hunter's,) and put the Marshall syndicate in possession of some of the choicest land in Northern Virginia. Not all questions were settled, however. The biggest issue left outstanding was rents, the status of back rents unpaid, and all the various rents, including quit rents, that had once been collected by Lord Fairfax as the proprietor of Virginia's Northern Neck. The Marshalls tried to gain these rents and found themselves embroiled in continuous litigation.[4]

The Marshalls wanted their claims founded not on the Compromise of 1796, because it made no mention of rents (and which could be repealed reopening the escheat proceedings), but the proprietor's title secured by the Treaty of 1783 and the Constitution. But, they needed to arrange a suit that would get around the Compromise of 1796, because any new case would come after the passage of that legislation. This was the context for the continuation of *Hunter* v. *Fairfax's Devisee* which had apparently ended in 1796, but had not been struck from the docket of the Virginia Court of Appeals. The suit was continued through hearings, decisions, and appeals to *Martin* v. *Hunter's Lessee* not by the state, because the status of the confiscated land was no longer in dispute, (or by David Hunter, who had no major interests involved after 1806, when he sold the land that was the subject of the controversy,) but by the Fairfax-Marshall side. They hoped that the judges of the Court of Appeals would not go beyond the record of the original state district court case to include the compromise.[5]

In *Hunter* v. *Fairfax's Devisee*, the Court of Appeals ruled against the Fairfax-Marshall side refusing to bar the Compromise of 1796 and entering it upon the record. By the compromise, the disputed land was deeded to Virginia in exchange for the state's allowing Fairfax to sell to the Marshall syndicate the land that was being escheated. The Marshalls had failed to sidestep the compromise. They also suffered an attack from the bench by Spencer Roane. He declared that, in the Compromise of 1796, the Fairfax-Marshall side had agreed to give up one half of the old proprietary domain, their claim to what had been confiscated, to get the other half, what the Marshall syndicate was buying, and now, they sought to throw out the compromise agreement to gain the whole. He contended that the state had never needed to work out a compromise. The British property could be taken within the power of the sovereign state of Virginia, and was unaffected by either the Treaty of 1783 or the Constitution.[6]

From the Marshalls' perspective, the Court of Appeals was becoming hostile to their interest. They appealed to the Supreme Court which ruled in their favor in *Fairfax's Devisee* v. *Hunter's Lessee*.[7] Due to his personal involvement, Marshall did not officially participate. Story gave the opinion of the Court. He ignored the Compromise of 1796, part of the record of the appeal from the Court of Appeals—which was contrary to Section Twenty-Five of the Judiciary Act of 1789—and went beyond the record to include the Jay Treaty. Finally, he made a pronouncement upon the common law of Virginia.[8]

The case was appealed to the Supreme Court in accordance with the Constitution and Section Twenty-Five of the Judiciary Act of 1789: because a question had been raised concerning the Constitution, treaty, or federal statute. Yet, Story's opinion was not based upon a construction of the Constitution, treaty, or federal statute, or a conflict between Virginia law and federal law. He ruled that Virginia's highest court had erred in determining the common law. An assertion of his view of an American common law, he was claiming that the Court was supreme in deciding state common law— though this was not expressly authorized by either the Constitution or an act of Congress. Story determined that Virginia had not properly confiscated the Fairfax land. Also, the state could no longer legally escheat any of it due to the Jay Treaty. This gave the Fairfax-Marshall side the right both to the land that had been confiscated and the land—previously being escheated—that was sold to the Marshall syndicate. The Marshalls finally received a solid judicial basis for their rights and claims to lands and rents under federal treaty.[9]

This decision was ample proof that Patrick Henry and the Anti-Federalists had been correct back in 1788 when they warned Virginians that federal judges could not be trusted to safeguard their interests against foreigners and would allow the reestablishment of the feudal Fairfax domain. They did have the consolation of knowing, however, that most of Story's opinion made for little more than poor federal-state relations.

In the law, it was irrelevant in that it gave to the Fairfax-
Marshall side a right to land that had been deeded to the state.
The Compromise of 1796 had been agreed to by all parties,
the legislation had not been reviewed and declared unconstitutional, and was still in effect. Story could have founded the
Fairfax-Marshall title originally in the treaties and the
Constitution, and then marked out how and to what extent
their compromise with Virginia had affected their title.
Instead, he ignored what was part of the record of the appeal
and awarded land that had long been deeded away. As a
result, Story's opinion appeared improper, anachronistic, and
high-handed. On the last point, he lectured Roane on the
value of due process of law as a protection for individual
rights.[10] Of course, confrontation between the federal and
state courts was part of Story's goal. And it was now Roane's
and the Virginia Court of Appeals' turn.

The judges of the Court of Appeals questioned a number of
points in Story's opinion. A good amount of the litigation
concerned state common law (neither touching upon the
Constitution, treaties, or federal statute) and no valid federal
jurisdiction could be claimed regarding it. They denied
Story's claim to be able to decide upon state common law.[11]
They contended that he had illegally discarded the
compromise legislation from the record of the appeal. And his
opinion was faulty in that the treaty that related to the issues
in the 1780s and early 1790s was the Treaty of 1783, not the
Jay Treaty.[12] There was a problem, also, in how the Virginia
court should comply with the ruling. Was it to return land to
Fairfax that had been deeded by him to the state? The
Virginia judges took the decision and Story's opinion as little
more than a challenge, and they intended to respond.[13]

The Court of Appeals raised the question: as the highest
state court, having made a final decision in a common law suit,
in *Hunter* v. *Fairfax's Devisee*, would they accept a reversal of
that decision by the Supreme Court through an appeal—
Fairfax's Devisee v. *Hunter's Lessee*—brought under Section
Twenty-Five of the Judiciary Act of 1789? The constitutionality of the section—and the appellate jurisdiction it authorized
—was the main point at issue in *Hunter* v. *Martin, Devisee of*

Fairfax. The basic problem they found in Section Twenty-Five was the interconnection of the federal and state governments in a way that violated dual sovereignty and went against the spirit of the Constitution. It allowed the Supreme Court to act as a final court of appeals for a state judiciary even regarding state common law. The two systems of government should be kept separate. If a party in a suit considered the United States Constitution, treaty, or statute to be involved, then this federal question should be placed before the federal judiciary at the commencement of the litigation. There should be no appeal from the state's highest court to the Supreme Court. Such an appellate power meant that, even in suits determined by state common law, the Supreme Court could send reversals back through the state courts to be carried out. After reviewing Section Twenty-Five of the Judiciary Act of 1789, the Virginia Court of Appeals declared it unconstitutional. Neither the Supreme Court's jurisdiction to hear *Fairfax's Devisee* v. *Hunter's Lessee* was recognized nor its reversal of the decision in *Hunter* v. *Fairfax's Devisee*.[14] The Court of Appeals denied that the Supreme Court alone determined the law of the land throughout the United States.

Roane, in his opinion, questioned whether federal judges should oversee the state judiciaries. Was there any doubt as to the ability of state judges or their sense of justice or impartiality in the law? Why had the Constitution obliged all state judges to swear an oath to uphold it unless state courts would have concurrent jurisdiction with the federal courts on constitutional matters?[15]

The Supreme Court responded, in *Martin* v. *Hunter's Lessee*, by upholding both its decision in *Fairfax's Devisee* v. *Hunter's Lessee* and the constitutionality of Section Twenty-Five. Story wrote the opinion of the Court. The problems that had been raised concerning Section Twenty-Five were dismissed. The Court did not act directly upon the states. When a case was appealed from a state court to the Supreme Court, and it was reversed, a state supreme court would be requested to see to having it executed or the Court would see to the execution itself. There would not be an attempt to compel the state judiciary to act. Also, Story defended the section using an historical argument. Since it had been acquiesced in by Congress, the Supreme Court, and the state judiciaries for twenty-five years without a challenge, it should be accepted as a proper means to establish appellate jurisdiction. The Court dismissed the distinction between a final appeal and a removal of a case from a state court at the commencement of the litigation. Both were applications of appellate power. It did not matter when an appeal was made to the federal judiciary, in the beginning, middle, or end of the litigation.[16]

Story defended appellate jurisdiction by citing the supremacy clause in the Constitution and by stressing the need for uniformity. Story knew that judges "in different states, might differently interpret a statute, or a treaty of the United States, or even the constitution itself." He states, therefore, without an "authority to control these jarring and discordant judgements, and harmonize them into uniformity, the laws, the treaties, and the constitution of the United States would be different in different states, and might, perhaps, never have precisely the same construction, obligation, or efficacy, in any two states." He believed that the "public mischiefs that would attend such a state of things would be truly deplorable. . . ." Story also attacked concurrent jurisdication on federal law by answering Roane's rhetorical questions. Yes, the drafters of the Constitution did expect that local prejudice and interests would bias the decisions of state judges detrimental to the good of the nation. State courts could not be entrusted with carrying out a federal supreme law of the land.[17]

Finally, Story refused to accept the objection that the Supreme Court should only decide questions of how to construe the Constitution, treaty, and federal statute, and not questions of state common law. Once the Court's jurisdiction was established—in the Fairfax cases by the relation to treaty—the Supreme Court did not have to distinguish between state and federal questions but could decide upon all of the questions on the face of the record of the case before them.[18]

Having declared that there must be one ultimate appellate court, the Supreme Court did not return the case to the Virginia Court of Appeals. This was wise, because, as in *Marbury*

v. *Madison*, the Court knew it could not have enforced a reversal. As matters stood, however, two courts had asserted their final opinions, and no single rule of law had been established. This litigation revealed the problem that the Supreme Court had in checking the states through its appellate jurisdiction. In the *Martin* case, the Court upheld Section Twenty-Five and set a constitutional law precedent for nationalism but failed to secure Virginia's compliance with its decision. The Court affirmed the original judgement of a state district court (at Winchester, Virginia) in favor of the Fairfax claims, but nothing came of this, and, therefore, this part of the litigation ended without the Supreme Court's ruling affecting the actions of the state.[19]

In terms of the law in Virginia, because the Supreme Court and the Virginia Court of Appeals had each made a decision, much depended on which one the state lower courts followed. They chose the state's highest court. This meant that the Supreme Court's decision, in practice, was null and void. It also meant that the Marshalls' personal involvement in the litigation would continue. And, in common law suits involving the former Fairfax lands, the claims based on a federal treaty were not recognized, which kept open the status of the rents (because this was not mentioned in the Compromise of 1796). For the Marshalls, there was little to be gained in appealing another case to the Supreme Court as long as the state judiciary remained uncooperative.[20]

Martin — or at least its outcome — was frustrating for Story and Marshall. Direct confrontation with the states, or having to move via Section Twenty-Five appeals through the state courts, allowed the state courts to thwart and undermine the rulings of the federal judiciary. It involved just the kind of diversity in America's judicial system that infuriated Story. He was discouraged by the decline of nationalism after the Era of Good Feelings. He and Marshall were concerned about the state-rights doctrines advanced by Roane and the Virginia Court of Appeals which became popular in Virginia and were spreading to other parts of the South and West. Marshall believed it was a return of Anti-Federalism, a desire to return to the Confederacy of the 1780s or to dismember the union, and Story agreed. The Constitution of the United States, Story wrote to Marshall, is "a frame of government and not a petty charter granted to a paltry corporation for the purpose of regulating a fishery or collecting a toll." If the state-rights constitutional doctrines "prevail, in my judgement there is a practical end of the Union." Story prayed "that the Supreme Court will continue fearlessly to do its duty." He began this duty, to defend the Constitution against these new doctrines, with his opinion in *Martin*. During the era of the Jacksonians and the Taney Court, he could only hope that *Martin* would become a nationalist precedent, and that, eventually, his nationalism would prevail over state rights.[21]

Story had, perhaps, forced the differences in the Fairfax litigation to achieve a confrontation over the issue of state rights. It can be said that he was trying to take the high ideological plane. Or, it can be said that, indeed, he only took the high ideological plane. He moved at a theoretical level delivering an opinion with little substance in the facts and law of the case. The abstract quality about his nationalist opinions in the Fairfax litigation is interesting given his preference for law that was rational and scientific.[22] His ideas on the common law as a science complemented his belief that nationalism and the common law could be joined, that the latter could be a force to serve the former, and that there was one American common law. He had assumed a federal common law jurisdiction in the Fairfax cases. The common law would provide a way to resolve the problems faced by the Court in *Martin* not being carried out. Story's ideas and opinions on a federal common law, which coalesced twenty-six years later in *Swift* v. *Tyson*, pointed to a way to bypass the state courts. *Swift* was brilliant, because, by not directly challenging the states, Jacksonians failed to notice its potential threat to state courts. While *Martin* was met by an uproar of opposition and was never carried out, *Swift* was carried out, and, in time, became the basis for the national law of America, the federal common law.

The federal common law issue had been brought to the forefront, in 1798, when the Jeffersonian Republicans criticized the Federalists for claiming that the Sedition Acts were an improvement on the English common law. Did that mean

there was a federal common law? The Republicans vehe-
mently denied there was. They contended that the common
law was brought to America from England during the colonial
period.   It was modified by the statutes of the colonial
legislatures and by the colonial courts' constructions of the
law.   The common law developed separately in each colony,
and, after 1776, each state. There was no general common law
that existed apart from the state governments. The lack of a
federal common law was not altered by the Constitution or by
the First Congress in the Judiciary Act of 1789. All federal law
was derived from the Constitution, treaties, and the statutes of
Congress. This was accepted by the Marshall Court in *United
States* v. *Hudson and Goodwin*. On this issue, the Court calmed
the Republican state righters. The Jeffersonians believed that,
if there was a national common law, separate from any grant
by the Constitution or Congress, then, first, the federal courts
could lay claim to a vast jurisdiction, like the English courts,
and, second, this law would be supreme over state common
law in the federal courts in each state.[23]

The analogy of the states and counties shows the problem
the Republicans faced. The state courts had appellate jurisdiction over the county courts, and the full jurisdiction of the
common law limited only by a state's constitution, legislature,
and the United States Constitution. There was not a separate
common law for the counties and one for the states. There
was only one legal realm in each state. Republicans were
afraid that even if a federal common law was restricted by the
Constitution and modified by Congress, there would then be
one American common law, one American legal realm, and
that, as common law cases were appealed to the federal judiciary, the state courts would become similar to county courts in
states, merely a lower level of courts within the same legal
realm, with one common law, determined by the highest court
of that realm. If there was an American common law, it would
be determined by the Supreme Court. The Federalists could
then achieve in the judiciary what they had failed to do in the
other branches: to subvert America's federalism by reducing
the states to the status of counties.

Despite Republican protests to the contrary, the Federalist justices who had upheld the Alien and Sedition Acts had thought there was a federal common law, and Story agreed with them. Although the common law brought to America from England had been modified by each colonial legislature, the principles remained the same as in England. In its fundamental nature, there was one common law. Thus, after 1776, there was an American common law, and, after the ratification of the Constitution, there was a federal government that could use it.[24] But, Congress did not authorize a federal common law, and the Marshall Court did not assume it. Story would find a way to establish it, instead, through his construction and application of the common law as a rational and scientific law.

"In truth, the common law, as a science, must be for ever in progress; and no limits can be assigned to its principles or improvements." "It is its true glory, that it is flexible, and constantly expanding with the exigencies of society; that it daily presents new motives for new and loftier efforts; that it holds out forever an unapproach[able] degree of excellence; that it moves onward in the path towards perfection, but never arrives at the ultimate point." These ideas were not commonly shared. Many who were afraid of a federal common law also were opposed to just such a scientific and constantly progressing law. Story's whole view of the law as rational and scientific, progressing toward perfection, and improving society, was the framework for *Swift*.[25]

Story set out his guiding principles in his "Inaugural Discourse" upon accepting the position as professor of law at Harvard. He stated that law was founded on reason. Most fundamental was the law of nature; then in importance was the law of nations, or international law; then equity. He acknowledged that many a common lawyer dreaded these kinds of law separate from the common law as being the law of lords, arbitrary and tyrannical. But he saw such law as "almost uniformly rational and just in its conclusions." He most admired the rules in the common law that could as easily be found in Rome, Paris, London, and Washington.[26]

It is interesting to compare him with his Southern, Republican judicial antagonist in the Fairfax litigation, Spencer

Roane. Story, in contrast to Roane, wrote commentaries on the law showing the scientific way to understand the common principles of the law. Roane was a judge of customary law who believed there were great principles, but did not see himself as expounding a rational system of law founded on those principles. Story's line of thought led to a single, rational law that science could discern, through commercial and international law, the law of nations, to the law of nature, of nature's God. He emphasized the international and commercial law, and equity and Roman law. Roane lived in a world where the law of nations and international law rarely applied. He was a provincial common law judge who opposed the use of the law as an agent of change to reform society or for economic development. He saw the law as a protection of individual liberty, property rights, and the interests of localities and the states in the federal system. Law, for Roane, was a negative, defensive, or protective force. He did not share Story's more positive and progressive vision — and, in fact, opposed legal reforms in his home state of Virginia. Roane was a defender of state sovereignty and separate legal realms for each state. Story was an expounder of a federal common law.[27]

Story found his general system for a federal common law in the commercial and maritime law. "[T]his part of our jurisdiction . . . is the golden chain, which connects the nations of the earth, and binds them together in the closest union. It comes home to every man's business . . . and is commendable for its sound morals, its flexible adaptations, and its enlightened policy. Much of its excellence, it must be admitted, is the growth of modern times." England was almost the last to receive this custom of the sea, sanctioned as law on the Continent. "The old common lawyers repelled it with a sullen inhospitality and indifference." England caught up with the Continent and now shined in this kind of law. England's "commercial law has attained a perfection, order, and glory, which command the reverence of the whole world." The rules of the customary commercial law were generally followed by all nations engaged in commerce. In England, and the American states, they had become a new and growing part of the common law.[28] Story had only to apply them in the federal courts.

Section Thirty-Four of the Judiciary Act of 1789, which governed common law trials in the federal courts, stated that "the laws of the several states, except where the constitution, treaties, or statutes of the United States shall otherwise require or provide, shall be regarded as rules of decision in trials of common law in the courts of the United States in cases where they apply." In most legal areas, where the common law varied from state to state, there was no question about how the federal courts were to proceed. But, in deciding a question in commercial law, where federal and state judges drew upon the same principles, were federal judges to be bound by the decisions of state judges? Story answered in the negative. He implemented his ideas in cases in the circuit court in admiralty and commercial law, and, finally, almost unnoticeably, set down his reasoning in an opinion of the Court, in *Swift* v. *Tyson*.[29]

Swift v. *Tyson* began as a dispute involving an investment company in New York and land speculators in Maine. Joseph Swift sued George W. Tysen, based on diversity of citizenship, in the Federal Court for the Southern District of New York.[30] At issue was whether or not a bill of exchange could satisfy a preexisting debt. No New York statute related to the subject, but, by the state's common law, there were grounds for restricting payment of a bill of exchange if elements of fraud were involved. The federal district court, following New York law, ruled against Swift, who appealed to the Federal Circuit Court for the Southern District of New York. Again, the court followed New York law and Swift lost. He appealed to the Supreme Court. Swift's lawyers, which included Daniel Webster at one point, argued that where there was an absence of state statute, on cases to be determined by the generally accepted rules of commercial law, federal judges were not bound by state common law. The word "law" in Section Thirty-Four of the Judiciary Act of 1789 was interpreted as referring only to state statute and state judicial construction of state statute, and not to common law rules laid down by a state court.[31]

Story wrote the opinion of the Court. He affirmed the new interpretation of Section Thirty-Four. Federal judges were not bound by state common law where the general principles of commercial law were used by them and state judges alike, and where a state had not passed statutes on the subject. Section Thirty-Four did not apply "to questions of a more general nature, not at all dependent upon local statutes or local usages of a fixed and permanent operation, as . . . especially to questions of general commercial law, where the state tribunals are called upon to perform the like functions as ourselves, that is, to ascertain, upon general reasoning and legal analogies, what is the true exposition of the contract or instrument, or what is the just role furnished by the principles of commercial law to govern the case." He stated, with "instruments of a commercial nature, the true interpretation and effect whereof are to be sought, not in the decisions of the local tribunals, but in the general principles and doctrines of commercial jurisprudence." This was "not the law of a single country only, but of the commercial world." *Swift* established a federal common law specifically in commercial law.[32]

There was no state-rights opposition to this Taney Court decision. After all, the Court did not declare a general federal common law, and, in commercial law, in common law suits, the federal courts would follow state law when statutes pertained and would follow a state court's construction of those statutes. This would actually have allowed states to pass statutes modifying the commercial law and restricting the actions of federal judges in federal district courts in their state. But, how would it be in the interest of a state to have its commercial law different from most other states and foreign countries engaged in commerce? That would seriously discourage commercial activity with the state. The general acceptance of *Swift* shows that Story was probably correct in believing that a federal, commercial common law well served most state and business interests.[33]

Swift had two dimensions. First, it embodied the ideas of the day involving commercial law. Second, it secured a foothold for Story's old Federalist view that there was an American common law. The decision did not appear to be revolution-

ary. Indeed, if it had, Jacksonians would have rejected it.
Story had bided his time and finally had made his common
law theory the law. In the end, the common law, as a growing,
rational, and scientific law, had won. And Story, having
achieved his goal, did not envision any harm resulting from it.
But, once established, could the new federal common law
remain specifically limited to the commercial law set down in
Swift?

The federal common law did not challenge the states
through the 1840s and 1850s. There was, however, a problem
which would develop into a long running controversy. If a
general law existed separate from the statutes of Congress and
the statutes and common law of the states, then would the federal judges be able to show restraint in using it? The attempts
of the Taney Court to base the new law on the Constitution —
so that it would not be a general, unchecked, usurpation of
power — only created another problem. Because the Constitution was superior to state law, the new common law could be
interpreted as also being superior to state law. The way was
paved for the Court to move beyond the bounds of state
statute. Also, what could bar the Court from moving beyond
commercial law? A nationalist Court and Congress, during the
Civil War and Reconstruction period, and pressure from the
rising national corporations, would press this development
toward its logical conclusion.[34]

Congress expanded diversity jurisdiction to include cases
where local prejudice might work against a plaintiff, and
creditors and corporations purposely established businesses, or
worked through associates, in other states to secure diversity
jurisdiction. Businessmen and their lawyers favored a transformation of *Swift*. They argued that the common law was a
general law that existed separate from territorial sovereigns,
and that, when interpreted by the Supreme Court, there was a
single American common law. These arguments were slowly
accepted by the Court. The development of the new *Swift* doctrine — which was endorsed by the American Bar Association —
was completed by 1887 in *Bucher* v. *Cheshire Railroad Co*. The
extent of federal jurisdiction was increased in two ways. First,
if the general common law was used in both state and federal

courts, because the federal government was superior to the states, federal courts were not bound by state statute. States only created problems by maintaining a law different from that of the federal courts. Second, what had begun as an exception, a commercial law, had become general. Far from being the rules of how to construe commercial contracts and negotiable paper, this federal common law encompassed torts, bonds, and over twenty other doctrines.[35]

It can be said that Story only intended *Swift* to establish a commercial federal common law. But, he had been an advocate of the establishment of a general federal common law as well. The first stage of the development of *Swift* then, in becoming a general common law, simply brought about what he had hoped the Court or Congress would have done from the start. After the Civil War, the growing *Swift* doctrine continued to serve two of his goals: increasing the power of federal courts vis a vis state courts, and building the nation.

Where would the process end, however? Would the general common law continue to expand while centralizing power, as the Jeffersonian Republicans had believed it would? Individual or state rights had been their major concern, and, in the late nineteenth century, the rights of noncorporate interests were added. The Jeffersonian Republicans had not shared Story's vision of a uniform, scientific law expounded by federal judges, that would unify America into a nation, and build the economy. They were afraid of the consequences of a law of science and reason wielded by the federal judiciary. What were the limits of reason? What would check a court with a law understood through reason and with the force of the common law? If the Constitution and Congress had not authorized the Court to develop either a federal common law or a commercial law of reason, then would the Constitution act as a check upon that Court? If not, in entering a realm without limits, the Court would be moving beyond America's constitutionalism.

The *Swift* doctrine continued to expand, and, because states enacted statutes to regulate corporations, there was a growing divergence between federal and state common laws. The resulting phenomenon, with two common laws in each state, allowed for forum shopping. Corporations could bypass state law through diversity jurisdiction. More than the state courts, the federal judiciary tended to support creditors against debtors, and corporations against regulation, labor, and liability claims. In the late nineteenth century, the Court and the *Swift* doctrine were criticized for political reasons by various groups from Populists to Progressives, and, for purely legal and constitutional reasons from within the legal profession.[36]

Justice Oliver Wendell Holmes, who built a reputation on his dissents, contended in *Black and White Taxicab and Transfer Co.* v. *Brown and Yellow Taxicab and Transfer Co.* that each state had drawn upon and modified the English common law and had developed its own law through statute and court opinions. There was no other law, abstract and transcendent, that existed separate from sovereign governments. Holmes stated, it "is very hard to resist the impression that there is one august corpus, to understand which clearly is the only task of any Court concerned. If there were such a transcendental body of law outside of any particular state but obligatory within it unless and until changed by statute, the Courts of the United States might be right in using their independent judgement as to what it was. But there is no such body of law. The fallacy and illusion that I think exist consist in supposing that there is this outside thing to be found." Law, as found in the courts, "does not exist without some definite authority behind it." The common law "is not the common law generally but the law of that State existing by the authority of that State without regard to what it may have been in England or anywhere else." Holmes declared that the *Swift* doctrine was fallacious and unconstitutional.[37]

In *Erie Railroad Co.* v. *Tompkins*, in 1938, the Court struck down *Swift*.[38] Louis Brandeis wrote the majority opinion. He stated that the Court was not ruling Section Thirty-Four of the Judiciary Act of 1789 unconstitutional—but Story's interpretation of it. Law in the state was not just statute but the pronouncements of the state's highest court. Brandeis stated, "except in matters governed by the Federal Constitution or by Acts of Congress, the law to be applied in any case is the law of the State. And whether the law of the State shall be declared by its Legislature in a statute or by its highest court in a decision is not a matter of federal concern. There is no federal general common law."[39]

Brandeis recognized that Story's intention had been uniformity, but the "persistence of state courts in their opinions on questions of common law prevented uniformity." The result was uncertainty and forum shopping. "In attempting to promote uniformity of law throughout the United States, the doctrine had prevented uniformity in . . . the law of the state." Of course, much of this had gone far beyond Story's original opinion. Nonetheless, the *Swift* doctrine was a logical extension of Story's claim that there was a common law separate from the law of particular governments. Because of this logic, Brandeis and the Court chose not to narrow the doctrine back to Story's specific, commercial common law. This would have left open the chance of a later Court restoring the *Swift* doctrine. To make the rule clear, the exception could not stand. It was necessary to throw out the *Swift* opinion to be rid of the doctrine. There was no federal general common law, and that included commercial law.[40]

There is little doubt, Story had not intended to develop a legal doctrine that undermined the Constitution he so revered, and that ran counter to the principles of American constitutionalism which he had done so much to develop and to expound. Although he had advocated the development of a general federal common law, separate from sovereign states, and the logic in *Swift* was being carried out, he may well have been repelled by the lack of uniformity in "forum shopping" and the conflict between the state and federal common laws. In the commercial law, Story had found the rational law that could become the consensus among the courts. In its transformation beyond the commercial common law set out in Story's original opinion, the general federal common law only resulted in conflict. There was no consensus, no uniformity, nor rationality.

Given Story's confrontational opinions, such as *Martin*, however, would the federal-state conflict resulting from the *Swift* doctrine have greatly disturbed Story if he was confident that the federal judiciary would win against the states, and that a uniform law would result through the defeat of state sovereignty and state rights? His continuous dealings with Jacksonians, state righters and nullifiers, and the trends of the Taney Court, set the context for much of Story's career. In *Martin*, he had wanted a uniform law, with the Supreme Court supreme in declaring it, and this had included common law as well as statute, treaties, and the Constitution. *Martin* and *Swift* were both ways to try to achieve his rational and national goals for the law. One alternative after *Swift's* transformation would have been to continue the logic of the doctrine to its conclusion by compelling all state courts to follow the common law set down by the federal courts. America would have one legal realm, with a single, uniform common law. That would have joined the national law, the federal common law of *Swift*, with the national judicial supremacy of *Martin*. Would Story have been repelled? In the final analysis, was he not like a Hamilton who was ready to use the Constitution to achieve ends beyond the Constitution? Story looked to that law, lofty and excellent, that advanced on "the path towards perfection."[41]

Notes

1 Joseph Story, "A bill further to extend the judicial system of the United States," mss., in William W. Story, ed., *Life and Letters of Joseph Story* (Boston: Charles C. Little and James Brown, 1851) 2 vols, 1:293-94; *Erie Railroad Co. v. Tompkins*, 304 U.S. 65 (1938).

2 Story, "A bill further to extend the judicial system," in Story, ed., *Life and Letters*, 1:294-95.

3 Ibid., 1:293-96. Story noted an interesting comparison between the federal judiciary with county courts. "Are the Judicial Courts of the United States so utterly destitute of all character, as that the ordinary powers, which the most common County Court possesses should be denied to them?" He could only hope that Congress would give the federal judiciary all the jurisdiction arising under the Constitution, treaties, and laws of the United States. Ibid., 1:295.

4 An Act concerning lands lying in the Northern Neck, 10 December 1796, in Samuel Shepherd, ed., *The Statutes At Large Of Virginia, From October Session 1792, To December Session 1806*, 3 vols. (Richmond: 1835; reprint ed., New York: AMS Press Inc., 1970) 2:22-23; on the purchase of the Fairfax estates by the Marshall syndicate, see the editorial notes in Charles T. Cullen, Herbert A. Johnson, et. al., eds., *The Papers of John Marshall*, multi-vol. (Chapel Hill: University of North Carolina Press, 1974-) 2:140-49 and 5:228-36; and see my "John Marshall Versus Spencer Roane: A Reevaluation of *Martin v. Hunter's Lessee*," *Virginia Magazine of History and Biography* 96 (1988):297-314.

5 Ibid.

6 *Hunter v. Fairfax's Devisee* (1809), 1 Munford (Va.) 218. Roane believed that all that the state had accomplished in the Compromise of 1796 was to receive land it had already rightfully possessed in return for giving up land it was in the process of rightfully gaining.

7 This was not the final move of a plan by Marshall to enjoin battle between the Supreme Court and the Virginia Court of Appeals. Neither as a land dispute litigant nor as the chief justice could he have expected a quick and conclusive victory. He and his brother were concerned, because they could easily find themselves on the winning side as makers of a constitutional law precedent and on the losing side as landholders in Virginia.

8 Story included the Jay Treaty, because it confirmed the articles in the 1783 treaty, which protected British claimants from actions taken against them because of their alien status, and it applied to any kind of escheat action, unlike the Treaty of 1783, which, it could be argued, was restricted to unlawful confiscations. *Fairfax's Devisee v. Hunter's Lessee* (1813), 7 Cranch 602.

9 Ibid.

10 Ibid.

11 *Hunter v. Martin, Devisee of Fairfax* (1814), 4 Munford (Va.) 1. The opposition to a general or federal common law is discussed below. See Note 23.

12 *Hunter v. Martin, Devisee of Fairfax* (1814), 4 Munford (Va.) 1. Marshall later realized that the use of the Jay Treaty in this case instead of the Treaty of 1783 had been a mistake. John Marshall to James Marshall, 9 July 1822, Marshall Papers, Library of Congress.

13 *Hunter v. Martin, Devisee of Fairfax* (1814), 4 Munford (Va.) 1.

14 Ibid.

15 Ibid.

16 *Martin v. Hunter's Lessee* (1816), 1 Wheaton 304. Story later claimed, regarding the *Martin* opinion, that "Marshall concurred in every word of it." Story to Ticknor, 22 January 1831, Story, ed., *Life and Letters*, 2:48-49.

17 *Martin v. Hunter's Lessee* (1816), 1 Wheaton 304.

18 Ibid.

19 Ibid.; John Alfred Treon, "*Martin v. Hunter's Lessee*: A Case History" (Ph.D. Diss., University of Virginia, 1970), 246.

20 On their problems with the rents and the continuous litigation, see my "John Marshall Versus Spencer Roane."

21 Story to Marshall, 27 June 1821, in Charles Warren, "The Story-Marshall Correspondence," *William and Mary College Quarterly*, 2nd Series, 21 (1941):6-8; Marshall to Story, 26 March, 17 May, and 13 July 1819, ibid., 2-4; and Henry Wheaton to Story, 19 August 1824, Papers of Joseph Story, Library of Congress.

22 For another example of Story working in a legal vacuum, see *Terrett v. Taylor* (1815), 9 Cranch 43. Peter Wallenstein's work on the glebe cases complements mine on the Fairfax litigation. His ideas were advanced in a paper, "Appellate Justice in the Early Republic," delivered at the

1990 meeting of the Society for Historians of the Early American Republic.

23 See St. George Tucker, *Examination of the Question, How Far the Common Law of England is the Law of the Federal Government of the United States?* (Richmond: John Dixon, 1800) included in an appendix in his edition of *Blackstone's Commentaries* (1803; reprint ed., New York: Augustus M. Kelley, 1969). *United States v. Hudson and Goodwin* (1812), 7 Cranch 32.

24 Story, "A bill further to extend the judicial system," in Story, ed., *Life and Letters*, 1:298-99.

25 Story, *A Discourse Pronounced Upon The Inaugural of the Author, as Dane Professor of Law in Harvard University* (Boston: Hilliard, Gray, Little, and Wilkins, 1829), 33.

26 Ibid., 41-51.

27 Ibid. On Roane's ideas in contrast to Marshall's and Story's, see my "John Marshall Versus Spencer Roane."

28 Story, *Discourse*, 51-53; Daniel Webster had similar sentiments asserting that the commercial law was "a system of most admirable utility, certain, complete, and uniform, to a degree of perfection, approaching the end of all that human wisdom may be expected to reach." A review of Wheaton's reports, in Andrew J. King, ed., *The Papers of Daniel Webster: Legal Papers* (Hanover, NH: University Press of New England, 1989), 3:212.

29 Section Thirty-Four of An Act to Establish the Judicial Courts of the United States, generally known as the Judiciary Act of 1789, 24 September 1789, Richard Peters, ed., *The Statutes At Large of the United States of America* (Boston: Little, Brown, and Company, 1846-54), 1:73-93. Story's reinterpreting of Section thirty-Four is seen in *Van Reimsdyk v. Kane* (1812), U.S. Circuit Court in Rhode Island, 28 *Federal Cases* 1062 (No. 16,871); he advanced his view on a federal common law of crime in *U.S. v. Coolidge* (1813), U.S. Circuit Court in Massachusetts, 25 *Federal Cases* 619 (No. 14,857), which was reversed by the Supreme Court in *U.S. v. Coolidge* (1816), 1 Wheaton 415; and on his advancing the general commercial law in admiralty jurisdiction, see *De Lovio v. Boit* (1815), U.S. Circuit Court in Massachusetts, 7 *Federal Cases* 418 (No. 3,776).

30 In the court report, "Tysen" was misspelled as "Tyson." *Swift v. Tyson* (1842), 16 Peters 1.

31 Ibid.

32 Ibid.

33 On the commercial law practices of the day in the state and federal
    courts, which created the receptive mood for *Swift*, and on the gradual
    development of the *Swift* doctrine, see Tony Freyer, *Harmony and Disso-
    nance: The Swift and Erie Cases in American Federalism* (New York: New
    York University Press, 1981); and also see Randall Bridwell and Ralph
    U. Whitten, *The Constitution and the Common Law: The Decline of the Doc-
    trines of Separation of Powers and Federalism* (Lexington, MA: D. C. Heath
    and Company, 1977).

34 Freyer, *Harmony and Dissonance*.

35 Ibid.

36 Ibid.

37 Opinion of Oliver Wendall Holmes, in *Black and White Taxicab and
    Transfer Co. v. Brown and Yellow Taxicab and Transfer Co.* (1928), 276 U.S.
    518.

38 In Hughestown, Pennsylvania, Harry James Tompkins was walking
    alongside a track of the Erie Railroad Co. when, he claimed, something
    extending from a passing train, probably an open door, struck him. By
    Pennsylvania common law, he was a trespasser, and the railroad com-
    pany was not liable for his injury. Because the company's headquarters
    was in New York, Tompkins could enter his suit through diversity
    jurisdiction in the United States District Court for the Southern District
    of New York. His lawyers argued that the court should not use Penn-
    sylvania common law but the *Swift* doctrine's general common law. The
    court gave judgement in accord with the latter, and the company
    appealed to the United States Circuit Court for the Second Circuit.
    Tompkins again won, and the company appealed to the Supreme
    Court. *Erie Railroad Co. v. Tompkins* (1938), 304 U.S. 65.

39 Ibid.

40 Ibid. *Erie* established that America did not have a general common law
    the origins of which transcended government and the extent of which
    was unlimited. Along with the common law of each state, what
    remained was a federal "common law" that was developing from Court
    precedents arising from federal statutes. This process has continued,
    and, indeed, beginning with the New Deal, there has been an enor-
    mous increase in the volume of federal statutes. This is law originating
    in Congress, however, and not Story's law of reason.

41 Story, *Discourse*, 33.

Roger B. Taney:
A Great Chief Justice?

Kenneth M. Holland

How should history remember Roger B. Taney? The question is not a simple one. On the one hand, Taney is perhaps the most vilified Chief Justice the Supreme Court has known. An 1865 detractor said of him, "as a Jurist, or, more strictly speaking, as a Judge, in which character he will be most remembered, he was, next to Pontius Pilate, perhaps the worst that ever occupied the seat of judgment among men."[1] Charles Sumner prophesied that he would be "hooted down the page of history."[2] On the other hand, many twentieth-century commentators have agreed with Robert J. Harris that "Taney's standing as a Chief Justice is second only to that of [John] Marshall."[3] In 1969, Fred Graham placed Taney below just two other chief justices, Marshall and the retiring Earl Warren.[4] Sixty-five law school deans and professors of law, history, and political science in 1970 rated the first one hundred justices to sit on the Supreme Court. Taney was one of the twelve justices placed in the top category.[5] The dramatic shift in the assessment of Taney's tenure on the Court is in large part explained by reactions to two of his opinions, *Dred Scott v. Sandford* (1857)[6] and *Charles River Bridge v. Warren Bridge*[7] (1837). Apart from the applause received from the South, Taney's "infamous" opinion in *Dred Scott* was nearly universally execrated by his contemporaries, who jubilated in exposing its historical inaccuracies, misstatements of law, and faulty logic. Scholars today speak no better of its argument. In the words of a prominent historian of American law, "no decision in the Court's long history has been so thoroughly reviled, then and now."[8] Students of the Supreme Court consider the decision to have been the single greatest error ever made by that lofty institution, a "self-inflicted wound" with which the Court damaged its reputation and authority.[9] The decision weakened the Court's prestige so much that it was ignored by President Lincoln and the Reconstruction Congress.[10] The closest it has come to receiving a kind word from late twentieth-century scholarship, which is much charmed by the doctrine of cultural relativism, is that it was an accurate expression of the racist sentiment rampant in the country in the 1850s and therefore we should not blame Taney, a product of the times in which he lived, too much.

During the battle between President Franklin Roosevelt and what he termed "the nine old men" of the Supreme Court over the extent of Congress' power under the Constitution to limit economic freedom, Taney surprisingly became the darling of political liberals.[11] In the *Charles River Bridge* case, Taney had departed from Marshall's strict enforcement of the obligation of contracts and ruled that where an ambiguity exists in a contract between private enterprisers and the public the Court must rule in favor of the public. Taney's opinion in favor of the Massachusetts legislature, which had chartered the Warren Bridge, was used by supporters of the New Deal to argue that in conflicts between congressional efforts to promote the public interest and property rights vested in individuals and corporations the Supreme Court should support Congress. The Supreme Court did in fact eventually agree, and this is today the law of the land.[12]

Taney's present high reputation is based not just on this one case but on an assessment of his leadership of the Court over a twenty-eight-year period. Henry Abraham, for example, speaks glowingly of his accomplishments, which included "enhanc[ing] the role of the states as governmental and philosophical entities," "guid[ing] his Court along pathways of conciliation and compromise virtually devoid of dogmatism and ploys," and "achieving governmental concord and constitutional understanding."[13] However, in order to reach this level of praise, Abraham and Taney's other twentieth-century apologists must discount his *Dred Scott* opinion, to the point of treating it as a "monumental aberration" and lamenting that "it is a pity that Taney is so often remembered by that case."[14]

The aberration view of his conduct was popularized by Chief Justice Charles Evans Hughes, when in September 1931 he unveiled a bust of Taney at Frederick, Maryland, and lavishly lauded his service on the Court, speaking of *Dred Scott* as "a well-intentioned mistake."[15] His champions have even found an excuse for Taney. Justice John McLean's extremist anti-slavery dissenting opinion, written to further his presidential ambitions, they say, forced Taney and the majority to take an equally extreme pro-slavery position.[16]

The aberration theory, of course, is problematic in assessing the greatness of any justice, for one assumes that the author himself did not regard any one opinion, no matter how despicable or unsatisfactory later generations might find it, as eccentric and somehow not really "his." In Taney's case, it is even more dubious, given the consistency in all of his opinions dealing with slavery and race.[17] Don Fehrenbacher, moreover, has shown that the thesis that Taney was forced by McLean to take an extremist position is a myth and that, in fact, Taney welcomed the opportunity presented by *Dred Scott* to settle once and for all the questions of Congress' power over slavery and of Negro citizenship.[18]

The aberration theory is not only historically inaccurate but also unfair to Taney's reputation, for his entitlement to inclusion in the pantheon of great justices rests, in my opinion, primarily upon the leadership he displayed as Chief Justice during the Court's consideration of the *Dred Scott* appeal and in the nature of the opinion he wrote for the majority in that case. Granted that Taney's constitutional argument in *Dred Scott* is unconvincing, his superiority lies in the fact that he did not practice judicial self-restraint, that he was the first Chief Justice to persuade the Court to invalidate a major national policy enacted by Congress, and that he was the first jurist to appreciate the full potential of the Supreme Court as a legislative body. Today liberals and conservatives take the Court's political function for granted, but that the Court would assume this role was not at all clear when Taney took the oath as Chief in 1836. As Abraham acknowledges (without appreciating *Dred Scott's* contribution to the process of the consolidation of judicial power) during Taney's tenure the Supreme

Court's "position as the logical, ultimate, and fair-minded arbiter of the Constitution was fully secured."[19] Moreover, the view that Taney inflicted a grievous wound upon the Court obscures the fact that he set in motion a trend that resulted in an explosion of judicial policymaking in the 1870s and 1880s that has continued to the present. As Stanley Kutler has shown, one must be careful to distinguish between public reactions to the *Dred Scott* decision and its author from public attitudes toward the kind of Supreme Court the decision heralded.[20] The Chase and Waite Courts that succeeded the Taney Court held a very different view of their role than that of the three preceding Courts under Jay, Ellsworth, and Marshall. Taney was neither a practitioner of judicial self-restraint nor a judicial activist. He represents a vision of the Supreme Court as a policy formulating institution superior to Congress, the President, the state legislatures, and public opinion, yet restrained by the text of the Constitution and the intention of its framers.

The Legitimation of Judicial Review

It took 250 years for the principle of judicial invalidation of major legislative acts to win public acceptance in the United States. The first settlers brought with them in the 17th century the legacy of the struggle of the English courts for independence from the Parliament and Crown. The judicial protagonist in this contest, Chief Justice Sir Edward Coke, had stated early in the century, "It appears in our books, that in many cases, the common law will controul acts of parliament, and sometimes adjudge them to be utterly void, for when an act of parliament is against common right and reason, or repugnant, or impossible to be performed, the common law will controul it, and adjudge such act to be void."[21] Coke's attempt to place parliamentary enactments under judicial supervision failed, however, with the Glorious Revolution of 1689 which culminated in an agreement between the Parliament and William and Mary in which the monarchy acknowledged the principles of parliamentary sovereignty and supremacy.

The American constitutions, however, departed from the British model in some important respects. They were written, often contained constitutionally entrenched bills of rights, and, most importantly, separated the powers of government among three co-equal branches. The question immediately arose as how to resolve conflicts over the distribution of powers. Relying on Coke's dictum in *Bonham's Case*, some in the states advocated giving the judiciary authority to invalidate acts of the legislatures. Opinion, however, was divided, and the judges moved cautiously. For example, the Mayor's Court of New York City in 1784 rejected such a power:

> The supremacy of the legislature need not be called into question; If they think fit positively to enact a law, there is no power which can control them. When the main object of such a law is clearly expressed, and the intention is manifest, the judges are not at liberty, although it appears to them to be unreasonable, to reject it; for this were to set the judicial above the legislative, which would be subversive of all government.[22]

In a case from Virginia decided in 1782 by the Court of Appeals, *Commonwealth v. Caton*, the presiding justice, Edmund Pendleton, doubted that the state courts could void a legislative act "without exercising the power of legislation, from which they are restrained by the same Constitution." In another opinion in the same case, however, George Wythe admonished that "if the whole legislature . . . should attempt to overleap its bounds, prescribed to them by the people, I, in administering the public justice of this tribunal will meet their united powers; and, pointing to the constitution, will say, to them, here is the limit of your authority: and hither, shall you go, but no further."[23] Exercises of this power were rare and highly controversial in the states when the Constitutional Convention met in Philadelphia in 1787.[24]

Not only did separation of powers give rise to demands for judicial review but also the second great departure from the British model, federalism, or the division of powers between two levels of government. The arrangement demanded some mechanism for resolving the inevitable conflicts. Many options were discussed at the Convention, including giving Congress the power to overrule acts of the state legislatures contrary to the federal Constitution. Jefferson, not a delegate, proposed submitting such disputes to the sovereign, the people, in the form of a referendum. In the Kentucky Resolution of 1799, he proposed the doctrine of nullification, which would allow a state to reject the application within its boundaries of federal laws it regarded as unconstitutional. Others preferred giving the Supreme Court the power to nullify unconstitutional state laws. This was a mechanism familiar to the Americans, for acts of the colonial legislatures could be appealed to the Judicial Committee of the Privy Council in London, which had the power to declare them null and void, and did so 265 times between 1680 and 1780.[25]

The Constitution itself contains no explicit authorization to the federal courts to invalidate acts either of the state or federal assemblies. The delegates debated the propriety of such a power, with Francis Mercer of Maryland, for instance, saying he opposed the judges having such a power, for "laws ought to be well and cautiously made, and then be uncontroulable."[26] On the other hand, Luther Martin of Maryland thought that the judges, as to constitutionality, would have "a negative on the laws."[27] The focus of the debate was on state laws contrary to the federal constitution, with some reference to acts of Congress encroaching on the judiciary.[28] Some speakers favored associating federal judges with the President in a council to advise him in the exercise of his veto power. Again the primary intent was to give the judges the ability to protect their jurisdiction against legislative infringement. Although the proposal was defeated, President Washington established the precedent, that lasted until the Jackson Administration, of limiting the veto to bills the President deemed unconstitutional. He did not rely upon the Supreme Court to perform the checking function.

The views of James Madison, the architect of the Constitution, are of special relevance. In his discussion of the securities in the Constitution against laws contrary to justice and the public interest, Madison both on the convention floor and in *Federalist* #10 and #51 said nothing about the courts playing the role of constitutional guardian. He argued that the rights of minorities would be protected by the extent of territory made possible by federalism, the wisdom of the lawmakers ensured by the principle of representation, and the diversity of economic interests generated by the commercial nature of the economy. Alexander Hamilton was perhaps the most forceful exponent in Philadelphia and in *Federalist* #78 of the full power of judicial review.

The lack of consensus on the prudence of judicial review among the delegates is reflected in the language finally adopted. Article VI states, "This Constitution, and the Laws of the United States which shall be made in Pursuance thereof . . . shall be the supreme Law of the Land; and the Judges in every State shall be bound thereby, any Thing in the Constitution or Laws of any State to the Contrary notwithstanding." The meaning of "made in Pursuance thereof" is ambiguous, for it could refer to laws passed in accordance with the forms set out in Article I, section 7, requiring passage by both chambers and presentation to the President, or to laws which are within the limits set out on Congress' power. The supremacy of the Constitution is asserted with regard to the states, not to Congress. There is the implication that a state judge must invalidate a state law contrary to federal law, and Article III suggests that if a litigant claimed that a state law was repugnant to the federal Constitution and lost he could appeal to the United States Supreme Court. Article III, section 2, states that "the judicial Power [of the United States] shall extend to all Cases . . . arising under this Constitution, the Laws of the United States, and Treaties." There is no textual basis, however, for judicial review of acts of Congress.

The Supreme Court waited only a few years to assume the power to invalidate acts of the state legislatures. In *Ware v. Hylton* (1796)[29] and *Clerke v. Harwood* (1797),[30] the Court struck down two minor state enactments. It was not until the later years of the Marshall Court, 1825-1835, however, that such exercises of federal judicial power became common.[31] Chief Justice Marshall took the momentous step of pushing judicial review one step further in an opinion joined by all members of the Court in which he claimed for the Court the power to declare acts of Congress unconstitutional. Significantly, he did not rely upon the Constitution's language but upon logic. The conclusion of his syllogism in *Marbury v. Madison* (1803)[32] was that the courts must hold statutes repugnant to the fundamental law null and void. What is often overlooked is the narrowness of the Court's holding. Marshall invalidated a minor section of an act establishing the federal court system, the Judiciary Act of 1789. It authorized the Supreme Court to issue writs of mandamus, a power that the courts in England possessed. Marshall held that this provision allowed William Marbury to bypass the lower federal courts and go directly to the Supreme Court to request the Court to issue a writ of mandamus directing the Secretary of State, James Madison, to deliver his commission as a justice of the peace for the District of Columbia. The provision was unconstitutional because, said Marshall, it enlarged the original jurisdiction of the Supreme Court, a jurisdiction which is carefully circumscribed in Article III, section 2 and which Congress has not power to alter by ordinary legislation. The Supreme Court was doing precisely what Elbridge Gerry had said it could do when faced with legislative incursions on its constitutional powers. The first exercise of judicial review over a federal statute, thus, was a form of judicial self-defense. The legitimacy of such a power is strengthened when compared with the mechanisms provided by the Constitution for the Congress and the President to safeguard their constitutional powers against usurpation by a competing branch. The President is given the veto power, and the Congress enjoys the power of impeachment. This second type of judicial review thus can be defended as an expression of the constitutional device of checks and balances. Thus, the power of judicial review over legislative, or executive, attacks on the judiciary plausibly can be implied. The Supreme Court under its first three Chief Justices, Jay, Ellsworth, and Marshall, developed the Court's powers this far but no further. Their courts did not strike down an act of Congress not dealing with the integrity of judicial power.

The *Dred Scott* case presented a very different kind of question, the constitutionality of a major piece of federal legislation, the Missouri Compromise of 1820, which had nothing to do with the powers or independence of the judiciary. This type of bold exercise of judicial power was highly problematic. Jefferson, one of the most popular presidents, had consistently opposed such a power, regarding it as an infringement on the sovereignty of the people. Justice John B. Gibson, in *Eakin v. Raub*, an 1825 decision of the Supreme Court of Pennsylvania, insisted that "the oath to support the Constitution is not peculiar to the judges, but is taken indiscriminately by every officer of the government," concluding that it is a "postulate in the theory of our government . . . that the people are wise, virtuous, and competent to manage their own affairs."[33] Taney's opinion for the Court established at last the novel principle in Anglo-American jurisprudence that the Supreme Court is superior to the people's elected representatives and possesses the final word on questions of national policy. Table 1 underscores the magnitude of Taney's innovation by distinguishing three types of judicial review, noting the date of their initial exercise, and the relative level of their legitimacy.

Table 1 Types of Judicial Review

Judicial Review of:	Initial Exercise	Level of Legitimacy
State laws	*Ware v. Hylton* (1796)	High
Federal laws encroaching on judicial power	*Marbury v. Madison* (1803)	Medium
Federal laws setting national policy	*Dred Scott v. Sandford* (1857)	Low

The Dred Scott Case as the Prototype of Judicial Policymaking

In *Dred Scott* the Supreme Court promulgated two policies designed to affect in significant ways millions of Americans in the future. They were: (1) Slaveholders shall be permitted to bring their human property into any of the territories of the United States, regardless of the wishes of the settlers dwelling in the territory; and (2) Negroes, whether slave or free, because of their race cannot become citizens either of the United States or of the state in which they reside. The scope, generality, and prospective character of these pronouncements set the Court's holding sharply apart from the norm of judicial decisionmaking. As Pendleton had said in 1782, in Britain and the United States judges were confined to adjudication and were not expected to "exercis[e] the power of legislation."[34] Adjudication is the resolution of the legal conflict between the parties to the case before the court. It is retrospective in nature; the adjudicator seeks to discover the truth concerning events that occurred in the past between the parties. It is case-specific; the adjudicator is interested only in the facts of this particular dispute. It is rule-oriented; the adjudicator seeks to find and apply the appropriate pre-existing rule to the facts as found by trial. It is remedy-focused; the adjudicator, if he rules in favor of the plaintiff, attempts, at common law, to make him whole again through an award of compensation or, in equity, to prohibit harm or further harm from occurring. Along one dimension, Marshall adjudicated Marbury's dispute with Madison and Taney adjudicated Scott's dispute with Sandford. Marshall ruled that Marbury was entitled to his commission but the law provided no remedy for his wrong. Taney held that Scott was still a slave and the property of Sandford. The Chief Justices, however, had other goals in mind than determination of the fates of Marbury and Scott. Marshall invalidated a minor section of the Judiciary Act, and Taney struck down a major piece of national legislation.

Taney's decision in *Dred Scott* was qualitatively different than any of the Marshall Court decisions. *Marbury* did not intrude into any question before the Congress and had no impact on national policy. Whether the Supreme Court could issue writs of mandamus under its original jurisdiction was a technical issue that did not divide the country along partisan lines. Whether slavery would be excluded from the territories and the process of its elimination thereby irrevocably set in motion was a question that had been before the Congress continuously since debate over the Kansas-Nebraska Bill of 1854, that had destroyed the Whig Party, that had given birth to its successor, the Republican Party, and thus that sharply divided the country along partisan and sectional lines. It was an issue on which passions had been whipped to fever pitch and over which men were willing to die. It was the issue over which the Civil War, with its hundreds of thousands of casualties and immense destruction, was to be fought.

The issue of Negro citizenship was not nearly as salient or divisive as the future of slavery in the territories. There was little sympathy among Democrats or Republicans, Southerners or Northerners, for racial equality. Yet, even here a number of New England states had granted citizenship to their Negro residents and believed that policy toward persons of African descent was a matter for each state's legislature, not the United States Supreme Court. The wrenching and often violent aftermath of the Fourteenth and Fifteenth Amendments, which granted blacks civil and political rights, for many decades denied, reveals just how much was at stake in the resolution of this policy issue.

Taney did not act entirely on his own initiative. The Supreme Court began its career as a policymaking institution in 1857 because a majority of the Court accepted the invitation of the nation's elected public officials to do so. This observation in no way diminishes the novelty or audacity of Taney's redefinition of the Court's role, for he could have refused to respond favorably to the demands that the Court take this burdensome issue off the presidential and congressional shoulders. The Court became a superlegislature because that is what the legislature wanted. The Court became the final arbiter of policy disputes because that is what those entrusted with responsibility for policymaking demanded. As Lincoln said in his famous House-Divided speech,[35] the nation could not remain half-slave and half-free, but the nation was unable to choose its destiny and left it to the high court. In other words, the political system designed by Madison in some important respects failed, its failure giving rise, as Tocqueville had foreseen,[36] to the judicialization of American politics.

During the 1856 presidential campaign both Democrats and Republicans recast the issue of slavery in the territories in constitutional terms in order to prepare the issue for judicial resolution. The Democrats united on a platform that said whether Congress could exclude slavery from the territories depended on the extent of Congress' powers under Article IV, section 3 "to dispose of and make all needful Rules and Regulations respecting the Territory or other Property belonging to the United States." Although Southern and Northern Democrats came to opposite conclusions on this question, "all agreed," said Judah P. Benjamin in a speech before the Senate on May 2, 1856, "that it was prejudicial to the best interests of the country that the subject of slavery should be discussed in Congress" and "that every question touching human slavery, or human freedom, should be appealable to the Supreme Court of the United States for its decision."[37] The Republicans also felt the pressure to convert their political policy into a constitutional principle. "They accordingly adopted also the argument of Salmon P. Chase and certain other party radicals that slavery was illegal in the federal territories by virtue of the due process clause of the Fifth Amendment."[38] The purpose, says Fehrenbacher, "was to reinforce the expectation already widespread among Democrats that the fundamental sectional differences over slavery would ultimately have to be settled in the courts."[39] There was nothing inevitable about this development. The party leaders could have continued to regard the matter, as they had done since 1820, as a moral and political one unsuitable for adjudication. By the 1850s, the dynamics of the modern party system and the aspirations of men like Stephen A. Douglas to make national politics a career (forces continuing to operate today to encourage legislators to delegate hard policy choices to the judiciary[40]) generated demands upon the Court that Taney chose not to resist.

Nor are Presidents immune from the pressure to "pass the buck" to the Supreme Court. Democratic nominee James Buchanan, an anti-slavery man who ran successfully on a pro-slavery platform in 1856, hoped that the Supreme Court would use the *Dred Scott* case as a vehicle for resolving the slavery question in favor of the South, expecting that Northern Democrats would rally behind the Court, thus isolating the Republicans, who, as a party founded for the single purpose of stopping the spread of slavery, would no longer have a reason for existence. Upon a request from the president-elect, Justice John Catron of Tennessee told Buchanan the line-up of the justices in the decision that Chief Justice Taney would announce two days after Buchanan's inauguration. On March 4, 1857, Buchanan informed the country that the Supreme Court would soon still the agitation over slavery in the territories that had marked American politics for more than thirty years.

The legislative nature of Taney's opinion was but one of its novel features. Turning on its head the abolitionists' reliance upon the Fifth Amendment's prohibition against government deprivation of a person's "life, liberty, or property, without due process of law," Taney held that, with respect to the Missouri Compromise, "an act of Congress which deprives a citizen of the United States of his . . . property, merely because he . . . brought his property into a particular Territory of the United States . . . could hardly be dignified with the name of due process of law."[41] This was a major innovation, because Taney was using, for the first time by a Supreme Court justice,[42] the due process clause to invalidate a law itself and not its application. In English and American law, the guarantee of due process was aimed at judges and prosecutors and directs them to provide, first, notice to persons charged with a crime or civil offense, so that they can prepare a defense, and, second, a hearing before an impartial tribunal in which they have an opportunity to present their defense. Legislatures are not part of the audience of this ancient right. At one stroke, Taney had significantly enlarged the scope of judicial power by finding a standard in the Constitution of substantive fairness. This reinterpretation of the clause complemented the national policymaking role assumed by the Court in *Dred Scott*, for the Fifth Amendment is directed at the federal government not the states.

How significant were Taney's innovations? The decision did not in fact settle the territorial question as the Democratic politicians had hoped. In the campaign debates with Lincoln on the Illinois prairies in 1858, Douglas, the leading Northern Democrat, distanced himself from Taney's reading of the Constitution by insisting that the people of a territory had the right, under the principle of popular sovereignty, to exclude slavery if they so wished. The South immediately cried "betrayal," the Northern and Southern wings of the Democratic Party split, each nominating a candidate in the 1860 presidential election and thus ensuring a Republican victory, Southern secession, and a civil war. The Court thus failed in its primary goal of providing a final solution to the territorial issue. The critics of Taney's opinion, notably Associate Justice Benjamin Curtis in a dissenting opinion and Lincoln in a speech at Springfield, Illinois, delivered on June 26, 1857, revealed numerous historical inaccuracies, misstatements of fact, fallacies in logic, and convolutions in constitutional exposition. Among Taney's most egregious errors were his interpretation of the Declaration of Independence, several clauses in the Constitution—including the three dealing with slavery, the one defining Congress' power over the territories, and those dealing with citizenship—and the history of white treatment of Negroes in the United States. Taney's main dubious assertions were that the phrase "all men are created equal" in the Declaration did not include Negroes; the states had no power to make Negroes citizens; the framers of the Constitution were emphatically pro-slavery and made no distinction between slavery and other kinds of property; even though the Congress under the Articles of Confederation had the power to ban slavery in the Northwest Territories, the Congress under the Constitution does not possess any such power in the territories acquired after 1787; and that Negroes were much better treated in 1857 than they had been during the Revolution and its immediate aftermath. The opinion was thus a failure in a second sense, i.e., it failed to convince the reader.

What is often overlooked, however, in the process of exposing *Dred Scott's* shortcomings is the extent to which its critics accepted the Court's bid to become a third policymaking branch of government. Lincoln addressed the Court's ambition squarely:

The candid citizen must confess that if the policy of the government, upon vital questions, affecting the whole people, is to be irrevocably fixed by decisions of the Supreme Court, the instant they are made, in ordinary litigation between parties, in personal actions, the people will have ceased, to be their own rulers, having, to that extent, practically resigned their government, into the hands of that eminent tribunal.[43]

Lincoln, in fact, acquiesced in the Court's claim to be the supreme and final policymaker. He agreed that Republicans believed that the Supreme Court's "decisions on Constitutional questions, *when fully settled*, should control, not only the particular cases decided, but the general policy of the country, subject to be disturbed only by amendments of the Constitution." The *Dred Scott* case, however, in his opinion had not met that condition:

If this important decision had been made by the unanimous concurrence of the judges, and without any apparent partisan bias, and in accordance with legal public expectation, and with the steady practice of the departments throughout our history, and had been in no part, based on assumed historical facts which are not really true; or, if wanting in some of these, it had been before the court more than once, and had there been affirmed and re-affirmed through a course of years, it then might be . . . factious, nay, even revolutionary, to not acquiesce in it as a precedent.[44]

Thus, Lincoln conceded that if the Supreme Court had considered more than once the policy issues presented by Dred Scott's bid for freedom and had consistently adhered to its reading of the Constitution, the political branches and the public would have been bound by it as national policy. The only means available to Congress and the people to overcome such judicial legislation, admits Lincoln, would be a constitutional amendment. Given the composition of the Court in 1857 and Buchanan's appointment of Democrat Nathan Clifford, an apologist for slavery, in 1858, the Taney Court, if the Civil War had not intervened, would almost certainly have reiterated its position on questions relating to slavery and race in a series of cases between 1857 and 1864, the year of Taney's death.[45]

Even so, Taney's *Dred Scott* opinion was vindicated and accepted as binding national policy. The Thirteenth, Fourteenth, and Fifteenth Amendments, ratified respectively in

1865, 1868, and 1870, explicitly undid Taney's holdings on slavery and Negro citizenship. In other words, the Congress and state legislatures responded to judicial policies they found objectionable in precisely the way Lincoln said they would if the Supreme Court were granted the right to "control . . . the general policy of the country."

Influence of *Dred Scott* on Subsequent Courts, 1865-1900

The contrast between the sequel to *Marbury v. Madison* and that to *Dred Scott* is striking. Following the Court's invalidation of part of the Judiciary Act of 1789 in 1803, no federal statute became the victim of judicial review until the *Dred Scott* decision, 54 years later. Obviously, Marshall had failed to legitimize judicial sovereignty. In the 52 years following *Dred Scott*, however, the Supreme Court declared unconstitutional 32 acts of Congress.[46] Under Chief Justice Melville Fuller, the Court found five federal statutes unconstitutional in a single decade, 1889-1899. "This great expansion of judicial review in the late nineteenth century," says Lawrence Friedman, "pivoted on the 'due process' clause."[47] Any law a majority of the Court found "unfair," "unreasonable," or "arbitrary," could be nullified under the doctrine of substantive due process. Typical of the Court now comfortable in its new role was *The Civil Rights Cases* (1883),[48] in which the Court held the Civil Rights Act of 1875 to be an unconstitutional infringement on the liberty of owners of public accommodations, such as hotels, theaters, and restaurants. The Court, in effect, promulgated a national policy of racial discrimination.

Was Taney a Judicial Activist?

"Judicial activism" is a term coined in the twentieth century by social scientists to describe departure by judges from the traditional adjudicative role. To the extent that the term applies to broad policymaking by the courts, it certainly applies to the Taney Court. To label John Marshall an activist is far more problematic, given his unwillingness to abrogate a piece of major congressional legislation.[49] Those judges who carry the activist sobriquet in the twentieth century, however, approach the Court's mission in some ways quite differently than Taney. The distinctions are so substantial that it is probably not appropriate to place Taney in their category, nor, as we shall see, in the category of advocates of judicial restraint. These terms as applied to the judiciary, activism and restraint, are peculiar to the twentieth century.

The root of judicial activism is German legal realism of the late nineteenth century. The American legal realists characterized all law as intrinsically subjective. Rejecting what they termed the theory of "mechanical jurisprudence," the realists taught that judges do not find or discover the law but make it and that judicial interpretation reflects more the personal characteristics of the judge than the facts peculiar to the case and the applicable law.[50] Nevertheless, the pattern of interpretation is not idiosyncratic. The constantly shifting law crafted by judges reflects society's ever changing needs. By definition, say the realists, there can be no conflict between social utility and the law.

The U.S. Supreme Court, whose justices, by the 1890s, were heavily influenced by what came to be called later "sociological jurisprudence" rendered a pattern of decisions, best exemplified by *Lochner v. New York* (1905),[51] in which it invalidated scores of state and federal laws regulating business, such as minimum wage, maximum hour, and child labor laws, on the grounds, fundamentally, that they would be bad for the country. The first activist judges were political conservatives, attempting to preserve economic freedom from what they perceived as regulatory strangulation. The justices paid little attention to the language of the Constitution or its framers' intentions. In *Lochner* the Court struck down a New York law setting maximum hours for bakers as a violation of the employer's and baker's "liberty of contract," a right nowhere mentioned in the Constitution, invoking the doctrine of substantive due process, which permits the Court to rule on the constitutionality of a statute even if it conflicts with no specific clause of the Constitution. The clash between a Court dedicated to laissez-faire economic principles, wielding the due process clause of the Fifth and Fourteenth Amendments, and Franklin D. Roosevelt, whose New Deal was premised on government intervention in the marketplace, resulted in the president's request to Congress, following his landslide victory in the 1936 election, for authority to appoint immediately six new members to the Supreme Court and the Court's subsequent decision to yield to presidential pressure to sustain the New Deal program.

Soon after the 1937 crisis, which resulted in a temporarily tamed Supreme Court, judicial activism re-emerged, but in a form far more acceptable to the nation's political leaders. In a footnote to an otherwise unremarkable case, *U.S. v. Carolene Products Co.* (1938),[52] the Court announced that although it would henceforth defer to the legislature's economic policies, it would presume to be unconstitutional laws that infringed upon fundamental political and personal rights, such as the franchise and freedom of speech, or that discriminated against members of "discrete and insular" racial or religious minorities. By the 1950s, the Court's new role as champion of the underdog became firmly established, resulting in repeated clashes with the Congress and state legislatures.

The decision marking the supplanting of the judicial activism of the right by the activism of the left was *Brown v. Board of Education* (1954),[53] arguably the single most momentous judicial decision since *Dred Scott*. State laws requiring separation of the races in the public schools, said the Court, were repugnant to the equal protection clause of the Fourteenth Amendment. Emerging from this use of a clause originally directed at the discriminatory enforcement of laws was the doctrine of "substantive equal protection." In a companion case, *Bolling v. Sharpe* (1954),[54] the Court struck down the racial segregation laws of the District of Columbia on the grounds that they offended the due process clause of the Fifth Amendment. Due process, said the Court, includes an equal protection element. What distinguishes *Brown* and *Bolling* is the nearly total lack of attention in Chief Justice Warren's opinions either to the meaning of the words of the Fifth and Fourteenth Amendments or to the intent of their framers. As he explains in the *Brown* opinion,

Reargument was largely devoted to the circumstances surrounding the adoption of the Fourteenth Amendment in 1868. It covered exhaustively consideration of the Amendment in Congress, ratification by the states, then existing practices in racial segregation, and the views of proponents and opponents of the Amendment. This discussion and our own investigation convince us that, although these sources cast some light, it is not enough to resolve the problem with which we are faced. At best, they are inconclusive.[55]

In the justices' conference on the merits of the cases, the Chief Justice allegedly brushed aside the niceties of constitutional exegesis and attempted to reduce the issues before the Court to the simple question, "What does justice require us to do?" Warren's perceived lack of need to engage in textual or historical analysis also accounts for the brevity of the opinions—remarkable, given the importance of the cases for millions of Americans. Another peculiar feature of the school segregation cases was the Court's reliance on social science research. Constitutional rights were anchored in the shifting sands of the findings of social psychologists regarding the effect of separate schooling on academic performance. *Brown* became a model for the activism of the left and its influence can be seen in later Warren and Burger Court decisions dealing with school prayer, reapportionment, busing, affirmative action, abortion, and other policy matters.

Taney's approach to judicial policymaking stands in sharp contrast to that of Warren and Justice Rufus Peckham, author of the Court's opinion in *Lochner*. Taney's opinion is not only quite lengthy, he even wrote a supplement to it in order to respond to its critics. The length was due to the care with which he analyzed the meanings of the relevant constitutional provisions and sought out the intent of their framers. The sheer amount of historical exploration is one of the opinion's most remarkable features. Textual and historical questions were especially important to Taney, for, unlike John Marshall, Peckham, or Warren, he did not employ higher law norms as a standard for judging the constitutionality of legislation. Taney, in fact, was the first legal positivist to serve as Chief Justice.[56] Law's authority, he believed, was derived from the will of the sovereign. The judge's function is to execute that will, regardless of his opinion concerning its wisdom or goodness. Nothing could be further from the activist's tenets than Taney's statement that

> If any of [the Constitution's] provisions are deemed unjust, there is a mode prescribed in the instrument itself by which it may be amended; but while it remains unaltered, it must be construed now as it was understood at the time of its adoption. . . . As long as it continues to exist in its present form, it speaks not only in the same words, but with the same meaning and intent with which it spoke when it came from the hands of its framers, and was voted on and adopted by the people of the United States. Any other rule of construction would abrogate the judicial character of this court, and make it the mere reflex of the popular opinion or passion of the day.[57]

Although often credited with introducing the doctrine of substantive due process into American constitutional law, the due process clause did not serve as a higher law in Taney's jurisprudence as it did in Peckham's and Warren's. Taney's use of the clause in *Dred Scott* is tentative, carries very little of the argument's weight, and is more closely tied to the historical meaning of the due process right than its employment by twentieth-century activists. The Constitution, according to Taney, prohibits the deprivation of life, liberty, or property except by due process of law for the same reason that it prohibits *ex post facto* laws and unreasonable seizures and guarantees the privilege of the writ of *habeas corpus*, viz., government cannot deprive anyone of his property "who [has] committed no offense against the laws,"[58] except in a taking for public use, which requires payment of "just compensation." In Taney's view, the Missouri Compromise violated procedural, not substantive norms, for the migrating slaveholder was afforded neither notice nor the right to a hearing before his property was dispossessed by summary means, simply upon crossing the border from Missouri to Kansas.

Is Taney an Advocate of Judicial Restraint?

Taney's refusal to invoke higher law norms in reading the Constitution and his insistence on the central role of framers' intent in the interpretive undertaking have led many students of the Court to categorize him as a proponent of judicial restraint. Thus, according to Abraham, knowing "how to exercise judicial self-restraint" was one of Taney's principal virtues.[59] Again, although Taney shares some of the characteristics associated with justices such as Oliver Wendell Holmes, Jr., Felix Frankfurter, and William Rehnquist, in the end the advocates of restraint have more in common with the proponents of activism than with Taney.

Political liberals were not always champions of judicial activism. In fact, they were its first critics. Holmes, Frankfurter, and Louis Brandeis shared the views of activists Warren, William Brennan, and Thurgood Marshall that constitutional values, like all moral values, reflect historical processess that are continuously transforming American society.[60] The liberal advocates of judicial restraint were legal realists who accepted the ineluctability of progress and the consequent obsolescence of the values of previous generations. The dispute between Holmes, Brandeis, and Frankfurter, on the one hand, and the activists of either the right or the left, on the other, was over the role of judges in the process of enlightening the masses as to the direction in which history was headed. The advocates of restraint in the 1910-1940 period believed that popularly-elected legislatures are likely to be the most progressive public institution, for in the clash of competing interests represented in the legislative assembly an accommodation will emerge that is much more likely to maximize social utility than any policy choice made by a handful of unaccountable jurists removed from the current of social change. By the 1950s, however, the state legislatures and Congress had lost their reputation for progressivism and were regarded by Warren, Brennan, and other advanced thinkers as sources of ignorance, repression, and illiberalism.

The influence of legal realism on the judicial restraint school is well illustrated by statements of Chief Justices Charles Evan Hughes and Harlan Fiske Stone. In 1907 Hughes pronounced, "we are under a Constitution, but the Constitution is what the judges say it is."[61] The consequences of the subjective quality of the basic law were spelled out by Stone in 1936:

> While unconstitutional exercise of power by the executive and legislative branches is subject to judicial restraint, the only check on our own exercise of power is our own sense of self-restraint. . . . Courts are not the only agency of government that must be assumed to have capacity to govern. . . . For the removal of unwise laws from the statute books appeal lies not to the courts but to the ballot and to the processes of democratic government.[62]

By sharp contrast, Taney felt restrained by the Constitution, whose words had an objective meaning which the Court was bound to observe in cases raising constitutional issues.

From the restraint point of view, such an understanding of the Supreme Court's duty was dangerous, for it would inevitably produce decisions which the justices thought were dictated by the language of the Constitution but which would be imprudent with respect to the welfare of either the country or the Court. In several of his works, scholar Alexander Bickel, an eloquent apologist for judicial self-restraint, counsels the Court to avoid principled decisions on controversial policy issues.[63] Such issues, he says, are best resolved by means of compromise. The attempt to do what the Constitution or justice require will often divide the nation and lead to a political backlash against the Court. The *Dred Scott* case is Bickel's principal example of the dangers of reaching principled decisions.[64] In Taney's opinion, by contrast, it is entirely unacceptable for a Supreme Court justice to allow the will of the sovereign expressed in the fundamental law of the Constitution to be thwarted by a fear for the Court's fate or a belief that negotiated settlements are superior to declarations of legal right.

Conclusion

Roger Taney's claim to greatness as a justice of the Supreme Court rests in his fulfillment of what had been hitherto only theoretical discussion of a role for the Court as a national policymaking institution. On March 6, 1857, the Supreme Court became a major player in the legislative process, and neither the Court nor the nation have looked back since. The Court attempted to resolve once and for all time the slavery question because a majority of the people and their representatives demanded a judicial resolution. *Dred Scott* represented the culmination of a tendency inherent in the American democracy, astutely perceived by Tocqueville in the 1830s—the judicialization of politics. In the 1930s and again in the 1960s, the unpleasant side effects of the principle of judicial supremacy on policy issues have led to intense constitutional soul-searching. Do we really want government by nine old men? Taney's *Dred Scott* opinion, even with its share of deficiencies, provides a superior alternative to his heirs' understanding of the judicial role. Eschewing the doctrines of both judicial restraint and judicial activism, Taney taught that judges are restrained by the Constitution, whose interpretation must be anchored in the text and the framers' intent. Yet, he did not hesitate to abrogate *erga omnes* congressional legislation repugnant to the basic law, which he conceived as the will of the people, subject to change only by an alteration in that will proclaimed in a constitutional amendment. For Taney, constitutional interpretation and judicial policymaking were one and the same activity. His opinion in *Dred Scott*, that for which he has been most reviled and which his apologists prefer to think of as a "monumental aberration," is the true warrant for his inclusion in the national pantheon.

Notes

1 Anonymous, *The Unjust Judge* (New York, 1865), p. 65.

2 Charles Sumner, *Congressional Globe*, 38 Cong., 2 Sess., 1012 (February 23, 1865).

3 Robert J. Harris, "Chief Justice Taney: Prophet of Reform and Reaction," *Vanderbilt Law Review* 10 (February 1957) 227.

4 Fred Graham, "180 Years of Chief Justices," *New York Times*, June 24, 1969, p. 25.

5 Henry J. Abraham, *Justices and Presidents: A Political History of Appointments to the Supreme Court*, 2nd ed. (New York: Oxford University Press, 1985), p. 9. Respondents were asked to rank the first ninety-six justices on a continuum from "great," through "near great," "average," "below average," and "failure." The other eleven justices rated "great" were: John Marshall, Brandeis, Holmes, Black, Story, Harlan I, Hughes, Stone, Cardozo, Frankfurter, and Warren. The results were initially published in Albert P. Blaustein and Roy M. Mersky, *The First One Hundred Justices: Statistical Studies on the Supreme Court of the United States* (Hamden, Conn.: Shoe String Press, 1978).

6 19 Howard 303 (1857).

7 11 Peters 420 (1837).

8 Lawrence M. Friedman, *American Law: An Introduction* (New York: W. W. Norton, 1984), p. 185.

9 Charles Evans Hughes, *The Supreme Court of the United States* (New York, 1928), pp. 50-51.

10 President Lincoln, for instance, defied Chief Justice Taney's writ of habeas corpus directing him to deliver a Southern sympathizer arrested for treason and held in Fort McHenry in Baltimore. *Ex parte Merryman*, 17 Fed. Cas. No. 9487 (1861). In the words of Edward Corwin, "During neither the Civil War nor the period of Reconstruction, did the Supreme Court play anything like its due role of supervision, with the result that during the one period the military powers of the President underwent undue expansion, and during the other the legislative powers of Congress." "The Dred Scott Decision in the Light of Contemporary Legal Doctrines," *American Historical Review*, 17 (1911): 68-69.

11 Taney's rehabilitation is best evident in the following New Deal biographies: Carl B. Swisher, *Roger B. Taney* (New York: Macmillan, 1935); C. W. Smith, Jr., *Roger B. Taney: Jacksonian Jurist* (Chapel Hill: University of North Carolina Press, 1936); and B. W. Palmer, *Marshall and Taney: Statesmen of the Law* (Minneapolis: University of Minnesota Press, 1939) and in Felix Frankfurter's book, written during the presidential campaign of 1936, *The Commerce Clause Under Marshall, Taney and Waite* (Chapel Hill: University of North Carolina Press, 1937).

12 The announcement came in Footnote #4 of *United States v. Carolene Products Co.*, 304 U.S. 144 (1938).

13 Henry J. Abraham, *Justices and Presidents: A Political History of Appointments to the Supreme Court*, 2nd ed. (New York: Oxford University Press, 1985), pp. 100-101.

14 Abraham, *Justices and Presidents*, pp. 100-101. It was Charles Evans Hughes who popularized the aberration view of Taney's conduct in *Dred Scott* in his *The Supreme Court of the United States* (New York, 1928).

15 Charles Evans Hughes, "Roger Brooke Taney," *American Bar Association Journal*, 17 (1931), 785-790.

16 Alexander M. Bickel, *Politics and the Warren Court* (New York: Harper & Row, 1965), p. 135.

17 See his pro-slavery opinions in *Prigg v. Pennsylvania*, 16 Peters 539, 627-628 (1842); *Groves v. Slaughter*, 15 Peters 449, 508-509 (1841); and *Strader v. Graham*, 10 Howard 82, 93-94, 97 (1850).

18 Don E. Fehrenbacher, *The Dred Scott Case: Its Significance in American Law and Politics* (New York: Oxford University Press, 1978), pp. 309-314.

19 Abraham, *Justices and Presidents*, p. 100.

20 Stanley I. Kutler, *Judicial Power and Reconstruction Politics* (Chicago: University of Chicago Press, 1968), pp. 1-29.

21 *Bonham's Case*, 8 Coke Rep., 114a.

22 *Rutgers v. Waddington* (1784), in J. B. Thayer, *Cases on Constitutional Law*, vol. I, pp. 63, 69-70.

23 *Commonwealth v. Caton*, 4 Call 5 (1782). David John Mays, *The Letters and Papers of Edmund Pendleton* (Charlottesville, Va.: University Press of Virginia, 1967), vol. II, p. 422.

24 Leonard Baker, *John Marshall: A Life in Law* (New York: Macmillan, 1974), pp. 382-387.

25 A. M. Schlesinger (pere), "Colonial Appeals to the Privy Council," *Political Science Quarterly*, 28 (1913), 279-297, 433-450.

26　Farrand, vol. II, pp. 298-299.

27　Farrand, vol. II, p. 76.

28　Elbridge Gerry said the judges will have "a sufficient check against encroachments on their own department by their exposition of the laws, which involved a power of deciding on their constitutionality." Farrand, vol. I, p. 97.

29　3 Dallas 199 (1796).

30　3 Dallas 342 (1797).

31　*The Constitution of the United States of America: Analysis and Interpretation*, Senate Document, 99-16, 99th Congress, 1st session (Washington, DC: GPO, 1987).

32　1 Cranch 137 (1803).

33　*Eakin v. Raub*, 12 S. & R. (Pa. S. Ct.) 330 (1825).

34　Quoted in Mays, *Papers of Edmund Pendleton*, vol. II, p. 422.

35　Abraham Lincoln, *Speech Accepting the Republican Senatorial Nomination, 1858*, in Richard N. Current, ed., *The Political Thought of Abraham Lincoln* (Indianapolis: Bobbs-Merrill, 1967), pp. 94-103.

36　In 1835 Alexis de Tocqueville acutely noted the trend that would culminate in the *Dred Scott* opinion, observing "there is hardly a political question in the United States which does not sooner or later turn into a judicial one." *Democracy in America*, ed. J. P. Mayer and Max Lerner, trans. George Lawrence (New York: Harper & Row, 1966), p. 248.

37　*Congressional Globe*, 34th Congress, 1st session, p. 1093.

38　Fehrenbacher, *The Dred Scott Case*, p. 202.

39　Fehrenbacher, *The Dred Scott Case*, p. 202.

40　See, for example, Steven V. Roberts, "Congressmen and Their Districts: Free Agents in Fear of the Future," in Dennis Hale, ed., *The United States Congress: Proceedings of the Thomas P. O'Neill, Jr., Symposium*, pp. 65-84.

41　*Dred Scott v. Sandford*, 19 Howard 393, 450 (1857).

42　In 1856, the New York Court of Appeals, in *Wynehamer v. People*, declared unconstitutional as violating due process a state prohibition law not because of procedural defects but because it destroyed vested rights in liquor. This was apparently the initial appearance in American law of the doctrine of substantive due process. See Charles Hartshorn Maxson, *Citizenship* (New York, 1930), p. 350.

43 Abraham Lincoln, "First Inaugural Address, 1861," in Current, ed., *Political Thought of Abraham Lincoln*, pp. 175-176.

44 Abraham Lincoln, in Roy P. Basler, ed., *The Collected Works of Abraham Lincoln* (New Brunswick, N.J., 1953-1955), vol. II, p. 401. Emphasis added.

45 Abraham, *Justices and Presidents*, p. 113.

46 *The Constitution of the United States of America: Analysis and Interpretation*, Senate Document, 99-16, 99th Congress, 1st session (Washington, DC: GPO, 1987).

47 Lawrence M. Friedman, *American Law: An Introduction* (New York: W. W. Norton, 1984), p. 186.

48 109 U.S. 3 (1883).

49 For elaboration of this view, see Wallace Mendelson, "Was Chief Justice Marshall an Activist?" in Stephen C. Halpern and Charles M. Lamb, eds., *Supreme Court Activism and Restraint* (Lexington, MA: D. C. Heath, 1982), pp. 57-76.

50 See, for example, Roscoe Pound, "Mechanical Jurisprudence," *Columbia Law Review* 8 (December 1908): 605-623.

51 198 U.S. 45 (1905).

52 304 U.S. 144, 152-153 (1938).

53 347 U.S. 483 (1954).

54 347 U.S. 497 (1954).

55 *Brown v. Board of Education*, 347 U.S. 483 (1954).

56 See Kenneth M. Holland, "Roger Taney," in Morton J. Frisch and Richard G. Stevens, eds., *American Political Thought*, 2nd ed. (Itasca, IL: Peacock Publishers, 1983), pp. 170-184. Illustrative of his rejection of natural law is this passage from an 1853 opinion: "It can never be maintained in any tribunal in this country, that the people of a state, in the exercise of the powers of sovereignty, can be restrained within narrower limits than those fixed by the Constitution of the United States, upon the ground that they may make contracts [in violation of] fixed and immutable principles of justice." *Ohio Life Insurance and Trust Co. v. Debolt*, 16 Howard 428-429 (1853).

57 *Dred Scott v. Sandford*, 19 Howard 303, 426 (1857).

58 *Dred Scott v. Sandford*, 19 Howard 303, 450 (1857).

59 Abraham, *Justices and Presidents*, p. 100.

60 See Richard G. Stevens, "Felix Frankfurter," in Frisch and Stevens, eds., *American Political Thought*, pp. 337-360.

61 Charles Evans Hughes, *Addresses*, 2d ed. (New York: Putnam, 1916), p. 185.

62 *United States v. Butler*, 297 U.S. 1, 78, 88 (1936).

63 Alexander M. Bickel, *The Least Dangerous Branch* (Indianapolis: Bobbs-Merrill, 1962) and *The Supreme Court and the Idea of Progress* (New York: Harper & Row, 1970).

64 Alexander M. Bickel, *Politics and the Warren Court* (New York: Harper & Row, 1965).

The Evolution of John Marshall Harlan the Elder

Linda C. A. Przybyszewski

Justice John Marshall Harlan the Elder, who served on the Supreme Court from 1877 until 1911, is perhaps best known today for his lonely refusal to agree to the legality of racial segregation. Harlan dissented in both the *Civil Rights Cases* in 1883 and in *Plessy v. Ferguson* in 1896.[1] It was Harlan in *Plessy* who coined the phrase "Our Constitution is color-blind." And in that same case he reminded his fellow judges in stirring words that racial inter-dependency was of a piece with common citizenship:

> The destinies of the two races, in this country, are indissolubly linked together, and the interest of both require that the common government of all shall not permit the seeds of race hate to be planted under the sanction of law.[2]

To many blacks at the turn of the century, Harlan become a judicial hero; Frederick Douglass, for example, wrote him letters of praise, and the African Methodist Episcopal church of Washington, DC held a memorial service when he died in 1911.

John Harlan's strong words in those two dissents ensured a revival of interest in him among historians and others when the Supreme Court delivered *Brown v. Board of Education* in 1954 and declared segregation in the public schools to be unconstitutional.[3] Still, there has been no full-length biography of Harlan, and what articles have been written have tended to neglect evidence from the private papers.[4] In the absence of such biographical information the *Brown* decision might lead one to think that Harlan's greatness lay in his ability to discern the modern path of equality. Harlan's color-blind rule does offer an invaluable contribution to 20th-century debates on the interpretation of the 13th, 14th and 15th Amendments.[5] However, it would be a mistake to see him as a man ahead of his time, as a 20th-century liberal mysteriously born in 1833.

To the contrary, Harlan was steeped in political and family traditions which he only reworked under the pressure of events. We can discover his greatness in the fact that the modifications which he made of inherited ideas led him to offer his new fellow citizens rights and protections which his colleagues would deny them. Appropriately enough for our setting here in the South, I am going to focus on how the peculiar institution of slavery influenced Harlan, and how he modified his understanding of slavery in the light of constitutional change, yet how antebellum patterns of racial thought persisted in his mind even into the 20th century.

Those who know Harlan only as the judicial champion of black civil rights may be surprised to learn that the Harlan family were slaveholders from the border state of Kentucky. John Harlan inherited slaves upon the death of his father in 1863 and accepted unquestioningly his right to hold property in human beings. Indeed, immediately after the Civil War, the future Supreme Court justice defended slavery and condemned the Republican plan for federal civil rights guarantees. In searching for the reason why John Harlan eventually chose to support emancipation and citizenship for blacks, we come to the ironic explanation that he did so in part by reference to the paternalistic ethic which the Harlan family claimed had guided their actions during the period when they owned slaves. In embracing the revolutionary change of legal equality, Harlan assented to the rule of law and displayed a concern with constitutionalism reminiscent of the old Whig party.[6] More distinctively and unexpectedly, he was preserving one aspect of paternalism — namely, its insistence on interracial goodwill and forbearance from the abuse of physical power. Of course, paternalism was inherently hierarchical, and this aspect of his family's ethic acted as a brake on Harlan's legal thought and caused him to break his rule of color-blindness more than once. Some changes in race relations were too great for even a repentant slaveholder to accept.

*   *   *   *   *

We should began with a caveat on sources. Very few contemporary family papers survive from the period surrounding the Civil War, and none contain any explicit account by John Harlan about how he made his decision to support black civil rights. So we have to make the most of what does exist while being careful in how we deal with documents in which members of the Harlan family recall events of previous decades.

Family tales read meaning back into past events, so they may tell us more about how people wished to remember the past than about how the past actually was.[7] At least we can check the plausibility of such stories against facts of which we are sure. Such memories cannot give us a picture of the reality of the antebellum Harlan household—in particular, they cannot tell us whether slavery was as benign as the family made it out to be—but they can indicate the shape of the family identity and consequently the interplay between that identity and John Harlan's decisions during his political and judicial careers.

Before the Civil War the Harlans were a lawyering family with strong Whig political connections. John's father James Harlan was a crony of Henry Clay and held numerous state and federal offices. At their home outside of Frankfort, Kentucky on what they called Harlan hill, a dozen slaves worked under the direct supervision of some member of the family, either in the house, in the adjoining flower and vegetable gardens, or at the barn where hogs were raised. While the family was part of the Kentucky elite, and owned a greater number of slaves than was typical in that state, the Harlans were not of the plantation aristocracy associated with the Deep South.

When the war came, John Harlan and his father James worked to push Kentucky to the Union side when it teetered on the narrow wall that its legislature called "neutrality."[8]

Once the border state had declared itself on the Union side, Harlan joined the Union army and raised a regiment which he led into battle. Upon the death of his father in 1863, he resigned his commission to take over the family law firm.[9]

Harlan remained politically active yet frustrated since he was part of an increasingly confused alliance of white men who defended the Union yet rejected the decisions of Lincoln's administration. The Union Army had made itself obnoxious to white Kentuckians in several ways, such as commandeering supplies, suppressing dissent, and interfering with elections. By far the most provoking federal action was the freeing of black slave military recruits and their families. White Kentuckians shared Harlan's view that the president's administration had substituted the illegitimate goal of emancipation for the original one of union. Why, as he once asked rhetorically of an Indianian crowd in 1864, had the people of the Union states risen against secession? "It was for the high and noble purpose of asserting the binding authority of our laws over every part of this land." He had scarcely to remind them that "it was not for the purpose of giving freedom to the Negro."[10] Harlan opposed Lincoln's re-election in 1864 as did the majority of Kentucky voters.

Harlan declared Lincoln's Emancipation Proclamation an unconstitutional interference with the state's power to define property rights in slaves. In 1865 he complained in a public letter that the national government had transgressed its rightful powers by freeing slaves and had left the state to cope with "the ruinous effects of such a violent change in our social system."[11] Harlan insisted that the value of slave property at stake was less relevant than the political principle. If only a dozen slaves lived in Kentucky, he declared, he would still oppose the Thirteenth Amendment as "a flagrant violation of the right of self-government."[12] He saw no paradox in invoking republican principles to defend slavery, nor did the Kentucky legislature which declined to ratify the 13th Amendment. That same year Harlan urged whites to organize to prevent blacks from gaining political rights.[13] Harlan and other white Kentucky Unionists had fought the war to prevent the secessionists from destroying the Union, but now the federal government was threatening one of the principles that underlay it.

By 1871, however, Harlan had abandoned his opposition to emancipation and equal rights. We find him in that year in the town of Livermore, Kentucky, now a Republican candidate for governor again making a political speech. He was now ready to condemn "the institution of African slavery" as "the most perfect despotism that ever existed on this earth." He declared himself glad that slavery was gone and that "these human beings are now in possession of freedom, and that that freedom is secure to them in the fundamental law of the lands, beyond the control of any state." Harlan's voice must have rang out over the crowd as he gloried in the fact of emancipation: "I rejoice that it is gone; I rejoice that the Sun of American Liberty does not shine upon a single human slave upon this continent. . . ."[14]

During that same speech at Livermore, Harlan confessed what every informed voter in Kentucky must have known: his about-face on the question of slavery. "It was true that I was at one time in my life opposed to conferring these privileges [of citizenship] upon [blacks]," he acknowledged to the crowd. Pointing to the upheavals that all Kentuckians had withstood during and after the war years, Harlan answered his detractors with "Let it be said that I am right rather than consistent."[15] In so saying, Harlan sold himself short because he supported black civil rights for the rest of his days.

In comparing these two political speeches, one naturally wonders what triggered the change in Harlan's position. How did he come to see freedom and citizenship for blacks as "right"? Why did he find it so right that he never lapsed into his former position even when the majority of whites of both regions became indifferent or hostile to black citizenship by the turn of the century?

There were a number of reasons which fed into the ethic of paternalism mentioned earlier. Like other white Kentucky Unionists, Harlan had condemned the secessionists, as his father had the abolitionists, as lawless proponents of disorder. When he defended slavery and the Union, he perceived no contradiction because both were supported by law. But once the Constitution was amended by the 13th and 14th Amendments, emancipation and racial equality *were* the law of the land and to defy this fait accompli was to fall into the ranks of the lawless and the violent.

Many white Kentuckians were happy to join such ranks. Throughout the late 1860s and early 1870s, bands of marauding whites—called Regulators, or after their leaders, Rowzee's Band, Skagg's Men—ran rampant over the Kentucky countryside attacking white and black alike.[16] In March of 1866 the Freedmen's Bureau reported to Congress that organized bands "have driven the freedmen entirely out of certain sections" and had begun to threaten white Unionists as well.[17] The campaign of white terrorism led a group of Frankfort blacks to petition Congress for protection. In order to prove their case, the group detailed sixty-four attacks which had occurred in the space of two years.[18] White gangs also harassed the Northerners who came south to teach in Freedmen's Bureau schools.[19] Terrorism had a tremendous impact upon the black population: about 30,000 blacks left the state from 1860 to 1870, a number out of all proportion to other border-state migrations.[20]

The connection between white terrorism and the Democratic party was often times a close one. As a Union state, Kentucky could not be reconstructed although some of its white males had battled for secession. Ex-Confederate native sons returning to Kentucky streamed into the Democratic party which continued to oppose black citizenship, in contrast to the Republicans who supported equal rights and the federal power to enforce them.

Faced with the choice between these two parties Harlan relied in part on his father's Whiggish dislike of the party of Jefferson.[21] Harlan's decision to continue his political career as a Republican rested also on his revulsion to the reign of white terror.[22] Condemnation of the Klan and other white riders became a common theme of his political rhetoric. In the speech he made at Livermore, he warned his audience that "these KuKlux are enemies of all order" and endangered the liberty and property of citizens both black and white.[23]

But few white Kentuckians seem to have shared Harlan's disgusted reaction to this violence as evidenced by his failure to win the governorship in 1871 and 1875.[24] If a Whiggish devotion to peace and good order were enough to explain Harlan's move to Republicanism, what of all the other former Whigs who refused to join him and satisfied their consciences with frowning quietly upon violence? Our search for the source of Harlan's decision-making must thus dig into the personal. For it seems to lay in his family's vision of itself as the practitioners of a benign, even beneficial, form of paternalistic slave-holding. Harlan's rejection of violence and disorder fed into his family's identity.

Central to the Harlan family's understanding itself was a story dating from long before the war about how James Harlan and his young son John encountered a slave-driver while on their way to church.[25] According to Malvina Harlan, these good Presbyterians found themselves sharing the main street of Frankfort with a "brutish" white slave-driver whose "badge of office was a long snake-like whip made of black leather, every blow from which drew blood."[26] His charges were a group of black slaves, the healthy adults chained together and their children and their elders walking unbound before them. She testified to James's discomfort at the brutal reality of slavery: "The sight stirred my Father-in-law to the depths of his gentle nature." He and his son John saw before them "the awful possibilities of an institution which, in the division of family estates, and the sale of the slaves, involved inevitably the separation of husband and wife, of parent and children . . ."[27]

In the restrained manner of a gentleman who did not like to make a fuss in a public street on the Sabbath, James Harlan gave the slave-driver a piece of his mind. "My Father-in-law could do nothing to liberate the poor creatures then before him," Malvina explained, "but he was so filled with indignation that any one calling himself a man should be engaged in such a cruel business that, walking out to the middle of the street and angrily shaking his long fore-finger in the face of the 'slave-driver,' he said to him, 'You are damned scoundrel. Good morning, sir.' " It was the closest thing to "swearing" that young John had ever heard from his father's mouth. "After having thus relieved his feelings," Malvina continued, "he quietly pursued his way to the House of Prayer."[28] With that said, she or another family member would sit back and wait for a murmur of appreciation from their audience.

Modern listeners to such a tale find the gesture of protest a small one in light of the far more courageous and dramatic actions of Kentucky abolitionists such as Cassius M. Clay or the founders of Berea College, but it loomed large in the family's collective imagination. James Harlan's curse was impressive enough to earn him biblical stature in their eyes: "like some Old Testament prophet he seemed to be calling down Heaven's maledictions upon the whole institution of Slavery."[29]

Let us consider the significance of the tale to these would-be paternalists before appraising its accuracy. James Harlan's anger is prompted by the spectacle of blacks laboring under less benevolent care than that which he provided his own slaves. There in the street, Malvina tells us, James Harlan was reminded that "the peculiarly close relations that existed between Master and slaves in the case of the best type of Slaveholders in the South"—i.e. the kind of relations allegedly found in the Harlan household—were an ideal not always reached.[30]

Malvina Harlan's memoirs, written in 1915 in a tribute to her husband, described life in the slave-holding Harlan household as idyllic.[31] The races are stratified yet live in happy interdependence. Work is scarcely mentioned, punishment never. In the memory of the Harlan family, the institution of slavery appears more a system of social welfare than a means of production. Blacks and whites make up an integrated, and inalienable household. The slave-driver was the villain of the Harlan legend because his job, the selling of slaves, marked a personal tragedy for blacks and an institutional failure for whites.

The sale of slaves shattered black families physically while demonstrating the fragility of white paternalism. The Harlan family effaced the original sin of purchase by insisting that James had inherited slaves, and that Harlans of the later generations neither bought nor sold them. When John Harlan recalled decades later those slave-time "practices that were horrible to the rights of the Christian man," it was the destruction of families that came to his mind as it did in the telling of the slave-driver story. Neither physical brutalities nor cheating laborers of their hire made as great an impression on his memory as the sight of a slave family "divided and separated" by sale on the courthouse steps: "the father sold to one man and the mother to another in a distant part of the country, and the children sold one by one, and separated, one to be sent to one state, and one to another . . ."[32] The mutual affection and obligations that paternalists like the Harlans believed they had fostered between themselves and their slaves could not survive the ever-present threat of this scattering. When masters exercised their right to trade in slaves, the notion of an inter-racial "family" (in the Latin sense of the word) died. By his very existence, the slave-driver betrayed the hopes of white paternalists; he embodied "the worst aspects of the system," as Malvina said.[33]

By telling the story of the slave-driver, the Harlan family disassociated themselves from the cruelties of the slave system even as they acknowledged the fact of their complicity. It may seem an obvious point, but one doesn't run across historical documents written by "bad" masters. It is always *someone else* selling slaves or abusing them, never the writer or the writer's kin or friends.[34] An early historian of life under slavery in Kentucky exhibited this tendency by absolving the entire state from the sin of cruelty. He argued, "that in Kentucky, Negro servitude was generally on a higher plane than in the States to the south and the treatment of slaves was much more humane."[35] We may discern some truth to that statement in light of the origins of the phrase "being sold down the river," but we still should question the likeness of the portrait drawn by the Harlans.[36]

Because so few contemporary documents survive, and nothing from the hands of the slaves themselves, we cannot know whether Harlan slaves were in fact ever beaten or sold. We do know that James was no radical on race (he once assured a political ally that "he who applies [the term Abolitionist] to me lies in his throat"), but his family remembered him primarily as a man who eased the cruelties of the slave system.[37] There are some indications that the Harlans were more liberal than other whites in racial matters. James Harlan defied public criticism by arguing freedom cases for blacks who complained of being held in bondage illegally.[38] Legal rights came before white supremacy to his Whiggish eyes. Also he took into his home a quadroon slave named Robert James Harlan (later reputed by one newspaper account to be his illegitimate son)[39] and allowed him "unusual freedom" even sending him to school along with his sons.[40] Robert attended class until "someone informed the school authorities of the fact" of his color and thereafter he was "taught the elements of an education by Mr. Harlan's older sons. . . ."[41] Robert and John remained friends and political allies all their lives.[42]

Putting aside the as yet unanswerable question of his origins, Robert's presence must have made an indelible mark on the Harlan family's memories. He represented physically the interdependence of the two races, while his personal history after leaving the household proved that race did not preclude success. Free to travel on his own, Robert made a fortune during the Gold Rush of 1848 and finally settled down in Cincinnati to a political and business career after paying five hundred dollars for formal freedom papers.

So what facts we do know suggest that the incident probably in fact occurred, even though the two recorded accounts we have of the tale date from the early 20th century (John's version from 1908 and Malvina's from 1915). After all, James Harlan's curse was a small challenge to the system of slavery. His target was a member of a lowly class of white men whose work was necessary to the peculiar institution, yet who endured the general scorn of their "betters."[43] It seems less likely that the tale was invented to make sense out of John Harlan's eventual support for black civil rights than that the memory of that day helped him to make his decision.[44] Harlan may have magnified the significance of the incident, and ignored contradictory events, thus turning it into a legend—

that is, a story with a basis in fact yet an exaggerated meaning. In doing that, however, John Harlan had made a choice.

Even before Harlan's political about-face, there were indications of the seriousness with which he took paternalism. The settling of estates was a major reason for the sale of slaves and an entirely excusable one in white eyes. Yet John Harlan shrank from the elemental hypocrisy of such an act when his father died in 1863. Rather than allow his father's slaves to be sold, John Harlan took on the debts which their price would have covered.[45] More than other whites, he seems to have abided by the paternalist ideal.

The political and judicial course which John Harlan chose to follow may be the best proof of the strength of paternalism as an ethical ideal in the Harlan household. When it came time to decide what to do after the war, John's memory of his father—who had chosen his son's profession at birth by naming him as he did, in whose legal and political footsteps his son had followed unprotestingly—must have served as an example. Harlan had learned to equate white supremacy with good-will between the races; in the post-war political chaos, these two values were detached from one another. It was either white supremacy and white terrorism on the one hand, or legal equality and inter-racial good-will on the other. He had to pick one value out of the package he had inherited from his father. How could the boy who remembered his father's disgust with the brutality of a white slave-driver become a man willing to embrace a political company which ran down and murdered blacks in the dead of night? So John Harlan joined the Republican party despite its minority status in the state, and he continued to demand protections for blacks in the exercise of their civil rights long after he was through seeking their votes.[46]

The family's combined devotion to law and forbearance in the exercise of power rang like a chime through their lives. Decades later, John Harlan gave his son James a lesson about bullying that reverberated with the ideas and language used by his wife in condemning the slave-driver as unworthy of manhood. Harlan was expressing his disappointment that his son John Maynard was thrown out of Princeton for hazing which at that time consisted of a general assault on some freshman for defying social conventions. "You can rely on it," Harlan wrote to his middle-son James, "if you find any boy in your class who is continually & deliberately pulling indignities upon others, he is a mean cowardly fellow who will turn pale & cower when confronted by a brave, self-respecting, justice-loving comrade who has the courage to resent personal insult."[47] Above all, Harlan bemoaned the state of John Maynard's "manliness." He, the son, was trying to pass the patriarch's lesson on to the grandson. Anyone worthy of calling himself a man did not brutalize others regardless of their rank. In fact a true American male who loved justice had a duty to fight those who did abuse power.[48]

Harlan had never wanted emancipation, but it had come, as had civil rights regardless of color. In the late 1860s in Kentucky, a white who continued to reject black freedom and black rights ended up making black survival itself impossible. The result was a lowering of white standards of behavior to a level Harlan thought contemptible. Ironically, the only way he could find to preserve white honor and some semblance of the paternalistic ethos of the antebellum era was by embracing a party that championed revolutionary legal changes. The Democratic party was intolerable to a man who had prided himself on the kind treatment of his "servants." Even the shock of emancipation could not dislodge the habits of his upbringing. And just as Harlan could not abandon the remembered standard of goodwill and care exercised by the best type of slaveholder, neither could he completely surrender its inherent assumptions of hierarchy and separation.

The singularity of Harlan's fight for equal rights at the ballot box and on the bench should not blind us to the traditional shape his racial thought took. To see him as a man before his time sunders him unnaturally from the sources of his social thought. The civil rights doctrine for which Harlan is still known today—"the Constitution is color-blind"—did not always guide his decisions.

True, the judge spoke out against racial segregation in public accommodations in no uncertain terms.[49] He also protested with disgust when his brethren allowed his home state of Kentucky to outlaw inter-racial private education. "Have we become so inoculated with prejudice of race," he asked his brethren incredulously, "that an American Government, professedly based on the principles of freedom, and charged with the protection of all citizens alike, can make distinctions between such citizens in the matter of their voluntary meeting for innocent purposes simply because of their respective races?"[50] He voiced his frustration in several peonage cases when the majority of the Court refused to act for jurisdictional reasons despite what Harlan called evidence of "barbarities of the worst kind against negroes."[51] By these actions, the judge gained the gratitude of the Gilded Age's black population.

However, when racial integration came too close to social intermixing for the comfort of a man raised in a slaveholder's household, Harlan let by laws that used race as a classification in clear contradiction to the color-blind rule which he had articulated.[52] He assented to a sophistical decision which allowed a state to punish inter-racial adultery more severely than same-race adultery.[53] He delivered a ruling that came close enough to authorizing segregation in the public schools (although Harlan explicitly denied such an intent) that it was later used for exactly that purpose.[54] In the jury discrimination cases, Harlan's faith in local institutions gave racist administrators more than the benefit of the doubt. When black defendants accused officials of excluding their race from juries, Harlan asked for evidence that was virtually impossible to obtain.[55] He seems to have overestimated local officials' loyalty to the color-blind rule just as in first advocating it he had assumed, wrongly as it turned out, that he himself would be able to live with all of its consequences. Harlan's jurisprudence as a whole could not produce the inter-racial polity which his color-blind rule dictated. Even under radically altered legal presumptions, some aspects of paternalistic thought survived long after the death of slavery.

If we turn again to Malvina Harlan's memoirs, we find a description of John's relationship with a black in the post-war period which proves that as late as 1900 neither the slaveholder nor the slave were yet dead. Her account suggests how paternalism had permanently affected John's thinking and indicates the consequent limitations it had on his vision of the race relations in a free, republican society. Other historians writing about the judge have neglected this portrayal of John's working relationship with James Jackson, a "court messenger" assigned by the Supreme Court to help with menial tasks, yet it seems to be the sole available depiction of Harlan in personal intercourse with a black in the post-war era.

Slavery, or rather "the fine Old Maryland family in which he was brought up as a slave in the antebellum days" endowed Jackson with "dignified and courtly manners," Malvina Harlan tells us. As in her portrait of the slave girl who gloried in her mistress's fineries, Malvina described with pleasure Jackson's success at personal self-effacement before John:

> By the time Jackson had been in the service of my husband for two or three weeks, he had so thoroughly identified himself with my husband and all our family interests, that, whenever he spoke to others about my husband or addressed him personally, he always used the pronouns, "We," "Us," and "Ours."[56]

While speaking of the female slaves who acted as maids to the white women in the Harlan household, Malvina had noted that "the familiarity was never abused by the maid, and the real affection which each had for the other showed itself in many ways."[57] So she praises Jackson similarly because "while he was on peculiarly friendly and even affectionate terms with his employer, he never for one moment forgot his place, nor the respect that was due from him to all the members of the family." Jackson "was in a real sense a member of our household," and accompanied the family to Murray Bay in Canada where John gathered the "Harlan tribe" every summer.

"Jackson took so much pride in all the members of 'The Family'," Malvina assures us.[58] She delights in recounting Jackson's reaction to the news that her son John Maynard had won a golf tournament at the resort:

> with his kindly, ebony countenance fairly shining with affectionate pride, [Jackson] grasped my son's hands in both of his and said, "Mr. John, *when* will *these people* around here understand what kind o' stock *we* come from?"[59]

Obviously, Jackson was accustomed to the emotional structure and expectations of a paternalist slave household. The two men were devoted to one another, Malvina tells us. And at John's deathbed, Jackson, having served fifteen years in their midst, mourned alongside the family.

*   *   *   *   *

Modern listeners are uncomfortable in hearing about Jackson and the judge. Certainly there was nothing in it to inspire our admiration for Harlan as a man before his time. Paternalism was a surprisingly persistent pattern in the Harlan family even as it moved through space and time from James Harlan's antebellum slave-holding household to the Supreme Court Justice's Gilded Age home. We can invoke it in estimating Harlan's greatness, however, by noticing how other whites put the same ideals to entirely destructive uses.

Southern whites used the idea of paternalism to gloss over the cruelties of slavery without bothering to preserve that aspect of it which had so captured the imagination of the Harlan family: paternalism's insistence upon inter-racial goodwill. Like the Harlans, most whites of the post-war period concentrated on the vision of the contented slaves and the benevolent master, yet unlike John Harlan they rejected the constitutional fact of legal quality, preferring to remain "gloomily reactionary" as one historian of the South has put it.[60] Romanticization of the Old South allowed white northerners and southerners to reconcile their former martial differences at the expense of the freed people.[61] Both southern and northern whites joined in celebrating the virtues of plantation life.[62] By positing slavery as the proper status for blacks, whites ended by excusing racial terrorism as the inevitable result of the upsetting of the system.[63] If only blacks knew their proper place, then whites would not need to remind them with violence.

This kind of thinking encouraged egregious lapses of legal justice. The administration of the law reflected the ugly fact which gave the lie to the Supreme Court's declaration in *Plessy* that accommodations assigned by race could be "separate but equal"—in fact the accommodations provided to each race almost never were physically equal. The lack of equality was mirrored in the administration of the law in other areas. Whites attempted to coat unequal justice with a gloss of fairness. The result was a sometimes pathological system of local administration which winked at its own and others' wrongdoings.[64]

One of the reasons Harlan proved to be a great justice was his refusal to use paternalism to excuse these wrongs. Instead, his memory of paternalism fused with his commitment to constitutional order. Harlan's familial myths concerning paternalism—the way in which the household functioned, the slave-driver incident—combined with a kind of constitutional myth that portrayed the founding fathers in the same light as his own father. Just as James Harlan was said to have opposed slavery even while participating in it, so the founders were egalitarians at heart if not in fact. The judge made a point of telling the law students he lectured to that many of the leading southern revolutionaries, although slave-holders themselves, had criticized slavery from the start.

Harlan believed that the Civil War generation had fulfilled the founders' wishes and the country's destiny; just as he had followed his own father's path in finally joining the Republican party. The 13th, 14th and 15th amendments to the Constitution were a kind of revelation of the document's essential meaning. Harlan once told his students when discussing the 14th amendment that "Equality before the law . . . is the fundamental underlying principle upon which our constitution rests, and it rests there securely. It never will be changed, as I think."[65] By this verbal sleight-of-hand, Harlan placed an amendment, by definition an addition to a document, at the very base of the republican structure of government. All else appeared to be built upon it. To Harlan's mind, racial equality fulfilled the country's providential mission even as it fulfilled the personal ethic taught in the Harlan household.

This dual influence—the constitutional and the familial—produced the dissents for which Harlan is known today. Harlan thus offered blacks a more equitable treatment than most of his fellow judges were willing to give. At the same time his record of justice was imperfect. Like all people, Harlan carried the burden of his personal history into new and unexpected circumstances. His greatness lay in not allowing its weight to cripple his moral sense as he struggled into the future.

Notes

1 *Civil Rights Cases* 109 U.S. 3 (1883), *Plessy v. Ferguson* 163 U.S. 537 (1896).

2 *Plessy,* 559, 560.

3 *Brown,* 349 U.S. 294 (1954). See Loren Beth, "Justice Harlan and the Uses of Dissent," *American Political Science Review* 49 (December 1955): 1085-1104. The *Kentucky Law Journal* devoted a whole issue to Harlan after *Brown* with articles by Alan F. Westin, David G. Farrelly, Florian Bartosic and Henry J. Abraham, 46 (Spring 1958). For a prophecy of *Brown,* see Richard F. Watt and Richard M. Orkiloff, "The Coming Vindication of Mr. Justice Harlan," *Illinois Law Review* 44 (1949): 13-40.

4 Alan Westin's early work on Harlan is the exception to that rule.

5 Harlan's analysis in *Plessy* of the meaning of *Dred Scott v. Sanford,* 19 Howard 393 (1857) offers the kind of principled argument based on precedent and history that Herbert Wechsler could not find in the modern desegregation cases, "Toward Neutral Principles of Constitutional Law," *Harvard Law Review* 73 (1959): 10-35. See also Monte Canfield, Jr.'s " 'Our Constitution is Color-blind': Mr. Justice Harlan and Modern Problems of Civil Rights," *University of Missouri at Kansas City Law Review* 32 (Summer 1964): 292-321.

6 See Chapter 2 of Daniel Walker Howe's *The Political Culture of the American Whigs,* (Chicago: University of Chicago Press, 1979).

7 See the *Journal of American History's* special issue on "Memory and American History," 75 (March 1989); also the commonsensical results from the social scientists' research into the question of memory, Michael Ross and Michael Conway, "Remembering One's Own Past: The Construction of Personal Histories," in Richard M. Sorrentino and E. Tory Higgins, eds., *Handbook of Motivation and Cognition: Foundations of Social Behavior* (NY: Guilford Press, 1986): 122-44.

8 The old but standard work on Kentucky during this period is E. Merton Coulter's *The Civil War and Readjustment in Kentucky* (1926; reprint, Gloucester, MA: Peter Smith, 1966). See also Daniel Stevenson, "General Nelson, Kentucky and Lincoln Guns," *Magazine of American History* X (August 1883), 118; JMH, autobiographical essay entitled "Civil War of 1861 . . ." JMH Papers, Library of Congress, Manuscript Division (hereafter cited as LC), Reel 8, #332.

9   While Harlan's resignation coincided with Lincoln's Emancipation Proclamation, the alcoholism of his only surviving brother indicates that his presence in the firm was a necessity.

10 From a speech at New Albany, Indiana, 4 October 1864 apparently a transcript from a newspaper report, quoted in the best of the articles published on Harlan, Alan F. Westin's "John Marshall Harlan and the Constitutional Rights of Negroes: The Transformation of a Southerner," *Yale Law Journal* 66 (April 1957), 651.

11 JMH letter to Coombs, *Lexington Observer and Reporter*, 1 June 1865, quoted in Louis Hartz's survey of the newspaper evidence on Harlan, "John Marshall Harlan in Kentucky, 1855-1877," *Filson Club Quarterly* 14 (January 1940), 29.

12 *Cincinnati Gazette*, 2 August 1865, quoted in Coulter, 279-280.

13 JMH letter to Coombs, *Lexington Observer and Reporter*, 1 June 1865, quoted in Hartz, 29.

14 Speech given at Livermore, Kentucky, 26 July 1871 reprinted in "General Harlan's Republicanism," *Louisville Daily Commercial* (editorial), 1 November 1877, typed copy, JMH Papers, LC, Reel 24, #004.

15 Ibid.

16 Coulter, 359; his Chapter XVI, "The Negro, The Freedmen's Bureau, and Organized Violence" is marred by the argument that if the Bureau had not antagonized whites, the Bureau would not have been needed to protect blacks.

17 House Executive Documents, 39th Congress, 1st sess., No. 70, p. 202, quoted in Allen W. Trelease, *White Terror: The Ku Klux Klan Conspiracy and Southern Reconstruction* (New York: Harper & Row, 1971), xlv.

18 The period was from November of 1867 to December of 1869, W. A. Low, "The Freedmen's Bureau in the Border States," in Richard O. Curry, ed., *Radicalism, Racism, & Party Realignment: The Border States During Reconstruction* (Baltimore: John Hopkins Press, 1969), 254-255.

19 George R. Bentley, *A History of the Freedmen's Bureau* (Philadelphia: University of Pennsylvania Press, 1955), 182.

20 W. A. Low, "The Freedmen's Bureau in the Border States," in Richard O. Curry, ed., *Radicalism, Racism, & Party Realignment: The Border States During Reconstruction* (Baltimore: John Hopkins Press, 1969), 255.

21 JMH to son Richard D. Harlan, autobiographical letter, 4 July 1911, JMH Papers, LC, Reel 32, #5.

22 Westin contends that "perhaps more than anything else" Democratic violence swayed Harlan's decision, 659.

23   Speech given at Livermore, Kentucky, 26 July 1871 reprinted in "General Harlan's Republicanism," *Louisville Daily Commercial* (editorial), 1 November 1877, typed copy, JMH Papers, LC, Reel 24, #004. See also speech at Elizabethtown in 1875, #008.

24   Kentucky did not elect a Republican governor until 1895.

25   Malvina Shanklin Harlan, "Some Memories of a Long Life, 1854-1911," JMH Papers, LC, Reel 16, #116 (hereafter cited as "Memories"). James Morrow retold John's version of the story in an article called "Talks with Notable Men: John M. Harlan Associate Justice United States Supreme Court," which differs in minor details, *Washington Post*, Sunday, 25 February 1906, p. 6.

26   "Memories," #118.

27   "Memories," #118.

28   "Memories," #118+.

29   "Memories," #118+.

30   "Memories," #155. The question of the reality of paternalism, of course, has been taken up by many historians of slavery, including Stanley Elkins, Kenneth Stampp, Fogel and Engerman, and Eugene Genovese.

31   We can, I think, take Malvina's descriptions as those shared by her husband of some 50 years. The beginning and ending dates in the title of her memoirs derive from her relationship with John: 1854 is the year she met him, and 1911 the year he died. Upon his death, she consoled herself with the knowledge that she could "truthfully say, that never *knowingly* did I do anything that I thought he would not approve!" MSH to her children, 27 October 1911, JMH Papers, LC, Reel 1, #718. The memoirs were written in this same spirit.

32   JMH, Constitutional Law Lectures, 7 May 1898, JMH Papers, LC. Hereafter cited as Lectures. I am preparing an edition of these lectures delivered at George Washington University in 1897-1898.

33   "Memories," #118. Malvina uses the term slave-driver, but as they were generally black, she must have meant a slave-trader.

34   See for example, Jennie C. Morton, "Life in Kentucky in the Days of Negro Slavery," *Register of the Kentucky State Historical Society* 5 (January 1907): 44-46.

35   See Ivan Eugene McDougle, "Slavery in Kentucky, 1792-1865," Ph.D. diss., Clark University, 1918, p. 2, who is taken to task by Frederic Bancroft, *Slave-Trading in the old South* (Baltimore, MD: J. H. Furst

Company, 1931), 128-134. See also John Winston Coleman, Jr., *Slavery Times in Kentucky* (Chapel Hill: University of North Carolina Press, 1940), 245.

36 Kentucky's non-plantation economy, which may have lessened the brutality and impersonality endured by slaves because so few of them were fieldhands, was the reason why so many slaves were exported from the state to more southern climes. Paternalism sprang from the same source as the auction block. In addition to Bancroft, see T. D. Clark, "The Slave Trade Between Kentucky and the Cotton Kingdom," *Mississippi Valley Historical Review* 21 (1934): 331-342.

37 James Harlan to D. Howard Smith, 5 August 1851, Frankfort, KY, JMH Papers, LC, Reel 2, #39.

38 James Harlan to D. Howard Smith, 5 August 1851, Frankfort, KY, JMH Papers, LC, Reel 2, #39.

39 The *Cincinnati Daily Gazette* of 15 October 1881, p. 4 col. 1, contained an editorial that read: "Colonel Harlan, on the paternal side, is a son of one of the best Kentucky families." I thank Professor J. Morgan Kousser for this citation, although we disagree on how to weigh the evidence. Walter J. Simmons says Robert came to the Harlan household at the age of eight, *Men of Mark, Eminent, Progressive and Rising*, (1887; reprint, New York: Arno Press and the New York Times, 1968); while Robert McStallworth names James Harlan as his father, see Rayford W. Logan and Michael R. Winston, ed., *Dictionary of American Negro Biography*, (New York: W. W. Norton & Company, 1982), 287. See also Joel Williamson, *New People: Miscegenation and Mulattoes in the United States* (New York: The Free Press, 1980), especially Chapter 1.

40 Simmons, 613.

41 Robert J. Harlan's obituary, *Cincinnati Enquirer*, 22 September 1897, p. 6; Simmons, 613.

42 Robert Harlan interceded on behalf of a Harlan who had assaulted a black civil servant, see 5 November 1871, Cincinnati, OH, JMH Papers, LC, Reel 1, #33; and discussed Hayes's disappointing race policy with John, 1 June 1877, Cincinnati, OH, JMH Papers, LC, Reel 4, #466.

43 Slave traders were condemned by all whites at least theoretically, Bancroft, 365 ff.

44 Contrast this judgment with Robert E. McGlone's conclusions about a legend told by the family of John Brown, "Rescripting a Troubled Past: John Brown's Family and the Harpers Ferry Conspiracy," *Journal of American History* 75 (March 1989): 1179-1200.

45 "Memories," #155.

46   Harlan's judicial opinions disprove Thomas Lewis Owen's characterization of him as an unprincipled political hack, although it is true that Harlan's civil rights decisions were purer than his political pronouncements, Owen, "The Pre-Court Career of John Marshall Harlan," M.A. thesis, University of Louisville, 1970.

47   JMH to James Harlan, 8 October 1881, Washington, DC, JMH Papers, LC, Reel 1, #185.

48   For a fuller exploration of the meaning of manhood to the Harlans, see Linda C. A. Przybyszewski, "John Marshall Harlan's Great Expectations: Lawyering Sons in the Republic," Law & Society Association Annual Meeting, Berkeley, CA, 2 June 1990.

49   Besides his well-known dissents in the *Civil Rights Cases*, 109 U.S. 3 (1883) and *Plessy v. Ferguson*, 163 U.S. 537 (1896), Harlan opposed the pro-segregation decisions which turned on questions of interstate commerce: see *Hall v. De Cuir*, 95 U.S. 485 (1878), which pre-dates Harlan's arrival to the bench where the Court declared a Louisiana desegregation law an unconstitutional burden on interstate commerce and segregation a reasonable rule for a private owner to make in the face of congressional silence on the subject; *Louisville, New Orleans, & Texas Railroad Company v. Mississippi*, 133 U.S. 587 (1890) where the Court held that a state-ordered segregation system did not interfere with inter-state commerce, Harlan dissents; *Chiles v. Chesapeake & Ohio Ry. Co.* 218 U.S. 71 (1910) a Kentucky segregation law, which actually forced an inter-state black traveler to change cars at its borders, deemed a reasonable regulation that does not interfere with interstate commerce, Harlan dissents.

50   *Berea College v. Kentucky*, 211 U.S. 45, 69 (1908).

51   *Clyatt v. U.S.*, 197 U.S. 207, 223 (1905); McKenna concurred in Harlan's dissent.

52   While Harlan ridiculed white supremacists for their obsession with the question of color, he also rejected "assimilation," see Linda C. A. Przybyszewski "The Republic According to John Marshall Harlan: Race, Republicanism, and Citizenship," Ph.D. diss., Stanford University, 1989, pp. 82-94, 144-150.

53   *Pace v. Alabama*, 106 U.S. 583 (1883).

54   *Cumming v. Richmond County Board of Education*, 175 U.S. 542 (1899). His friend Justice William Howard Taft cited *Cumming* to allow state segregation in the schools in *Gong Lum v. Rice*, 275 U.S. 78 (1927).

55   See *Neal v. Delaware*, 103 U.S. 370 (1880), Harlan delivers and *Bush v. Kentucky*, 107 U.S. 110 (1882), Harlan delivers, for example. For a close analysis of the jury trial cases, see Benno C. Schmidt, Jr., "Juries, Jurisdiction, and Race Discrimination: The Lost Promise of *Strauder v. West Virginia*," *Texas Law Review* 61 (May 1983) 1401-1499.

56 "Memories," #228-9.

57 "Memories," #115.

58 "Memories," #230.

59 Emphasis hers, "Memories," #229-230.

60 George C. Rable contrasts this with "union men, carpetbaggers, and blacks [who] displayed a great deal of flexibility in dealing with the revolutionary upheavals of the Civil War and Reconstruction," in "Bourbonism, Reconstruction, and the Persistence of Southern Distinctiveness," *Civil War History* 29 (June 1983), 138. See also George Fredrickson on the multiple uses of racial romanticism, *The Black Image in the White Mind: The Debate on Afro-American Character and Destiny 1817-1914* (1971; reprint, Middletown, CT: Wesleyan University Press, 1987), 97-129.

61 Gaines M. Foster, *The Ghosts of the Confederacy: Defeat, the Lost Cause, and the Emergence of the New South* (New York: Oxford UP, 1986), 121, 145ff; and David W. Blight, " 'For Something Beyond the Battle Field': Frederick Douglass and the Memory of the Civil War," *Journal of American History* 75 (March 1989): 1156-1178.

62 See Paul H. Buck, *The Road to Reunion 1865-1900* (Boston: Little and Brown, 1937), 196-235; Rollin G. Osterweis, *The Myth of the Lost Cause, 1865-1900* (Hamden CT: Archon Books, 1973): 24 ff; Thomas L. Connelly and Barbara L. Bellows, *God and General Longstreet: The Lost Cause and the Southern Mind* (Baton Rouge: Louisiana State University Press, 1982), 50ff.

63 The pro-slavery ideology of the post-war period strongly resembled that which had flourished in the antebellum years; compare William Sumner Jenkins *Pro-Slavery Though in the Old South* (Chapel Hill: University of North Carolina Press, 1935) with John David Smith, *An Old Creed for the New South: Proslavery Ideology and Historiography, 1865-1918* (Westport, CT, Greenwood Press, 1985), 17-67.

64 See for example, William Cohen, "Negro Involuntary Servitude in the South, 1865-1940: A Preliminary Analysis," *Journal of Southern History* 42 (February 1976): 31-60; C. Vann Woodward, *Origins of the New South 1877-1913* (Baton Rouge: Louisiana State University Press, 1951, 1971), 212-215; Edward L. Ayers, *Vengeance and Justice: Crime and Punishment in the Nineteenth Century South* (New York: Oxford UP, 1984). And for the 20th century, see Gunnar Myrdal, et al, *An American Dilemma: The Negro Problem and Modern Democracy*, 2 vols., (New York: Harper & Row, 1944), 547-569; Dan T. Carter, *Scottsboro: A Tragedy of the American South* (Baton Rouge: Louisiana State University Press, 1969).

65 Lectures, 26 March 1898.

Oliver Wendell Holmes and the Democratic Foundations of the First Amendment

Patrick Garry

Throughout American history, freedom of speech has been one of the most intensely debated issues on the national agenda. Although the Constitution explicitly carries a protection for free speech, the meaning and nature of this protection has remained unsettled to this day. And despite the two-centuries existence of the Bill of Rights, the history of civil liberties in America seems more filled with villians than with heroes.

Until recently, Oliver Wendell Holmes unquestionably occupied the hero category. He held that honor since his famous dissent in *Abrams v. U.S.* in 1919.[1] In that dissent, Holmes argued that the First Amendment prohibited punishment of speech critical of the government. He articulated for the nation an eloquent defense of free expression. Though the Court did not immediately accept Holmes's views on free speech, his theory of the First Amendment set forth in the *Abrams* dissent would influence the development of civil liberties law throughout the twentieth century.

Holmes has been called the "legendary father of modern First Amendment jurisprudence."[2] He was the Court's most frequent spokesman on constitutional matters; and his judicial opinions remain among the best known ever written.[3] Revisionist historians, however, have drawn a different picture of Holmes and his free speech views.[4] They point to opinions written by Justice Holmes prior to *Abrams* — opinions like *Schenck v. U.S.* — in which he failed to recognize First Amendment rights and the value of free speech.[5] Using contemporary standards, these revisionists argue that Holmes should be categorized as "conservative" or "restrictive" on civil liberties.

In part, the revisionist critics of Holmes are correct. Some of his decisions, particularly *Schenck*, reflect a restrictive view of the First Amendment—a view, incidentally, entirely consistent with prevailing legal views at the turn of the century. Yet the critics seem to ignore the transformation made by Holmes in his views on free speech and the manner in which he accomplished his transformation. With his *Abrams* dissent, Holmes offered a new and expanded vision of free speech and its value to a democratic society—a view that would eventually lead to the more libertarian First Amendment decisions by the Supreme Court in the 1960s and 1970s.

Thus, the debate over the "correct" labelling of Holmes as either a "liberal" or "conservative" ignores the lasting impact that Holmes had on the First Amendment. His change in free speech views from his restrictive *Schenck* opinion in 1919 to his more enlightened *Abrams* dissent later that same year foreshadowed the judicial transformation of First Amendment law that would occur fifty years later.

Justice Holmes in his *Abrams* dissent also demonstrated that majority rule and democratic processes were not always contradictory to individual free speech values. He articulated a theory of democratic society which required for its survival the maintainence of a system of free expression—an open "marketplace of ideas." This theory, in turn, supported Holmes's "marketplace of ideas" view of the First Amendment which provided a social justification for free speech. Thus, Holmes's incorporation of social and political values into First Amendment theory paved the way for a more protective free speech law. He essentially discovered and used democratic arguments to create a constitutional doctrine protective of speech rights. In *Schenck*, for instance, Holmes treated democratic and free speech values as contradictory—a treatment later reversed in his *Abrams* dissent. Indeed, perhaps Holmes's greatest accomplishment in the free speech area was to begin a reconciliation of the long-standing conflict perceived between democratic rule and individual freedom.

The story of Holmes's transformation in free speech views from *Schenck* to *Abrams* tells in a capsule the story of America's constitutional transformation in free speech law in the twentieth century. Holmes's evolution of a free speech theory served as both a guide for and a preview of the later liberalization of First Amendment interpretations in the courts. It is this transformation and his pioneering First Amendment theory in *Abrams* that makes Holmes a champion of the First Amendment.

Holmes's initial free speech views flowed almost instinctively from his judicial philosophy of democratic law. Although Holmes's views of democratic government eventually provided the key to his later-developed free speech views, they initially presented an obstacle to his vision of a protective theory on civil liberties. Thus, Holmes's judicial philosophy on majority rule and democratic values forms an essential element in the evolution of his First Amendment views. As will be seen, his philosophy constituted both an obstacle, initially, and a stimulant, subsequently, to his free speech theory.

Oliver Wendell Holmes, Jr. was appointed to the U.S. Supreme Court in 1902 by President Theodore Roosevelt and came to the Court after serving nearly twenty years on the Supreme Judicial Court of Massachusetts. Appointed by a "progressive" president in the "Progressive" era, Holmes during his thirty-year tenure on the Court gave his judicial support to much of the progressive legislation challenged there. While the majority of the Court during that period often struck down such legislation as child labor laws on the grounds that it violated rights of property and contract, Holmes supported the democratic power of the majority to legislate on behalf of the general welfare.[6]

Holmes held an ardent belief in democracy and majority rule, and concentrated his legal theory on eliminating obstacles to the will of the majority. Since the only body empowered to make law was the legislature, a judge's duty as seen by Holmes was to uphold the majority rule.

This view of the judicial role therefore required judicial restraint and legislative deference. Only when a law explicitly violated the Constitution did the Court have the authority to eschew the majority will and overturn legislation.   Thus, Holmes's philosophy implicitly contained a presumption of constitutionality.   His opinions demonstrated a willingness to "allow the legislative will to prevail in all but extraordinary circumstances."[7]

Holmes opposed what today would be called "activist" tampering with the Constitution.[8] To Holmes, the discovery of new rights in the Constitution violated the judicial role.   As one scholar has noted, Holmes did not believe in rights and was skeptical of all arguments that began with the assertion of rights.[9] He feared that the creation of "rights" through judicial activism had led people who no longer could control the legislature to look to the courts for fulfillment of their political agenda.   Judicial activism, according to Holmes, resulted in undemocratic law.

Holmes's philosophy of restraint pitted him against the majority of the conservative Court which actively used the contract clause to overturn progressive legislation.   Unlike Holmes, most of the justices mistrusted the majority will and feared its effects on property and commercial interests. Indeed, up until the first free speech cases in 1919, the majority of cases handled by Holmes at the Supreme Court in which individual rights were pitted against democratic legislation involved the property interests and "rights" of the wealthy elite, who strove to maintain the status quo and to prevent legislative experimentation to address the social problems of the time. This opposition to change and to the general welfare, according to Holmes, constituted an unnatural use of law.   Thus, much of Holmes's early judicial experience with individual interests involved the Court's use of them to strike down progressive legislation that infringed on the property interests of a select few.

Holmes's judicial philosophy of restraint did not obviously orient him toward protecting the rights of the minority. Indeed, in *The Common Law* published by Holmes in 1881, he argued that conflicts between individual rights and national welfare should be resolved in favor of the latter: "No society has ever admitted that it could not sacrifice individual welfare to its own existence."[10]

Holmes's early opinions involving individual rights also demonstrated his bias toward social interests and against individual rights.   In *Commonwealth v. Davis*, a case which he decided while sitting on the Massachusetts Supreme Court, Holmes denied any constitutional problems with a conviction of an individual who had been arrested for preaching on the Boston Commons.[11] Finding no constitutional implications in the case, Holmes focused only upon the meaning of the statute allegedly violated.   Thus, by presuming constitutionality, Holmes could avoid any constitutional interpretations or any inquiry into individual rights.[12]

In *Patterson v. Colorado*, a 1907 case in which a newspaper that had published articles attacking the conduct of the Supreme Court of Colorado had been cited for contempt, Holmes again dismissed the constitutional challenges and stated that the First Amendment speech protections "do not prevent the subsequent punishment of such as may be deemed contrary to the public welfare."[13] A year later, in ruling upon the propriety of a union leader's arrest and detainment under a state governor's order of martial law, Holmes found no deprivation of due process.[14] He reasoned that "the ordinary rights of individuals must yield to . . . the necessities of the moment."

Finally, in a case reaching the Court after the outbreak of World War I, Holmes once again demonstrated his presumption of constitutionality and his apparent indifference to individual rights.   In upholding the conviction of a newspaper editor who had violated a state statute by criticizing a law against nude sunbathing, Holmes stated that the role of the Court was not to look at a statute in a light that would define it as a violation of the Constitution.[15] Instead, the judicial role obligated the Court to find a way to read the statute as constitutional. The benefit of the doubt as to constitutionality went to the legislature.

As these decisions show, and as Paul Murphy has argued, Holmes's early judicial career was "marked strongly by a spirit of permissive majoritarianism and a commitment to judicial self-restraint.[16] According to Murphy, "Holmes was fairly well in tune with the growing tendency in twentieth-century

America toward community control, with its corresponding limitation upon individual freedom."[17] In Holmes's early philosophy, social order would always come before liberty and the individual.[18] In 1918, he explained his approach to free speech by reasoning that a nation would always protect itself against the expression of dangerous views as readily as it would against the spread of small pox. "Free speech stands no differently than freedom from vaccination," he told Judge Learned Hand.[19]

Thus, as the nation entered World War I and embarked upon a domestic campaign against political dissidents, Holmes's legal philosophy had not prepared him for the challenges to the First Amendment that subsequently occurred. His theory of democratic law and majority rule blinded him to the protection of civil liberties. Yet while this obsession with majority rule initially obstructed his development of a theory of free speech, it ultimately provided the key to a more protective view of free speech set forth in his *Abrams* dissent.

A second obstacle to Holmes's development of a protective theory of free speech prior to *Abrams* lay in the prevailing legal views toward free expression. During the war period, the right of expression in the United States was subjected to restrictions more widespread and more intensive than at any other period except perhaps the slavery controversy in the pre-Civil War South.[20] National paranoia and insecurity resulted from America's entry into the war, the Bolshevik Revolution, and the domestic turmoil caused by rapid changes in industrial, urban, labor and immigration conditions. The period marked the beginning of an extensive use of federal power in controlling speech and in harassing critics and suspected dissidents.[21]

During this period of national hysteria, Congress enacted two important statutes placing limitations upon press and speech. The Espionage Act adopted on June 15, 1917 carried two principal censorship provisions: it imposed felony sanctions on anyone who attempted to cause insubordination in the armed forces or to obstruct the enlistment and recruiting operations of the armed forces. The amendment to the Espionage Act, which became law on May 16, 1918, and which was often referred to as the Sedition Act of 1918, was more comprehensive and general in character. It was enacted at the insistence of a general public alarmed at the activities of pacifist groups, certain labor leaders, and a few over-publicized radicals. The law made it a felony to "incite mutiny or insubordination in the ranks of the armed forces," to "disrupt or discourage recruiting or enlistment service, or utter, print, or publish disloyal, profance, scurrilous, or abusive language about the form of government, the Constitution, soldiers and sailors, flag, or uniform of the armed forces . . ."

Approximately two thousand cases arose in the federal courts involving the Espionage Act alone.[22] Consequently, this period in American history formed the testing ground for the First Amendment. With the widespread restrictions against expression, the courts were faced for the first time with the task of defining freedoms of speech when those freedoms conflicted with national security concerns. Eventually, a case came to the Supreme Court asking for a ruling on the constitutionality of the Espionage and Sedition Acts. The case, *Schenck v. U.S.*, involved an appeal from a conviction of socialists who, in violation of the Espionage Act, had circulated antidraft and antiwar leaflets.

The *Schenck* case presented the U.S. Supreme Court its first opportunity to interpret and apply the First Amendment. The case marked the first time in the Court's 130-year history that anyone attempted to use the First Amendment as a shield against government prosecution; and it was the first time the Court considered federal legislation in relation to the constitutional right of free speech. This absence of First Amendment precedent and lack of experience with free speech issues posed a third obstacle to Holmes's free speech thinking.

The void of First Amendment precedent in 1919 left free speech with weak and untested defenses in the face of strong public demands for restrictions. Moreover, the public desire to control speech occurred within a void of any consensus on or commitment to the values underlying the First Amendment. According to Paul Murphy, few Americans "doubted that freedom could be restricted when it served no constructive public function; and laws of libel, defamation, conspiracy,

slander, and malicious intent (provided) clear legal restraints."[23] Consequently, few judges, including Holmes, were
prepared for the assault on free speech: the First Amendment
arsenal was bare.

Holmes was assigned to write the opinion for the Court in
Schenck. Given his judicial philosophy and his approach to
individual rights, as well as the prevailing views of free speech
and the lack of First Amendment precedent, Holmes's opinion
came as no surprise. In many ways, it was consistent with his
prior judicial career.

In a unanimous opinion the Court upheld the convictions
and the constitutionality of the Espionage Act. It was in this
decision that Holmes created the well-known doctrine of
"clear and present danger" and here that he coined the
metaphor of comparing seditious speech to falsely shouting
fire in a theater: "Free speech would not protect a man in
falsely shouting fire in a theatre, and causing a panic." When a
nation was at war, he added, "many things that might be said
in time of peace are such a hindrance to its (war) effort that
their utterance will not be endured so long as men fight." The
constitutional test was "whether the words used are used in
such circumstances and are of such a nature as to create a
clear and present danger that they will bring about the
substantive evils that Congress has a right to prevent." Under
Holmes's application of the "clear and present danger" test,
however, the focus was on the possible consequences of the
speech rather than on the content of the speech itself.

In *Schenck*, the Court essentially adopted the traditional
Blackstonian belief in the common-law crime of seditious
libel.[24] The decision thus established an exception to the constitutional admonition against congressional interference with
speech: when words create a "clear and present danger" to the
national interest during a time of war, they cannot be protected by any constitutional right. This view, however, lacked
any recognition that speech could serve broader social interests and that society could be harmed if denied the benefits of
the ideas which the prohibited speech might contain.[25]

The *Schenck* decision flowed naturally from the make-up
and orientation of the Court. With the exception of Holmes

and Brandeis, the members of the Court were dedicated to upholding the rights of property and to preserving civil order. They believed that radicals and political dissidents posed a serious threat to society.[26] Given this fear of radicalism, the justices viewed free speech as "subject to the restraints which separate right from wrong-doing."[27]

The lack of First Amendment precedent and free speech experience also influenced the outcome in *Schenck*. Jeremy Cohen concludes that this lack of experience and precedent clouded Holmes's view of the First Amendment implications of the case.[28] Instead, according to Cohen, the Court focused upon the more narrow questions involving the violation of the specific statutes.[29] In presuming the Act constitutional, Holmes concentrated primarily on the commission of a criminal act proscribed by Congress, and only summarily dealt with free speech.[30]

Holmes devoted little effort in his opinion to interpreting the meaning of the First Amendment. As Cohen argues, ample evidence suggests that the Court had not yet seriously considered a comprehensive theory of the First Amendment. For instance, Louis Brandeis later spoke with Felix Frankfurter about *Schenck* and said, "I have never been quite happy about my concurrence in (*Schenck*). I had not then thought the issues of freedom of speech out."[31] Thus, as Cohen argues, the Court reached a conclusion in *Schenck* that had a direct bearing upon the First Amendment, even though it did not provide a serious discussion of the First Amendment prohibition against the abridgment of speech or of the free speech implications of the Espionage Act.[32]

At the time of *Schenck*, therefore, Holmes was "quite insensitive to any claim for special judicial protection of free speech."[33] This insensitivity undoubtedly arose in part from the absence of any clear theory of free speech. When *Schenck* came to the Court, the sparse free speech doctrines were unsophisticated and lacking in detailed specificity.[34] The primary justifications for free speech consisted of the nineteenth century libertarian notions of individual liberty and autonomy. Thus, in deciding free speech issues in the early twentieth century, judges essentially weighed national security interests against the right of the individual to speak his or her mind. Nor surprisingly, as a Civil War veteran injured in three different battles, Holmes enthusiastically supported national security interests during wartime and easily concluded in *Schenck* that individual rights must yield when society felt threatened.

Holmes's First Amendment thinking had not yet developed to a point where the balance in *Schenck* would tilt toward upholding free speech. As with the other justices, Holmes had not envisioned free speech as carrying enough constitutional value to raise it to the level of certain national interests. Unlike the majority of the Court, however, Holmes would acquire such a vision of free speech during the months following *Schenck*. In his *Abrams* dissent, Holmes would devise a free speech theory providing greater weight to free speech values on the judicial scales.

One week after the Court issued its *Schenck* opinion, Holmes authored two more opinions for the Court involving the Espionage and Sedition Acts.[35] These marked the last time he would agree with the Court's approach to abridgments of free speech.

These opinions brought Holmes much criticism, particularly from individuals he respected. Consequently, this criticism rather quickly sharpened his concern with the law of civil liberties.[36] In the months following *Schenck* and preceding *Abrams v. U.S.*, which would be heard by the Court in October of that same year, Holmes received an intense education on free speech theory from respected judges and legal scholars. This education prompted Holmes to reconsider his views on the First Amendment and eventually to write one of the most eloquent defenses of free speech in his *Abrams* dissent.

Holmes not only set out to reconsider his free speech views at a time when the prevailing political and legal attitudes strongly discouraged such an endeavor, but he also discovered a free speech theory which elevated the importance and value of free expression and which later in the century greatly contributed to the liberalization of First Amendment law. His reconsideration of free speech in 1919 produced for Holmes a rationale of why speech had to be protected in a democratic society; whereas in *Schenck* he saw only the conditions in which speech could be restricted. It was from the critics of his *Schenck* opinion that Holmes learned the democratic foundation and rationale for free speech.

Learned Hand criticized Holmes's application of the "clear and present danger" test in *Schenck* and proposed a more protective standard in his correspondence with Holmes shortly after the decision. To Hand's criticism, Holmes replied, saying, "I don't quite get your point," and adding that he could not see any difference between Hand's direct incitement test and his own clear and present danger standard.[37] In response to Hand's disagreements with *Schenck*, Holmes stated that he did not "know what the matter is, or how we differ." The undeveloped nature of Holmes's First Amendment thinking at that time prevented him from comprehending the implications of his *Schenck* ruling and the parameters of a more protective free speech theory.

Ernest Freund, of the University of Chicago Law School, also denounced the clear and present danger test articulated in *Schenck*. He published a harsh attack in the May 3, 1919 issue of *The New Republic*. According to Freund, the decision would foster intolerance. "Tolerance of adverse opinion is not a matter of generosity," he concluded, "but of political prudence."[38]

The most vigorous and comprehensive criticism, however, came from Zechariah Chafee. Chafee, a professor of law at Harvard, argued that the clear and present danger test constituted a piece-meal approach to free speech problems: one which failed to provide a rational guide to courts faced with different types of free speech restraints in the future.[39] In proposing a general theory of free speech, Chafee argued that the true meaning of freedom of speech lie in its contribution to democratic society. According to Chafee, the discovery and spread of truth on subjects of general concern constituted one of the most important purposes of society and government; and such discovery was only possible through free and unlimited discussion. To Chaffee, the social interest in the attainment of truth required a system of free speech protected by the First Amendment.

Chafee's argument hit a receptive note with Holmes. It gave Holmes a greater rationale — a democratic argument — for protecting speech. No longer should speech be protected only because individuals should be free to say and do whatever they liked, free speech should be protected because it was necessary for the survival of democracy. Just like military strength, free speech protected American society and government. Thus, Chafee had explained how free speech could weigh more heavily on the judicial balance with social interests such as national security.

Holmes became strongly attracted to the "truth" argument for free speech.[40] Although Holmes did not accept the individual libertarian views of Hand or Freund, he did through his reading of history and political philosophy become more convinced of the value of free speech in acquiring social truth.[41] This view of speech also fit with Holmes's view of truth. He was skeptical of absolute truth, and believed only that the clash of conflicting beliefs would produce "the natural outcome of a dominant opinion."[42]

Holmes not only read Chafee's writings on free speech, but met with him during the summer of 1919. By this time, Holmes was seriously reconsidering his free speech views.[43] Recognizing that while certain national interests might call for limitations on speech, Holmes now saw that those limitations had to be weighed against the social interest in obtaining truth. By merging the individual's freedom of speech with the healthy functioning of democratic government, Holmes had discovered a view of the First Amendment consistent with American democracy and serving vital social values.

This new view of free speech found expression in Holmes's dissent in *Abrams*. In that dissent, Holmes articulated an expansive view of the First Amendment protections, the importance of which arose from Holmes's logical construction of a free speech theory. He based his protection of speech not simply on a literal reading of the First Amendment, but upon a rational theory of the value of free speech in a democratic society. By constructing this democratic foundation to the First Amendment, Holmes created the blueprints for the subsequent building of free speech rights in the twentieth century.

In *Abrams v. U.S.*, the Court upheld the constitutionality of the Sedition Act.[44] Justice Clarke wrote the majority opinion, joined by all the other justices except Holmes and Brandeis. In its decision issued on November 10, 1919, the Court upheld the convictions of appellants charged with publishing and distributing pamphlets attacking the government's expeditionary force to Russia. The pamphlets denounced the capitalistic government of the United States, called on the allied armies to cease murdering Russians, and asked for a general strike to achieve this purpose. In upholding the convictions, the Court applied the "clear and present danger" test and held that the purpose of the pamphlets was to "excite, at the supreme crisis of the war, disaffection, sedition, riots, and . . . revolution."

Based upon the *Schenck* precedent as it was, Clarke's *Abrams* opinion was very much like one Holmes might have written eight months earlier. Holmes, however, had now moved away from that precedent.

Holmes authored a vigorous dissent and offered an eloquent and moving defense of free speech.[45] He more strictly applied the standard used in *Schenck* and found no clear and present danger posed by the expressions of the appellants. He warned that the clear and present danger test as applied by the Court could in the future be used to prohibit all vigorous criticism of the government. Holmes concluded his dissent with a powerful articulation of the philosophy of free speech in a republican society and a discussion of the connection between freedom of speech and the search for truth:

> Persecution for the expression of opinions seems to me perfectly logical. If you have no doubt of your premises or your power and want a certain result with all your heart you naturally express your wishes in law and sweep away all opposition. To allow opposition by speech seems to indicate that you think the speech impotent, as when a man says that he has squared the circle, or that you do not care wholeheartedly for the result, or that you doubt either your power or your premises. But when men have realized that time has upset many fighting faiths, they may come to believe even more than they believe the very foundations of their own conduct that the ultimate good desired is

better reached by free trade in ideas—that the best test of truth is the power of the thought to get itself accepted in the competition of the market; and that truth is the only ground upon which their wishes safely can be carried out. That, at any rate, is the theory of our Constitution. It is an experiment, as all life is an experiment. Every year, if not every day, we have to wager our salvation upon some prophecy based upon imperfect knowledge. While that experiment is part of our system I think that we should be eternally vigilant against attempts to check the expression of opinions that we loathe and believe to be fraught with death, unless they so imminently threaten immediate interference with the lawful and pressing purposes of the law that an immediate check is required to save the country.[46]

By incorporating the attainment of truth rationale into free speech theory, Holmes reached a more speech-protective application of the "clear and present danger" test.[47] Holmes did not simply apply more strictly the clear and present danger test articulated in *Schenck*, he incorporated the truth rationale into his theory, which then mandated a more protective application. This incorporation put free speech on a more even level with the forces seeking to repress it. Thus, while the defenders of free speech formerly offered only individual liberty arguments, Holmes now showed how speech was vital not only for individuals but for society as a whole. Under Holmes's views, speech should no longer be restricted just because of the claim that it might jeopardize national interests; indeed, the restriction of speech in itself would threaten the democratic marketplace of ideas. The *Abrams* dissent advanced the idea that dissenting speech served the government's interests, since the truthful basis of governmental measures could only be tested in the marketplace of ideas.

Holmes's change of views between *Schenck* and *Abrams* has been well documented by scholars and historians. While at the time of *Schenck* Holmes was "quite insensitive to any claim for special judicial protection of free speech, . . . it was not until his famous dissent in *Abrams* that Holmes put some teeth into the clear and present danger formula."[48] That dissent reflected his belief that the First Amendment established a national policy favoring a search for truth, while balancing social interests and individual interests.[49]

Although Holmes's reconsideration of his free speech views after *Schenck* may have been prompted by the criticism he received from people like Hand and Chafee, his transformation to a more protective theory resulted from his formulation of the marketplace theory of the First Amendment. While in the summer of 1918 he insisted that free speech was no different than freedom from vaccination, Holmes in November of 1919 articulated the vital need for free speech in a democratic society.[50] Indeed, in 1918 Holmes had seemed impervious to Hand's arguments that the tendency to silence dissenters should be tempered in the interest of the search for truth.

His dissent in *Abrams* brought Holmes a mixture of praise and criticism. Roscoe Pound, Dean of Harvard Law School, assured Holmes that the dissent was "a document of human liberty."[51] Zechariah Chafee described the dissent as a "magnificent exposition of the philososphic basis" of the First Amendment."[52] Many in the legal community, however, deplored the dissent. One such criticism appeared in an article written by Professor John H. Wigmore, one of the most widely respected legal scholars in America.[53] Wigmore disagreed that the speech at issue in *Abrams* could be justified by any reference to a search for truth. He saw the real danger not in the government's suppression of speech, but that a misplaced reverence for free speech would be used to protect the treacherous thuggery of impatient and fanatical minorities.

Despite Wigmore's fears, American courts in the 1960s, at a time of even more domestic turmoil, would adopt an even more protective view of the First Amendment. And no danger would come to pass from the "treacherous thuggery of impatient and fanatical minorities."

Notwithstanding the furor of criticism over the *Abrams* dissent, Holmes's marketplace theory of the First Amendment subsequently had a lasting impact on constitutional law. Court decisions in the 1930s and 1950s and 1960s would generally adopt the view of the First Amendment set forth in the Holmes dissent.[54] Indeed, Holmes's marketplace theory would become a principal judicial guide rule in First Amendment cases.[55] The transformation of Holmes between his opinion in

Schenck and his dissent in *Abrams* provided for future generations the key to a more rationale and consistent theory of the First Amendment. Indeed, his marketplace of ideas metaphor would throughout the twentieth century characterize the role of free speech in American law. Moreover, this marketplace theory would also form the basic concept of press freedom during the twentieth century.

Justices continued to invoke the *Abrams* dissent to support free speech well into the 1960s. Not until June of 1969, in *Brandenburg v. Ohio*, did the Court decide that the "clear and present danger" test, even in its mort libertarian form, was not sufficiently speech-protective.[56] In *Brandenburg*, the Court adopted instead a more speech protective test—the direct incitement test. Yet this decision still incorporated the marketplace theory of the First Amendment articulated by Holmes in his *Abrams* dissent.

The *Abrams* dissent has led many to see Holmes as a champion of free speech and the First Amendment.[57] As one historian has noted, the *Abrams* dissent contributed "to a process of judicial reconsideration which eventually placed freedom of speech on a firmer constitutional basis.[58] Constituting the first statement by a Supreme Court Justice that the government could not deal with the act of speech as it would with any other act, the dissent laid the ground for a "new jurisprudence that would give superordinate status to the communicative freedoms."[59]

Holmes, a believer in majority rule, had found a way in *Abrams* to expand the First Amendment protections given to individual speech and to reconcile the values underlying civil liberties and democratic government. With that dissent, Holmes squarely rebutted and opposed the restrictive judicial trend involving free speech. He not only gave the first constitutional defense of free speech, but through his marketplace theory he showed future generations how to finally achieve a more enlightened constitutional protection of free expression. The legacy of the *Abrams* dissent exists in the development of American civil liberties in the twentieth century. Our present open society, resting on communicative freedoms, owes much to the labors of Holmes.[60]

Notes

1 *Abrams et al. v. United States*, 250 U.S. 616.

2 Richard M. Abrams, "Oliver Wendell Holmes and American Liberalism," *Reviews in American History* 19 (March 1991), 86-97, p. 86.

3 Sheldon Novick, "Justice Holmes and Roe v. Wade," *Trial* (December 1989) 58-64.

4 By 1962, scholars had begun a reconsideration of Holmes, prompted by Yosal Rogat's publication of "Mr. Justice Holmes: A Dissenting Opinion," *Stanford Law Review* 15 (1962-1963), 254. A synopsis of the revisionist views of Holmes's speech opinions appears in Yosal Rogat and James M. O'Fallon, "Mr. Justice Holmes: A Dissenting Opinion – The Speech Cases," *Stanford Law Review* 36 (July 1984), 1349-1406. The authors argue that Holmes was not the great liberal he was once thought to be. The authors also argue, as this author recognizes, that Holmes's free speech decisions prior to his *Abrams* dissent displayed no special concern for the protection of dissident speech.

5 *Schenck v. United States*, 249 U.S. 47.

6 Holmes's support of progressive legislation, as the revisionists argue, may not have resulted from his "liberal" or "progressive" political views, but rather from his judicial philosophy. Indeed, contrary to the expectations of Theodore Roosevelt, who appointed Holmes to the Court, Holmes was neither a progressive nor a reformer – though he often ruled as one. Abraham, Henry J., *Justices and Presidents* (New York: Oxford Univ. Press 1985), p. 159; Burton, David H., *Oliver Wendell Holmes, Jr.* (Boston: G. K. Hall & Co. 1980), p. 93.

7 Burton, *Holmes*, p. 79.

8 Walter Robert Goedecke, *Change and the Law* (Tallahassee: Florida State Univ. Press, 1969), p. 166. For more discussion on Holmes's judicial philosophy, see Oliver Wendell Holmes *The Common Law* (1881), ed. Mark DeWolfe Howe (Boston: Little Brown & Co., 1963); Roscoe Pound, "Judge Holmes's Contributions to the Science of Law," *Harvard Law Review* 34 (March 1921); Henry M. Hart, Jr., "Holmes' Positivism – An Addendum," *Harvard Law Review* 64 (April 1951), 929-39; Mark DeWolfe Howe, "The Positivism of Mr. Justice Holmes," *Harvard Law Review* 64 (February 1951), 529-46; and Holmes, "The Path of the Law" – a lecture given by Holmes on January 8, 1887 to Boston Univer-

sity School of Law; Pohlman, H. L., *Justice Oliver Wendell Holmes and Utilitarian Jurisprudence* (Cambridge: Harvard Univ. Press 1984); and Novick, Sheldon M., *Honorable Justice: The Life of Oliver Wendell Holmes* (Boston: Little, Brown 1989).

9   Goedecke, *Change and the Law*, p. 166.

10 Holmes, *The Common Law*, pp. 36-8.

11 *Commonwealth v. Davis*, 162 Mass. 510 (1895).

12 This view found expression in several of Holmes's decisions, and particularly so in *Baily v. Alabama*, 219 U.S. 219, 248 (1911).

13 *Patterson v. Colorado*, 205 U.S. 454 (1907).

14 *Moyer v. Peabody*, 212 U.S. 78 (1908).

15 *Fox v. Washington*, 236 U.S. 273 (1915).

16 Paul L. Murphy, *World War I and the Origin of Civil Liberties in the United States* (W. W. Norton & Co., New York: 1979), p. 186.

17 Ibid, p. 187.

18 Holmes to Learned Hand, June 24, 1918, in Gerald Gunther, "Learned Hand and the Origins of Modern First Amendment Doctrine: Some Fragments of History," *Stanford Law Review*, XXVII (1975), 757.

19 Ibid.

20 Norman Dorsen, Paul Bender, Burt Neuborne, *Political and Civil Rights in the United States* 4th Ed., (Boston: Little, Brown and Company 1976), p. 31.

21 Many historians have remarked that the wartime repression did not arise from genuine fears of German subversion or of some international Communist conspiracy for revolution, but from anxieties over widespread challenges to traditional American culture. The harshness of the industrial system, the seemingly titanic waves of eastern and southern European immigrants, the rise of urban slums all contributed to the divisive pressures on social order and traditional cultural and social norms. Consequently, "most of the custodians of culture, beset already by intellectual attack and worried by signs of sexual, racial, and other kinds of insurrection, linked the Allied Cause with the defense of all they valued, and thereby added the last element needed to produce a really big explosion." Henry F. May, *The End of American Innocence* (1959), p. 354.

22 Alfred H. Kelly and Winfred A. Harbison, *The American Constitution: Its Origins and Development* (New York: W. W. Norton & Co., 1976) 5th Ed., p. 632.

23 Paul Murphy, *The Meaning of Freedom of Speech*, (1972) p. 12.

24 Murphy, *The Origin of Civil Liberties*, p. 266.

25 Ibid., p. 267.

26 Richard Polenberg, *Fighting Faiths: The Abrams Case, the Supreme Court, and Free Speech* (New York: Viking Penguin, 1987) p. 198; see also Robert M. Cover, "The Left, the Right, and the First Amendment: 1918-1928", *Maryland Law Review* XL (1981), 354.

27 This view of the First Amendment was described by Edward D. White, and is set forth in Robert B. Highsaw, *Edward Douglass White: Defender of the Conservative Faith* (Baton Rouge, 1981), p. 154.

28 Jeremy Cohen, *Congress Shall Make No Law: Oliver Wendell Holmes, the First Amendment, and Judicial Decision Making* (Ames, Iowa: Iowa State University Press, 1989).

29 Cohen, *Congress Shall Make No Law*, p. 17.

30 Ibid., p. 88.

31 Quoted in Alexander Bickel, *The Supreme Court and the Idea of Progress* (New Haven: Yale Univ. Press, 1978), p. 27.

32 Cohen, *Congress Shall Make No Law*, p. 100.

33 Gunther, "Learned Hand," p. 720.

34 Murphy, *Origin of Civil Liberties*, p. 39.

35 In *Frohwerk v. U.S.*, 249 U.S. 204 (1919) and *Debs v. U.S.*, 249 U.S. 211 (1919), the Court upheld convictions under the Espionage and Sedition Acts. Both decisions were based on the *Schenck* precedent.

36 Fred D. Ragan, "Justice Oliver Wendell Holmes, Jr., Zechariah Chafee, Jr., and the Clear and Present Danger Test for Free Speech: The First Year, 1919," *Journal of American History* 58 (June 1971), 39-43.

37 Gunther, "Learned Hand," pp. 758-60, 741.

38 Ernest Freund, "The Debs Case and Freedom of Speech," *The New Republic* 19 (May 3, 1919): 13; Ernest Freund, "The Debs Case," *The New Republic* 19 (May 31, 1919): 152.

39 Chafee's criticisms of the *Schenck* decision appeared in Zechariah Chafee, "Freedom of Speech in War Time," *Harvard Law Review*, XXXII (June 1919), 932-73.

40 Ibid., p. 227.

41 Ibid.

42 *Lochner v. New York*, 198 U.S. 45, 76 (1905) (Holmes, J., dissenting).

43 Polenberg, *Fighting Faiths*, p. 223.

44 250 U.S. 616 (1919).

45 Holmes's dissent has been called "intense and brilliant" even by the revisionist critics of his free speech opinions. Rogan and O'Fallon, "Mr. Justice Holmes," p. 1383.

46 250 U.S. at 630-1. This discussion of liberty of expression has been called "the greatest utterance of intellectual freedom by an American, ranking in the English tongue with Milton and Mill." *The Mind and Faith of Justice Holmes* 306 (M. Lerner ed. 1943).

47 Gunther, "Learned Hand," p. 743; and see Cover, "The Left, the Right, and the First Amendment," p. 373.

48 Gunther, "Learned Hand and the Origins of Modern First Amendment Doctrine: Some Fragments of History," *Stanford Law Review* 27 (1975) p. 719. See also Rabban, "The Emergence of Modern First Amendment Doctrine," *University of Chicago Law Review* 50 (1983) pp. 1207-9, in which the author discusses Holmes's move from a restrictive construction in *Schenck* to a more protective position in the *Abrams* dissent.

49 Fred D. Ragan, "Justice Oliver Wendell Holmes, Jr., Zechariah Chafee, Jr., and the Clear and Present Danger Test for Free Speech: The First Year, 1919," *Journal of American History* 58 (June 1971), 43.

50 The *Abrams* dissent, as unremarkable as it may seem from a modern perspective, represented a significant departure from the prevailing view, which Holmes had expressed so starkly to Laski in 1918: that government could constitutionally impinge on speech for good cause as readily as it could impinge on any other right—perhaps even more readily, indeed, than it could on the rights of private property. O. W. Holmes, Jr., to Harold Laski, 7 July 1918; quoted in Richard Polenberg, *Fighting Faiths*, p. 212. For more of the correspondence, see Mark DeWolfe Howe, ed., *Holmes-Laski Letters*, abridged edition by Alger Hiss (Vol. 1, 1963), p. 116.

51 Pound to Holmes, November 26, 1919, Holmes MSS, Reel 26.

52 Zechariah Chafee, "A Contemporary State Trial," *Harvard Law Review*, XXXIII (April 1920), 769.

53 Wigmore, John H. "Abrams v. U.S.: Freedom of Speech and Freedom of Thuggery in War-time and Peace-time," *Illinois Law Review* XIV (1920), 539-561.

54 Dorsen, *Political and Civil Rights in the United States*, p. 44.

55 Kelly, *The American Constitution*, p. 633.

56 *Brandenburg v. Ohio*, 395 U.S. 444.

57 Cohen, *Congress Shall Make No Law*, p. 116.

58 Polenberg, *Fighting Faiths*, p. 370.

59 Abrams, "Oliver Wendell Holmes," p. 87.

60 Abrams, "Oliver Wendell Holmes," p. 94.

Louis D. Brandeis: Pioneer Progressive

Marguerite R. Plummer

There is little doubt that when President Woodrow Wilson appointed Louis D. Brandeis to the U.S. Supreme Court in 1916, he did so in recognition of the fact that the growing Progressive movement in the country would be a crucial factor in the success or failure of his bid for reelection. In Brandeis, Wilson found a Progressive activist, a "people's attorney," a Jeffersonian Democrat who deplored bigness in business and government, and a legal craftsman with a reformer's vision of a society in which politics and the law allowed people to control their own environments and maximize the chances of fulfilling their potential.[1] What Wilson accomplished in appointing Brandeis was to place on the Court not only a Progressive with a penchant for social reform, but one whom legal experts and scholars would consistently rank as one of the greatest U.S. Supreme Court justices.

Brandeis was born of Jewish middle class parents, emigrants from Czechoslovakia, in Louisville, Kentucky, on November 13, 1856. His family's values—education, culture, idealism, morality, ambition, political awareness—would leave "clear imprints on his mind."[2] Brandeis' experience of growing up in Kentucky during the Civil War, seizing the opportunity to attend Harvard Law School, mingling with the elitist Brahmin society in Boston, developing a large corporate law practice during the Industrial Revolution, and then embarking on a career of social activism during the height of the Progressive movement, not only exemplified the American dream of success but personified the changing shape of the American legal system.

The Industrial Revolution brought about significant changes in the practice of law. New demands were being made on the judicial system to interpret contract law, labor relations and labor conditions, interstate commerce and transportation systems, federal and state government regulations and procedures, all involving individual rights, states' rights, an expanding federal government and business interests. In this milieu of changing and conflicting interests, Louis D. Brandeis was realizing his American Dream: he made his fortune as a corporate attorney with a vast understanding of business and economics, and, at the same time, gained a reputation as "the people's lawyer," concerned with protecting the rights of the individual from the avarice of big business and the encroachment of big government.

Brandeis' crusade for individual rights first drew national attention with an article on "The Right to Privacy" written by Brandeis and his law partner, Samuel Dennis Warren, Jr., for the December 1890 *Harvard Law Review*. Disgusted by the tactics of sensation-seeking photographers and journalists who thrived on the "gossip trade," as Brandeis called it, and those who appealed to a prurient taste for details of sexual relations, Brandeis and Warren presented their case for the individual's right "to be let alone." The impact of the article was significant. Dean Roscoe Pound of the Harvard Law School observed, more than 26 years later, that despite the absence of any discussion about potential conflict between the right to privacy and the right to a free press, the article "did nothing less than add a chapter to the law."[3]

By 1928, ten years after Brandeis became a Supreme Court justice, he would again stand up for individual rights against the United States Government itself in *Olmstead v. U.S.* (277 U.S. 438). In the *Olmstead* case, the lower court ruled that evidence obtained by the federal government through secret wire-tapping of the telephones in chief offices and residences of co-conspirators in crime, where no trespass on private property was involved, did not violate the constitutional rights of the defendants. The case was appealed on the ground that the government's wire-tapping of private telephone conversations constituted unreasonable search and seizure in violation of the

Fourth Amendment. Though the Supreme Court upheld the decision of the lower court, Brandeis wrote a vigorous dissent, insisting that the clauses in the Constitution guaranteeing protection to the individual against abuses of power must be adaptable to the changing world; that, since advances in science and technology had placed "subtler and more far-reaching means of invading privacy" in the hands of government, the law must be capable of "wider application than the mischief that gave it birth" (472-73). In this case, according to Brandeis' dissenting opinion, the government had violated both the Fourth Amendment (the prohibition against unjustified search and seizure) and the Fifth (protection against self-incrimination), in the invasion of the "sanctities of a man's home and the privacies of his life" (483). In a very forceful argument, Brandeis stated a principle that would earn him the name of prophet: "If government becomes a lawbreaker, it breeds contempt for the law; it invites every man to become a law unto himself; it invites anarchy."[4]

Before Brandeis was appointed to the Supreme Court, his political and social activism drew national attention and made powerful enemies who would fight against his confirmation with all the strength that money could amass. Former President William Howard Taft, whose anger still festered because of Brandeis' representation of *Colliers* magazine and Louis Glavis, the whistleblower in the Senate hearing on the Ballinger-Pinchot Alaskan land controversies during Taft's administration, signed an opposing petition containing the signatures of seven former presidents of the American Bar Association.

The Boston Brahmins, former friends and allies, were unforgiving of Brandeis for representing both sides of cases in disputes between industry and labor. Brandeis' statement that he was "attorney to the situation" was to the traditional Bostonians a ridiculous assertion. In the case of the *United Shoe Company,* Brandeis alienated a number of the Boston attorneys because he joined in an antitrust suit against a company he formerly represented, using in his arguments information that many felt to be privileged by the confidential client-attorney relationship. Despite the attacks on his character during the lengthy Senate hearings, no wrongdoing was proved by his detractors, and on June 1, 1916, he was confirmed by the Senate by a vote of 47 to 22.

Brandeis' stature on the Court was enhanced by the so-called "Brandeis brief," a technique developed by Brandeis in which he combined facts and social theory in support of his constitutional philosophy. The first case before the Supreme Court in which the Brandeis brief was used was *Muller v. Oregon,* 208 U.S. 412 (1908), before Brandeis' appointment. He entered the case not as a mere friend of the court, but, rightly perceiving that the Court would pay little attention to him as *amicus curiae,* he asked that Alice Goldmark, his sister-in-law who helped prepare the brief, secure his appointment by the attorney general of Oregon as co-counsel for the defense. Since the state attorney general was already filing a brief detailing the legal arguments, Brandeis wrote a 113-page brief comprising quotations of facts and scientific reports detailing the dangers to women's physical and moral health of excessively long hours of hard work. For the first time, the Supreme Court was asked to accept the truth of "diverse factual material" and sociological data outside the record of the case. The Court upheld the Oregon statute and cited Brandeis' brief in the opinion.[5]

Brandeis' use of facts outside the record in the *Muller* brief "became the norm in litigating social issues." The "ultimate triumph" of the Brandeis brief, according to Melvin I. Urofksy, writing in *Brandeis and America,* was in the case of *Brown v. Board of Education,* 347 U.S. 483 (1954), in which additional studies and reports confirming the harm to Negro children of isolation in segregated schools had a strong impact on the decision of the Supreme Court in striking down the "separate but equal" doctrine previously enforced.[6]

Another constitutional issue that was a priority for Brandeis was the protection of the right to freedom of speech and the right to education, for he felt that education was the key to the intelligent exchange of ideas and good government. One of the earliest cases in which Brandeis figured on the Supreme Court was *Pierce v. U.S.,* 252 U.S. 239 (1920), in which Brandeis wrote a dissenting opinion arguing that free speech was an expression of the "fundamental right of free men to strive for better conditions through new legislation and new institutions." Disgusted at times by some of the Court's rulings abrogating individual rights, Brandeis remarked on occasion that the Fourteenth Amendment should be repealed because, in his view, the Court had used it to strike down the states' rights to enact experimental economic legislation. He advocated use of the amendment only to ensure that state legislatures observed procedural regularities and to protect fundamental rights in a democratic system. Although he supported Justice Holmes' test of "clear and present danger" in wartime, Brandeis asserted his belief that the right of free speech should never be denied in peacetime except in the case of incitement to immediate unlawful action.[7]

In *Whitney v. California,* 274 U.S. 357 (1927), Brandeis wrote a concurring opinion that seemed to contradict his views on the right of free speech. But a technicality in that case presented an obstacle which Brandeis could not overcome. The distinction in the *Whitney* case arose from the failure of the plaintiff to challenge the factual basis of the state law under which she was convicted. As Paper noted in his discussion of the case in *Brandeis,* the United States Supreme Court at that time did not assert its power, in cases arising from state courts rather than lower federal courts, to "step in and correct fundamental errors" when the parties had not raised the issues.[8] Therefore, the Supreme Court limited its consideration to the issues raised in the appeal and upheld the state court's conviction in the *Whitney* case.

The Court ruled that the California statute did not violate the Equal Protection Clause of the Fourteenth Amendment when it was used to protect the public peace against the plaintiff, Whitney, who had joined the Communist Labor Party in expectation of aiding and abetting the commission of a crime. In Brandeis' concurring opinion, he supported the court's ruling that the exercise of the fundamental rights—"right of free speech, right to teach, right of assembly"—must be subject to restrictions in order to protect the state from "serious injury, political, economic or moral."[9]

In his fight against bigness in business and government, Brandeis sought to restrain the growth of oppressive trusts. He wrote a series of articles on the banking interests for *Harper's* magazine, which were published in 1913 as *Other People's Money*. Brandeis sought the vigorous enforcement of the Sherman Antitrust Act and was the principal draftsman for the Clayton Antitrust Act of 1914, which brought into being the Federal Trade Commission. The 1929 stock market crash and the subsequent depression were no surprise to Brandeis, the prophet with the "curse of bigness" message. (It is interesting to note that *Other People's Money* has been dramatized in a play with that title, by Jerry Sterner, and that a movie based on the play, produced and directed by Norman Jewison and starring Danny DeVito, was released in 1991.)

When Franklin D. Roosevelt succeeded to the Presidency, Brandeis advised and consulted with him as freely as he had with Wilson. Roosevelt's advisers were divided, however: some advocated more centralization of government and consolidation of business; others, like Brandeis, sought to reduce the size and power of both. Most New Deal legislation, therefore, represented a compromise. While the consolidationists claimed the programs were working, Brandeis saw the National Recovery Act and the Agricultural Adjustment Act as going from bad to worse. The National Recovery Act reached the Supreme Court first in the *Schechter* case and the unanimous Court invalidated the law because of its excessive delegation of power to the Presidency. It was a stunning blow to President Roosevelt when the whole Court, even the progressives like "Old Isaiah" Brandeis and Benjamin Cardozo, voted against the centerpiece of his New Deal economic reforms.

On the same day, May 27, 1935, the Court struck down the Frazier-Lemke Act providing relief for mortgagors—not because of lack of sympathy with the intent but because the act was so poorly written. Brandeis, never one to criticize without offering a remedy, counseled and advised through Felix Frankfurter and others in the White House, so that Roosevelt's subsequent reform measures embodied many of Brandeis' ideas and reflected careful attention to the possibility of judicial review.

When the conservative majority on the Court continued to strike down all reform measures, including those promulgated by the states, Roosevelt overreacted and introduced a bill to implement his scheme to pack the court with justices who would be more favorable to his programs. Brandeis fought against the measure in order to help preserve the independence and integrity of the judiciary. Brandeis, in contrast to the impatient President Roosevelt, believed that persistent and consistent argument and education would eventually bring about a more progressive attitude on the Court.

And in some instances Brandeis was right. In the 1930s, the Court would consistently reinterpret the "due process" clause of the Fourteenth Amendment as to freedom of speech and a free press, generally following the dissenting opinions of Brandeis in the 1920s. The "prudent investment theory of valuation," as set forth in a 1923 Brandeis dissent, was validated in 1933, which alleviated some of the economic problems of the public utilities. And in 1937, the Court reversed its decision on the legality of wiretapping by federal officers.[10]

Other opinions of Brandeis, "the great dissenter," were enacted into law and/or validated by the Court. State and federal restrictions on the use of injunctions in labor disputes were finally enacted and upheld by the Court. The "yellow-dog contract," in which workers had to promise not to join a union, was nullified by the Norris-LaGuardia Act. The National Labor Relations Act of 1935 incorporated ideas from a number of Brandeis' dissenting opinions in cases decided by the Court. And in 1937, in *West Coast Hotel v. Parrish*, the Supreme Court validated the minimum wage legislation which Brandeis had argued for as early as 1914.

In addition to labor conditions, Brandeis was a zealous leader in establishing savings bank insurance and unemployment insurance. During the latter decades of his life, he devoted an immense amount of energy as well as money to the Zionist movement. Never a practitioner of the Jewish religion, he nevertheless led the fight to establish a Jewish state in Palestine and organized American Jewry to support it with money and political influence.

The progressive trend in the United States Supreme Court which culminated in the liberalism of the 1960s and 1970s bears testimony to Brandeis' influence during the 23 years he served on the Court. Though his name was often cited in tandem with Justice Holmes, Brandeis was much more than a junior partner; he was a pioneer in progressivism. When he retired on February 13, 1939, barely two years before his death, the whole country acknowledged his greatness for establishing the "legal bases for a truly living law."[11] And in 1972, the *Journal of the American Bar Association*, whose members had fought against his Senate confirmation, reported a poll of 65 experts that ranked Louis D. Brandeis as the second-greatest justice in the history of the Supreme Court.[12]

Notes

1 Lewis J. Paper, *Brandeis* (Citadel Press, 1983), p. 4.

2 Philippa Strum, *Louis D. Brandeis: Justice for the People* (Harvard University Press, 1984), p. 5.

3 Paper, *Brandeis*, p. 34, quoting William Prosser, "Privacy," in 48 *California Law Review*, p. 383 (1960).

4 *Olmstead v. U.S.*, 277 U.S. 438, at 472-3, 483.

5 Paper, *Brandeis*, pp. 165-6.

6 *Brown v. Board of Education*, 347 U.S. 483 (1954): Historical references cited in Footnote 4, p. 489; social science and psychological studies cited in Footnote 11, pp. 494-5, of the Court's Opinion written by Mr. Chief Justice Warren.

7 Paper, *Brandeis*, p. 287.

8 Paper, *Brandeis*, p. 286.

9 *Whitney v. California*, 274 U.S. 357, at p. 373.

10 Melvin I. Urofsky, *Louis D. Brandeis and the Progressive Tradition* (Little Brown & Co., 1981), p. 167.

11 Urofsky, *Louis D. Brandeis and the Progressive Tradition*, p. 171.

12 Albert P. Blaustein and Roy M. Mersky, "Rating Supreme Court Justices," *American Bar Association Journal*, 58 (November, 1972), pp. 1183-1189.

Benjamin Cardozo:
Pathfinder for Progress

Marguerite R. Plummer

Benjamin Nathan Cardozo was born on May 24, 1870, to a family of Sephardic Jews with a history in America that reached back to the mid-1700s. In 1932, Cardozo became the second Jew to sit on the nation's Supreme Court through an appointment that has come to personify the idea of merit selection.

As much as ten years earlier, Cardozo, who published the highly-regarded volume, *The Nature of the Judicial Process* (1921), was considered a potential candidate for the high court. But the circumstances were never right. In 1930, Cardozo's name was at the top of the recommended list submitted by Justice Harlan Fiske Stone to President Herbert Hoover. Instead, Hoover nominated Court of Appeals Judge John Parker for the vacancy. Parker was rejected by the Senate and Owen Roberts was then nominated and confirmed for the position.

When another vacancy occurred on the Supreme Court two years later, Cardozo still seemed to be a long shot for the position. The first Jewish Justice, Louis Brandeis, remained on the Court and Cardozo's appointment would mean two of the nine justices on the highest court in the land would be Jews. Also, there were already two sitting justices from New York, Cardozo's state, where he had attained an illustrious reputation on the New York Court of Appeals. In geographic terms, his appointment would produce a court with one-third of its members from one state.

Despite those barriers, Cardozo's legal reputation generated such support that the Republican Hoover, who remained unhappy over the Senate's narrow rejection of Parker, found it wise politically to nominate the New York Democrat. Merit and politics thus came together to elevate Cardozo to America's supreme judicial body. During his relatively brief term of service (1932-1938), when the Supreme Court justices were predominantly conservative, Cardozo's legal brilliance and progressive philosophy served to blaze a trail toward a more progressive interpretation of the law of the land in later years.

Cardozo's influence for social awareness was even more important because he served during the Great Depression when the Court was seeking a path through the legal morass of test cases challenging the New Deal programs and reforms initiated by President Franklin D. Roosevelt as he sought to lead the country out of economic depression and into recovery. As a pathfinder for progress, Cardozo frequently took the broad view of legislation and voted to support government efforts toward social and economic progress, because in his view, the law was deemed an instrument for the advancement of society. It was, in his words, "a body of rules and principles and standards which in their extension to new combinations of events are to be sorted, selected, molded, and adapted in subordination to an end."[1]

For example, in the Supreme Court's first significant decision on the emergency legislation enacted by a state to combat the severe economic depression, Justice Cardozo heartily concurred in the five to four decision upholding the Minnesota Supreme Court's ruling in *Home Building & Loan Association v. Blaisdell*, 290 U.S. 398 (1934). The Minnesota Supreme Court had declared the Minnesota Mortgage Moratorium Act constitutional when it was challenged on the grounds that the property rights of creditors were protected by the federal Constitution, which denied to the individual states the right to pass any laws impairing the obligation of contracts. The emergency legislation, limited to two years' duration, extended the time allowed to a mortgagee to pay his debt, thereby bringing relief to numerous home owners who were facing foreclosure on their homes.

The U.S. Supreme Court upheld the Minnesota Supreme Court's ruling that the state legislature had the right to declare a limited moratorium on mortgages to avoid anarchy and maintain stability and, furthermore, the state was justified in the invasion of private contracts in order to preserve peace and stability. Justices Sutherland, Van Devanter, Butler and McReynolds, the strict constructionists on the nation's highest court, were all in accord in dissent, with Justice Sutherland writing a vigorous opinion deploring an attitude among the majority justices that seemed to him to be paving the path toward destruction of the Constitution.

The Minnesota case was not necessarily a precedent for the approval of all the actions of the liberal New Deal Congress. However, with the three liberal Justices—Cardozo, Brandeis and Stone—and sometimes progressive/sometimes conservative Justice Roberts supporting Chief Justice Hughes, the narrowly won Minnesota decision gave rise to the hope that President Roosevelt's National Recovery Act and other economic recovery measures would be upheld when the almost certain challenges occurred. As Joseph Pollard has noted, had President Hoover appointed a conservative judge instead of Cardozo to succeed Justice Holmes, there is little doubt that the Minnesota case would have gone the opposite way and that subsequent efforts of the federal government to bring the nation out of economic depression would have been jeopardized.[2]

From a different angle, another challenge to economic recovery legislation that came before the U.S. Supreme Court emerged from New York's Milk Control Act. In *Nebbia v. New York* (291 U.S. 502), the court dealt with the legislation which gave the state's milk control board price-fixing power. In another five to four decision in the same alignment as the Minnesota case, the Supreme Court upheld the New York statute though it meant a departure from precedent which had consistently denied such price-fixing power in any industry other than a public utility. The private property rights guarded by a substantive due process interpretation of the Fourteenth Amendment were thus again subordinated to the social welfare and need to preserve order, despite the dissenting justices' claim that the Constitution guaranteed to private entities freedom from government interference.

Justice Cardozo was, without doubt, gratified to see the Court adapting the law to his philosophy and that of the much admired Justice Holmes, that "the Constitution should not be used to shield private property from legislative regulation in the public welfare."[3] Equally gratifying, perhaps, was seeing the New York court cite in support of their decision a number of Cardozo's opinions in analogous situations which arose during the eighteen years he sat on that court.

Following the cases involving state emergency measures, the Supreme Court had to address those testing the constitutionality of the federal measures promulgated by President Roosevelt and his New Deal Congress. In January of 1935, *Panama Refining Co. v. Ryan* reached the court. Though not a true test of the merits of federal acts to regulate industry and achieve economic recovery per se, the case did hold serious implications for the overall exercise of power by the national government. The critical question to be decided was whether Congress had unconstitutionally delegated its legislative powers to President Roosevelt when it granted to the President authority to restrict interstate shipments of oil in excess of state quotas and to act as he saw fit to halt the flow of "hot oil."

The problem centered on the hurriedly written Section 9(c) of the Recovery Act, which failed to specify either a policy for the President or the conditions under which the President was empowered to impose restrictions on the oil business. The argument hinged on whether the preliminary declaration of purposes set forth as the rationale for the emergency act limited the transfer of power in Section 9(c) sufficiently to make it legal. Here, only Justice Cardozo supported the government's argument. For the Court majority, the preliminary statement could not be read into Section 9(c). Chief Justice Hughes wrote the opinion declaring Section 9(c) invalid because such transfer of lawmaking power from Congress to the President was in violation of the Constitution.

Though he agreed in principle that the Congress could not part with its constitutional function, Justice Cardozo wrote a vigorous dissent. True to his pragmatic philosophy of the law, he supported a broad interpretation rather than the limited and narrow focus on Section 9(c). His dissent reiterated his support for the actions of Congress and the President to meet the desperate needs of the nation. His view of the law as organic in nature and of the Constitution as a flexible document led him to see the statute more broadly.

On the other hand, Justice Cardozo did not approve of presidential dictatorship, and under no circumstances could he be labeled a "rubber stamp" for FDR on the Supreme Court. When the *Schechter* case testing the National Recovery Act itself came up for decision on May 27, 1935, a unanimous Court declared the Act unconstitutional because it far exceeded the limits of power vested in the government regarding matters of commerce. Justice Cardozo, concurring in the opinion written by Chief Justice Hughes, called the sweeping grants of legislative power to the President a case of "delegation running riot."[4]

On the same day, in another unanimous decision, the Court struck down the badly written Frazier-Lemke Act in *Louisville v. Radford* (295 U.S. 590), although the progressive justices were in sympathy with the purposes of the measure to provide relief to mortgagors. When successive rulings invalidated the National Recovery Act and the Agricultural Adjustment Act's processing tax (though the three progressive justices—Brandeis, Stone and Cardozo—dissented on the latter), the first New Deal based on FDR's New Nationalism concept virtually came to an end. Immediately, President Roosevelt initiated other reform measures developed with an eye to judicial review. The conservative justices had tasted blood, however, and they consistently voted against the government, which stymied FDR's reforms and led to his attempt in 1937 to pack the court with more supportive judges—an effort which failed in Congress.

Other momentous decisions affecting the economic recovery and the move toward more socially conscious interpretation of the Constitution were the so-called "Gold Clause Cases" (*Norman v. B & O R.R. Co.*, 294 U.S. 240; *Nortz v. U.S.*, 294 U.S. 317; *Perry v. U.S.*, 294 U.S. 330). The challenge to the Roosevelt administration's financial policy was a serious one and a national chaos seemed imminent. Looking at the oil field decision, some business leaders believed that the Supreme Court would disapprove of the national industrial recovery program as a whole. They perceived an opportunity to have the Court declare invalid the Congressional Resolution which abrogated the gold clauses in both private and government bonds. These gold clauses were written promises to pay both principal and interest in gold upon demand of the bondholder, which, in effect, contravened the policy of Congress and the President in restructuring the nation's finances to achieve economic recovery through devaluation of the dollar. As Pollard indicates, "the magnitude of the problem, the vast amount of money involved, [and] the possible plight of both government and private companies" faced with continuing increases in debt during an unprecedented depression, "combined to make this case one of the most momentous in the history of the Supreme Court."[5]

Finally, by yet another five to four vote, the Supreme Court upheld the power of Congress to abrogate the gold clause in private bonds; though the Court denied Congress the power to repudiate its own promise in the government bonds, the ruling necessitated a showing that actual damage was suffered by reason of the government's breach of contract, so the result was the same as if it had been upheld. Chief Justice Hughes delivered the opinion, again joined by Justices Brandeis, Stone, Roberts, and Cardozo, with the conservative four holding tightly to strict constructionism in a bitter dissent written by Justice McReynolds.

In a later New Deal case (*Holyoke Power Co. v. Paper Co.*, 300 U.S. 324), Justice Cardozo wrote the majority opinion upholding the money measures of the emergency banking act, citing as precedent the "gold clause" rulings. Cardozo noted that the obligation was for payment of money, not for the delivery of gold, and he said that "the disappointment of expectations and even the frustration of contracts may be a lawful exercise of power when expectation and contract are in conflict with the public welfare." He quoted Justice Hughes' opinion that

> "Contracts, however express, cannot fetter the Constitutional authority of the Congress. Contracts may create rights of property, but when contracts deal with a subject matter which lies within the control of the Congress, they have a congenital infirmity" (citing *Hudson Water Co. v. McCarter*, 209 U.S. 349, 357).[6]

In 1937 Justice Cardozo wrote the majority opinion affirming the validity of the Social Security Tax against a challenge based on the Fifth Amendment. He mentioned the Great Depression, the high unemployment rates, the inability of states to give relief, and declared:

> The problem had become national in area and dimensions. There was a need for help from the nation if the people were not to starve. It is too late today for the argument to be heard with tolerance that in a crisis so extreme the use of the moneys of the nation to relieve the unemployed and their dependents is a use for any purpose narrower than the promotion of the general welfare. (*Steward Machine Co. v. Davis*, 301 U.S. 548, 586-7.)

Again in 1937, Justice Cardozo wrote the opinion in *Helvering v. Davis* upholding the validity of the Social Security Act's Old Age Benefits. Expressly stating that the Act does not contravene the limitations of the Tenth Amendment, and that Congress is empowered to spend money in aid of the general welfare, Cardozo added, "the concept of general welfare is not static but adapts itself to the crisis and necessities of the times."[7]

Justice Cardozo seemed intent on moving the Supreme Court away from the strict constructionist precedents and toward a socially aware interpretation of the Constitution. He voted consistently for centralization of power in the federal government, which, in effect, would enable the establishment of extensive social welfare programs in the 1960s and 1970s. In his study of Justice Butler, D. J. Danelski offers a scalogram of cases involving government and the economy for the critical 1935 Term, which indicates the votes for and against the government of each of the Supreme Court Justices in eighteen cases which came before the Court. In all eighteen cases, Cardozo voted for the government. Brandeis and Stone, the other two progressives, voted seventeen times each in favor of the government. It should be noted that the government prevailed in only four of the eighteen cases, as the conservative justices persisted in voting against the federal reform legislation.[8] Throughout his tenure on the Court, Cardozo would consistently vote in favor of federal supremacy and limited power to intervene in commerce, industry and private contracts to effect economic and social reform.

Cardozo's support of the government was rooted in his pragmatic philosophy of the law as dynamic rather than static, and as an instrument to be used for the advancement of society. He agreed with Justice Brandeis that the law should be informed and vitalized by "the contemporary conditions, social, industrial, and political, of the community of the affected."[9] This strong sense of the need for social accountability on the part of the law explains in part Cardozo's continuing influence as a great justice into the era of the 1960s and 1970s, another time of great social change.

Cardozo's influence on the interpretation of law over the decades is documented in a recent study by Richard A. Posner. He measures greatness in terms of the popularity of Cardozo's written opinions among lawyers and judges, as evidenced by the number of citations of cases in which Cardozo wrote majority or concurring or dissenting opinions, in comparison with the number of citations to opinions by contemporary colleagues on the Court. One section of this empirical study focuses on 127 opinions written by Justice Cardozo during his six years on the Supreme Court, as compared to the opinions written during the same period by his two progressive contemporaries, Justices Louis Brandeis and Harlan F. Stone.[10]

Moreover, Posner examines the citations of opinions in blocks of time as follows: Citations up to 1945, those from 1945-50, then by decades, 1950-1960, 1970-1980, and 1980-1989. This incremental approach enables a measure of the popularity of Cardozo's opinions to emerge in a changing relationship to those of Brandeis and Stone. Surprisingly, Posner's study reveals that Cardozo's opinions were cited more heavily than those of Brandeis throughout, and also surpassed Stone's in all periods except the citations prior to 1945. Equally surprising is the indication that the citations of Cardozo's opinions increased from decade to decade after 1945-50.[11] His increased popularity coincides with major social changes and reinterpretations of the Constitution and the Bill of Rights. On the rights front, of course, Cardozo's 1937 opinion in *Palko v. Connecticut* (302 U.S. 319) outlined the path of selective incorporation that would guide the Court for decades to come. Interestingly, though, Cardozo's honor roll of rights to be protected from state action was much more limited than that produced by the later Warren court.

Posner also went on to compare the Cardozo citations to the three progressive justices on an average basis rather than total, and found that since 1970, Cardozo's opinions have been followed more often than those of either Brandeis or Stone. Posner notes that during Cardozo's brief tenure on the Supreme Court, he wrote more opinions than either Brandeis or Stone, despite the fact that he was the most junior justice on the Court. Posner insists that this superior productivity itself "is a valid factor in measuring judicial quality."[12] When comparing Cardozo's average number of citations to randomly selected opinions of other contemporary justices on the Supreme Court, Posner's analysis renders a finding that Cardozo's citations, while below that of the average judge, still outrank those of Brandeis and Stone. And when the citations to opinions written as a state court justice are added to the federal opinions, Cardozo again rises to dominance.[13]

For even more recent affirmation of Cardozo's reputation as a great justice among scholars, lawyers and judges, see the study presented in this volume by Robert C. Bradley of Illinois State University.

Considering that Cardozo was a junior justice and served only six years, and that he was one of the so-called liberal "pariah group" of justices, his continued popularity, as evidenced by case citations and rankings by attorneys, judges, and scholars is phenomenal. Like his predecessor, Justice Holmes, he had an understanding of the law and the writing ability necessary to earn the respect of his colleagues. He was unquestionably concerned with adapting the law to serve the public good. He consistently voted for federal supremacy and in favor of social experiments in legislation that would promote the public welfare. Mr. Justice Cardozo, "a liberal mind in action,"[14] not only established some precedents for later progressive rulings, but he broke ground for the pathway to judicial activism which was traveled by the Supreme Court decades after his death.

Notes

1 Benjamin N. Cardozo, *The Growth of the Law* (Westport, Connecticut: Greenwood Press, 1973), p. 55.

2 Joseph P. Pollard, *Mr. Justice Cardozo: A Liberal Mind in Action* (Westport, Connecticut: Greenwood Press, 197), p. 308.

3 Pollard, *Mr. Justice Cardozo*, p. 14.

4 *A. L. Schechter Poultry Corp. v. U.S.*, 295 U.S. 495, 554.

5 Pollard, *Mr. Justice Cardozo*, p. 315.

6 *Holyoke Power Co. v. Paper Co.*, 300 U.S. 324, 341.

7 *Helvering v. Davis*, 301 U.S. 619, 640-1.

8 D. J. Danelski, *A Supreme Court Justice is Appointed* (New York: Random House, 1964), p. 185.

9 *Truax v. Corrigan*, 257 U.S. 312, as quoted in Cardozo, *The Growth of the Law*, p. 117.

10 Richard A. Posner, *Cardozo: A Study in Reputation* (Chicago: The University of Chicago Press, 1990).

11 Posner, p. 87.

12 Posner, p. 88.

13 Posner, p. 89.

14 Pollard, title.

How Liberal Was
Chief Justice Hughes?

Roger W. Corley

In July 1937, Irving Brant, journalist and later public servant, historian and professor, wrote an article in the *New Republic*, "How Liberal is Justice Hughes."[1] This was in the wake of Franklin D. Roosevelt's failed court-packing proposal and the "switch in time that saved nine." Brant was very critical of Hughes, maintaining that he called himself a liberal but acted otherwise. Certainly Charles Evans Hughes was one of our great statesmen, serving as Governor of New York, Associate Justice of the United States, Secretary of State, and Chief Justice. He also served on numerous boards and commissions and none questions the selfless contributions he made, but what of his liberalism?

Liberalism *per se* could easily be the subject of another study so I will not dwell on that for too long. Rather I choose to fall back on Harlan F. Stone's *Carolene Products* doctrine; legislative will in the economic realm is to be obeyed unless totally unreasonable, but at the same time, infringements on civil rights or liberties will be severely questioned. This may well be objected to, but it is from the period when Hughes was at the peak of his career and comes close to what Irving Brant had in mind.[2] This should suffice for domestic policy; for foreign policy I am offering collective security and non-interventionism as the criteria.

Hughes was born in 1862 to a Baptist clergyman and his school teacher wife. He was a very precocious child, reading at three and translating the Bible from Greek at seven. Much of his early schooling was at home, at the knee of his mother, but he also excelled at primary and secondary institutions. Too young for New York's City College, he was sent to Hamilton (today's Colgate) University. He there fell in with possibly corrupting influences, which caused him to question if he wished to be a minister, and he was redirected to safer Brown University in 1878. His record was outstanding and he used his photographic memory to merit election to Phi Beta Kappa as a junior. There were two flaws in his character, at least as far as his parents were concerned; he wrote essays for other students, for pay, and he had decided against a career in the ministry.[3]

Graduating from Brown at nineteen, the five foot eleven, 130 pound beanpole looked even younger. Yet he sought and somehow secured a teaching job at Delaware Academy, Delhi, New York. He grew a beard at this time to appear older. Charles began reading law with a local attorney and was awarded a meager scholarship to Columbia University Law School. He supplemented this with employment with the United States Attorney's office. Graduating with honors, he was chosen as a clerk by the prestigious law firm of Walter Carter. He struggled through the days, quizzed at Columbia Law at night, and was awarded a junior partnership within a year. Columbia made him a lecturer. Two years later he became a partner and shortly after married his boss's daughter.[4]

Hughes frequently suffered from ill health and had to retire to teach again or to go on long vacations abroad. He was so slim that he could not purchase life insurance, but he began to exercise and play golf and he got his weight up to a healthy 165 pounds. Meanwhile, when he worked as an attorney, he was very successful for his corporate clients. He mixed in the better social circles in New York City and was very successful and well known, so it was natural that public service should seek him out. In 1905 he was asked to serve as counsel for the New York legislature's Stevens Committee investigating gas rates. He uncovered mismanagement and overcharges and recommended lower rates and the creation of a state public service commission. Some of this was accomplished and Hughes was asked to serve another committee, the Armstrong Committee, as it investigated the insurance industry. Again he uncovered mismanagement; there were high executive salaries, low benefits to policyholders, and few dividends to stockholders. There was much corporate and political pressure applied against him, but he refused to relent or be bought off by a nomination as a candidate for Mayor of New York.

The exposure did little to the insurance industry except effect a change in management, but it propelled Hughes into the political limelight. President Theodore Roosevelt called him to Washington to aid in an examination of the coal industry and pressed him to run in the 1908 New York gubernatorial campaign. The Republican Party leaders chose Hughes because they needed an attractive, popular candidate. He campaigned as a progressive and especially supported a public service commission. He got strong financial support from the business community and handily defeated publisher William Randolph Hearst.

Under his leadership, New York enacted a workmen's compensation law and established a strong public service commission. He secured legislation ending racetrack gambling, but failed to gain a direct primary. He was a capable administrator who made good appointments, quarreling with the President and party bosses over patronage. He vetoed cheap streetcar fares, as had Grover Cleveland, and he opposed the Income Tax Amendment as too sweeping. He easily won reelection.[5]

As a Governor from a large "swing" state, he was naturally considered as a Presidential candidate, but Roosevelt and Hughes had squabbled, and the mantle fell on William Howard Taft. Hughes readily campaigned for the successful Taft. The new President liked him both personally and politically. When Justice David Brewer died in 1910, Taft offered Hughes the appointment as his replacement, noting that he could become wealthy in private practice, but that if he went on the Court, he might later be appointed Chief Justice.[6] Hughes accepted and was rapidly confirmed by a unanimous voice vote.

The United States Supreme Court was at the height of its progressive period; whether listening directly to the election returns, or indirectly reflecting them in the appointments of

Roosevelt, Taft, and Woodrow Wilson, the Justices were accepting most of the new reform legislation emanating from the state and national legislatures. The new judge soon fell in with the rest of his colleagues and became a leader in voting with progressive majorities, in writing progressive opinions, and in dissenting with the other reform minded brethren.[7]

In evaluating any one judge's role on an appellate court, it must be noted that his voting record and even the opinions that bear his name may not fully reflect his real views. Liberal judges are often assigned conservative opinions, and vice versa. The opinion may have been altered to keep an essential vote. A threatened dissent might change key wording. The published document may be a committee report. A jurist may logroll in a strategic or tactical maneuver. A judge may play a "game" to maximize his power. Finally, there may be silent submission, for one cannot dissent in too many cases and still be effective when it counts.[8]

Hughes joined progressive majorities in extending the federal police power.[9] He supported usually conservative Willis VanDevanter's broad definition of the commerce power in the *Second Employers' Liability Cases*,[10] and joined a dissent in a case overturning a "yellow-dog" contract law.[11] He supported greater powers for the Interstate Commerce Commission,[12] and delivered the majority opinions in the *Minnesota Rate Cases* and the *Shreveport Rate Cases* which gave virtually unlimited powers to the commission.[13] Hughes also voted to give states greater regulatory powers.[14] In the area of civil liberties he wrote majority opinions against a state peonage law,[15] against a law requiring Pullman accommodations only for whites,[16] and against a law restricting the employment of aliens.[17] He joined Oliver Wendell Holmes Jr. in a dissent, which he helped to write, attacking the conviction of Leo Franks in a scene dominated by a mob.[18] His first tenure on the Court coincided with its peak of progressivism and one scholar found him to be more liberal at this time than Holmes.[19]

In 1916 though, he resigned to accept the Republican nomination for the Presidency. The author of Hughes' "authorized but not . . . official biography," and the candidate both denied that the call was sought after,[20] however, their documentation is not conclusive. Further, it is inconceivable that a twentieth century candidate of a major party could be chosen without his consent, much less without his ardent cooperation. He was one of the few progressives in the party who was neither identified with the Taft debacle nor tainted by the Bull Moose campaign in 1912. He had a difficult campaign as Woodrow Wilson had led his party to the left domestically and to peace in foreign policy. He was somewhat burdened with Roosevelt's bellicosity and continued alienation of progressives. Wilson won a very narrow victory. Hughes and his biographer blamed defeat on the peace campaign, but Arthur S. Link asserts the swing of progressive, social justice voters to the President was just as important.[21]

Hughes returned to New York to practice law; his name and stature brought numerous corporate clients. He argued cases locally and in Washington, and was active in party politics, especially in the 1918 Congressional elections. He supported the bipartisan war effort, heading the Draft Appeals Board in New York and investigating the Army aircraft scandal. He defended Truman Newberry successfully against charges that he had bought an election, but also defended John L. Lewis in a labor dispute, and tried to gain reinstatement for Socialists who had been expelled from the New York Legislature. In the conflict over the Versailles Treaty and the League of Nations, Hughes supported the League, but also insisted on reservations. His name was barely mentioned as a potential Presidential candidate in 1920 and after Warren G. Harding won the nomination, he campaigned for him, although he insisted we could still participate in the League of Nations.[22]

Harding won the greatest landslide victory up to that time, and in spite of the fact that the new President-elect was equivocal on the League, he nominated Hughes to be his Secretary of State. The new Secretary was given a free hand for the most part but he operated under the limitations of a Congress, especially the Senate, which had just strongly defeated Wilson's League, he confronted an ever encroaching Commerce Department, and he faced a public mood of strong nationalism. As far as the League was concerned, Hughes avoided any actions that might require congressional approval, but he did send unofficial observers and the United States thus participated in conferences dealing with such issues as the international opium trade and white-slavery. Since the Senate had rejected the Versailles Treaty, separate treaties ending the war were concluded with Germany, Austria, and Hungary. Fearing Japanese power in the Pacific, and a naval armaments race with Great Britain and Japan, Hughes, after overcoming strong U.S. Navy resistance, astounded the world at the Washington Naval Conference by proposing significant reductions in the navies of the major world powers. Treaties accomplishing this as well as the ending of a British-Japanese alliance, and support for the sovereignty of China were negotiated and ratified. This brought about better relationships with Japan, but in spite of Hughes' protests, the Congress insulted Japan in 1924 by restricting oriental immigration. He did not directly deal with the War Debt-Reparations issue, but was able to operate outside the Congress and secure the Dawes Plan for lower interest, longer term payments on the debt. He opposed the recognition of the Soviet Union because of a lack of guarantees of restoration of American property, but, at Harding's insistence, we recognized Mexico, even though there were less than adequate assurances protecting United States' investments there. With Sumner Welles as his Division Chief for Latin America, a policy of withdrawal from the Caribbean, which anticipated Franklin D. Roosevelt's Good Neighbor Policy, was begun, but Hughes could never bring himself to deny a right to intervene because of the need to protect our citizens. The United States concluded a treaty with Colombia in 1921 to assuage its hurt over the Panama Canal, but oil greased that through. The nation did aid in the settling of a number of border disputes in Latin America but the Senate refused to accept the World Court protocol. With Hughes lobbying extensively, Congress passed the Rogers Act in 1924 which established the career foreign service and improved both the quality and morale in that enterprise. All deny that Hughes had any knowledge of the Harding scandals and he stayed on after the President's death, but resigned on

March 4, 1925 claiming he could not afford to remain in public service.[23]

He returned to a prominent New York law firm and was again recognized as a leader of the bar. He represented many large corporations in appearances before the Supreme Court, yet also advised the State Department and participated in Pan-American Conferences. He helped to found the National Conference of Christians and Jews, and aided in the reorganization of New York State's government. By 1928 he had recouped his fortune and was able to accept an appointment to the Permanent International Court of Justice. In that year, Hughes was mentioned as a Presidential possibility, but he declined and worked for Herbert Hoover's election. He was considered for a Cabinet position, particularly Secretary of State, but he was not interested.[24]

Early in 1930, a rapidly failing Chief Justice Taft was persuaded by his family to resign. All on the same day, February 4, Taft's resignation was received and Hoover nominated Hughes to replace him. To many he was the obvious choice; Associate Justice from 1910 to 1916, Presidential candidate in 1916, Secretary of State, etc. However, he was 68, much above his oft-stated ideal of 60, his son was Solicitor-General and would have to resign, and there might be trouble in the Senate. It has been charged by Henry F. Pringle, Drew Pearson and Robert S. Allen, Frederick B. Wiener, and others, that Justice Harlan F. Stone was preferred and that the offer to Hughes was a formality which was expected to be refused. Hoover later stoutly denied this, as did Attorney General William D. Mitchell, and Hughes, but there are some discrepancies as to dates and as to whether Justices Pierce Butler and Van Devanter were consulted. However, although he was a member of the "medicine-ball cabinet," and a fishing companion of the President, Stone had recommended a liberal such as Benjamin N. Cardozo to Hoover and Mitchell. The role of Taft and the Taft wing of the Court seems important; they feared a dangerous radical, progressive President (Hoover), might appoint an "extreme destroyer of the Constitution," and so preferred Hughes to Stone.[25]

The "Sons of the Wild Jackass" in the Senate, a progressive-insurgent group which included William E. Borah, George Norris, Burton K. Wheeler, and Robert LaFollette, perceived the Hughes appointment in much the same fashion as the Taft supporters; not only had he betrayed his former liberal record on the Court by resigning to run for the Presidency, but he had become the servant of monopolistic, corporate wealth. Of particular concern was the fact that Hughes' firm had represented the railroads in the recent, unpopular, anti-regulatory decision of the Court in *St. Louis and O'Fallon R. Co. v. U.S*, and that Hughes had personally made forty-four appearances before the Court since leaving the State Department, all for corporations. Joseph P. Harris links the reception of Stone's appointment in 1925, Charles Beecher Warren's unsuccessful appointment as Attorney General in 1925, Hughes's struggle, and the defeat of the appointment of John J. Parker to the Supreme Court later in 1930, in "Opposition by Senate Liberals to the Appointment of Conservatives." The growing unpopularity of President Hoover was also a factor. In spite of his supposed ideology, Hughes was just too prestigious for the Senate to turn down; after brief hearings and vituperative debate, he was confirmed fifty-two to twenty-six. Senate liberals certainly perceived Hughes as a conservative.[26]

A Chief Justice on an appellate court, but especially the United States Supreme Court, has unique opportunities for leadership, if he takes them. In the 1930's, in conference, the chief spoke first and was followed in descending order of seniority. Voting proceeded up from the junior Associate Justice and the chief voted last. If in the majority, the chief assigned the opinion. He could lead the Court if he had sufficient character, knowledge, and personality. Hughes came to conference with few notes, yet, aided by his photographic memory, he succinctly stated all the issues in a case, leaving little else to be said. Some resented this, especially Stone. Felix Frankfurter later said that Hughes conducted the Court the way Toscanini conducted an orchestra.[27]

Taking office on February 24, 1930, he inherited Taft's Court. Because of the conservative appointments of Warren Harding and Calvin Coolidge, this was a Court which had resurrected nineteenth century doctrines such as substantive due process and dual federalism. A federal child-labor law,[28] a minimum wage law for the District of Columbia,[29] a state law regulating bread weight,[30] a state law establishing a court to prevent strikes in essential industries,[31] and state laws regulating ticket sales,[32] employment agencies,[33] and gasoline prices,[34] were all declared unconstitutional. The Federal Trade Commission,[35] and the Interstate Commerce Commission,[36] major progressive establishments, both found their activities restricted. The Court was not too ardent in its defense of civil liberties,[37] although one adverse decision did lay the basis for future advances,[38] and the dissents of Louis D. Brandeis, Holmes, and Stone provided further foundations for later advances. In general the Taft Court was very restrictive on state experimentation, preferred no taxation to the possible risk of dual taxation, and cast aside twelve federal statutes and about fifty state laws.

Brandeis, Holmes and Stone were usually opposed by Taft and the rest of the Court, so Hughes appointment could not effect any changes, but Edward T. Sanford died later in 1930, and Judge Parker was named to succeed him but was not confirmed by the Senate. Owen J. Roberts, the prosecutor of the Teapot Dome scandals, then secured easy and rapid acceptance. In 1932, Holmes resigned, to be replaced by Benjamin N. Cardozo, who tended to vote in much the same fashion as the man he replaced. Thus from the time of Roberts' appointment there were a bloc of three liberals, Brandeis, Holmes-Cardozo, and Stone; a bloc of four conservatives, Butler, James C. McReynolds, George Sutherland, and Van-Devanter; and an uncommitted Roberts and Hughes.

The major issue to confront the Court was the New Deal and control of the national economy. Here Hughes' record is mixed; he voted for federal programs in six out of eleven cases up to June 1937. He wrote opinions supporting the government in the Gold Clause cases,[39] and went along with the dissent in the railroad retirement case,[40] and absolutely refused federal power in the "hot oil,"[41] and N.I.R.A. case, where he wrote the opinion.[42] He supported a unanimous majority in voiding a federal mortgage moratorium act,[43] and opposed the A.A.A.,[44] and the Guffey-Snyder Act,[45] although perhaps he did this to avoid another much criticized five to four majority. He supported a limited consideration of the T.V.A.[46] and joined a dissent over the municipal bankruptcy act.[47] In 1937 he supported the Wagner Act,[48] and Social Security,[49] and later voted for the second A.A.A.,[50] and the Fair Labor Standards Act.[51]

In cases involving state control of the economy much is made of *Nebbia v. N.Y.*,[52] and *Home Building and Loan v. Blaisdell*[53] as being indicative of an early willingness of the Court to accept new dogma, and then of *Morehead v. Tipaldo*[54] and *West Coast Hotel v. Parrish*[55] as demonstrating the switch that marks the constitutional revolution of 1937. These last two cases were decided in June 1936 and March 1937. In between Franklin D. Roosevelt was re-elected in a landslide and shortly thereafter proposed his court-altering plan. In that these cases were heard in court and discussed and voted on in conference before the President made his proposal, but after the election, it is clear that court-packing could not have influenced the decisions, but that elections returns might have.[56]

Elections aside however, the court under Hughes had begun making switches as early as 1930. A bread-weight statute similar to the one cast aside by the Taft court was upheld.[57] A minimum wage was upheld in the *West Coast Hotel* case, and price control was upheld in the *Nebbia* case. In the *Blaisdell* case, a mortgage moratorium, though limited and under judicial control was allowed, although in every previous depression stay laws had been declared unconstitutional. Bankruptcy, insolvency, and business reorganization statutes at the state level, which contained provisions previously unacceptable, were also allowed.[58]

More realistic attitudes toward state taxation were taken in the 1930s. Under Taft, as noted above, the Court seemed to prefer avoidance of all taxes rather than the possibility of dual taxation. Under Hughes, just the opposite was true. New rules were devised to more fairly measure the commodity to be taxed, and to determine the situs of a taxable object.[59] Attempts to impose graduated taxes on chain stores were upheld.[60] The income tax received mixed treatment but a tax on rents was allowed, the Court cast aside the doctrines that income from without a state could not be taxed, and that federal employees were immune from state income taxes.[61] Interstate commerce had been a barrier to state taxation but the Court began to accept taxes that burdened such trade as long as it was not discriminatory.[62]

Public utility rates also brought many cases to the Court. Under Taft, in 1929, in the *O'Fallon* case, McReynolds upheld "reproduction cost," which favored carriers, as the basis of rate setting. Under Hughes the doctrine was more realistic and led to lower rates. Procedural errors were allowed if the rate were fair.[63] As far as motor vehicles were concerned states were granted virtually unlimited authority to regulate as long as it were conditioned on safety. Even Sutherland overruled an opinion he had written in 1926,[64] and allowed requiring private carriers to be certified.[65]

In general the Hughes Court began exemplifying significant deference to the states in their economic experiments. In 1938 they went so far as to overturn *Swift v. Tyson*,[66] which had established a federal common law in 1842 and had attempted to impose uniform federal authority.[67] On the other hand though, the Court in the 1930s began to take a very solicitous attitude toward political and civil liberties.

Using the Fourteenth Amendment as a limitation on state action in regard to First Amendment and Sixth Amendment rights the Court struck down a number of state statutes and overturned convictions. In *Near v. Minnesota*,[68] a law censoring newspapers was put aside and in *Stromberg v. California*,[69] a "red flag" law was struck down. In the Scottsboro Boys case,[70] right to counsel in capital cases was established. Picketing became a protected form of free speech,[71] as did the right to assemble,[72] and the right to distribute religious pamphlets.[73] Dissident political minorities found the protection of the "clear and present danger" doctrine when they tried to sell their ideas.[74] Furthermore Hughes made access to the Supreme Court easier by the increased use of *in forma pauperis* petitions for certiorari.

After June 1937, when VanDevanter resigned, Roosevelt had many chances to make appointments to the Court and that body increasingly reflected a New Deal bias. But Hughes and Roberts wrought significant changes well before 1937. Hughes as chief was largely responsible for the promulgation of new court rules of criminal procedure and a complete, new set of Federal Rules of Civil Procedure. He also fostered the enactment of a statute setting up the Administrative Office of the United States Courts, a device designed to provide for a more uniform course of judgments, especially in the District Courts. By 1941, Hughes at 79, was ready to step down. He recommended Stone as his successor and retired to a well deserved rest.[75]

How liberal was Hughes? As an investigator he seems to have been most active in the politics of exposure; but that was an important part of progressivism. As Governor he secured a very strong public service commission whose findings were reviewable only as to law, another meaningful progressive issue. He was about as progressive as any Eastern Governor, but it is interesting that Massachusetts at this same time introduced Savings Bank Insurance, something New York did not achieve until Herbert Lehman. As Associate Justice Hughes ranks very high and his commerce and civil liberties opinions and votes would make him an outstanding liberal. As Secretary of State the result is mixed; he began retrenchment in Latin America although he would not deny the right of the United States to intervene, but he was less than strong when it came to collective security. While at the time the treaties he negotiated seemed significant, they do not now, and he failed, as did so many others, to see how our tariff policies affected the rest of the world. He has been rated third among Secretaries of State behind John Quincy Adams and William H. Seward. Incidentally, the Harding revisionists now try and say that all of the foreign policy was Harding's.[76]

He was much criticized for serving corporate wealth, but he also defended minorities and gave many years of underpaid and unpaid public service. As Chief Justice he led the Court through a very stormy period and at times lacked grace in doing so. But he confronted a conservative bloc of four that needed only one vote, usually supplied by Roberts, to triumph. Hughes had to win Roberts over to his way if liberalism were to succeed. Whether he were playing the "Hughberts" game or avoiding the biting dissents of Brandeis, Cardozo or Stone, in the early New Deal cases when Hughes voted with the liberals, he wrote the opinion himself, and when he dissented, he let someone else write. This was Irving Brant's main point; Hughes portrayed himself as a liberal, but often voted otherwise. Much is made of Roberts' switch, but Hughes also switched; he wrote an opinion in the *Schechter* case which retained the fiction of "indirect effects on commerce," yet his opinion in the *Jones and Laughlin* case completely overturned that doctrine.[77] It should be noted that the "sick chicken" case was decided unanimously and was also predicated on excessive delegation and inadequate standards. Beyond that the liberals voted against other New Deal legislation, but in the *Schechter* case Hughes was still using nineteenth century doctrines.

In the lesser noted cases involving states, Hughes was a liberal and here the turning point is 1930 when he was appointed. He was never quite so supportive of states as was Brandeis, Cardozo or Stone, but there was a dramatic increase in approval of state economic legislation after Taft resigned. Hughes was certainly never as liberal as the Roosevelt appointees, in fact after 1937, the Court moved to the left, and he did not, but he did preside over the constitutional revolution in that year. As far as civil liberties is concerned, Hughes ranks very high, and not only do cases such as *Powell v. Alabama* mark the beginning of the changes in criminal procedures that reached fruition under Earl Warren, but Hughes opening up access to the Supreme Court is also very important. He has been rated sixth among the twelve great justices.[78] This does not differentiate between his two periods of service on the Court, nor does it deal with his liberalism. Perhaps it is safest to rate him as a "near great" liberal much like the man who appointed him and Roberts, Herbert Hoover.[79]

Notes

1 LCI (1937) 295-98, 329-32.

2 *United States v. Carolene Products*, 304 U.S. 144 (1938), at p. 151, especially fn 4; and letter from Irving Brant to the author, October 29, 1974.

3 Charles Evans Hughes, *Autobiographical Notes* (ed. David J. Danelski and Joseph Tulching, Cambridge, 1973); Samuel-Hendell, *Charles Evans Hughes and the Supreme Court* (New York, 1951); Merlo J. Pusey, *Charles Evans Hughes* (2 vols., New York, 1951); Dexter Perkins, *Charles Evans Hughes and American Democratic Statesmanship* (Boston, 1956); and Robert F. Wesser, "Charles Evans Hughes and New York politics, 1905-1910," (Unpublished Ph.D. dissertation, University of Rochester, 1961) all provide ample details on the life of Hughes.

4 Ibid.

5 Ibid.

6 Chief Justice Melville Fuller died soon after but Taft reneged, at least in part because he feared that 48 year old Hughes would live a long life and 66 year old Edward White, whom he did appoint, might not live too long and Taft could achieve his "all-consuming ambition" to himself become chief. Henry J. Abraham, *Justices and Presidents: A Political History of Appointments to the Supreme Court* (2nd. ed., New York, 1985), pp. 169-70.

7 Harding Coolidge Noblitt, "The Supreme Court and the Progressive Era, 1902-1921," (Unpublished Ph.D. dissertation, University of Chicago, 1955), pp. 232-33.

8 Slip opinions, Harlan F. Stone Papers, Library of Congress; Alexander Bickel, *The Unpublished Opinions of Mr. Justice Brandeis* (Cambridge, 1957); Walter F. Murphy, "Marshalling the Court: Leadership, Bargaining and the Judicial Process," *University of Chicago Law Review* XXIX (1962) 640-72; and Glendon A. Schubert, *Quantitative Analysis of Judicial Behavior* (Glencoe, IL, 1959), pp. 190-210.

9 *Hipolite Egg Co. v. U.S.*, 220 U.S. 45 (1911), and *Hoke v. U.S.*, 227 U.S. 308 (1913).

10 223 U.S. 1 (1912).

11   *Coppage v. Kansas* 236 U.S. 1 (1915).

12   *U.S. v. Atchison, Topeka, and Santa Fe* 234 U.S. 476 (1914).

13   230 U.S. 352 (1913) and 234 U.S. 342 (1914).

14   For example: *Chicago, Burlington & Quincy Railroad v. McGuire*, 219 U.S. 549 (1911); *Purity Extract & Tonic v. Lynch*, 226 U.S. 192 (1912); *Sturges & Burn v. Beauchamp*, 231 U.S. 120 (1913); and *Price v. Illinois*, 238 U.S. 446 (1915).

15   *Bailey v. Alabama*, 219 U.S. 219 (1911).

16   *McCabe v. A.T.S.F.*, 235 U.S. 151 (1914).

17   *Truax v. Raich* 239 U.S. (1915).

18   *Franks v. Mangum*, 237 U.S. 309 (1915).

19   Noblitt, pp. 229-33, 239.

20   Pusey, pp. viii, 315-29; and Hughes, pp. 178-81.

21   Pusey, pp. 315-62; Hendel, p. 68; Hughes, pp. 236-37; and Link, *Wilson: Campaigns for Progressivim and Peace, 1916-1917* (Princeton, 1965), pp. 160-64.

22   Pusey, pp. 367-405; Hendel, pp. 71-73; and Perkins, pp. 80-87.

23   Pusey, pp. 411-618; Perkins, 95-140; Robert K. Murray, *The Harding Era: Warren G. Harding and His Administration* (Minneapolis, 1969), pp. 227-75; and Eugene P. Trani and David L. Wilson, *The Presidency of Warren G. Harding* (Lawrence, KS, 1977), pp. 109-69. Hughes may not have been Harding's first choice.

24   Hendel, p. 77; Pusey, pp. 619-49; and Hughes pp. 362-66.

25   Walter H. Newton, "Letter to the Editor," *New York Times*, December 18, 1938, IV, 9; Abraham, 197-98; Leo Pfeffer, *This Honorable Court: A History of the United States Supreme Court* (Boston, 1965), p. 286; Henry F. Pringle, "Profile: Chief Justice," *New Yorker* (July 13, 1935), p. 19; Drew Pearson and Robert S. Allen, *Nine Old Men* (New York, 1936), pp. 74-75; Herbert Hoover, *Memoirs* (3 vols., New York, 1951, 1952), III, 375-76; exchange of letters between Mitchell and Pusey, October 1949, William DeWitt Mitchell Family Papers, Minnesota Historical Society; Pusey, pp. 650-59; Henry F. Pringle, *The Life and Times of William Howard Taft* (New York, 1939), p. 967, citing a letter from Taft to Horace Taft, December 1, 1929, Taft Papers, Library of Congress, and p. 1044, citing Taft to C. P. Taft March 12, 1929, Taft Papers; Alpheus T. Mason, *Harlan Fiske Stone: Pillar of the Law* (New York, 1968), pp. 262-83; Mason, *William Howard Taft: Chief Justice* (New York, 1964), p. 190n, citing a memo of John Bassett Moore, February 20, 1930, Moore

Papers, Library of Congress; David Burner, *Herbert Hoover: A Public Life* (New York, 1975), p. 212; and Frederick Bernays Wiener, "Justice Hughes' Appointment-the Cotton Story Re-Examined," *Yearbook 1981* (Washington, 1981), pp. 79-91.

26 Ray Tucker and Frederick R. Barkley, *The Sons of the Wild Jackass* (Boston, 1932); Abraham, pp. 198-99; Claudius O. Johnson, *Borah of Idaho* (New York, 1936), pp. 449-50; Pringle, "Profile," pp. 19-29; Pfeffer, p. 287; Robert S. Allen and Drew Pearson, *More Merry-Go-Round* (New York, 1932), pp. 62, 65, 78; 297 U.S. 461 (1929); and Joseph P. Harris, *The Advice and Consent of the Senate: A Study in the Confirmation of Appointments by the United States Senate* (New York, 1969), pp. 115-32.

27 Felix Frankfurter, "Chief Justices I Have Known," *Virginia Law Review*, XXXIX (1939), 901-02.

28 *Bailey v. Drexel Furniture*, 259 U.S. 20 (1922).

29 *Adkins v. Children's Hospital*, 261 U.S. 525 (1923).

30 *Jay Burns Baking Co. v. Bryan*, 264 U.S. 504 (1924).

31 *Wolff v. Court of Industrial Relations*, 262 U.S. 522 (1922).

32 *Tyson & Bros. v. Banton*, 273 U.S. 418 (1927).

33 *Ribnik v. McBride*, 277 U.S. 350 (1928).

34 *Williams v. Standard Oil Co.*, 278 U.S. 235 (1929).

35 *F.T.C. v. Curtis Publishing Co.*, 260 U.S. 568 (1923).

36 *St. Louis and O'Fallon Railway Co. v. U.S.*, 279 U.S. 461 (1929).

37 *Whitney v. California*, 274 U.S. 357 (1927).

38 *Gitlow v. New York*, 268 U.S. 652 (1925).

39 *Perry v. U.S.*, 294 U.S. 330 (1935); *Norman v. Baltimore & Ohio Railroad Co.*, 294 U.S. 240 (1935); and *Nortz v. U.S.*, 294 U.S. 317 (1935).

40 *Railroad Retirement Board v. Alton*, 295 U.S. 330 (1935).

41 *Panama Refining v. Ryan*, 293 U.S. 388 (1935).

42 *Schechter Bros. Poultry v. U.S.*, 295 U.S. 495 (1935).

43 *Louisville Bank v. Radford*, 295 U.S. 555 (1935).

44 *U.S. v. Butler*, 297 U.S. 1 (1936).

45 *Carter v. Carter Coal*, 298 U.S. 238 (1936).

46 *Ashwander v. T.V.A.*, 297 U.S. 288 (1936).

47 *Ashton v. Cameron Water District*, 298 U.S. 513 (1936).

48 *N.L.R.B. v. Jones & Laughlin Steel Corp.*, 301 U.S. 1 (1937).

49 *Stewart Machine Co. v. Davis*, 301 U.S. 548 (1937).

50 *Mulford v. Smith*, 307 U.S. 38 (1939).

51 *U.S. v. Darby*, 312 U.S. 100 (1941).

52 291 U.S. 502 (1934).

53 290 U.S. 398 (1934).

54 298 U.S. 587 (1936).

55 300 U.S. 379 (1937).

56 Felix Frankfurter, "Mr. Justice Roberts," *University of Pennsylvania Law Review*, CIV (1955), 311-17; and John W. Chambers, "The Big Switch: Justice Roberts and the Minimum Wage Cases," *Labor History*, X (1969), 44-73.

57 *Peterson Baking v. Bryan*, 290 U.S. 570 (1934).

58 *Richmond Mortgage & Loan v. Wachovia Bank & Trust*, 300 U.S. 124 (1937); *United States Mortgage v. Matthews*, 293 U.S. 232 (1934); *Jennings v. United States Fidelity and Guaranty*, 294 U.S. 216 (1935); and *Pobreslo v. Boyd*, 287 U.S. 528 (1933).

59 *Johnson Oil Refining v. Oklahoma*, 290 U.S. 158 (1933); *Virginia v. Imperial Coal Sales*, 293 U.S. 15 (1934); *Wheeling Steel v. Fox*, 298 U.S. 193 (1936); and *Southern Natural Gas v. Alabama*, 301 U.S. 148 (1937).

60 *State Board v. Jackson*, 283 U.S. 527 (1931); *Great A&P Tea Co. v. Grosjean.* 301 U.S. 412 (1937); and *Fox v. Standard Oil Co.*, 294 U.S. 87 (1935).

61 *New York ex rel. Cohn v. Graves*, 300 U.S. 308 (1937); *Madden v. Kentucky*, 309 U.S. 83 (1940); and *Graves v. New York ex rel. O'Keefe*, 306 U.S. 466 (1939).

62 *Monamotor v. Johnson*, 292 U.S. 86 (1934); and *Wiloil v. Pennsylvania*, 294 U.S. 169 (1935).

63 *Los Angeles Gas & Electric v. Railroad Comm.*, 289 U.S. 287 (1933); and *Lindheimer v. Illinois Bell Telephone*, 292 U.S. 151 (1934).

64 *Frost v. Railroad Commission*, 271 U.S. 583.

65 *Stephenson v. Binford*, 287 U.S. 251 (1932).

66 16 Peters 1.

67 *Erie Railroad Co. v. Tompkins*, 304 U.S. 64.

68 283 U.S. 697 (1931).

69 283 U.S. 359 (1931).

70 *Powell v. Alabama*, 287 U.S. 45 (1932).

71 *Senn v. Tile Layers Union*, 301 U.S. 468 (1937); *Thornhill v. Alabama*, 310 U.S. 468 (1937); and *American Federation of Labor v. Swing*, 312 U.S. 321 (1941).

72 *Hague v. C.I.O.*, 307 U.S. 496 (1939).

73 *Lovell v. Griffin*, 303 U.S. 444 (1938).

74 *DeJonge v. Oregon*, 299 U.S. 353 (1937; and *Herndon v. Lowry*, 301 U.S. 242 (1937).

75 Pusey, pp. 683-90, 773-91.

76 Perkins, p. 139; David L. Porter, "The Ten Best Secretaries of State and the Five Worst," *The Rating Game in American Politics: An Interdisciplinary Approach*, William D. Pederson and Ann M. McLaurin (eds)., (New York, 1987), pp. 86-90; and Murray, pp. 373-75.

77 Schubert, pp. 192-210.

78 Albert P. Blaustein and Roy Mersky, "Rating Supreme Court Justices," *The Rating Game*, pp. 132-33; and Blaustein and Mersky, *The First One Hundred Chief Justices* (Hamden, Connecticut, 1978), pp. 37, 43.

79 See Burner cited above and Joan Hoff Wilson, *Herbert Hoover: Forgotten Progressive* (Boston, 1975).

William Howard Taft, Charles Evans Hughes and the Permanent Court of International Justice

Michael Dunne

1. Introduction Diplomatic historians often refer to the years between the First and Second World Wars as the period of American interwar isolationism. For historians of domestic law the same period marks the shift from the jurisprudential dominance of conservative legalism to liberal realism. Such are the broad, conventional patterns; and though scholars have analyzed (or "deconstructed") these problematical terms and their ideological origins, the essential accuracy of the characterization cannot be seriously challenged. For all the economic internationalism of the interwar years, the foreign policy of the United States was conducted unilaterally—the key element in isolationist thinking; while bench, bar and graduate school forwarded the process of historicizing or con-textualizing common, statute and even constitutional law—a process perhaps more familiarly known as the study of the sociology of the law. In the case of foreign relations, the political turning-point of the interwar years is often seen to come between the onset of the Great Depression during 1929 and the multiple crises of 1931 (the *annus terribilis*, in Arnold Toynbee's phrase); in domestic legal history, the shift is likely to be identified with the resignation of William Howard Taft as Chief Justice of the US Supreme Court and his succession by Charles Evans Hughes early in 1930.[1]

The coincidence, the symmetry even of these events merits investigation; but any possible causal interrelationship cannot be simply inferred. After all, the crisis years of 1929-1931 are alleged to have induced international political reaction; while at home the Crash and the New Deal are traditionally represented as nuturing progressive jurisprudence, even if under duress in the notorious Supreme Court "packing" episode of 1937. Yet again the overlapping tenure of the Justices works against sudden philosophical breaks in the Court's jurisprudence. Finally we may note that the height of international legal realism was reached in 1931 with the World Court's decision on the Austro-German Customs Union case; but in this instance the so-called realism effectively undermined the prestige of the World Court and became an additional argument for its American opponents to remain aloof. This, in brief, is the context in which we shall examine the roles of Taft and Hughes in the interwar years.

Section 2   The main stages in the public life of William Howard Taft and Charles Evans Hughes are well known. Taft, born in Cincinnati in 1857, came of an influential family, his father Alphonso holding political, legal and ambassadorial posts in the Grant and Arthur administrations. After undergraduate years at Yale, law school back in Cincinnati and private legal practice, Taft's career rans as follows, in his own brief account:

> 1. Three years on the state bench. 2. Two years solicitor general, U.S. 3. Eight years presiding judge, U.S. Circuit. 4. Four years Court of Appeals, Sixth Circuit. 5. Four years secretary of war. 6. Four years president. 7. Eight years Kent professor, Yale University. . . .

There was also Taft's service as the first Governor-General of the Philippines; and, the culmination for Taft, the Chief Justiceship of the US Supreme Court from 1921-1930. As he said soon after his appointment by President Harding:

> I love judges and I love courts. They are my ideals on earth of what we shall meet afterward in Heaven under a just God.[2]

As President from 1909-1913 Taft exerted enormous influence on the Supreme Court he himself came to lead, appointing six Justices in four years to the three each appointed by Theodore Roosevelt and Woodrow Wilson; and he is authoritatively credited with having "engineered" the appointment of "at least" three other Justices once he himself became Chief Justice.[3] But in purely personal terms, Taft's most successful appointment was that of Edward D. White. On the death of CJ Melville W. Fuller in 1910, Taft bypassed Associate Justice Charles Evans Hughes (the favoured candidate and Taft's junior by five years) and elevated White (Taft's senior by some twelve years) from the Associate ranks—an unprecedented promotion. The gamble paid off. Living well into his seventies, CJ White died in May 1921, leaving Warren G. Harding an opportunity to repay Taft for his help in the 1920 presidential election campaign. The "lifelong aspirant" was able "at last" to enter the "sacred shrine" as Chief Justice.[4]

Hughes's time would also come, when he succeeded Taft as Chief Justice in 1930. Before then Hughes had had an outstanding career by any standards. Born in Glen Falls, NY, in 1862, Hughes studied at Madison (renamed Colgate) University, Brown and the Columbia Law School. There followed very lucrative private legal practice and Chairs at Cornell and the New York Law School; but widespread public recognition came only with Hughes's work as special counsel to the New York legislature's investigation of utility companies. This appointment became for Hughes the stepping-stone to the Republican gubernatorial nomination and his subsequent defeat of William Randolph Hearst in the 1906 election in a largely personal victory. Two years later Hughes was again adrift of the State Republicans—but in the wrong direction. Even so he was re-elected to Albany, just as Taft was succeeding to Roosevelt in the 1908 presidential campaign. Hughes did not, however, stand for a third term as Governor, having been nominated to the Supreme Court by President Taft in April 1910 and then confirmed without difficulty by the Senate.

If the judicial elevation of White to thwart Hughes had been unprecedented in 1910, Hughes himself set another "first." In 1916 he resigned from the Supreme Court to accept the Republican presidential nomination. As is well known, Hughes failed to defeat Wilson—but by a slim majority in the Electoral College. (This was something of a legacy of the 1912 campaign. Roosevelt's Bull Moose running-mate, Governor Hiram Warren Johnson of California, was fiercely opposed to Hughes and helped swing his State for Wilson, so tipping the balance in the Electoral College.)[5] Four years later, when the Republicans recaptured the White House, Hughes (like Taft) was repaid for services rendered in the election campaign. Within hours of the inauguration, Hughes was first nominated by Harding and then unanimously confirmed by the Senate as Secretary of State.

Section 3   Harding's debt to Taft and Hughes lay in their successful efforts to prevent the GOP splitting over the League of Nations. The story has been told at length elsewhere; so we can be selective in the following account.[6]

Both Taft and Hughes had been spoken of as eminently suitable members to join the American delegation travelling to Paris to negotiate the treaties ending the First World War. (Roosevelt was simply too frail and cantankerous to be a serious candidate to represent the Republicans; and he died shortly before the Peace Conference opened.) Hughes's claim was essentially his recent role as party standard-bearer; Taft's credentials were much greater. He had tried as President to advance the scope of international arbitration; and he had later been a founding and very senior member of the League to Enforce Peace (LEP), established in 1915 as the American version of the transatlantic movement which prefigured the League of Nations itself. Neither man (as we now know) was chosen for the American Delegation to Negotiate Peace; and Wilson's concession to bipartisanship was the appointment of a Republican career diplomat, Henry White.[7] Remaining at home, Taft and Hughes carefully monitored the negotiations. Both men agreed that the Draft Covenant of the League of Nations, published on 14 February 1919, needed amending to include: the right of withdrawal; an American veto-power in the League Council; the reservation of "domestic" questions from the competence of the League; and an explicit defence of the Monroe Doctrine. The only serious disagreement between the two men was over Article X, which Taft (true to his LEP background) accepted in principle, while Hughes was opposed to it from the outset. In the event, the final text of the League Covenant gave verbal protection to the common concerns of Taft and Hughes (<u>via</u> Articles I, V, XV and XXI respectively);

but Article X—for Wilson the "backbone," or even the very "heart" of the Covenant—remained in place substantially unaltered.[8]

Taft and Hughes also disagreed on who exactly was to blame for the double failure of the revised Covenant to win a two-thirds majority in the Senate during the voting in November 1919 and March 1920. Hughes blamed Wilson more than the Senate; while Taft blamed Wilson, Wilson's unconditional supporters, Henry Cabot Lodge and the "strong reservationists," and the "irreconcilables"—in other words, all those who for different reasons had refused to compromise and get the basis of the Covenant accepted. As Taft wrote to the Democratic (now Minority) Leader, Senator Gilbert M. Hitchcock of Nebraska:

> The treaty, even with the reservations, represents enormous progress toward better conditions as to peace and war in the world.

Like the British and French governments and the nascent League Secretariat, Taft particularly and Hughes to a lesser extent thought that virtually any American conditions attached and passed with the Covenant were preferable to its total rejection.[9]

The controversy over the Covenant did not end in March 1920: it became the central if muddled issue of the succeeding presidential campaign between the Republicans led by Harding and the Democrats under another Ohioan, Governor James M. Cox. But whatever the meaning of the "solemn referendum" on public opinion towards the League of Nations, one thing was clear. Harding had won the endorsement of Taft, Hughes and other leading party activists, notably *via* the famous Declaration of Thirty-One Pro-League Republicans, as being the only candidate (backed by the only party) who could effect ratification of the treaty by modifying the terms of Article X.[10] The statement, whether genuine or disingenuous, had the desired result. The GOP did not split as it had in 1912; Hiram Johnson and the other Republican Irreconcilables were held in check; and the White House was recaptured.

One provision of the Covenant had not aroused any real controversy or serious opposition in the debates of 1919-1920.[11] Article XIV of the Covenant read:

> The Council shall formulate and submit to the Members of the League for adoption plans for the establishment of a Permanent Court of International Justice. The Court shall be competent to hear and determine any dispute of an international character which the parties thereto submit to it. The Court may also give an advisory opinion upon any dispute or question referred to it by the Council or by the Assembly.

Herein lay the constitutional origins of the Permanent Court of International Justice (PCIJ), the so-called first World Court, comparable to the mandate given in Article III, Section 1 of the US Constitution to establish the federal judicial system. The particular roles of Taft and Hughes in advancing the cause of the World Court form the subject of the rest of this chapter.

Section 4 The establishment of a *permanent* bench of judges to adjudicate international disputes according to an agreed body of law and practice was a judicial goal sought by the victorious, defeated and many neutral States at the close of the First World War. Both the militant and pacific wings of the world-wide peace movement wanted to advance the work of the two Hague Peace Conferences of 1899 and 1907, which had set up a system of judicial arbitration to effect *ad hoc* resolutions of inter-state conflicts. For many lawyers and diplomats agreed that the weakness of the resulting Permanent Court of Arbitration (PCA) was precisely that it lacked the permanency, the physical and jurisprudential continuity of domestic courts.[12]

Although the US Senate twice rejected the Covenant, the major League Powers nevertheless hoped for American membership in the proposed new court. (The United States was a participant in the PCA.) Indeed there were those inside and outside the League who believed that American membership in the future court would not be a simple substitute, a *pis aller*, but rather a stage on the way to eventual full membership in the League itself. To help achieve one or both of these goals, the League invited a leading American to help in the drafting of the Court's Statute (or constitution) in the Summer of 1920. That man was Elihu Root.

Root's career rivalled that of Taft and Hughes. To select only the highlights: Root had served as Secretary of War and State under Roosevelt; had then been a Senator from New York; was a panel-member of the PCA; had been a leading figure in the American Society of International Law since its founding in 1906; was the first President of the Carnegie Endowment for International Peace; and for these and other contributions to diplomacy and international law he had been awarded the Nobel Peace Prize in 1912. Later Root was prominent in the League to Enforce Peace. Now, in 1920, he was seventy-five years old and regarded as the outstanding conservative Republican statesman. He it was who worded both the ambiguous Republican plank on the League and later the Declaration of Thirty-One; and it was his presence on the drafting committee of the Court Statute at The Hague during the Summer of 1920 which led many propagandists to dub the emerging institution the "Root Court."[13]

Contemporaneously with Harding's election the League members finalized the text of the Court Statute and agreed a formula which allowed not just League members but original signatories of the Covenant, scilicet the United States, to adhere to the Protocol of Signature to which the Court's Statute was attached. For the next fifteen years the question of American membership of the PCIJ and the implications for membership of the League itself were major controversies in and concerning Washington; and for diplomatic historians they have become a touchstone of American interwar isolationism.[14]

Section 5 Despite many historical allusions to the World Court issue in interwar politics, even the basic outlines of the narrative are obscure and often confused.[15] To understand the special contribution of Taft and Hughes this larger pattern needs a brief survey. Yet in a topic involving not only the constitution and functioning of an international court but also politics in Washington, Geneva and The Hague (homes of the League and Court respectively), and major foreign capitals, precision and nuance should be at a premium. With the caveat that the following sketch is cast in very broad terms, we can distinguish three main chapters. First there was a five-year period ending in the winter of 1925-1926, during which the terms of American membership in the Court were formulated and then approved by both the Coolidge administration and the Senate: a genuine example of executive-legislative partnership. Then came three more years, in which time the League twice analyzed these conditions and gave its own qualified acceptance in September 1929. The final chapter was the longest; and it ended with the Senate casting a vote (constituting a plurality but not the needed two-thirds majority) against the League's compromise in January 1935. Such, in capsule, is the outline story. For us, though, the perspective is different and starts in the winter of 1920-1921 with the publication and acceptance by the League members of the Court Statute (the so-called Root Court).

Though Root's contribution to the creation of the PCIJ has been exaggerated, he deserves credit for helping to solve a problem which "had baffled and defeated" previous attempts to create a permanent court.[16] How would the judges be elected? The Great Powers (in contemporary language) demanded their own individual voice and vote on the bench; while the smaller States needed to participate in numbers somehow if the court were to be genuinely multinational. Yet it was impossible practically for each to be represented. Root's solution was a variant of the Connecticut Compromise adopted at Philadelphia during the drafting of the US Constitution. The eleven judges and their four deputies would be elected by concurrent votes of the League Council and Assembly. In the Council the Great Powers (or Permanent Members) dominated politically—and, initially, were meant to dominate numerically; while in the Assembly each member had an equal vote— though States represented in both chambers had a vote in each. The Connecticut Compromise was relevant, Root argued, because it proved that the conflicting principles of sovereign equality (represented in the US Senate and the League Assembly) and political, actual inequality (as in the population criterion for the House of

Representatives) could be blended harmoniously in one constitutional system to achieve equity.[17]

Important in itself for the establishment of the Court, Root's argument for the novel electoral procedure was relevant to the question of American adherence. Was it conceivable that the United States would consent to join without participating in elections to the bench—elections which were confined to members of the League? A related, though uncontentious issue was the possibility of an American citizen sitting on the bench. Under the Court Statute citizens of *any* State could be elected, provided they had been nominated by panel-members of the PCA; nor was it necessary for the nominators to be Americans. In short, an American could indeed be elected on to the bench and without the American panel-members necessarily nominating the candidate.

There were, however, two other major, interconnected problems. Since the Statute had been approved by the League, was derived from the Covenant, and was viewed by many authoritative people as a means of maintaining the Peace Settlement, could the United States both claim a role in amending the Statute and yet disclaim any obligations arising from the numerous Paris peace treaties—all the while participating in Council-Assembly elections?

Finally there were two other issues. One was the size of any American financial support for the Court. This was a federal, constitutional matter as much as an international one, because funding would need to be authorized by Congress and might not be pre-committed. The other query was over the right of withdrawal, which was not specified in the Statute but which was (as we have seen) a successful demand made by the Americans on the Draft Covenant.[18]

Undoubtedly the most paradoxical element in the initial debate over American relations with the PCIJ was the lack of any controversy over the right to use the Court, ie being a willing litigant before the bench. This facility was available to the United States *qua* signatory of the Covenant (Statute: Article XXXV). At issue, of course, would be the political decision to resort to the Court. And what if there were no American judge on the bench? Then the United States had the right (as did all litigants: Article XXXI) to nominate a judge *ad hoc*. Moreover the United States could not be haled before the Court willy-nilly: such so-called compulsory jurisdiction was a function Signatory States accorded to the Court if they wished, on the terms they individually set. (The "Optional Clause" allowed signatories to cede such jurisdiction in general terms and reciprocally: Article XXXVI.)

To contemporaries such complex detail was overshadowed by the larger question of American membership of the League. Proponents and opponents of this ulterior goal readily described the campaign for adherence to the Court as a "staging-post," a "back door" to the League. Early in the 1920s Taft was inclined to this strategy; while Hughes was more cautious, believing that the anti-League forces were still powerful and alert; and he was less prepared than Taft to risk splitting the Republican party, even on the Court campaign — let alone to push for the League. Root was somewhere between the two; while Harding was even more hesitant than Hughes and judged everything by domestic, political, especially re-election standards. Harding's position was not surprising: he had won the nomination in 1920 because he was acceptable to the Irreconcilables; and yet he had then been endorsed by the Thirty-One Pro-League Republicans. The rift ran through the Cabinet, with Secretary of Commerce Herbert Hoover (another of the Thirty-One) even more keen on the League than Taft; while the Secretary of the Interior, Albert B. Fall of New Mexico, was a former Irreconcilable.[19] In such a politically delicate situation Secretary of State Hughes and Chief Justice Taft began to advance the cause of American membership in the PCIJ.

Section 6 For a year after Harding's inauguration Hughes moved cautiously. He wanted to quieten Irreconcilable fears, not least to smooth the way for the Treaty of Berlin in the Autumn of 1921 (concluding the war with Germany in lieu of the Treaty of Versailles) and then prepare for the Washington Disarmament Conference from November 1921-February 1922. (The Treaty and the Conference were seen as potential points of attack on the administration for aligning with the League.)[20] Similarly Hughes was happy for the American

PCA-panelists not to submit nominations for the Court's first elections by the Council and Assembly. In the event, their favoured candidate, John Bassett Moore, was nominated by the Italians and comfortably elected on to the bench in September 1921. But in conciliating the mainly Republican Irreconcilables, Hughes annoyed the pro-Leaguers, who were mainly Democrats, notably the editor Hamilton Holt, as well as fellow-signatories of the Declaration, especially George W. Wickersham and A. Lawrence Lowell. In July 1922 denunciations of Hughes for reneging on the commitments of the 1920 campaign filled the press; and Hughes was obliged to defend his own name and that of the State Department.[21]

Three issues had been brought into the public view: American relations with the League in general; participation in the PCIJ; and the specific matter of the PCA-panelists' failure to submit any nominations. Our present concern must be with the second issue, the prospects of the United States "shar[ing] in the maintenance of the Court" (as Hughes phrased it). He insisted that he had always "advocated the judicial settlement of justiciable controversies between nations," and thus implied that the newly-established PCIJ satisfied these broad goals. But, Hughes added, there was "no prospect" of American participation in the Court

> until some provision is made by which, *without membership of the League,* this Government would be able to have an appropriate voice in the election of Judges [emphasis added].

Utterly reasonable in itself, Hughes's published response discreetly neglected the one factor which might have mollified Ham Holt & Co. For Hughes had already begun to explore diplomatically the framing of just such a "provision" for American adherence to the Court. Moreover Hughes had not only put out secret feelers abroad; he was using as an intermediary someone he described as "one of the most eminent and influential friends of the league." The anonymous negotiator was William Howard Taft.[22]

In June-July 1922 Taft, a keen administrator, visited Great Britain. His primary and expressed purpose was to study judicial procedure; and he used the columns of the *ABA Jour-*

nal to declare that he would steer clear of political controversies. But before Taft left the United States he was briefed on exploring the possibilities and means of US adherence to the PCIJ. Once he had arrived in London, Taft's initial soundings were not promising to his British counterparts: Lords Grey, Balfour, Robert Cecil and Phillimore. (The latter two had been heavily involved in the drafting of both the Covenant and the Court Statute; while Cecil and Balfour were active in official League business and in the major British lobby-group, the League of Nations Union.)[23] Taft began by suggesting that the Court be made "a separate institution" from the League. Clearly this was non-starter; for though the two bodies were distinct and functioned under different constitutions, there were interdependent, even if not co-ordinate. Later discussions, however, revealed that the British and American governments (the former acting as an intermediary for the League collectively) could agree that only two substantive problems were at issue: 1) American participation in the Court's elections and 2) freedom from any obligations under the Covenant. Paradoxically the main difficulty lay in the procedure for realizing these principles.

Back from Great Britain, where he had been feted by the social, political and academic establishment, Taft acted as the transmission point between Hughes, Root, Balfour, Cecil and Phillimore—a role all the more important when Hughes was absent from Washington celebrating the centenary of Brazilian independence. Now that the notion of separating the Court from the League had been laid to rest, the various negotiators came up with three different schemes. Root initially favoured an executive agreement granting the US government electoral rights to the Court and legal immunity from the Covenant. This method appealed to him because he feared that any congressional, especially senatorial, involvement would re-open the League controversy and offer the chance of either a simple legislative rejection or—more likely—prolonged crippling through the attaching of wrecking reservations. Taft for his part thought in terms of amending the Court Statute, since only textual changes to the Court's constitution could possibly placate the anti-League forces in the Senate. As he put it to Root: such alterations to the Court's fundamental structure were a "psychological necessity in dealing with our Bitter Enders." Between these two widely divergent American views came the final proposal of the British negotiators, backed in turn by the League Secretariat as well as judges and officials at The Hague. There should be no amendments to the Court Statute (and *a fortiori* to the Covenant).   Rather the United States should declare its acceptance of the Protocol of Signature (whereby the Member States had established the Court) through a formal treaty, approved by a two-thirds vote of the Senate; and with the specific conditions of American adherence detailed in appropriate reservations. (It may be noted that this was precisely the method used unsuccessfully with the Treaty of Versailles.) As Cecil authoritatively informed Taft: "any reasonable suggestion made by America would be immediately accepted"—by the League! And the greater the difficulty in securing such legislative approval, the firmer, more substantial would be the ultimate American commitment. Furthermore, Cecil implied, such a success would allow the Harding administration to shake loose from the Irreconcilables' veto.

> Such final endorsement by both branches of the American Government would give the Executive far greater freedom . . . in co-operating with the Court, and would demonstrate that co-operation with the Court had entered into the very fibre of American foreign politics.[24]

A full history of the Court and the League would show that Taft and his Anglo-American collaborators had not worked alone in devising the basic formula of US adherence. Judge John Bassett Moore, doyen of American international lawyers, and a later occupant of his seat on the bench, Manley O. Hudson, had both also been active at The Hague and Geneva respectively. Senior officials of the League, notably the British Secretary-General Eric Drummond and the head of the Legal Section, Joost van Hamel of The Netherlands, had woven their cautious, collective ideas together and allowed them to reach Washington, London and The Hague, from where the Court's Swedish Registrar, Ake Hammarskjold, had developed close links with pro-Leaguers like Hudson.   Yet despite all this activity, what is so striking is the degree of independence, even isolation, in which the various groups worked; and, even, in the case of Taft and Hughes, the lengths they went to conceal their purpose. For example, the American ambassador in London, George Harvey, was kept in complete ignorance of the Court negotiations; but then he had been a leading and vociferous opponent of the League in 1919-1920. (Harvey's posting to the Court of St James's was another pay-off by Harding for services rendered against the League.)[25] Yet Taft's role should not be minimized. Its importance lay less in the detail of his drafting, in the formalities of the terms ulti-mately devised. Rather his contribution lay in the trust that Hughes, Harding and Root could place in his robust yet discreet personality, his earlier history as an advocate of the political function of the League and the general judicial reso-lution of international disputes, his influence in conservative, regular Republican circles, his public status at home and abroad—all qualities, experiences and connections which rendered Taft so authoritative an ambassador in official British eyes.

Section 7 The results of the secret negotiations conducted by Taft & Co. now needed to be carefully publicized. If the Senate was to give its approval to so delicate and controversial a scheme, it had to be conciliated. (Even the passage of the Treaty of Berlin and the pacts deriving from the Washington Conference showed the continuing influence of the Irreconcil-ables.) Certainly, as Hughes told Taft on the latter's return, "friends of the League" had been "gunning for him" to take action on the Court Protocol; but there could be no chance of a two-thirds majority in the Senate if the anti-Leaguers and the undecided were provoked by a surprise move.[26]

Hughes decided to work through Henry Cabot Lodge (still Chairman of the Foreign Relations Committee), who faced a tricky re-election campaign in Massachusetts. Hughes would make one of his rare mid-term campaign speeches for Lodge; and, in the same endorsement, float the broad lines of the proposed senatorial resolution of adherence.[27] With Lodge so neatly compromised and with Harding (needing Regular support) backing Hughes's stance, the Secretary of State could feel confident that the Republican Irreconcilables would be marginalized in the eventual debate. (Almost all the Democrats could be relied upon to support adherence.) But this was not the whole of the plan: there was also the question of timing. With the agreement of Harding and Taft and the acceptance of Moore, Hughes delayed the formal submission of the proposed terms of American adherence until the last week of February 1923, ie at the close of the fourth and last legislative Session of the Sixty-seventh Congress.[28] It is not simple hindsight gained from reading backwards from our own knowledge of what actually happened to realize that Hughes's timing virtually guaranteed that there would be no effective senatorial action until the opening of the *next-but-one* Congress, viz. the Sixty-ninth Congress, scheduled to convene in December 1925. The reasoning goes as follows. Nothing would be achieved in the current, lame-duck, Fourth Session of the Sixty-seventh Congress. The First Session of the Sixty-eight Congress would be geared up to the 1924 presidential election campaign; and with the Insurgents in the Republican party having done well in the recent mid-term elections, their disruptive effect upon administration programmes would carry on into the Second, lame-duck, Session, ending in March 1925. Only in December 1925, with the start of the Sixty-ninth Congress (elected in 1924) would there be any chance—and that not guaranteed—of a calm (understand: favourable) debate on the Court Protocol. The process of delaying action on the Court—procrastination invariably attributed to the opponents of membership—was thus begun quite deliberately by its avowed supporters.[29]

Section 8   That story of delay lies beyond our present concerns. Instead it remains to detail and discuss the terms specified by Secretary Hughes in February 1923; and then to conclude with Hughes's final efforts on behalf of American entry into the World Court.

In his letter of transmission for President Harding to lay before the Senate, Hughes set out the four formal "conditions and understandings" which should govern American "adhesion" to the Protocol establishing the Permanent Court of International Justice.

1. That such adhesion shall not be taken to involve any legal relation on the part of the United States to the League of Nations or the assumption of any obligations by the United States under the Covenant of the League of Nations constituting Part I of the Treaty of Versailles.

2. That the United States shall be permitted to participate through representatives designated for the purpose and upon an equality with the other States members respectively of the Council and Assembly of the League of Nations in any and all proceedings of either the Council or the Assembly for the election of judges or deputy judges of the Permanent Court of International Justice, or for the filling of vacancies.

3. That the United States will pay a fair share of the expenses of the Court as determined and appropriated from time to time by the Congress of the United States.

4. That the Statute for the Permanent Court of International Justice . . . shall not be amended without the consent of the United States.[30]

The bulk of Hughes's letter contained his rationale for adherence and explanations of these four paragraphs (which would later be called the Hughes-Harding conditions). The preceding narrative has explained the general thinking behind the Hughes-Harding formula; but what of Hughes's own arguments?

One preliminary point to note is that Hughes, confident in his personal judicial and rhetorical skills, composed the brief very much on his own. There is little evidence of departmental input into the final document. Moreover, Hughes worked on it at home when "laid up with the grippe."[31] Both factors may account for some weaknesses in the argumentation; though it must be said that Hughes's biographers and pro-Court scholars have found no fault with the document. But it is indisputable that a fundamental flaw runs through Hughes's brief; and this was his confusion of two different methods for resolving international disputes: the political and the legal.

It does not take advanced scholarship to realize that the line between law and politics is blurred and contentious. But such a distinction was frequently expressed in the debate on the World Court. Indeed, Root's involvement in the establishment and advocacy of the new court derived in large measure from his desire to move beyond the arbitral system of the existing Hague Court towards the judicial determination of inter-state conflicts. To Root, Hughes and the like, the crucial distinction lay between the political or diplomatic compromise of rival claims (arbitration) and the disinterested pronouncement and enforcement of legal rights (adjudication). Whether such a categorical and abstract separation can hold absolutely and in practice is not for us the issue. Rather, in this particular case, Hughes's analysis posited the distinction and then wandered between the opposing principles, particularly in his favourable allusions to the "time-honored policy" of the US government in promoting "the peaceful settlement of international controversies," a policy which was now taken to entail supporting the PCIJ, as it had been "invest[ed] . . . with a jurisdiction which conforms to American principles and practice. . . ." The rhetoric of Hughes's brief implied that such "American principles and practices" were strictly legal, in purist terms; and they therefore could be identified *both* with the tradition of American diplomatic practice *and* the jurisprudence and procedure of the new World Court. In fact, the PCIJ was established along lines which conformed far more to an arbitral system; and which, in three quite obvious ways, conflicted with American legal ideals. One was the Court's constitutional rejection of the principle of precedent (*stare decisis*). The second was the Court's lack of so-called compulsory or obligatory jurisdiction: parties consented to appear before the Court; it could not arraign them—a key feature of domestic or municipal courts. The third deviation lay in the PCIJ's function of providing advisory opinions on a reference from the League of Nations.[32]

If these three areas can be regarded as posing procedural conflicts with American "principles and practice," there was also the question of the fundamental or basic law to be applied by the PCIJ. Textually and politically the obvious candidates were the treaties collectively known as the Paris Peace Settlement; and throughout the drafting and completion of the Court Statute in 1920 the majority of the drafters and the League under whose aegis they worked stressed the role of the new court in functioning as the interpretative, the juridical voice of the League. To draw the obvious analogy with the US federal system: the PCIJ was to act as the ideological guardian of the international political order established in 1919-1920; just as the federal judicial system, and especially its Supreme Court, has been perceived as the custodian of the principles and institutions established in the constitutional debates and decisions of 1787. (Advocates and opponents of American membership in the World Court frequently adduced this analogy.)[33]

Hughes was not able to resolve these argumentative difficulties. It would remain for international law specialists, which Hughes was not, to accept these distinctions between American ideals and practice on one side and the origins and purposes of the PCIJ on the other and *then* go on to say that the new court offered a chance to develop an international jurisprudence and procedure which might yet be shaken free of the particular and regrettable historical-political origins; and which, indeed, might become so more readily *provided* the United States could join — precisely the position of Judge Moore (and, initially, his star pupil and later close friend, Edwin M. Borchard of Yale).[34]

Whatever Hughes's forensic skills, his domestic political sensitivities were still alert. Tucked away in the body of the letter to President Harding and not specified or enumerated in the proposed "conditions and understandings to be made a part of the instrument of adhesion" was a provision which gave the Senate a crucial role in determining American use of the Court as a means of *arbitration*. Taking up the point that the Court exercised no "compulsory jurisdiction," Hughes stated that the Harding administration had no intention of conceding such a power to the Court. Rather the government would maintain the traditional "position . . . that there should be a special agreement for the submission of a particular controversy to arbitral decision." Two separate issues were involved: one was the government's function in defining "the questions for adjudication" by a *compromis*; the other was the implication that the Senate would be involved, through the treaty-making power, in formulating the particular terms of any *ad hoc* reference to the Court. Contemporaries would surely remember that the Senate had been reluctant to lose this prerogative under earlier arbitration schemes.[35]

President Harding expressed himself perfectly pleased with Hughes's brief and the proposed conditions; and though he publicly requested early senatorial approval, in his private correspondence he admitted he did "not really expect" this in the short time before the adjournment.[36] Some weeks later Harding, Hughes, Root and Hoover all gave major addresses in favour of the Court. But the overall effect was vitiated by Lord Robert Cecil, who was on a lecture-tour of the United States and gave numerous speeches stressing and praising the League connection.[37] Indeed Harding judged that public opinion — let alone insurgent Republican senatorial feeling — was moving so strongly against the League's Court that he began "wiggling and wobbling" (in his language) until in a dramatic speech in St. Louis towards the end of June he "bloviated" into an equivocal, ambiguous but basically actual renunciation of Hughes's proposals and revived Taft's "separation" scheme with a call for the "court's complete independence of the league."[38]

Hughes's reaction to Harding's retreat at St. Louis can only be surmized. The Hughes Papers, his own memoirs, State Department files, his biographers — all ignore Harding's finesse. (Hudson and his contacts in the League and Court knew what was up: a deliberate, political "surrender" by a President anxious about being dumped at the 1924 convention.)[39] Thereafter, so long as he remained Secretary of State, Hughes kept a low profile on the Court issue. Whether discretion was the better part of valour, whether Hughes believed the chances of American adherence would be improved by his silence, we can only speculate. But there is no doubt that the agitated advocates of the time became increasing critical and frustrated. To the indictment over Hughes's backing of Harding in 1920 and then his abstention on the PCIJ nominations in 1921 they now added the charge of trimming in the interests of Harding's political future.[40] It was scarcely worth it. Within a few weeks of the St. Louis speech Harding was dead; and his successor, Calvin Coolidge, picked up the cause and brought it before the Senate with the original Hughes-Harding terms.

Section 9 As we have seen, full Senate action on the Court Protocol did not begin until December 1925. Neither Taft nor Hughes played any significant part on the fringes of the debate—though another Supreme Court Justice (and later Chief Justice) did. He was Harlan Fiske Stone, who was an intimate of Moore's and close to Coolidge and Hoover. Stone helped to create links between Moore, the administration and leading Senators: men such as William E. Borah (Idaho, Rep.), Chairman of the Foreign Relations Committee; the formal Democratic manager on the Court Protocol, Claude A. Swanson of Virginia; the chief Democratic proponent, Thomas J. Walsh of Montana; and Regular Republicans like Irvine L. Lenroot of Wisconsin and George Wharton Pepper of Pennsylvania. On the Floor of the Senate *four* more conditions were added to the Hughes-Harding terms. These new conditions troubled the pro-Leaguers, but not unduly; and they have annoyed later historians. In fact they were sponsored by the senatorial *proponents* of adherence and were immediately or subsequently endorsed by the Coolidge administration. One of these conditions was essentially procedural and caused no real concern to the League; two were re-statements of traditional American attitudes towards arbitration and adjudication; and only the remaining condition was a major obstacle: the reservation of an American veto on the use of the advisory jurisdiction—a power which the Permanent Members had *de facto* if not (as the Senate and Executive demanded) *de jure*.[41]

For more than three years the Coolidge and Hoover administrations tentatively, half-heartedly negotiated officially and unofficially (through Root again) with the League and the Court's member-States. This process lasted from March 1926 until September 1929. Whatever the merits (and even strict meaning) of the American demand for a veto-power over the advisory jurisdiction, the League refused to grant such a power unconditionally. The compromise offered (beguilingly called the Root Protocol, in an echo of 1920) became the new contentious issue. And then in 1931 this same advisory function, so long a rather theoretical concern, became the vehicle for the PCIJ's most important judgment in the Austro-German Customs Union case. In its ruling against the Customs Union the Court divided 8-7 but with four different opinions; and even some proponents of American adherence as well as supporters of the Court outside the United States could not overcome the suspicion that the judicial split was determined by the political position of the judges' governments.[42] Consequently, when the Court Protocols returned to the full Senate in 1935, the prospects were not promising.[43] The Americans had not secured the right to a veto, even though it was arguably more important than in 1926; while the political role of the Court under its parent League of Nations was more problematical in the troubled mid-1930s than in the years of apparent hope in the mid-1920s. On 29 January 1935 the Senate failed to approve by the necessary two-thirds majority almost exactly the self-same terms its predecessor had passed overwhelmingly in January 1926. In the popular phrase of the time, the World Court had been "defeated."[44]

Section 10 Between the high-point of January 1926, which saw the first, favourable Senate vote, and the subsequent negotiation of the Root Protocol, Charles Evans Hughes performed his last service to the PCIJ in general and the goal of American adherence especially. In April 1928 Judge Moore resigned; and it was widely acknowledged that an American must be on the Court bench to give domestic and international credibility to the campaign for US adherence. Moore, Root and Newton D. Baker (Woodrow Wilson's Secretary of War and a new PCA-panelist) nominated Hughes over some far less prominent candidates, like Edwin B. Parker (an international financial expert and Moore's original choice). As Manley Hudson and George Wickersham said: Hughes's election was certain — no other American's was. When Hughes agreed to be put forward, Taft was "perfectly delighted" and was completely confident Hughes would be successful.[45] Taft was right. In the September 1928 Hughes was elected unanimously by the League Council; while in the Assembly he won 41 of the 48 votes.

The timing of the elections meant that Hughes would not serve at The Hague until the Sixteenth (extraordinary) Session beginning May 1929; and he then served at the Seventeenth (ordinary) Session finishing later in September. There is no mistaking the praise Hughes received from his new colleagues and indeed throughout legal and diplomatic circles. Though not the equal of Moore as an international lawyer, Hughes's political standing was immeasurably greater: Governor of New York; Associate Justice of the Supreme Court; presidential candidate; and Secretary of State.[46] For authoritative observers Hughes's election brought the day of American adherence that much nearer; while to pro-League activists, at home and abroad, the coincidence of the election with the signing of the Kellogg-Briand Pact seemed to offer an effective alternative to straightforward American membership of the League, namely parallel action to enforce sanctions against aggressors indicted by the League.[47]

Whether Hughes would have stood in the Court's second general election in 1930 is doubtful for purely familial reasons; but (as we know) that difficult decision had not to be taken.[48] Very early in the year Hughes was nominated by Hoover to succeed Taft as Chief Justice of the US Supreme Court. Only the prestige of the post to which he was going could allay the regrets of his new colleagues: judges like the first three Court Presidents, Bernard Loder of The Netherlands, Max Huber of Switzerland and Dionisio Anzilotti of Italy. Hughes stayed in the United States to preside over the Supreme Court during the "decade of crisis" and oversee the evolution of a liberal judicial realism from the conservative legalism of Taft and his predecessors.[49] Anzilotti, for his part, was re-elected to the PCIJ and so remained to deliver his brilliant, realist "individual" (concurrent) opinion in the Austro-German Customs Union case—the judgment which grieviously damaged the prestige of the Court for the rest of the 1930s.[50] Such was the fate of the Court to which William Howard Taft and Charles Evans Hughes had brought the United States so close, working secretly and openly, vigorously and cautiously by turn.

Notes

I have tried to keep these notes to a minimum. Full citations and a bibliographical guide are provided in the works listed at ns. 14 & 17 below.

In the text I have retained original orthography, though this method produces a number of minor textual inconsistencies.

1 Arnold J. Toynbee, *Survey of International Affairs, 1931* (London: Oxford University Press, 1932), Part I. This annual series, published by the Royal Institute of International Affairs, provides the best contemporary analysis of the interwar period in English. An invaluable guide to (primarily) American materials is Justus D. Doenecke, *Anti-Intervention: a Bibliographical Introduction to Isolationism and Pacificism from World War I to the Early Cold War*. Garland Reference Library of Social Science, vol. 396 (New York & London: Garland, 1987). Studies of domestic legal trends are provided by: Alpheus Thomas Mason, *The Supreme Court from Taft to Burger* (Baton Rouge & London: Louisiana State University Press, 1979); Paul L. Murphy, *The Constitution in Crisis Times, 1918-1969* (New York: Harper & Row, 1972); William F. Swindler, *Court and Constitution in the Twentieth Century*, 2 vols. (Indianapolis: Bobbs-Merrill, 1969-1970).

2 Taft to Gus Karger, 19 May 1921: William Howard Taft Papers, Library of Congress; Henry J. Abraham, *Justices and Presidents: a Political History of Appointments to the Supreme Court*, 2nd ed. (New York & Oxford: Oxford University Press, 1985), p. 185.

3 Laurence H. Tribe, *God Save this Honorable Court. How the Choice of Supreme Court Justices Shapes Our History* (New York: Random House, 1985), pp. 128-29.

4 Taft to Karger, 20 March 1916: Taft Papers; Henry F. Pringle, *The Life and Times of William Howard Taft: a Biography*, 2 vols. (New York: Farrar & Rinehart, 1939), II, Chap. L; Alpheus Thomas Mason, *William Howard Taft: Chief Justice* (New York: Simon & Schuster, 1965), Chap. III; *idem*, "William Howard Taft," in Leon Friedman & Fred L. Israel, eds., *The Justices of the United States Supreme Court [1789-1969]. Their Lives and Major Opinions*, 5 vols. (New York: Chelsea House, 1969-1978), III, pp. 2103-121, esp. p. 2103.

5 The Hiram Warren Johnson Papers are in the Bancroft Library, University of California, Berkeley. His role in the 1916 election is disputed: see George E. Mowry, *The California Progressives*, (Berkeley:

University of California Press, 1951), esp. Chap. X and Spencer C. Olin, Jr., *California's Prodigal Sons: Hiram Johnson and the Progressives 1911-1917* (Berkeley: University of California Press, 1968), esp. Chaps. 10-12.

6   Randolph C. Downes, *The Rise of Warren G. Harding, 1865-1920* (Columbus: Ohio State University Press, 1970), esp. Chaps. 15 & 23.

7   White was extremely well qualified professionally; but he was *politically* unimportant.   The most recent, full-length sudies are: Arthur Walworth, *Wilson and his Peacemakers: American Diplomacy at the Paris Peace Conference, 1919* (New York & London: Norton, 1986) and Lloyd E. Ambrosius, *Woodrow Wilson and the American Diplomatic Tradition: the Treaty Fight in Perspective* (Cambridge: Cambridge University Press, 1987).

8   Taft, "Analysis of the League Covenant as Amended," *Public Ledger* [Philadelphia], 30 April 1919: reprinted in Theodore Marburg & Horace E. Flack, eds., *Taft Papers on League of Nations* (New York: Macmillan, 1920), pp. 313-21; Thomas A. Bailey, *Woodrow Wilson and the Great Betrayal* (New York: Macmillan, 1945), pp. 86, 116.

9   Taft to Hitchcock, 15 November 1919: Taft Papers; Pringle, *Taft: a Biography*, II, Chap. XLIX; Merlo J. Pusey, *Charles Evans Hughes*, 2 vols. (New York: Macmillan, 1951), I, Chap. 37; Betty Glad, *Charles Evans Hughes and the Illusions of Innocence: a Study in American Diplomacy* (Urbana & London: University of Illinois Press, 1966), Chap. 11.   The official British case was classically expressed in the public letter of Lord Grey: *The Times* [London], 31 January 1920, p. 13.

10   Taft himself did not sign the Declaration; but his brother Henry (a law partner of George W. Wickersham: see below at n. 21) did.   For Taft's explicit endorsement, see his "Foreword," 23 July 1920: Marburg & Flack, *Taft Papers*.   The best (though bitter) study of the Declaration remains: Samuel Colcord, *The Great Deception: Bringing into the Light the Real Meaning and Mandate of the Harding Vote as to Peace* (New York: Boni & Liveright, 1921), esp. Chap. 9.

11   E. M. Hood (Associated Press) to Arthur Sweetser, 27 July 1920: Arthur Sweetser Papers, Library of Congress.

12   Calvin DeArmond Davis, *The United States and the First Hague Peace Conference* (Ithaca: Cornell University Press, 1962); *idem*, *The United States and the Second Hague Peace Conference: American Diplomacy and International Organization, 1899-1914* (Durham: Duke University Press, 1976).

13   The major biography remains that by his young confidant, who would later go far; see Philip C. Jessup, *Elihu Root*, 2 vols. (New York: Dodd, Mead, 1938).   For 1920, see George Harry Curtis, "The Wilson Administration, Elihu Root and the Founding of the World Court, 1918-1921." Ph.D. diss., Georgetown University, 1972.

14 Michael Dunne, "Isolationism of a Kind: Two Generations of World Court Historiography in the United States," *Journal of American Studies* 21 (December 1987), pp. 327-51.

15 The classic account, misleading yet still frequently cited, is Denna Frank Fleming, *The United States and the World Court* (Garden City, NY.: Doubleday, Doran, 1945).

16 Manley O. Hudson, *The Permanent Court of International Justice, 1920-1942: a Treatise* (New York: Macmillan, 1943), p. 149. This study (by a judge of the PCIJ: see below at n. 25) is the most comprehensive in English.

17 For an elaboration of the argument in Section 5, see Michael Dunne, *The United States and the World Court, 1920-1935* (New York: St. Martin's, 1989), esp. Chaps. 2 & 3, where League, PCIJ, governmental and private sources are fully cited.

18 Root agreed with Taft and Hughes on requiring an American right to withdraw from the League: W. H. Hays (Chairman of the Republican National Committee) to Root, 24 March 1919 and Root to Hays, 29 March 1919: Elihu Root Papers, Library of Congress.

19 Clifford R. Lovin, "Herbert Hover, Internationalist, 1919-1923," *Prologue* 20 (Winter 1988), pp. 249-67.

20 Harding to Root, 6 September 1921: Warren Gamaliel Harding Papers, Ohio Historical Society, Columbus, Ohio.

21 The interchanges were later collected and published in a broadsheet by the Woodrow Wilson Democracy of New York, of which Ham Holt was president: copy in Manley Ottmer Hudson Papers, Harvard Law School Library. The Holt Papers are in the Mills Memorial Library, Rollins College, Winter Park, Florida.

22 Hughes to Edwin F. Gay, 1 August 1922: Charles Evans Hughes Papers, Library of Congress.

23 "The Chief Justice Abroad," *American Bar Association Journal* 8 (August 1922), pp. 455-56. Two valuable studies are Donald S. Birn, *The League of Nations Union, 1918-1945* (Oxford: Clarendon Press, 1981) and George W. Egerton, *Great Britain and the Creation of the League of Nations: Strategy, Politics, and International Organization, 1914-1919* (Chapel Hill: University of North Carolina Press, 1979). A major source for the following analysis are the records of the US Department of State, Record Group 59: National Archives, Washington, DC., esp. Decimal File 500. C114 for the PCIJ. These are cited below as NA. 500. C114/ plus item number (and date, where necessary).

24 NA. 500. C114/ 236-43 (July-November 1922), esp. Cecil to Taft [late October 1922] in Taft to Hughes, 16 November 1922; Taft to Balfour,

14 September 1922: *ibid.*, / 240, 236 1/2; Taft to Root, 16 November 1922: Root Papers.

25 Willis Fletcher Johnson, *George Harvey: "A Passionate Patriot"* (Boston: Houghton Mifflin, 1929), esp. p. 377.

26 Hughes to Taft, 1 August 1922: NA. 500. C114/ 236.

27 Hughes to Harding, 6 October 1922; Lodge to Hughes, 1 November 1922: Hughes Papers; *New York Times*, 31 October 1922, pp. 1, 4.

28 Hughes to Moore, 16 March 1923; Moore to Hughes, 4 April 1923: NA. 500. C114/ 247a.

29 Representative—and unfounded—complaints include Glad, *Hughes and the Illusions of Innocence*, Chap. 12 and Pusey, *Charles Evans Hughes*, Chap. 57.

30 Hughes to Harding, 17 February 1923: NA. 500. C114/ 225a. The text printed here is taken from US Department of State, *Foreign Relations of the United States*, 1923, I, pp. 10-17, esp. p. 17.

31 Hughes to Harding, 12 February 1923: Harding Papers.

32 The PCIJ's jurisdiction was, of course, a complex question. Two studies may be cited: J. P. Fockema Andreae, *An Important Chapter from the History of Legal Interpretation: the Jurisdiction of the First Permanent Court of International Justice, 1922-1940* (Leiden: A. W. Sitjhoff, 1948) and Michla Pomerance, *The Advisory Function of the International Court in the League and U.N. Eras* (Baltimore & London: Johns Hopkins University Press, 1973). For further references, see Dunne, *United States and the World Court*, esp., pp. 275-76, 282.

33 Thomas Willing Balch, *A World Court in the Light of the United States Supreme Court* (Philadelphia: Allen, Lane & Scott, 1918); James Brown Scott, *The United States of America: a Study in International Organization* (New York: Oxford University Press, 1920); and Charles B. Warren, "The Supreme Court and the World Court: 1832 and 1932," *International Conciliation* 289 (April 1933), pp. 175-90.

34 Moore to Hughes, 27 September 1922: NA. 500. C114/ 269. Taft regarded Borchard as a "real authority on international law" and an unsound "radical" on the US Constitution: Taft to Root, 21 December 1922: Root Papers. The Edwin Montefiore Borchard Papers are in the Sterling Memorial Library, Yale.

35 A general introduction is Hudson, *Permanent Court*, Chap. 20; and relevant to our concerns is the special study by John P. Campbell, Jr., "Taft, Roosevelt, and the Arbitration Treaties of 1911," *Journal of American History* 53 (September 1966), pp. 279-98.

36   Harding to Walter Wellman, 5 March 1923: Harding Papers.

37   See the hostile comments in Hearst's *New York American*, 21 April 1923: ed. "Lord Cecil Seeks to Lure U.S. into Entanglement;" Lodge to Root, 27 April 1923: Root Papers.   There is much material in the Cecil Papers, Add. Mss. 51095: British Museum, London.

38   *Address of the President of the United States on the I. C. J. at St. Louis, Thursday Evening, June 21, 1923* (Washington, DC.: GPO, 1923).   For the Hardingesque vocabulary, see, eg, Address to the Indianapolis Delegation, Marion, Ohio: 28 August 1920: Harding Papers.

39   Hudson to Cecil, 25 June 1923; Cecil to Hudson, 27 June 1923: Cecil Papers.

40   Raymond B. Fosdick, *Secretary Hughes and the League of Nations* (New York: privately published, 1924).

41   Moore to Francis Colt de Wolf, 23 December 1930: NA. 500. C114 [Advisory Opinions Special File] / 90; Moore to Hiram Johnson, 11 January 1936: Johnson Papers.

42   The contemporary literature is enormous; but representative of a disillusioned proponent is *New York Herald-Tribune*, 10 September 1931, p. 20: ed. "The Trouble with the World Court." The best, though not neutral, monograph remains Franz Vali, *Die deutsch-österreichische Zollunion vor dem Ständigen Internationalen Gerichtshof* (Vienna: Manz, 1932). The official record of the decision is Permanent Court of International Justice, Series A/B, Fascicule no. 41, *Customs Regime between Germany and Austria (Protocol of March 19th, 1931)*, 37-103.

43   There were now *three* Protocols; the original (1920) Protocol of Signature; and two Protocols deriving from the League-Signatory States' Committees and Conferences of 1929: the Protocol for the Accession of the United States of America and the Protocol for the Revision of the Statute.   These are conveniently printed (with other documents) as appendices in Alexander P. Fachiri, *The Permanent Court of International Justice: its Constitution, Procedure and Work*, 2nd ed. (London: Oxford University Press, 1932).   This is the best concise, contemporary, English-language study of the Court.

44   [Massachusetts] *Springfield Republican*, 30 January 1935, p. 10: ed. "Defeat of the World Court." The *Springfield Republican* (a favourite source for Fleming and Bailey: see ns. 8, 15 above) was highly regarded: John J. Scanlon, *The Passing of the Springfield Republican* (Amherst, Mass.: Amherst College, 1950).

45   Hudson to Hughes, 30 May 1928; Taft to Hughes, 22 June 1928: Hughes Papers; Arthur Sweetser to Huntington Gilchrist, 3 May 1928: Huntington Gilchrist Papers, Library of Congress.   This episode,

neglected in many biographies of Hughes, is narrated in Pusey, *Charles Evans Hughes*, Chap. 62. It may be noted that Moore, Hughes and their successor, Frank Billings Kellogg (another Secretary of State), set a record for resignations.

46   [John Fischer Williams], "The United States and the Permanent Court of International Justice," *British Year Book of International Law* 10 (1929), pp. 210-12.

47   Borchard to Moore, 11 January 1929: Borchard Papers; Edward L. Reed (Charge d'affaires, Brussels) to Secretary of State, 4 March 1929: NA. 500. C114/ 767; "League Paving our Way to World Court," *Literary Digest*, 14 September 1929, p. 12.

48   Pusey, *Charles Evans Hughes*, pp. 646-47.

49   Swindler, *Court and Constitution*, II, Part I.

50   Anzilotti, known as the "great dissenter," here made the Court majority. For the basis of his reputation, see *Opere di Dionisio Anzilotti* 4 vols. in 5 (Padua: CEDAM, 1955-1963), II, Part 2, pp. 593-767.

Chief Justice William Howard Taft

Henry B. Sirgo

William Howard Taft held jobs in both the executive and judicial branches of the United States government. Although he never served as a legislator, Taft vigorously and successfully lobbied the U.S. Congress as Chief Justice of the United States to dramatically increase the Court's control over its docket, the size of the federal judiciary and the compensation of federal judges and Supreme Court justices (WHT, "Circuit Judges and District Judges" 6/16/25). Virtually single-handedly, he brought about the movement of the Court from the Old Senate Office Building to its own new building, giving great care to the selection of its architect and location. Chief Justice Charles Evans Hughes cited Taft's pre-eminent role in this matter during the building's cornerstone-laying ceremonies in 1932 (Mason 1965, 133-37). Taft's unmatched record of achievement is even more remarkable in that it largely occurred in the early 1920s, when there were congressional efforts to curb the power of the federal courts (Goldman and Jahnige 1985, 230). He was an "activist" as an executive and judge in terms of promoting judicial causes, even if he remained a conservative by temperament.

Throughout his career Taft sought to advance the interests of lawyers as a way to protect western civilization, which he viewed as dependent on business for its sustenance. He wanted to enhance both the well-being of lawyers and business, and believed that the two achievements were totally compatible, given that members of the bar were, on average, the most highly compensated of all occupational groupings. As President he was able to secure substantial pay increases for members of the federal judiciary (Pusey 1952, 271). With feelings of ambivalence, because he could not nominate himself, and meticulous attention to the backgrounds and qualifications of candidates, he was able to elevate six individuals to the U.S. Supreme Court ("Chief Justice William H. Taft" 7/2/21). As of 1992, only George Washington and Franklin D. Roosevelt have exceeded that number.

His interest in the composition of the High Court continued until the end of his life, which virtually coincided with the end of his tenure on the Supreme Court of the United States. The Chief Justice wrote the following to his brother, Horace, several weeks prior to the latter's death and exactly four months prior to his own:

> My feeling with respect to the Court is that if a number of us die, Hoover would put in some rather extreme destroyers of the Constitution, but perhaps we are unduly exercised (WHT to Horace Taft 12/8/29).

In personal relationships, especially when dealing with lawyers and family members, William Howard Taft was at his best.

Except for his distinctive weight of 340 pounds, it is difficult to differentiate Taft from any of the other Taft family members. He was the son and grandson of judges; and the in-law, sibling and parent of lawyers, politicians and educators. A close-knit family, it is difficult to find in their correspondence any variance in outlooks, except for Mrs. Nellie Taft's preference for William to serve in the White House rather than on the U.S. Supreme Court. Taft twice declined appointment to the U.S. Supreme Court by President Theodore Roosevelt. The first time was because he believed that he was still needed in the Philippines, and the second time was because of Nellie's desire to see him serve as President of the United States (Mason 1965, pp. 23-27). She not only successfully communicated this desire directly to Will, but also convinced Roosevelt to urge Taft to remain in his position of Secretary of War (Ross 1964, 176).

Mrs. Taft was an uncommonly persuasive person whose command of literature was one reason William Howard Taft grew to love her. With a well-rounded intellect, she studied chemistry and German at the University of Miami (Ohio), and subsequently became a teacher (Ross 1964, 90). She was undoubtedly pleased that a major item on William Howard Taft's agenda in his capacity as Governor of the Philippines was the improvement of its educational system. Horace Dutton Taft, the brother who ran the Taft School in Connecticut, was close to his brother the public servant. They both held strong views about the importance of education for the proper functioning of democracy, whether in Cuba and the Philippines of the post-Spanish-American War period or in the United States. Unsurprisingly, William Howard Taft was immensely proud that his daughter earned the Doctor of Philosophy degree in history. For many years she served at Bryn Mawr (Ross 1964, 413). It is understandable that Taft's daughter was able to achieve so much. William Howard Taft, in his personal and governmental dealings, did not discriminate against individuals because of their sex, race, religion, party or regional origin.

As President

During his presidency, Taft was least reluctant to use the power of his office when it was to support members of the judiciary. This was in marked contrast to his behavior when asked to help the weakest members of society. For example, a committee of the Washington branch of the National Association for the Advancement of Colored People (NAACP), after that organization had conducted a lengthy and intensive investigation into lynching, presented the President with a resolution of the NAACP Executive Committee's call for federal action. Scholar Minnie Finch has written that "President Taft informed the committee that he could do nothing, since lynching was not a Federal offense but a matter to be left entirely to the individual states" (1981, 47). This rebuff took place despite the fact that blacks were a loyal component of the Republican coalition and that Taft served on another committee of the NAACP.

But Taft did vigorously intervene in state affairs when the well-being of the judiciary was at stake. Despite the urgings of Mayor Morris Goldwater of Prescott and Ben Heney, the former mayor of Tucson, he vetoed legislation admitting

Arizona into the Union because "its proposed constitution permitted the voters to recall state judges" (Peltason 1991, 148). Mayor Goldwater implored Taft to issue his declaration of statehood on February 12, 1912, President Lincoln's birthday, since Lincoln had issued the proclamation making Arizona a territory (Goldwater to WHT 1/31/12). Ben Heney was shocked that the better than three-to-one margin of approval for the constitution by the people of Arizona was being ignored by the President (WHT, Ben Heney Memorandum). Forty-two citizens of Jerome telegramed the President seeking his approval of the constitution and observing that, unlike the situation at Southern state constitutional conventions, the rights of Negroes had not been maligned. Arizona deleted the offensive clause, entered the Union and then adopted the same provision (Peltason 1991, 148-49).

Taft's lack of executive vigor in this matter is easier to understand if one considers the political issue behind his position. For example, Charles S. Wheeler of San Francisco, California, brought out these issues concerning his state's struggle with the "judicial recall threat":

> . . . socialists are using the radical element within the ranks of the Progressive Republicans to carry the judicial recall, their objective being to batter down the property guarantees of the state and Federal Constitutions (WHT, Wheeler to Wickersham 3/7/11).

William Howard Taft disdained expanded use of the ballot, whether it was the direct primary, the referendum or the judicial recall. Indeed, despite his many years of public service and subsequent lobbying activities as Chief Justice of the United States, he only ran for one office in his entire life, the presidency of the United States. And he vied for the Republican candidacy only after the insistence of President Theodore Roosevelt; yet within a few years, ideological differences led members of the Taft family to despise Roosevelt.

Henry W. Taft, the brother who was a Wall Street lawyer, was as infuriated as William Howard Taft at Theodore Roosevelt's outlandish proposal to limit the powers of state judges through his advocacy of the recall of judicial decisions. Henry W. Taft argued that such limitations would doubtless spread to the federal judiciary and lead to the demise of property and of democracy. He felt that neither anarchy, socialism nor communism would claim the United States; but rather a return to despotism (Henry W. Taft to WHT 5/24/10). Nor did Henry W. Taft relish having a brother as president, especially when he had to decline legal work because of editorial allegations of conflict of interest (Henry W. Taft to WHT 5/8/12).

William Howard Taft's restrictive view of presidential power (except in promoting judicial interests) and expansionist views of the Chief Justiceship (except in assisting the public welfare) grew out of his conservative upbringing. His entire career and personal philosophy were reproachful of the term "class"; nonetheless, he increasingly mounted a vigorous defense of the upper class. Consequently, it is little wonder that he became an Anglophile, being especially in awe of England's "wonderful legal procedure" (WHT to Chitty 5/9/23). Virtually all of the demands of his day for infringement on liberty of contract and other prerogatives of capitalists were calls for increased executive action. Thus, from his pro-business viewpoint, the paramount task of the judiciary was to prevent the implementation of "unwise" legislation and foolish regulations in this area.

Yet Taft was never as hostile toward change as some conservatives. As late as the 1908 presidential contest, he was far more scrupulous than President Roosevelt deemed wise in turning away large campaign contributions from big business executives, such as those of the Standard Oil Company (Sheldon to TR 9/22/08). Taft wanted to abide by the spirit as well as the letter of the 1907 Tillman Act, which outlawed political contributions by corporations (Wayne 1984, 36). Indeed, it was Taft's administration rather than Roosevelt's which won anti-trust suits against the American Tobacco Company and the Standard Oil Company ("Taft's Greatest Achievement" 4/3/12). In 1909, he even lent support to the call for an income tax amendment.

Taft also smashed precedents when he elevated Democrat Edward Douglass White to Chief Justice in 1910. White hailed from the outskirts of Thibodaux, Louisiana, and had served as a Confederate soldier at Antietam in the same battle in which Oliver Wendell Holmes fought as a Yankee. He was considered a progressive conservative. White was to return Taft's favor of his nomination by delaying his own retirement from the High Court and postponing serious surgery until Democrat Woodrow Wilson was out of the White House. White died in 1921, several days after his surgery (Karger 7/6/21). Unable to complete his college education at Georgetown University because of the outbreak of the Civil War, White had served the interests of the nation's most prominent Yale man exceedingly well (Highsaw 1981, 18-19).

Upon closer inspection of his background, it is not surprising that Taft could get along with a Catholic Democratic southerner. He himself had been denounced for his Unitarian faith and his opposition to prohibition on the grounds that laws should not be passed which cannot be enforced (Ross 1964, 201). Much of the impetus behind that movement did not concern questions of health but was instead based on disdain for immigrants who used alcohol and were culturally different from "mainstream Americans". Nonetheless, Chief Justice Taft adroitly used Prohibition to argue successfully for the expansion of the federal judiciary and the administrative reorganization of the federal judiciary.

His ability to adapt while maintaining adherence to conservative principles was also a hallmark of his relations with blacks. Taft's flexibility allowed him to assist the black community when doing so did not violate his views on federalism and executive restraint. When the fledgling NAACP requested that he withdraw a federal judicial nomination, he honored the organization's wish (White 1948, 105). President Taft also insisted that a unit of the Republican National Committee make special overtures to the black community during his unsuccessful presidential bid (Wilensky 1965, 53).

It is little wonder that Taft was so inept in seeking public office when Theodore Roosevelt shifted from being mentor to rival in the 1912 presidential campaign. Despite Taft's long public service, he had only contested two elections prior to 1912. Theodore Roosevelt knew how to use symbolism to appeal to the public and flourished in the presidential primaries of 1912; indeed, teddy bears are still going strong. Happily for Taft, he at least lived to see the ebbing of presidential primaries and died years before they returned in significant numbers. Although Roosevelt won nine primaries to Taft's one, he still lost the Republican nomination due to the party regulars' support of President Taft, particularly in the South (Wayne 1984, 11). President Taft ended up trailing Governor Wilson and Colonel Roosevelt in the general election. Yet Taft's political loss meant he could return to New Haven, the beloved home of his undergraduate alma mater.

As Professor

Law and education were traditionally the two dominant professions in the Taft family. Hence, it was perfectly natural that this former dean of the University of Cincinnati Law School would take simultaneous positions as a faculty member at both Yale College and Yale Law School following his presidency. He taught, wrote, championed the movement for the League of Nations. Upon U.S. entry into World War I, he traveled the nation to improve the morale of the troops ("Taft Off" 2/7/18). For instance, he spoke to one gathering of 2,500 black soldiers in San Antonio during "The Great War" ("War May Give Opportunities" 2/7/18).

Still, during this time period he yearned to be on the U.S. Supreme Court and maintained an abiding interest in its composition. Following the death of Justice Joseph R. Lamar in 1916, the *New York Times* and *Washington Herald* editorialized for Taft's appointment to the Court (Paper 1983, 212). Professor Taft could not anticipate his triumphant rival's being so generous, yet was still stunned when President Woodrow Wilson announced the nomination of Louis Brandeis for the position of Associate Justice on the Supreme Court of the United States on January 28, 1916 (Paper 1983, 212). Taft, along with other former presidents of the American Bar Association, issued the following statement:

To the Senate Committee on the Judiciary:

> The undersigned feel under the painful duty to say to you that in their opinion, taking into view the reputation, character and professional career of Mr. Louis D. Brandeis, he is not a fit person to be a member of the Supreme Court of the United States.

Dated, February 7th, 1916.

Wm. H. Taft.
Simeon E. Baldwin.
Francis Rawle.

Dated, March 12th, '16.

Joseph H. Choate.
Elihu Root.

(U.S. Senate 1916)

Taft never relinquished his disdain for what he perceived as Brandeis' radicalism. However, the Senate Judiciary Committee confirmed Brandeis by a margin of 10-8. The vote was cast along strict party lines on May 24, 1916 (Paper 1983, 238). And then, less than a week later, the full Senate confirmed Brandeis by a vote of 47 to 22 (Paper 1983, 238).

As Chief Justice

The election of Warren G. Harding in the 1920 presidential election helped pave the way for Taft to replace the ailing White. Harding and Attorney General-designate Harry M. Daugherty were both from Taft's native state of Ohio. Moreover, Secretary of State-designate Charles Evans Hughes had been appointed to the Supreme Court in 1910 by then-President William Howard Taft, and Taft had vigorously campaigned on Hughes' behalf when he served as the Republican party's presidential standard-bearer in 1916. The one person who might have raised opposition to Taft's nomination, Colonel Theodore Roosevelt, had died. Hence, when Taft was summoned to Marion, Ohio, in late 1920 to discuss the likely vacancy on the Supreme Court, the event was almost anticlimactic ("Taft Chosen" 7/6/21).

Interestingly, what little opposition there was to Harding's nomination of Taft to the position of Chief Justice of the

Supreme Court of the United States came predominantly from progressive Republicans ("Those Four" 7/3/21). Senators William Borah of Idaho, Hiram Johnson of California and Robert LaFollette of Wisconsin denounced him as too political and too judicially inexperienced to serve as Chief Justice of the Supreme Court. They were joined in the short-lived and futile effort by the populist Democratic Senator of Georgia, Tom Watson.

Although he had strongly desired a berth on the Court for many years, Taft's confirmation was swift and virtually painless. Within an hour and a half after the announcement of his nomination by President Harding, he was confirmed by the Senate. The nomination was especially popular with Southerners, who recalled that he had been responsible for the elevation of a Georgian and a Tennessean to the Court, as well as the elevation of Edward Douglass White of Louisiana from Associate to Chief Justice. The overwhelming majority of the press, especially in the South, applauded the nomination. But *The Nation* opposed it on the grounds that he lacked adequate courtroom experience, was prejudiced against immigrants and had not once "effectively protested during the war against the repeated violations of the Constitution by the Wilson Administration and numberless Federal officials" (7/16/21). The expression of such views and his earlier opposition to the Brandeis nomination underscore the ideological character of Supreme Court politics.

Once on the High Court, he would prove to be more discerning in his approach to "the law," including the area of civil liberties. For example, although he refused to interpret the Fourth Amendment as including telephone wire taps in the 5-4 decision of *Olmstead* v. *United States*, 277 U.S. 454 (1928), Taft joined the majority in 1925, when the Court for the first time held that a provision of the Bill of Rights was binding on state governments in *Gitlow* v. *New York* 268 U.S. 652 (1925). Writing for the seven-member majority, Justice Sanford held in this paradoxical case that speech which might tend to hurt a government at some time in the future could be curbed by a legislature, a notion which was discarded without comment in the 1930s. Holmes, in a dissent joined by Brandeis, maintained that the "Clear and Present Danger" doctrine established in *Schenck* v. *United States*, 249 U.S. 47 (1919), should have been observed. Nonetheless, Justice Sanford, with Taft's support, indirectly managed to establish that the freedoms of speech and of the press are applicable to the states under the due process clause of the Fourteenth Amendment (Feeley and Krislov 1990, 477). The principle has endured to the present day.

On the other hand, the due process clause of the Fourteenth Amendment became a favorite tool used by the Court to derail state legislation favorable to workers. The notion of liberty of contract was born in the late nineteenth century and reached its zenith during the years of the Taft Court (Berger 1977, 269-70). State efforts to regulate matters such as wages were deemed by the High Court to constitute an infringement upon the ability of an employer and a worker to contract with one another. For example, when it came to grappling with "substantive" due process' haphazard notion of "the distinction between business with and without a 'public interest,' " (Feeley and Krislow 1990, 333) no one reasoned more laboriously than Chief Justice Taft (Van DeVanter to WHT 5/23). In the case of *Chas. Wolff Packing Company* v. *Court of Industrial Relations of the State of Kansas*, 262 U.S. 522 (1923), Taft developed a three-part classification to determine whether a business were "clothed with a public interest" (262 U.S. 522). Assuming that one or more of these conditions existed, he elaborated on the conditions and circumstances that might justify legislative regulation of such businesses.

In a letter to his son Robert during the same term of the Court, he also indicated the arduousness of developing opinions dealing with interstate commerce and mused that "we shall have had the biggest term in the history of the Court, though I may be mistaken about this" (WHT to Robert Taft 6/10/23). Indeed, Taft himself had dealt with some of these issues in his first term on the Court. For instance, in *Bailey, Collector of Internal Revenue,* v. *Drexel Furniture Co.* 259 U.S. 20 (1921), writing for the majority with only Justice Clarke dissenting, the Chief Justice stated that "to regulate the hours of labor of children in factories and mines within the states was a purely state authority" and could not be subject to congressional regulation, even if it was under the pretext of taxation, when it merely involved the production and transport of ordinary goods in interstate commerce (259 U.S. 39). Jurisdiction in this and a great number of other important areas was reserved to the states by the Tenth Amendment (259 U.S. 38).

On the latter point, the Chief Justice maintained consistency when his dissenting opinion supported the constitutionality of a minimum-wage law for women in *Adkins* v. *Children's Hospital*, 261 U.S. 525 (1923). Writing for himself and Justice Sanford, he saw no distinction between the legitimacy of a state (or in this instance a District of Columbia) agency's regulation of hours, a practice whose constitutionality had previously been established by the Court, and the regulation of wages (261 U.S. 564). Writing for the majority, Justice Sutherland maintained that freedom of contract can be legislatively abridged "only by the existence of exceptional circumstances." He argued that "hours-of-service" laws were clearly related to health, a matter which came under the police power of the District of Columbia, in this instance, and of the states (261 U.S. 537). Wages were another matter to be settled by negotiations between workers and employers. The Fourteenth Amendment was a major source of interest and power for the Taft Court, as it would be for its successors (Berger 1977, 269-89).

The history of the Fourteenth Amendment indicates that its purpose was to help the newly freed blacks following the Civil War. Yet Taft failed to see it as requiring the Mississippi legislature to outlaw racial segregation in public schools (Pritchett 1984, 259). He held such a view despite the fact that he was probably one of the least biased public figures of his time. But he did see the Fourteenth Amendment as preventing the Oklahoma legislature from exempting farmers' cooperatives from taxes on cotton-ginning cooperatives. His point that the equal protection clause extends to privileges as well as to penalties is well-taken. Justice Holmes was joined in dissent by Brandeis and Stone (WHT 1929, "Cotton Gin Case"). Holmes observed that all but two states had passed legislation encouraging the formation of farmers' cooperatives. Additionally, the U.S. Congress had passed such legislation. For such a lovable and pleasant individual, William Howard Taft notably lacked empathy for individuals with backgrounds different from his own.

A native of Cincinnati, he also had little use for southwestern farmers who supported populist measures and candidates such as his vanquished 1908 Democratic rival, William Jennings Bryan. Taft was more at home in the Northeast during a time when regional voting patterns reached their apogee in United States politics, most notably with the Northeast displaying political conflict with the Western states. He felt organizations such as the American Federation of Labor should not have undue influence, and if workers had gumption they would be business owners. Moreover, he believed that once blacks acquired the right to vote, they should restrain from complaining (Shull 1989, 45).

Five NAACP cases came before the High Court during Taft's tenure as Chief Justice (Goings 1990, 14-15). Two of these had markedly different outcomes, but both were unanimous decisions. Writing for a unanimous Court in *Nixon* v. *Herndon Et Al,* 273 U.S. 536 (1927), Justice Holmes struck down a Texas statute which prohibited blacks from participating in Democratic primaries on the basis of the equal protection clause of the Fourteenth Amendment. He saw no need to even consider the implications of the Fifteenth Amendment since this statute was so clearly in violation of the Fourteenth Amendment (273 U.S. 541). "States may do a good deal of classifying that it is difficult to believe rational, but there are limits; and it is too clear for extended argument that color cannot be made the basis of statutory classification affecting the right set up in this case." Unanimous opinions were a hallmark of the Taft Court, and this was especially true in the NAACP cases. The Chief Justice was highly receptive to the advice of his brethren when writing majority opinions. In *Corrigan* v. *Buckley,* 271 U.S. 323 (1926), the validity of racially restrictive residential covenants drawn up by private parties was upheld. But such a scheme based on an ordinance in New Orleans was found to be unconstitutional in 1927, as had been held in a case involving a similar Louisville ordinance during the tenure of his predecessor, Chief Justice White. Holmes, writing for a divided Court in *Moore* v. *Dempsey*, 261 U.S. 86 (1923), found "due process of law" a fiction in the five-minute deliberations of all-white juries which had convicted black Arkansas tenant farmers of murder. Justice McReynolds, joined by Sutherland in dissent, argued that all of the requirements of due process, such as the formal filing of charges, had been fulfilled. McReynolds' was to be the only dissenting opinion written in one of the NAACP cases during the years of the Taft Court.

Olmstead v. *United States*, 277 U.S. 454 (1928) is the most fractious decision of the Taft Court, since it presented new questions born of technological progress. Did the use of an incriminating telephone conversation, gathered by means of a government wiretap as evidence in a criminal trial, violate the Fifth Amendment's protection against self-incrimination? Did the tapping of telephone wires constitute a search within the meaning of Fourth Amendment, and so require a warrant to be lawful? The Chief Justice, writing for the majority, answered no to both propositions. The petitioners had been convicted of violating the National Prohibition Act by running a massive bootlegging operation between the Seattle area of Washington state and British Columbia (277 U.S. 455). Taft concluded that since the conversations were voluntary, the Fifth Amendment was not involved. For Fourth Amendment protection to be invoked for an individual, there had to be "an official search and seizure of his papers or his tangible material effects, or an actual physical invasion of his house 'or curtilage' for the purpose of making a seizure" (277 U.S. 466). Holmes, Brandeis, Butler and Stone dissented. Such a diversity of opinion was unusual for the consensually-oriented Taft Court. The Chief Justice was unable to expand his view of the Fourth Amendment to afford constitutional protection to telephone conversations.

Nevertheless, Taft demonstrated adaptability during his tenure as Chief Justice. After Prohibition was embedded in the U.S. Constitution, he used it to justify expansion of the federal judiciary and the Department of Justice. Even so, he did fail to have enforcement jurisdiction shifted from the Department of the Treasury to the Department of Justice. Eliot Ness was not to lose his chance for fame. Taft maintained that the lesser capabilities of Treasury Department officials was a major reason for Prohibition's shortcomings. He was also distressed by the lack of enforcement enthusiasm displayed by state officials in such places as Alabama. Prohibition may have been a foolish law, but it was "the law" and had to be enforced for the sake of the constitutional system. In order to promote the well-being of the judiciary in the social order, Taft could not ignore the Congress.

Indeed, Taft was not only a flexible Chief Justice, but an effective lobbyist as well. He served as Chief Justice during most of the years of the greatest degree of Court-Congressional conflict in United States history (Katzman 1989, 10). He strongly influenced the development of the Judiciary Act of 1922, which provides the basis for the Judicial Conference, "the policymaking arm of the courts." This was accomplished even though the U.S. Supreme Court, through the use of judicial review, found numerous Acts of Congress unconstitutional from 1918 through 1936 (Katzman 1989, 7). Undermining the product of the main function of another institution while securing its cooperation in securing one's own institution's priorities was no mean feat. The Chief Justice demonstrated a grasp of the legislative process that could not have been much more impressive had he himself been a former member of the U.S. Congress (Mason 1965, 121-37).

The Chief Justice testified frequently before the House and Senate Judiciary Committees. Each time he did so, he had always previously achieved a virtual consensus among his colleagues on the High Court. The high degree of unanimity characteristic of Taft Court decisions was highly conducive to success in the legislative arena. Taft's years of regular attendance at the annual meetings of the American Bar Association and active participation in that organization throughout his adult life also enabled him to strongly influence the Congress in reorganizing the federal judiciary.

Conclusions

In sum, William Howard Taft was by temperament a conservative. Regardless of the position he occupied, he was flexible enough in his reasoning to uphold and promote the judiciary as the centerpiece of the United States government. For example, he championed the judiciary as chief executive although he believed in a conservative approach to presidential power, and as chief justice he was a strict constructionist in general, he became the Court's greatest lobbyist before Congress. In fact, the construction of the Supreme Court building itself was the ultimate legacy of the activity of this conservative jurist and remains a monument to his devotion to the law.

References

Berger, Raoul. *Government by Judiciary: The Transformation of the Fourteenth Amendment*. Cambridge, Massachusetts: Harvard University Press, 1977.

Burton, David H. *The Learned Presidency: Theodore Roosevelt, William Howard Taft, Woodrow Wilson*. Rutherford: Fairleigh Dickinson University Press, 1988.

Caplan, Lincoln. *The Tenth Justice: The Solicitor General and the Rule of Law*. New York: Alfred A. Knopf, 1987.

"The Chief Justice—A Mistaken Appointment." *The Nation*. July 16, 1921.

"Chief Justice William H. Taft." *San Francisco Journal*. July 2, 1921.

Cunliffe-Owen, Frederick. "Appointment of Taft Pleases Foreign Powers." *Globe & Commerce Advertiser*. July 25, 1921.

Feeley, Malcolm M. and Samuel Krislov. *Constitutional Law*. Glenview, Illinois: Scott, Foresman and Company, 1990.

Finch, Minnie. *The NAACP: Its Fight for Justice*. Metuchen, NJ: The Scarecrow Press, Inc., 1981.

Goings, Kenneth W. *The NAACP Comes of Age: The Defeat of Judge John J. Parker* Bloomington: Indiana University Press, 1990.

Goldman, Sheldon and Thomas P. Jahnige. *The Federal Courts as a Political System*. Third Edition. New York: Harper & Row, 1985.

Hicks, Frederick C. *William Howard Taft: Yale Professor of Law & New Haven Citizen*. New Haven: Yale University Press, 1945.

Hughes, Langston. *Fight for Freedom: The Story of the NAACP*. New York: W. W. Norton & Company, 1962.

Katzman, Robert A. 1989. "Judicial-Congressional Relations: A Primer" presented at a Bicentennial Research Conference on "Understanding Congress," sponsored by the Congressional Research Service, Washington, D.C.

Paper, Lewis J. *Brandeis*. Secaucus, New Jersey: Citadel Press, 1983.

Pritchett, C. Herman. *Constitutional Civil Liberties*. Englewood Cliffs, New Jersey: Prentice-Hall, 1984.

Pusey, Merlo J. *Charles Evans Hughes*. New York: Macmillan Company, 1952.

Ross, Ishbel. *An American Family: The Tafts—1678 to 1964*. Cleveland, Ohio: World Publishing Company, 1964.

Shull, Steven A. *The President and Civil Rights Policy*. New York: Greenwood Press, 1989.

"Taft's Greatest Achievement." *The Oregonian*. April 3, 1912.

Theodore Roosevelt Papers (TR). Series 1: Reel 85. Library of Congress. Letter from George R. Sheldon to the President. September 22, 1908.

"Taft Chosen Long Ago." *Boston Evening Transcript*. July 6, 1921.

Taft, William H. *The President and His Powers*. New York: Columbia University Press, 1916.

William Howard Taft Papers (WHT). Reel 254. Library of Congress. Letter from William H. Taft to Robert A. Taft. June 10, 1923.

William Howard Taft Papers. Series 6: Case Files. Reel 384. Library of Congress. Telegram from Citizens of Jerome to William Howard Taft. March 3-4, 1911.

William Howard Taft Papers. Series 6: Case Files. Reel 384. Library of Congress. Letter from Morris Goldwater to William Howard Taft. January 31, 1912.

William Howard Taft Papers. Series 6: Case Files. Reel 384 Letter from Charles S. Wheeler to George W. Wickersham. March 7, 1911.

William Howard Taft Papers. Series 6: White House Files. Reel 415. Memorandum concerning letter of Ben Heney.

William Howard Taft Papers. Series 7: Case Files. Reel 453. Library of Congress. Letter from Henry W. Taft to William Howard Taft. May 24, 1910.

William Howard Taft Papers. Series 7: Case Files. Reel 453. Library of Congress. Letter from Henry W. Taft to William Howard Taft. May 8, 1912.

William Howard Taft Papers. Series 15: 1924-1930. Reel 618. Library of Congress. "Letter from the Chief Justice to the Circuit Judges and the District Judges of the United States." June 16, 1925.

William Howard Taft Papers. President's Personal File: Box 8. Reel 454. Letter from William Howard Taft to Mabel T. Boardman. March 20, 1912.

William Howard Taft Papers. Series 7: Case Files. Reel 618. (1929) "Cotton Gin Case."

U.S., Senate, Committee on the Judiciary. *Hearing on the Nomination of Louis D. Brandeis.* 64th Congress, 1st session, 1916.

Vose, Clement E. "NAACP Strategy in the Covenant Cases." *Western Reserve Law Review* Winter 1955: 101-45.

Wayne, Stephen. *Road to the White House: The Politics of Presidential Elections.* Second Edition. New York: St. Martin's Press, 1984.

White, Walter. *A Man Called White: The Autobiography of Walter White.* New York: The Viking Press, 1948.

Wilensky, Norman M. *Conservatives in the Progressive Era.* Gainesville: University of Florida Press, 1965.

"Women Felicitate Taft." *New York Times.* July 12, 1921.

Justice William O. Douglas and the Wilderness Mind

James C. Duram

Many justices have been deeply involved in extramural activities while serving on the U.S. Supreme Court. None, however, have been as publicly conspicuous with their activities as the late Justice William Orville Douglas (1898-1980). During his thirty six year stay on the Court, Douglas, as both he and numerous Court watchers noted, found the supreme tribunal simply too confining to satisfy his widely ranging intellectual, political, and social interests.[1] One of the most important of these interests, certainly the one closest to his heart, was his love of the outdoors, particularly his affection for the rugged wilderness areas of this country. Douglas' attachment here was the result of his conviction that his wilderness experiences played a crucial role in shaping his values and his outlook towards life. Such interest, given Douglas' activist personality, assured that his advocacy of a wilderness-conservation ethic as an antidote to what he perceived as impending ecological disaster would emerge as one of the major themes in his writing. It underscored the continuing close connection between his experiences, beliefs and writing.

Many scholars insist that William O. Douglas' writings on wilderness values rank along with those on civil liberties as expressions of his fundamental beliefs.[2] His extensive writings on nature, ecology, and conservation contain much evidence that substantiates this view. His proposal that judicial protections be extended to wilderness areas as they had been to members of minorities and his outspoken advocacy of conservation revealed the intensity of his feelings on this subject.

Moreover, his writing served him well as an effective means of publicizing his beliefs.

Nature appears in Douglas' writings in all of its multidimensional complexity. He wrote with clarity about its roles as teacher, friend, enemy, emotional catharizing agent, mystery, and above all, something that could help man regain perspective on his place in the earth's environment. Though he fondly described its beauty, individuality and diversity, he also saw its brutal, demanding side. His own early experiences convinced him that nature challenged men to rise above their limitations and taught them how to live with their fears.[3]

Thus, whether he took his reader through a mountain canyon or on a visit to a favorite trout stream by means of his formidable descriptive powers, Douglas had a message. The wilderness must be preserved! The blend of this advocacy with his personal adventures in the outdoors gave Douglas an appealing way to get his message across. It lent authenticity to his discussions of the problems confronting those who sought to preserve our wilderness heritage.[4]

Douglas' subsequent exposure to the writings of John Muir and Aldo Leopold and his extensive citation of them in his writings reveal that their ideas reinforced what he had learned by experience. They strengthened his desire to immerse himself in the wonders of nature. Like them, he came to see man's proper place in the universe as within instead of above the natural order of things.[5]

His reputation as an antibusiness activist came as much from his advocacy of the wilderness ethic as from his behavior on the Securities Exchange Commission and the Supreme Court. Douglas was not a doctrinaire anticapitalist. He possessed a different set of values, one that rejected the hypocritical American attitude toward wilderness that praised its virtues while destroying it in the name of progress.

As the following excerpt from his last volume, *The Court Years* indicates, Douglas spared no one who threatened his conservationist position.

LBJ gave us "consensus conservation," which was designed to gain support from everyone and please all people. This was not the "conservation" of Theodore Roosevelt or FDR. Under them the Establishment did not get what it wanted. Under LBJ the Army Corps of Engineers and its dams never waxed stronger. Under LBJ the billboard industry scrapped most of our highway beautification program. Under LBJ water pollution was condemned, but industry had pretty much its own way when it came to cleaning up our lakes and rivers. "Consensus conservation" was the formula whereby LBJ gave the heritage of America away to the fat cats and the official vandals who have despoiled us. . . . what he meant by this he explained when he dedicated the Percy Priest Dam in Tennessee. That dam made a 420 mile lake where nearly half a million people could boat, camp, hike and swim. The dam destroyed the river, where people could also boat, camp, hike, and swim. . . . The Corps of Engineers, the Bureau of Reclamation, and TVA destroy river after river. The dams will in time silt in and be useless, the rivers will be gone forever, but the money spent in building the needless structures looks like a means to "progress" and people cheer.[6]

Douglas felt that there was too much at stake to permit the politics of consensus to be the chief determinant of our conservation policies. It permitted too much compromise of the preservationist ethic.

Of Men and Mountains: The Seminal Work

Douglas' love affair with nature proved to be a lasting one. It began in the Pacific Northwest in a time of personal crisis for him. His 1950 autobiography, *Of Men and Mountains*, presents the best explanation of the causes of his deep attachment to the outdoors.[7] It is a proper starting point for those seeking understanding of the essential assumptions in this aspect of his writings and the literary techniques that he developed to illustrate them. Most of those who reviewed *Of Men and Mountains* agreed that it is a clearly written volume marked by a personal, anecdotal, reflective style. It is a work that combines adventure with an autobiographical statement. Above all, it is the author's own explanation of the crucial relationship between his wilderness experience and the shaping of his personality.

Douglas was certainly not the first or most famous of a large number of Americans whose attitude toward life was profoundly influenced by close contact with nature. Few, however, were more profoundly influenced by it than he.

Writing in the foreword of *Of Men and Mountains* in reference to the continuing attraction of the rugged mountain wilderness areas of the Pacific Northwest, he asserted: "Here man can find deep solitude, and under conditions of grandeur that are startling he can come to know both himself and God" (p. ix). The work is thus philosophical in the sense that it illustrates the discoveries Douglas made about the meaning of life. He summarized the most significant lesson gained from his mountain experiences as follows: "I learned early that the richness of life is found in adventure. . . . But man is not ready for adventure unless he is rid of fear. For fear confines him and limits his scope" (p. x). His boyhood experiences, when he learned to overcome this fear had a lasting effect on his adult life.

The first two chapters of the work described the events of his early childhood that took place after his arrival in Yakima: his father's death, his family's poverty, his attack of polio, and his resentment about being teased about his withered legs. Interspersed in his narration are hints of his early attraction to the mountains including a moving description of the solace he received from viewing the dominating presence of Mount Adams at his father's funeral. The initial two chapters set the scene for the extended discussion of his increasing involvement with the mountain wilderness that followed.

Chapters 3 to 7 contain a moving description of how Douglas rebuilt the shriveled muscles in his legs and his own self-confidence by taking increasingly longer and higher hikes into the foothills and mountains. The chapters constitute a well-balanced description of how the recovery of strength in his legs increased his sense of self-reliance and his awareness of the wonders of the mountain wilderness where he walked. As he said when recounting the first time he walked twenty-five miles with a thirty-pound pack in one day: "I had conquered my doubts. So far as my legs were concerned, I knew I was free to roam these mountains at will" (p. 84). Triumph over his disability opened the way for other conquests. Descriptions of the way that these shaped his attitude toward life constitute the rest of the book.

Douglas also insisted that the brutal side of nature could have a therapeutic effect. In the chapter "Snow Hole" he related how he and some friends were caught in a blizzard and forced to survive by burrowing down into the snow beneath the snug of a fallen tree. While there, he came to the realization that: "When man holes up in snow, he returns to earth in a subtle way. . . . Man returns to the womb of the earth to live. . . . He escapes the reality of the world and lowers the tempo of his own life" (p. 290). Such experiences not only taught him self-reliance but gave him a deepened sense of introspection. (Little wonder that a number of professional politicians in the Democratic party argued against the selection of Douglas as FDR's running mate in 1944 on the grounds that he acted too much like a boy scout.)[8]

The Justice used the final chapter of the work to discuss the implications of his philosophy for what he perceived as the troubled American society of the 1950s. Beginning with the question of what one could gain from conquering high mountain peaks, he brushed aside the argument that it was merely a form of exercise. It was rather, he insisted, a spiritual experience, one where the individual tested the limits of his endurance. Citing Arnold Toynbee's argument that the growth of society was the result of successful response to challenge, he argued that the solutions to the challenges confronting Americans would require men who had lost the fear of living dangerously. Such were the kinds of men created by the challenges of the mountain wilderness. Douglas was convinced that he was one of them.

Though Douglas was to write numerous articles and several more books in defense of wilderness values, none of these approached *Of Men and Mountains* in terms of literary quality. It is a beautifully integrated volume that tells his story well and leaves the reader with a sense of understanding about the importance of wilderness values in the Justice's personality development. Though his subsequent works stated his case for wilderness preservation with the same mixture of descriptive material and philosophic arguments employed in *Of Men and Mountains*, Douglas' increasing concern about conservation and ecology brought a more strident, pleading quality to his later works. They also suffered from the haste with which they were written.[9]

The Sharpening Focus

The impact of Douglas' attachment to nature on his personality became increasingly evident is his numerous articles on the outdoors in the 1950s.[10] In these, he began to bring his beliefs about the wilderness-preservation ethic into sharper focus. As his awareness of the dangers of technologically related pollution grew, so did the militancy of his position. As he put it: "We deal with values that no dollars can measure.[11]

His increasing concern did not mean, however, that Douglas had abandoned his considerable descriptive powers. This was evident in the two wilderness books he published in 1960 and 1961. Each was an account of his journey through a major wilderness area. Each reflected his continued successful integration of his personal experiences and his preservationist ethic.

The first, *My Wilderness: The Pacific West*, is a descriptive celebration of his experiences in such wild areas as the Brooks Range in Alaska, Pacific Coast beaches, the middle fork of the Salmon River, the Olympic Mountains, and Douglas' beloved Willowas.[12] Taking up where he left off in *Of Men and Mountains*, he developed his narrative with a combination of personal anecdotes, natural and social history, and his beliefs on conservation and preservation. His mastery of detail is apparent throughout the work. This is true whether he is describing the place of the artic squid in the fragile ecosystem of the Far North or discussing the impact of the damming of the Middle Fork of the Salmon River. The major theme of the work is clear: wilderness areas should be left as undisturbed as possible.

Already Douglas' work showed movement towards what later became his advocacy of formal legal rights for wilderness areas. He spoke with approval of the great conservationist Aldo Leopold's remark: "The right to find a pasque-flower is a right as inalienable as free speech."[13] Douglas' preoccupation with preservation is evident throughout his writings on the outdoors. It was a view that brought him sharp criticism from those who sought to maximize public access to outdoor areas. What Douglas cherished here was something far beyond the realm of material values: it was the basis of his peace of mind. He was defending the preservation of what had become an important part of himself.

Destruction of wilderness areas was something that he took personally. As he observed while viewing a high meadow in the Cascades: ". . . an emptiness in life comes with the destruction of wilderness; that a fullness of life follows when one becomes on intimate terms with woods, peaks and meadows."[14] He saw no middle ground when it came to the question of preservation of wilderness. His persistent condemnations of road-building into or near wilderness areas must be understood from this perspective.

Thus, Douglas summarized the forces threatening wilderness in *My Wilderness: the Pacific West* and in its 1961 sequel, *My Wilderness: East to Katahdin*. Using the same format as in the former, he described his jaunts through Wilderness areas east of the Mississippi in the latter.[15] Douglas failed, however, in both volumes to articulate much in the way of a positive program to assure wilderness preservation. Nevertheless, he made it clear in both that he felt the situation was at a crisis point, something Douglas defined as a situation containing elements of both danger and opportunity. He hoped they would awaken the American people to the challenges confronting them in the realm of conservation. What was needed, he concluded, was a positive comprehensive program, one that would assure the place of wilderness in American life. This thinking led him eventually to conclude that wilderness preservation would require a formal bill of rights.

Wilderness-Rights Evangelism

Douglas' most comprehensive advocacy of the Wilderness preservationist ethic came in his 1965 work, *A Wilderness Bill of Rights*.[16] It was his most comprehensive answer to the challenges facing those who sought to preserve wilderness areas. His proposed solution was a controversial one premised on a unique legal hypothesis that received enthusiastic support from wilderness preservation groups and sharp criticism from those who hoped to gain more access to the wild lands.

The challenge, Douglas insisted, was to find a way to get more Americans to see the values of hiking and packing when powerful forces were pulling them in another direction. "The road is the main culprit, and it often has the demanding voice of a majority of the people behind it" (pp. 22-23). The continuation of such an approach would soon lead to a pattern of more people with more cars overwhelming the remaining wilderness areas unless some use limitations were created. He acknowledged the difficulty of creating such limits in a democratic society. He illustrated how preservationists could easily be condemned as elitist or as opponents of growth and progress, positions distinctly un-American. Douglas argued, however, that the defenders of wilderness advocated another set of values that were also distinctly American.

He reminded his readers that the U.S. Constitution also protected minority rights. The exponents of wilderness preservation were a minority. Observing that there was no constitutional guarantee that the 36.5 million acres of wilderness lands under federal control would be preserved, Douglas called for the creation of a Wilderness Bill of Rights.[17] He noted with approval Congress's firm four point definition of what constituted "wilderness" in the Wilderness Act of 1964. Its true meaning, though, went beyond the formal definition in the Act. To him, "Wilderness is the earth before any of its wildness has been reduced or subtracted" (p. 29). It was something whose true value far exceeded the worth of the resources it contained. Like Thoreau, Douglas took his stand on romantic-humanist grounds.

Douglas then discussed what would have to be done to achieve the creation of a conservation ethic among Americans. He called for education in conservation values in the early years. He hoped that such an approach would offset the land exploitation ethic currently dominating American thought. He urged that biologists, botanists, and ornithologists be placed on land use planning agencies. He called for the development of legal techniques that could be used to head off

developers when they threatened wild areas. His final suggestion was that conservationists try to make their beliefs a civic
cause and develop a united front against those who threatened
the wilderness areas. The publicity and debate over ecology in
the past decade indicate that his final suggestion has been at
last realized. One cannot help but wonder, however, whether
he would have been thrilled by the newly discovered devotion
to ecology being touted in the PR campaigns of so much of
corporate America.

In a final chapter that comprised nearly half of the work,
Douglas developed a more precise description of the specific
legal protections to be included in such an approach. Among
the major points that he emphasized was a more restrictive
definition of multiple use of wilderness areas to assure their
survival. Though he agreed that it was a pragmatic approach
when properly administered, he opposed its use as a cover for
various pressure groups to secure their economic ends, something he described as ". . . little more than private enterprise
engaged in boondoggling on the public domain" (p. 95). The
critical point, he emphasized, centered on who made the decisions on use and what priorities they used. Increasingly
distrustful of bureaucracy, he called for congressional rather
than more easily modified administrative designations of wild
areas. Other important specifics in Douglas' version of a
Wilderness Bill of Rights included severe restrictions on fenc-
ing public lands, motorized vehicles, boats, aircraft, mining
claims, industrial waste dumping, and damming of wild rivers
and wetlands.

Douglas was certain his proposed Bill of Rights would be
meaningless unless accompanied by the creation of a new
land-use ethic, one by which Americans learned ". . . to live
with the land, not off the land" (p. 150). His use of Aldo
Leopold's words from *A Sand County Almanac* underscored the
influence of his thinking on Douglas's approach.[18] Leopold
beautifully articulated what Douglas believed about the proper
relationship between man and nature.

That changed attitude toward land use would also involve
other basic changes. One of these, the impact of chemicals on
the biotic community, was a matter of critical concern to

Douglas. Referring to Rachel Carson's *Silent Spring*, (1962) he called for strict regulation of predator control programs and pesticides because of their harmful effect on the environment. His concern here was premised on his view of man as part of instead of something separate from the eco-system.

Douglas capped his discussion of his proposed Wilderness Bill of Rights by calling for a the creation of a new federal Office of Conservation. He cited the "vast Medley" of agencies such as the Army Corps of Engineers and the Bureau of Land Management whose actions affected conservation. His proposed office would represent the public interest in shaping the broader policies the exercise of their functions. It would provide the President advice and thus work to control the bureaucratic discretion that Douglas found so inimical to wilderness interests. (p. 173)

A Wilderness Bill of Rights marked the culmination of Douglas's defense of the preservationist land-use ethic. It reveals his mastery of the law and literature on that subject. He was brutally realistic and statistically very convincing in his depiction of the threat that technology posed to the shrinking areas of American wilderness and the dangers associated with the multiple use concept that had long dominated our conservation policies. As in other aspects of his writing, the challenge motif was very much in evidence in this work. He left the reader with a sense of foreboding about the implications of current trends and policies. So also, as in other aspects of his off the Court writing, he presented the reader with a counterplan that called for a radical departure from current policies. His belief that wilderness could be given statutory protection like the rights of minorities was especially significant. It represented his attempt to codify those values that he held so dear. Formal legal status would give the advocates of wilderness preservation a powerful, permanent weapon. Thus, *A Wilderness Bill of rights* presents a clear exposition of the basic assumptions underlying the preservationist position in a continuing debate over the best ways to use public recreation lands which still rages. The tenacity with which Douglas defended that position is indicative of the depth of his attachment to those values.

Warnings of Disaster

In 1967 Douglas reinforced the point he had made in *A Wilderness Bill of Rights* by focusing on the causes of the destruction of wilderness areas. He did this in *Farewell to Texas: A Vanishing Wilderness* by examining the situation in the wilderness areas of one state.[19] Written as the first volume in McGraw-Hill's American Wilderness Series, the work is marked by a return to the personal, anecdotal style that characterized his earlier "My Wilderness" volumes and his travel adventure works. The result was a much more readable book than a *A Wilderness Bill of Rights*, one that reinforced the message of that work quite effectively.

Farewell to Texas is a narration of Douglas's trips through the remaining wilderness areas of that state. In it he used general and natural history, and vignettes about the inhabitants of the wilderness areas to illustrate the natural grandeur that they possess. As one reviewer has noted, his descriptive powers were such that he succeeded in conveying to his readers a real feeling for the areas described.[20] The sense of appreciation that he evoked made it easier for him to plead the case for preservation.

With excellent use of contrapuntal writing, Douglas interspersed his descriptions of each wild area by pointing out the forces threatening its survival. His list of those contributing to the destruction of the natural beauty of Texas was a long one. It included public utilities armed with the power of eminent domain, federal agencies-especially the Army Corps of Engineers with its dam policies, stockmen who permitted overgrazing, lumber barons who clear cut, vandals, oil companies, poachers, and ranchers who used pesticides indiscriminately (pp. vi, 117). The resulting effect was a striking contrast between what was, what is, and what would become of Texas wilderness. He reinforced his own observations with references to such writers as J. Frank Dobie, John C. Duval, and numerous others who knew their native state intimately.

Douglas concluded sadly that time and powerful interest groups were working against those who were laboring to save the remaining Texas wilderness areas. He urged all-out support of continued federal and state efforts to create more areas such as the Big Bend National Park. His concluding pleas to save the remnants of Texas wilderness for future generations was one of his most eloquent in a long series of such statements (pp. 229-31). As in *A Wilderness Bill of Rights*, he emphasized the critical need for education in the conservation ethic, a task that he admitted would be most difficult given the popularity of the acquisitive side of American culture.

The disturbing situation he characterized in Texas was only the tip of the iceberg as far as Douglas was concerned. His increasing alarm about the costs of technology and our material culture created a growing interest in the dangers of pollution. As with his ideas on other aspects of the environment, it soon appeared in his writing. Man must act, he argued, before it was too late, not just for the sake of wilderness but before the earth was too damaged to support human life.

Douglas published his last book on conservation and the environment, *The Three Hundred Year War: A Chronicle of Ecological Disaster*, in 1972.[21] Though his goal was the same as in *Farewell to Texas*, his approach was quite different. What he tried to achieve in that volume by focusing on one state, he tried to accomplish in the *Three Hundred Year War* by a more generalized approach. It is an expository essay brimming with references to scientific authorities designed to lend credence to his frightening message: his increasing doubt about man's ability to reverse the pattern of ecological devastation that he had created.

The general causal forces that Douglas saw behind the continuing rape of the earth were the twin gods of technology and materialism, forces that played critical roles in the shaping of Western culture. As he noted: "Technology and the profit motive have carried us far down the road to disaster. It is indeed a desperate race to institute preventive controls that will save the ecosystem" (p. 168). The problem, he insisted, could not be laid solely at the door of business hunger for profits and the ineptitude of government bureaucracy. The American people also shared the blame because:

As a people we have no ecological ethic. We talk about Law and Order and we mean it when we say that burglaries, street crimes, holdups and the like must cease. But in a deeper sense we have a basic disrespect of law — unless the law restrains the other group, not our own (p. 10).

The search for means to overcome this attitude was a crucial part of Douglas' approach.

He was convinced that these traits were reinforced by the sanctity of the doctrine of economic growth in Western culture. (He also makes many references to the ecological sins of the Soviet Union caused by its pursuit of economic growth.) Relying heavily on the writings of Aldo Leopold, Barry Commoner, Jacques Costeau, and others as proof of the harmful effects of the blind pursuit of unrestricted economic growth, Douglas laid the groundwork for an alternative approach. He questioned the traditional equation of no economic growth with stagnation and decay, and argued that the fragile ecology of the earth would no longer support unrestricted growth. He urged Americans to become aware of their place in the ecosystem. Such an awareness, he thought, would hopefully lead to the creation of a standard of growth based less on output and more on improvement of the quality of life (p. 18).

As for the means to stem the headlong rush towards disaster, Douglas discussed the question of gaining standing to sue on behalf of defense of the environment. He cautioned against too much reliance on courts that were status quo-oriented and too easily swayed by "industrial lawyers" (p. 182). Ultimately more effective, he maintained, would be an approach that made conservation a messianic religion, one that motivated its believers to move beyond the public relations approach to one based on political action. Chief among the goals of this activism should be a less exploitative land-use ethic including high fines and prison sentences for those who violate pollution laws and public hearings on all major governmental conservation decisions (p. 183-185). In addition, all industries should be held to high antipollution standards to greatly reduce the obstructive capabilities of those who threaten to move to states and communities with less restrictive standards (p. 190).

Government sponsored retraining and reemployment in environmentally useful projects, he felt, would also cushion the economic impact of the transition.

The Three Hundred Year War is a fitting, though sad summation of Douglas's advocacy of ecological sanity, the conservation-land-use ethic, and wilderness preservation. The volume is a stunning example of how his hope struggled fiercely with his pessimism. It is his last concerted effort to get his fellow Americans to see what he saw so clearly. It is like so much of his writing, advocacy of his point of view, a position that made him a hero to ecologists and the *bete noir* of many federal bureaucrats and members of the American business community. He left his readers with the impression that his mind knew what his heart could not accept. Disasters such as Love Canal, Three Mile Island, and the Valdez spill seem to bear out the validity of his fears about the dangers of unchecked technological pollution.

One wonders how he would assess the current burgeoning interest in ecology, conservation, and wilderness preservation that he helped to stimulate with his writings. Although he would be pleased by the increased ecological awareness of Americans, he would most certainly be skeptical of the belated conversion of some of the country's worst industrial polluters to the ecology movement. Their blatant attempts to substitute public relations campaigns for action on this past Earth Day would not have escaped his notice or the passion invoked by his integrity.

The challenge motif which dominated so much of his writing is an important part of his lasting legacy. It propelled Douglas to off-the-Court activism, which, whether or not it violated the quasi canon of judicial modesty, provides a fascinating perspective on his basic beliefs. It reminds us also that our Supreme Court Justices are best understood when they are approached in the context of not only what they regarded as important in the course of their own lives, but how they translated these values into reality.[22]

Notes

1 William O. Douglas, *The Court Years, 1939-75* (New York: Vintage Books, 1981), p. 4; James C. Duram, *Justice William O. Douglas* (Boston: G. K. Hall-Twayne, 1981), pp. 130-132.

2 Stanley Mosk, "William O. Douglas," *Ecology Law Quarterly* 5 (1976): 229-32; Peter Wild, "Defender of Nature in the Nation's Highest Court," *High Country News*, January 27, 1978, pp. 1,4,5.

3 William O. Douglas, *Of Men and Mountains*, (New York: Harper and Brothers, 1950), pp. 109-23; *Go East Young Man*, (New York: Random House, 1974), pp. 41-54.

4 See his "Why We Must Save the Allagash," *Field and Stream*, July 1963, pp. 24-29, 57 for an outstanding example of this technique.

5 See Douglas' discussions of Muir and Leopold's ideas in his childrens' book, *Muir of the Mountains*, (Boston: Houghton-Mifflin, 1961), passim; and his *A Wilderness Bill of Rights*, (Boston: Little, Brown and Company, 1965), pp. 31-32, 34-35, 37, 42-43, 98-100, 151.

6 *Of Men and Mountains*, p. 318.

7 Subsequent page references to Douglas' works will be included in the text.

8 Transcript of Douglas' Interview by George E. Allen (May 15, 1969), p. 4, Harry S. Truman Presidential Library.

9 Monroe Bush, review of *A Wilderness Bill of Rights*, *American Forests*, October 1965, p. 38.

10 William O. Douglas, "My favorite Vacation Land," *American Magazine*, July 1952, pp. 38-41, 94-99; "Wilderness Trails of the Pacific Northwest," *Mademoseille*, April 1955, pp. 140-41, 194-97; "Man's Inhumanity to Land," *American Forests*, May 1956, p. 9.

11 William O. Douglas, *My Wilderness: The Pacific West* (Garden City, N.Y., Doubleday and Company, 1960), p. 168.

12 For a balanced critique of the work, see Howard Zahniser's review, *The York Herald Tribune Book Review*, November 6, 1960, p. 3.

13 *My Wilderness: The Pacific West*, p. 88.

14   Ibid., p. 165, see also pp. 189-90.

15   William O. Douglas, *My Wilderness: East to Katahdin*, (Garden City, N.Y., Doubleday and Company, 1961); For a balanced critique of the work, see Charle's Poore's review, *New York Times*, October 26, 1961, p. 33.

16   Page references are in text; For a balanced critique of the work, see Stewart L. Udall's review, *Natural History*, 75 (Fall, 1966): 6, 8.

17   Douglas notes that the idea for this came from a paragraph in the preamble of the Constitution of the American Camping Association. See Douglas' dissent in *Sierra Club v. Morton*, 405 U.S. 727 (1972), pp. 749, 752.

18   Aldo Leopold, *A Sand County Almanac: With Essays on Conservation from Round River* (New York: Ballantine Books, 1949 and 1953).

19   William O. Douglas, *Farewell to Texas: A Vanishing Wilderness*, (New York: McGraw-Hill, 1967. For a balanced critique of the work, see Pete A. Gunter's review, *Living Wilderness*, Spring/Summer 1967, pp. 48-49. Douglas received much assistance from President Lyndon Johnson and his friends in arranging the visits to Texas that became the basis of this book. See Jack Valenti to Dale Maalechek (June 4, 1965, and June 7, 1965), White House Central File: Name File, and William O. Douglas to Lyndon B. Johnson (March 7, 1966), "Famous Names" Collection, Johnson Presidential Library.

20   *Choice*, March 1968, pp. 77-78.

21   William O. Douglas, *The Three Hundred Year War: A Chronicle of Ecological Disaster* (New York: Random House, 1972). For a balanced critique of the work, see *Audubon Magazine*, May 1973, pp. 91-92.

22   Perhaps the best known of Douglas' activities on behalf of preservation was the important role he played in the long struggle to get the 180 mile long C&O canal turned into a national historic park that has become a mecca for hikers. See *Go East, Young Man*, pp. 212-213; and Melvin Urofsky, Ed., *The Douglas Letters* Bethesda, Md.: Adler and Adler, 1987), pp. 232, 236-240. Urofsky sees a "certain amount of irony" in Douglas' crusade for the C&O park, given his own personal preference for rugged untouched wilderness.

Hugo L. Black As A Great Justice

Henry J. Abraham

I

What renders a justice—for that matter any jurist—"great?" It is a daunting question, one that an enterprising duo of law professors, Albert P. Blaustein of Rutgers University and Roy M. Mersky of the University of Texas (Austin), endeavored to address in an intriguing exercise *cum* poll more than two decades ago. In what was arguably the primary extensive, systematized, formal study of the performance of the first 97 justices (from John Jay through the initial year of the incumbency of Chief Justice Warren E. Burger), 65 law school deans and professors of law, history and political science (including myself) were asked in June 1970 to pass judgment. We were requested to use a survey model employing the following categories: "great" (A); "near great" (B); "average" (C); "below average" (D); and "failure" (E). No other criteria, measurements, or research tools were either mandated or suggested. The sole other specific instruction provided by Professors Blaustein and Mersky was to "select the nine outstanding Justices of both centuries"—a stipulation that resulted in the selection of twelve "great" justices. The results were published in book form in 1978, entitled *The First One Hundred [sic] Justices: Statistical Studies on the Supreme Court of the United States*.[1] In the interim prior to publication, and since that time, a number of other studies and commentaries appeared in print,[2] in effect confirming closely the general rankings of the pioneering 1970 study, although some found additional "greats" and varied their categories. Definitions of "greatness," however, continued to be elusive, notwithstanding broad agreement on the adjective's entitled recipients.

On the other hand, the Blaustein/Mersky results had pointed to a compendium of qualities that characterized "greatness." All of the chosen twelve made significant, identifiable contributions to the development of law and its interpretation. Their agreed-upon success on the highest tribunal in the land was, in the observation of the two editors, the product of the following several combined qualities: "scholarship; legal learning and analytical powers; craftsmanship and technique; wide general knowledge and learning; character, moral integrity and impartiality; diligence and industry; the ability to express oneself with clarity, logic, and compelling force; openness to change; courage to take unpopular positions; dedication to the Court as an institution and to the office of Supreme Court justice; ability to carry a proportionate share of the Court's responsibility in opinion writing; and, finally, the quality of statesmanship."[3]

Who comprised the twelve "greats" selected by the 65 experts? They included four chief and eight associate justices, bracketing a period from 1801 through 1969. In chronological order they were: John Marshall, Joseph Story, Roger B. Taney, John M. Harlan (I), Oliver Wendell Holmes, Jr., Charles Evans Hughes, Louis D. Brandeis, Harlan F. Stone, Benjamin N. Cardozo, Hugo L. Black, Felix Frankfurter, and Earl Warren. Their period of service ranged from Marshall, Harlan, and Black's astounding 34 years each (exceeded since then only by William O. Douglas's 36 1/2 years and equalled by Justices Stephen J. Field and William J. Brennan, Jr., all three of whom were ranked as "near great") to Cardozo's all-too-brief six years on the Court. Only one of the twelve received all 65 votes—not surprisingly it was John Marshall. In second place was Brandeis with 62; Holmes was third with 61, followed by Black with 42, and Frankfurter with 41. It is interesting to note that whereas the "greats" spanned all but the first decade of the Court's then 180 years existence, the eight rated as "failures" (Willis Van Devanter, James C. McReynolds, Pierce Butler, James F. Byrnes, Harold H. Burton, Fred M. Vinson, Sherman Minton, and Charles Whittaker) served in a fifty-year period of the 20th century, ranging from 1911 through 1962. There were fifteen "near greats," 55 "average," and six "below average."[4]

Because he was the most recent among those named "great" to leave the Court (1971); because of his long tenure; because it was my great privilege to know him at least somewhat personally; and because he was such a fascinating, influential, towering figure, I have selected him as the example of a great justice I should now like to discuss in some detail.[5]

II

When Justice Van Devanter announced his retirement, the leading candidate for the vacancy was Joseph T. Robinson of Arkansas, the Democratic Majority Leader of the Senate. A faithful New Dealer who had supported every New Deal measure that F.D.R. had sent to Congress, the popular, hardworking Robinson had also been an early and key backer of the President's Court-reorganization bill. Everything pointed to his designation. F.D.R. had evidently promised him a Supreme Court seat, although not necessarily the first available one. But according to the then still high-riding Postmaster General and Democratic National Committee Chairman, James A. "Jim" Farley, Roosevelt had said that Robinson could count on being nominated.[6] And in an unusual move the Senate as a body endorsed the candidacy of its Democratic Leader. Yet F.D.R. had been forced to wait more than four years for that precious initial vacancy; now he would bide his time. He liked and was grateful to "Arkansas Joe"; still, there was just enough basic conservatism in Robinson's past to cast doubt on his "reliability." Then fate intervened: on July 14, while leading the floor fight for the Court-packing bill, Senator Robinson suffered a fatal heart attack. Roosevelt at once instructed Homer S. Cummings, his Attorney General, to canvass the field of other "suitables," keeping in mind that the nominee had to be absolutely loyal to the New Deal program. By early August the search had narrowed to four such loyal New Deal Democrats: U.S. Solicitor General Stanley F. Reed of Kentucky, Senator Sherman Minton of Indiana, Senator Hugo L. Black of Alabama, and Assistant Attorney General

Robert H. Jackson of New York. All four would become Supreme Court Justices eventually; it was Black's turn now (although there are assertions—firmly denied by Justice Douglas, for one—that F.D.R. offered Minton first refusal). "Jesus Christ!", exclaimed White House Press Secretary Stephen Early, when F.D.R. disclosed his choice to him late at night on August 11.[7] The President grinned—it had been a well-kept secret, indeed. Earlier that evening he had summoned Black to his White House study, showed him the nomination form he had filled out in long-hand himself, and chuckled, "Hugo, I'd like to write your name here." A happy Black nodded assent.[8]

Steve Early's reaction was understandable. At first glance there was precious little in the impoverished rural background of the then fifty-one-year-old Senator from Ashland, Clay County, the eighth (and last) child of a small-town rural merchant, to qualify him for the Supreme Court. True, he had had considerable experience as a lawyer among country sharecroppers, as a county solicitor, and as a police-court judge and prosecutor in Birmingham; moreover, he was a pillar of the church, had taught Sunday school at the Birmingham First Baptist Church for 16 years; he had read widely; and he had a lucid, profound mind. But was he *really* the best F.D.R. could do? The President of course knew precisely what he was doing: Black, now in his second term in the Senate, had not only demonstrated enthusiastic and outspoken support of the New Deal, but he had staunchly supported the Court-packing bill. Those two factors were decisive—but F.D.R. also happily noted that Black had a long and effective record of siding with "little people" and "underdogs", and that he was from a part of the country that he, F.D.R., wanted to see represented on the Court. He was also aware of Black's principled discipline and his astounding educational achievements. His nominee never finished high school, moving straight into the Birmingham Medical School at age seventeen, finishing the four-year program in three. Black then switched to the law, studying for three years at the University of Alabama School of Law at Tuscaloosa—where he was so bored that he took an *entire* liberal arts curriculum concurrently (!), graduating with high honors in 1907.[9]

The nomination's announcement was met with approbation by most of Senator Black's colleagues and most New Deal spokesmen throughout the land. Yet it also evoked loud protests from both public and private sources. The intellectual and soft-spoken liberal was portrayed as being utterly unqualified by training, temperament, and constitutional dedication; as being blindly partisan; as being a radical rather than a liberal; as being, in fact, a phony liberal when it was revealed that he had been a member of the Ku Klux Klan (K.K.K.) in the 1920s. Although F.D.R. denied any knowledge of a Black-KKK link in a September 14, 1937 press conference, Black recalled a converse fact: He had discussed his erstwhile membership with the President at the time of his formal nomination, F.D.R. telling Black not to worry about it, that "some of his best friends and supporters in the state of Georgia were strong members of that organization."[10] The press—no more a friend of the Senator's than of his President—roasted Black for "combined lack of training on the one hand and extreme partisanship on the other,"[11] with the *Chicago Tribune* declaring that the President had picked "the worst he could find,"[12] and the *American Mercury* called him a "vulgar dog." But the Senate, although treated to the somewhat unaccustomed spectacle of a public debate on the merits of a sitting member, quickly confirmed its colleague (who had been backed 13:4 in the Judiciary Committee) by a vote of 63:16 on August 17.[13]

When the verdict was in, Justice-designate and Mrs. Josephine Black sailed for a European vacation. In their absence, Ray Sprigle, a reporter on the *Pittsburgh Post-Gazette*, published a six-day series of articles repeating the known facts of Black's erstwhile K.K.K. membership. Although acknowledging written proof of Black's resignation from the Klan in 1925, Sprigle alleged that, in fact, Black-notwithstanding on-the-floor denials by such powerful non-Democratic colleagues as Senator W. E. Borah (R.-Idaho), for example—was still a member of the hooded organization, having been secretly elected to life membership in 1926. Black was besieged abroad by reporters, but he characteristically disdained any comment until he stepped before radio microphones on October 1, 1937, to make the eleven-minute statement that was heard by the largest radio audience ever, save for those who listened to Britain's Edward VIII's abdication "for the woman I love":[14]

> My words and acts are a matter of public record. I believe that my record as a Senator refutes every implication of racial or religious intolerance. It shows that I was of that group of liberal Senators who have consistently fought for civil, economic and religious rights of all Americans, without regard to race or creed. . . . I did join the Klan. I later resigned. I never rejoined. I have never considered and I do not now consider the unsolicited card given to me shortly after my nomination to the Senate as a membership of any kind in the Ku Klux Klan. I never used it. I did not even keep it. Before becoming a Senator I dropped the Klan. I have had nothing whatever to with it since that time. I abandoned it . . .[15]

The public was generally sympathetic and persuaded of his sincerity. Again characteristically, Justice Black — whose personality Gerald T. Dunne has aptly described as "steel wrapped in silk"[16] — said no more on the subject, refusing to discuss or reopen the matter during the remainder of his long life. "When this statement is ended," he had said, "my discussion of the question is closed." He meant it, and it was! Three days after the broadcast he donned the robes of Associate Justice — "he need not buy but merely dye his robes" was a favorite contemporary cocktail quip.[17]

Thus began a remarkable Supreme court tenure of more than thirty-four years. It was one marked by a distinction and an influence rare in the annals of the Court. How right the *Montgomery Advertiser* had been when it observed: "What a joke it would be on Hugo's impassioned detractors if he should now turn out to be a very great justice of the Supreme court. Brandeis did it when every Substantial Citizen of the Republic felt that Wilson should have been impeached for appointing him. . . ."[18]

III

Few jurists have had the impact on law and society that Justice Hugo Lafayette Black had. A constitutional literalist to whom every word in the document represented an absolutist command, he nonetheless used the language of the Constitution—"language plus history," he would avow—to propound a jurisprudence that has had a lasting effect on the development of American constitutional interpretation and law. It is one perhaps best characterizable as a blend of democratic populism and judicial strict constructionism. Black's contributions were seminal. They stand as jurisprudential and intellectual landmarks in the evolving history of the land for which he fought both literally and figuratively and loved so well—a devotion so touchingly and effectively manifested in his valedictory lectures, aptly entitled "A Constitutional Faith."[19]

In Harvard University's esteemed Paul Freund's view, Black was "without a doubt the most influential of the many strong figures" who sat on the Court during his thirty-four years of membership.[20] In that of the University of Chicago's Philip Kurland, only one other member, John Marshall, "left such a deep imprint on our basic document."[21] He fully met F.D.R.'s expectations, of course. But that was in the short run; the New Deal as such had spent its course by the end of the 1930s. In the long run Black's achievements encompass securing the central meaning of the Constitution and of the Bill of Rights. At the pinnacle of his legacy stands the now-all-but-complete nationalization of the latter, a doctrine known as "incorporation", i.e., its application to all of the states through the due process of law clause of the Fourteenth Amendment. In what was probably his most influential opinion in dissent, the *Adamson* case of 1947,[22] Hugo Black called for that nationalization, dramatically expanding and elaborating Justice Cardozo's pioneering dichotomous classification in the 1937 *Palko Case*[23] and Justice Stone's famed *Carolene Products* case Footnote Four.[24] He lost in *Adamson* by only one vote. But by constantly reiterating the theme of constitutional intent as he perceived it in the Fourteenth Amendment—"I cannot consider the Bill of rights to be an outworn eighteenth-century 'strait jacket,' " he had thundered in *Adamson*—and by his reading of the debates leading to the Amendment's adoption— he coaxed the Court step by step to his side. By 1969 the Warren Court had, with but minor exceptions, in effect, written its concurrence into constitutional law.[25]

It is generally agreed that the nationalization of the Bill of Rights was Black's most visible achievement; yet it is but one of the many that have rated him all but universal acclaim as one of the great justices.[26] Among those accomplishments were his leadership in propounding an "absolutist" theory of the First Amendment's freedom of expression guarantees[27] — always provided that he viewed the issue at hand as one involving freedom of *expression* rather than one of proscribable *conduct* — a theory based upon the *specific verbiage* of the Constitution that contributed heavily to the Warren Court's broadly liberal definition of obscenity, to its tough standards on proof in alleged libel and slander cases, and to its striking down of much of the "subversive activities" legislation of the McCarthy era; his assertive majority opinions defining a "contra-establishment" line of separation between Church and State; his tenacious, literal interpretation of the protective guarantees of the Constitution in the administration of justice, including the specific provisions against coerced confessions, compulsory self-incrimination, double jeopardy, and those defining the conditions of trial by jury and the availability of counsel — while the presence of the qualifying adjective "unreasonable" in the Fourth Amendment's "searches and seizures" safeguard provisions would not infrequently find him on opposite sides of his customary liberal allies, such as William O. Douglas; his victory over Justice Frankfurter in the arena of "political questions" that legalized the egalitarian representation concept of ("one man, one vote") now so broadly taken for granted. It prompted the acerbic Frankfurter to pronounce Black a "rural country bumpkin in judicial robes" who "delivers flapdoodle in the name of democracy."[28] Perhaps Black's most moving victorious opinion was written for a unanimous Court in the celebrated case of *Gideon v. Wainwright* (1963),[29] which overruled a decision of more than two decades earlier from which he had vigorously dissented:[30] *Gideon* enshrined the principle that any criminal defendant in a state was well as a federal proceeding who is too poor to pay for a lawyer has a constitutional right to be assigned one gratis by the government. For

Black the opinion represented the affirmation of another touching plea written twenty-three years earlier in the famed case of *Chambers v. Florida*. Still viewed as one of his most beautifully penned, it held for a unanimous Court that the confessions obtained by Florida authorities to condemn four black defendants to death were patently coerced and, therefore, a clear violation of due process of law. In the most celebrated passage, at the close of his opinion, Black wrote:

> Under our constitutional system courts stand against any winds that blow as havens or refuge for those who might otherwise suffer because they are helpless, weak, outnumbered, or because they are non-conforming victims of prejudice and public excitement. Due process of law, preserved for all by our Constitution, commands that no such practice as that disclosed by [the *Chambers* case record] shall send any accused to his death. No higher duty, no more solemn responsibility, rests upon this Court, than that of translating into living law and maintaining this constitutional shield deliberately planned and inscribed for the benefit of every human being to our Constitution — of whatever race, creed, or persuasion.[31]

One week after ill health compelled his retirement in September 1971 at eighty-five, Justice Black died — but not until he had had one last good argument about the incorporation of the Bill of Rights with fellow-fatally-ill-in-Walter-Reed-Hospital-long time Supreme Court colleague, John Marshall Harlan. Hugo Lafayette Black had written almost 1000 opinions during his thirty-four years of exemplary service. "The law," as one of those who knew him best wrote, "has lost a kindly giant."[32] Friends who called at a funeral home in Washington before his burial in Arlington National Cemetery received a poignant parting gift — a copy of the Constitution. On a desk bearing a book for visitors' signatures was a pile of small paperbound copies of the document Black had so often referred to as "my legal bible" — a copy of which he always carried in his suit pocket. He would have approved. Laid to rest with him in the simple pine casket were several of them. On a bench that she had placed adjacent to Justice Black's final resting place, his widow, Elizabeth Seay Black, had inscribed the words: "Here lies a good man." He was that, indeed, and a great Justice of the Supreme Court of the United States of America.

Notes

1 (Hamden, Conn.: Shoe String Press [Anchor Books]).

2 E.g., Stuart S. Nagel, "Characteristics of Supreme Court Greatness," 56 *American Bar Association Journal* (October, 1970); Richard Funston, "Great Presidents, Great Justices?", VII *Presidential Studies Quarterly* (Fall, 1977); Richard G. Zimmerman, "Nine Men of the Highest Court Are Judged," *The Times-Picayune*, July 30, 1980, Sec. 3, p. 8; an extensive *National Law Journal* survey (graded by 900 [!] law professors), December 1979; Sheldon Goldman, "Judicial Selection and the Qualities that Make a 'Good' Judge," 462 *Annals*, AAPSS (July 1982); "James E. Hambleton," The All-Time All Star All Era Supreme Court," 69 *American Bar Association Journal* (April 1983); and Gregory A. Caldeira, "In the Mirror of the Justices: Sources of Greatness on the Supreme Court," 10 *Political Behavior* 3 (1988).

3 Op. cit., fn. 1, pp. 50-51.

4 See my *Justices and Presidents: A Political History of Appointments to the Supreme Court*, 3d ed. (New York: Oxford University Press, 1992), Appendix A, pp. 412-14, for a convenient tabular account.

5 The remarks to follow borrow heavily from my *Justices and Presidents*, *loc. cit.*, esp. ch. 9, pp. 212-218.

6 *Jim Farley's Story* (New York: McGraw Hill, 1948), p. 86.

7 As quoted by Virginia Van der Veer Hamilton, *Hugo Black: The Alabama Years* (Baton Rouge: Louisiana State University Press, 1972), p. 275. (Mrs. Hamilton is the source for the Minton claim.)

8 *Ibid.*, p. 274.

9 Hugo L. Black, Jr., *My Father: A Remembrance* (New York: Random House, 1975), pp. 16-17.

10 Van der Veer Hamilton communications, H.L.B. papers, Library of Congress, MSS Drive, Box 31.

11 As the *Washington Post*, for one, put it in an editorial on August 13, 1937.

12 As quoted in 60 *Judicature* 7 (February 1977), p. 350.

13 Sixty Democrats and three Republicans—Robert La Follette (Wisconsin), Arthur Capper (Kansas), and Lynn J. Frazier (North Dakota)—voted aye, ten Republicans and six Democrats voted nay; and sixteen Senators abstained from voting—an uncommonly high number.

14 John P. Frank, *Mr. Justice Black: The Man and His Opinions* (New York: Knopf, 1949), p. 105.

15 *New York Times*, October 2, 1937, p. 1.

16 Gerald T. Dunne, *Hugo Black and the Judicial Revolution* (New York: Simon & Schuster, 1977), p. 43.

17 *Ibid.*, p. 274.

18 As quoted by Frank, *op. cit.*, fn. 12, p. 102.

19 Published as *A Constitutional Faith* (New York: Knopf, 1968).

20 "Mr. Justice Black and the Judicial Function," 14 *U.C.L.A. Law Review* 467 (1967), at 473.

21 "Hugo Lafayette Black: In Memoriam," 20 *Journal of Public Law* 359 (1971), at 362.

22 *Adamson v. California*, 332 U.S. 46.

23 *Palko v. Connecticut*, 302 U.S. 319.

24 *United States v. Carolene Products Co.*, 304 U.S. 144 (1938), at 152-53.

25 For a detailed description, see my *Freedom and the Court: Civil Rights and Liberties in the United States*, 5th ed. (New York: Oxford University Press, 1982), Ch. 3: "The Bill of Rights and Its Applicability to the States," pp. 38-117.

26 See Appendix A, *infra*.

27 See James J. Magee, *Mr. Justice Black: Absolutist on the Court* (Charlottesville: University of Virginia Press, 1980).

28 Quoted in John Noonan's book review of Gerald J. Dunne's *Hugo Black and the Judicial Revolution*, op. cit., fn. 16, in 9 *Southwestern Law Review* (1977), p. 1131.

29 372 U.S. 335.

30 *Betts v. Brady*, 326 U.S. 455 (1942).

31 *Chambers v. Florida*, 309 U.S. 227 (1940), and 241.

32 John P. Frank, "Hugo L. Black: He Has Joined the Giants," 58 *American Bar Association Journal* (January 1972), p. 25.

The Earl of Justice:
Warren's Vision for America

Norman W. Provizer
Joseph D. Vigil

In 1991, Clarence Thomas survived controversial confirmation hearings to become the sixth member of the Supreme Court nominated by the administrations of Ronald Reagan and George Bush. With Thomas on the Court, only Justice Byron White remained as a holdover from the days when Chief Justice Earl Warren presided over America's primary judicial institution.

Though the constitutional paths cut by the Warren Court were not completely repaved by the Burger and Rehnquist Courts that followed, they have and will continue to be altered by changing political realities. A cartoon that displayed an "Impeach Earl Warren" billboard sitting on top of the Supreme Court building may have been apocryphal but—by 1991—it was not at all pure fantasy.

The irony, of course, was that 1991 was also the year that marked the centennial of Earl Warren's birth. And it is Warren's name that will forever be connected to the judicial revolution that shaped the face of constitutional law during the last half of the 20th century—a revolution that is now in the midst of a Thermidor.

Earl Warren was born on March 19, 1891 in Los Angeles. Soon after, his family moved to Bakersfield, where his father was a repairman for the Southern Pacific Railroad. The son of immigrant parents from Scandinavia, Warren worked his way through an undergraduate and law degree at the University of California at Berkeley.

With the exception of a brief period of time right after law school, Warren spent his entire career in the public sector, moving from deputy city attorney of Oakland to deputy district attorney for that county. In 1938, the lawyer of lower-middle class origins and no middle name won the nomination for state attorney general in the primaries of the Progressive and Democratic parties as well as his own Republican organization; and in 1942, he continued his political rise by winning the California governor's race. He was twice re-elected to that position, gaining the Democratic nomination on top of his Republican selection in 1946.

On the national scene, Warren was Thomas Dewey's vice-presidential running mate in 1948 and supported Dwight Eisenhower at the 1952 Republican Convention after his own presidential aspirations stalled. That support provided the glue that would link Warren to the Supreme Court the following year.

Earl Warren owned an enduring passion for justice. He believed in equal opportunity for the disadvantaged so they could become part of the expanding American economic scene. He demonstrated a clear belief that all Americans were entitled to a broad vision of equal protection and due process of the law, no matter what their social standing, or color of their skin. He, and others, also knew public policy had failed to serve those ends for black and other disadvantaged Americans. As Chief Justice, from 1953 until 1969, Warren was placed into a leadership role at a time when several of the most controversial issues in constitutional law would come before the Court. The Warren Court issued watershed opinions on issues of obscenity, school prayer, libel and the criticism of public figures, criminal defendant rights, the desegregation of public facilities, school busing, gerrymandering, the right to privacy, equal protection doctrines, and the death penalty. And in what the Chief Justice considered to be the most important decision affecting constitutional law issued during his tenure, the Warren Court shattered the political questions doctrine as a barrier for injured parties in voting rights cases.

The common sentiment espoused by detractors is that the Warren Court was an activist body that played the role of a "super legislature." The critics charge that the Warren Court advocated position on civil rights and guaranteed freedoms that were not part of the "original intent" of the framers of the Constitution. From the political world, one of the primary detractors of the Warren Court was Richard Nixon. In the 1968 general election, Nixon campaigned on a plank of remaking the Court with nominees who were "strict constructionists." Nixon harshly criticized the Warren Court's decisions on criminal defendant rights, civil liberties and civil rights. His main attack concentrated on "activism" the judicial branch had engaged in: He argued that the role of the judiciary was strictly to interpret existing law, not to take any initiative in that field.[1]

Earl Warren began to have serious detractors during his first term on the Court. The John Birch Society focused its attention on the Chief Justice following his decision in *Brown v. Board of Education* — Topeka (1954). The Society mounted a billboard campaign to "Impeach Earl Warren." Warren was mildly amused with the campaign and reasoned that it kept the members' time and money occupied because he was not going to resign and there was not a legitimate fear of being impeached. Following the Brown decision Senator James O. Eastland (D-Mississippi), soon to become the powerful chairman of the Senate Judiciary Committee, declared that the Warren Court and the lower federal courts had destroyed the Constitution by disregarding the law. In a speech given to a Mississippi audience on August 12, 1955, Senator Eastland extolled the virtues of segregation and Southern life. Referring to the Brown decision, he told the audience, "You are not required to obey any court which passes out such a ruling. In fact, you are obligated to defy it."[2]

Southern congressmen and other segregationists had lined up in opposition to the Brown decision and began a political counterattack of the Warren Court. The United States Congress engaged the Court, in 1957, when the House voted 241-155 to limit the jurisdiction of the Supreme Court. The political maneuvering of Senate Majority Leader Lyndon B. Johnson provided a simple one-vote majority in beating down that House initiative, 41-40. Southern state legislatures then began a series of legislative maneuvers designed to impede the desegregation edicts of the Warren Court using a loophole created by the Court's own language "with all deliberate speed."[3] Still the Fifth Circuit Court of Appeals used the Brown decision as a bedrock of to overcome those Southern legislative initiatives that had been designed to nullify the effect of the desegregation orders.

In 1962, the Warren Court announced a key decision that affected discrimination as no other case had before and, arguably, ever again will, in terms of constitutional law. In *Baker v. Carr* (1962), the judiciary met legislative discrimination head on. In that case, the Court used the Fourteenth Amendment to rule that the issue of legislative reapportionment was justiciable and that the Court would now allow claims based upon the Equal Protection clause to be heard. Though the far-reaching nature of the decision in *Baker v. Carr* is understood by few, that decision opened the opportunity for redress of grievances that had previously been denied because of the political questions doctrine. The door to the Court had been pried open by Earl Warren.

The Issue of Race

For the majority of Court watchers and others, the decision in *Brown v. Board of Education* — Topeka (1954) is seen as the most important decision made during the tenure of Chief Justice Warren. Certainly, it was a decision that stands as watershed in the history of American constitutional law.

The framers of the Constitution and the Bill of Rights addressed the issues of slavery and racial segregation within the framework of maintaining the nation's political and economic stability. Slavery and racial discrimination were divisive issues and provided the spark that ignited this nation into a bloody Civil War. While the Thirteenth Amendment settled the issue of slavery, it, and the Fourteenth and Fifteenth Amendments that followed, did not satisfactorily settle the issue of racial discrimination.

There are those who argue that positive law cannot be made to end racism, just as Congress cannot legislate morality. Laws proscribe behavior that is considered criminally reprehensible. The act of legislating punishment for criminal conduct does not mean that all vices are outlawed, nor does it mean that all virtues are enhanced. The Court itself has said that a law need not be perfect to be constitutional. The Court requires only that there be a rational relationship between the classification created by the law and the means used to affect that group. This ends-means relationship is called the rational basis test. When using the rational basis test, the Court has decided that if the goal of the legislative enactment is constitutional, then the law is assumed constitutional because it is within the proper power of legislatures to enact legislative measures. The statutes passed by Congress and state legislatures both promoting and attacking racial discrimination are imperfect constructs that require legal critique.

The history of racial discrimination in America is compelling. At the Constitutional Convention it was declared that slaves were to be considered three-fifths of a human being in matters of legislative apportionment and direct taxation.[4] The Federalist Papers describe the three-fifths compromise as an expedient to the adoption of the Constitution.[5] In 1857, the Supreme Court decided the Dred Scott Case—a case Samuel Krislov aptly describes as one that "represents judicial review at its worst" and that "as much as any other single action, this helped lead to the Civil War."[6] Led by Chief Justice Taney, the Court ruled, 7-2, that blacks were not citizens, that Congress could not bar slavery from the new territories and that slaves who were taken to free territories did not become free because they were still considered property. The Thirteenth (1865) and Fourteenth (1868) Amendments effectively overruled the decision in the Dred Scott Case. In the Civil Rights Cases of 1883, the Court ruled, 8-1, that the Fourteenth Amendment prohibited the states from discriminating against blacks because of their race, but did not restrict private organizations from such discriminatory actions. The decision meant that the Court would allow private discrimination to take place in theaters, restaurants, hotels, transportation facilities and other areas related to private organizations. The Court felt that private action described was not subject to the prohibitions set forth in the Fourteenth Amendment and the Civil Rights Act of 1875 because even though the Act and the

Amendment did grant rights and privileges, they prohibited only state law and state procedure, and then only when the action affected those rights and national privileges.

In *Plessy v. Ferguson* (1896), the Court established the doctrine of "separate but equal" that ruled America for the next fifty-eight years. The Court, by a vote of 7-1, allowed states to legislate racial segregation so long as the separate facilities provided were equal. This case became the harbinger to a litany of law and custom designed to discriminate against blacks. In *Cumming v. Richmond County Board of Education* (1899) the Court allowed for separate but unequal school facilities. In that case, the Court approved the use of a white-only system and accepted the state's argument that it could not provide for the high school education of black teenagers because it did not have the money to build a separate school.

During the next half-century state and local governments responded with Jim Crow laws, grandfather clauses, poll taxes, and state sponsored violence against blacks. Property clauses were instituted to skirt the provisions of the Fifteenth Amendment. Property clauses were designed to disenfranchise blacks and minorities who did not own property. Grandfather clauses were instituted to reincorporate poor whites who did not own property. The clause would extend the right to vote to a person who was currently without property but who was delineated from anyone that had voted in previous elections (usually pre-1868). All of the actions were designed to intimidate ethnic and racial minorities, to prevent them from exercising their right to vote and to keep in place a state apparatus of discrimination. Racial and ethnic discrimination was not confined to the Deep South. Southwestern and Western states openly discriminated against peoples of Hispanic, Asian and Native American ancestry.

In only a few cases did the Court strike such provisions. In *Guinn v. United States* (1915) the Court struck down an Oklahoma grandfather clause for being violative of the Fifteenth Amendment. This decision was used as the basis to strike down grandfather clauses that were used in several other Southern states. In *Yick Wo v. Hopkins* (1886) the Court struck down a San Francisco ordinance that, in fact, discriminated against Chinese launderers. The ordinance was enacted under a public safety cloak and called for a prohibition against the operation of wooden laundries unless there was a grant of waiver by the board of supervisors. Ninety-seven percent of the Chinese laundries were in wooden buildings. White laundry owners were routinely given the waiver but Chinese launderers were not and the Court felt the ordinance was patently discriminatory and struck it down.

In addition to the states' efforts to disenfranchise and segregate minority groups, terrorism took place in the form of lynching and kangaroo courts. Both of these forms of terrorism were denials of due process and equal protection of the law.

Racism did not begin with *Plessy v. Ferguson* but it was the legal procreator of court doctrine that ruled America for nearly two-thirds of a century. The decision allowed legal tribunals to rule in favor of states' efforts to discriminate against blacks and minorities. With more than a touch of irony, the legal progenitor of racial discrimination in America became the nation's Constitution and its interpretation. The potential of the Civil War Amendments to affect change in the practice of racial and ethnic discrimination in this country was largely unrealized. The decision in *Plessy v. Ferguson* made blacks and other minorities subject to the doctrine of "not equal but separate" protection of the law. The decision stood until the Warren Court overruled it in 1954. Prior to *Brown v. Board of Education*—Topeka (1954), the Court was satisfied to apply the Plessy doctrine rather than rule on its constitutionality. The Court conveniently side-stepped the issue of the doctrine's constitutionality by deciding equal protection cases on a case-by-case basis, and then issuing orders for remedial action in the particular case. In *McCabe v. Atchison, T.&S.F. Railroad Company* (1914) the Court held that the practice of segregating dining cars may produce unequal service but its solution was to make the separate services more equitable. A quarter-century later, the Court refused to grant certiorari to a lower court case and thereby let stand a ruling that black teachers in Norfolk, Virginia should be paid the same salaries as their white counterparts if they did equal work, even though the school system was segregated.

In the cases of *Sweatt v. Painter* (1950) and *McLaurin v. Oklahoma State Regents* (1950) the Court began to constrict the definition of "separate but equal." In McLaurin, the Court said that a young black that had been admitted into a white graduate program must be accorded similar privileges as his white counterparts in the normal process of education. In this case, the student was placed in a room adjoining the lecture hall. The room was equipped with windows and air ducts so that he could hear the lecture and see the blackboard. The Court did not directly address the issue of "separate but equal." Instead, the Court granted specific relief to the black plaintiff. In a careful reading of the opinion in McLaurin one can see the looming specter that the Court was growing dissatisfied with the Plessy doctrine.

In Sweatt, the Court again skirted an overrule and relied on ordering a remedy only to the facts of the case. Homer Sweatt had been denied admission into the University of Texas Law School based upon his race. The state argued that a soon-to-be black law school would suffice to provide instruction on the fundamentals of law and provide the necessary resources for Mr. Sweatt to complete his studies. The trial court accepted that argument and gave the state of Texas six months to build the all-black law school. Mr. Sweatt refused to attend that school and pursued his case to gain admittance into the law school at the University of Texas. The appellate courts of Texas upheld the lower court decision and the remedy of a separate law school for blacks. The University of Texas Law School is well-respected. Mr. Sweatt knew this and wanted to attend. He appealed his case to the Supreme Court, and was vindicated. The Court ordered his admittance into the University's law program. The Court stated that the all-black law school was inferior to one at the University of Texas. The all-black law school was not accredited, did not have its own faculty or library; and other facilities such as scholarship programs, alumni associations, fraternities, were not present. While the Court opined that the equal protection clause of the Fourteenth Amendment required the University of Texas to admit Mr. Sweatt, and ordered compliance, it did not overrule the doctrine of "separate but equal." A careful reading of the Court's opinion however, showed its growing dissatisfaction with the Plessy doctrine. The issue was becoming ripe for fundamental reconsideration. What was needed was a new leader for a new day on the Court.

By 1952, a series of cases directly challenging segregated education were before the Supreme Court. The lead case was Brown and it was argued in 1953. The Court faced with internal divisions asked for reargument; but before that would take place, Chief Justice Fred Vinson died suddenly. Repaying a political debt, President Dwight Eisenhower named Warren as Vinson's successor. Thus during Warren's first term on the bench, the Court under his direction had the opportunity to override the Plessy doctrine, and the accompanying Jim Crow doctrines. The new Chief Justice provided clear leadership in Court conference and together with his clerks wrote the opinion of the Court. On May 17, 1954, a unanimous Court announced in Brown that Plessy had been wrongly decided and declared "separate but equal" was constitutionally impermissible. The Chief Justice described how Plessy had dealt with transportation and not education. He described how Sweatt dealt with schools that were separate, but equal, or were being equalized. The Chief Justice then swept aside the past and said that segregation and public education must be dealt with in present circumstance. He then reproduced the case history of segregation, including Sweatt, McLaurin and the facts of the case-at-hand. Then came the bombshell everyone had been waiting for. Warren read aloud:

> We come to the question presented: Does segregation of children in public schools solely on the basis of race, even though the physical facilities and other tangible factors may be equal, deprive the children of the minority group of equal educational opportunities? We unanimously believed that it does.[7]

The Chief Justice remembered that the word "unanimous" carried with it the connotation that the Supreme Court was making an affirmative statement for the entire country to recognize.[8] The early Warren Court had different-minded justices who were strong-willed and had opposing ideologies. There was a staunch liberal wing that was juxtaposed to the conservative members: Justice Frankfurter and Robert Jackson. There were distinct personality conflicts among the justices that, in earlier proceedings, had erupted into shouting matches. Under Chief Justice Warren's leadership this divided group agreed unanimously that the doctrine of "separate but equal" was inherently unequal and a violation of the Equal Protection clause of the Fourteenth Amendment. The strong leadership of Chief Justice Warren, in this important case, led to tranquility among a brethren whose relationship can be described as acrimonious, at best. Justice Frankfurter, renown for his personal dissatisfaction with Warren, wrote him on the day of May 17, 1954:

> Dear Chief: This is a day that will in glory. It's also a day in the history of the court, and not in the least for the course of deliberation which brought about the result. I congratulate you.[9]

From Justice Burton came this note:

> To you goes the credit for the character of the opinion which produced the all-important unanimity. Congratulations. . . .[10]

The type of leadership that Chief Justice Warren provided to the Court had not been present before and would not be present after. Chief Justice Fred Vinson had not been able to lead his court on this issue. And Chief Justice Warren Burger, despite *Alexander v. Holmes County Board of Education* (1969), quickly lost intellectual control of his Court and saw it decay into warring factions.[11]

The Warren Court had thrown out a government sanctioned public policy of racial segregation; and the following year, it ordered the implementation of its own policy. Critics of the Warren Court era charge that the Court acted as a "super legislature." This charge is accurate in the sense that the judicial branch of government acted to overturn a public policy that it had created nearly sixty years before. The executive and legislative branches had not acted to end segregation policies. President Eisenhower never endorsed the Brown decision, he never advocated the correctness of it, and warned that any concomitant violence would be in response to judicial activity and the executive branch could not be held responsible. When the state of Arkansas confronted the president on the issue of school desegregation, he ordered action only as a last resort.

Earl Warren provided the leadership to move the country away from a doctrine that established a national policy for almost two-thirds of a century. Blacks were simply not the equivalent of whites in the eyes of the law. The doctrine of "separate but equal" was known to be inherently unequal but it took Earl Warren, as Chief Justice of the United States, to outlaw the practice, and then to make new policy. State legislatures were using de jure and de facto discriminatory methods knowing that legal challenges would be expensive and lengthy. States, in fact, were content to fight the battle in and out of local, state and federal courts because they never lost on the fundamental issue—that is until Warren and the Brown case.

Into The Political Thicket

The declarations of the Supreme Court affect public policy in several ways. The Court can mandate certain types of legislation by declaring other pieces of legislation unconstitutional. It can define the parameters of what is constitutionally permissible, in statute, as well as the practice of custom. If the legislative branch, be it local, state or national, passes an act deemed by the Supreme Court to be repugnant to the Constitution, that act will fall. If custom, such as racial segregation, is deemed inherently unconstitutional, the Court can act to outlaw such de facto systems of behavior, within the public domain. The Court becomes an advisor by issuing opinions on what is acceptable, and what is unacceptable, under its interpretation of the Constitution. In other areas, the Court has developed doctrines affecting the right to privacy; the right of substantive and procedural economic due process; the right to equal protection of the law; the right to suffrage; and foreign policy. Within those broad areas of decisions, an agenda for public policy has been established by the Court using its power of judicial review.

Second only to the power of judicial review is the power of the Court to determine what cases will be heard. Before a court can exercise its judicial power in a case, the litigant bringing the cause must first be able to show damages or threat to a legal right, and then a determination by the Court must be made as to whether or not the damaged party has standing to sue on a justiciable issue within the Court's jurisdiction.

Prior to *Baker v. Carr* (1962) The Court had imposed the barrier of the political questions doctrine against affected plaintiffs in reapportionment cases. Succinctly, the political questions doctrine denies standing to parties because the justiciable issue is political in nature; or is constitutionally directed to Congress, or the president; or would require a policy determination by the Court; or would, upon Court adjudication, cause embarrassment to the Court, Congress or the president; or is of a nature of an unusual need (which generally means foreign affairs). Chief Justice Warren felt that the application of the political questions doctrine to the issue of legislative malapportionment was little more than Court "timidity."[12] Justice Frankfurter had written the opinion in the reapportionment case of *Colegrove v. Green* (1948) that slammed shut the door to the courthouse because he felt the issue was too far into the political thicket. The canons of judicial interpretation invited the invocation of the political questions doctrine in the case of *Baker v. Carr* and its progeny.

In 1962, the state of Tennessee had one of the most malapportioned state legislatures in the nation. Malapportionment existed, to some degree, in at least forty other states. In Tennessee, there had been a population shift from the rural areas to the inner cities. The apportionment of legislators did not follow the population shift and instead adhered to the schematic that had been drawn up at the beginning of the century. Reapportionment schemes that were supposed to be drawn from census data never passed the legislature and likely never would because rural districts would not relinquish their power in the state legislature. Even the districts as they were drawn up in 1901 were described as being contrary to constitutional formula and the representatives were apportioned in an arbitrary and capricious manner. There was no judicial review of states' malapportionment because the Court had decided to impose the political questions doctrine barrier and instructed affected individuals to seek relief in the legislature. This was very unlikely because redistricting required that individual districts of states would have to vote to give up their power. Rural districts had shown no proclivity to do this and the Warren Court decided to take up the issue.

Archibald Cox argued the case as Solicitor General, and Justice Frankfurter registered his dissent at Justice William Brennan's majority opinion. Both Cox and Frankfurter were men who believed in the philosophy of judicial restraint and each felt genuine respect for the canons of judicial interpretation. In *Baker v. Carr* the Court decided that malapportionment was a denial of the Equal Protection clause of the Fourteenth Amendment, and was therefore justiciable before the Court. This legal reasoning clashed head-on with the ideals of Justice Frankfurter. He issued a stinging rebuttal in his dissent. He lambasted the majority for overruling his opinion in *Colegrove v. Green*. Even though Frankfurter's stance in Colegrove was not controlling, he felt that it was. He noted that the Court was breaching the political questions doctrine that he had laid down in *Colegrove* and that the new ground it was embarking upon was tantamount to rewriting the Constitution. He stated that the issue in *Baker v. Carr* involved the Guaranty clause of the Fifteenth Amendment, not the Equal Protection clause of the Fourteenth Amendment, and for that reason was not justiciable. While his dissent is lucid, and bears the earmarks of constitutional scholarship, it is pregnant with the diatribe of a man angry and hostile. He charged the six-man majority in Baker with acting within the abstract and hypothetical and of missing the issue completely.

Baker v. Carr is considered a watershed in allowing equal protection claims to be heard by the Court when juxtaposed against the political questions doctrine. It shattered the barrier that the doctrine imposed for blacks, and others who sought redress against state legislatures that were denying the one-person, one-vote principle by gerrymandering. It also presented a precedent for future Court majorities to embrace when seeking to shatter further the doctrine used as barrier for judicial redress. Following it, there would come: *Gray v. Sanders* (1963), in which the one-man, one-vote doctrine was articulated; *Wesberry v. Sanders* (1964), in which the doctrine was extended to Congressional districts; and finally, *Reynolds v. Sims* (1964), in which the Supreme Court challenged forty state legislatures to redraw boundaries for both of their houses in compliance with the one-man, one-vote dictum. The Reynolds decision was written by Warren and set to rest the various issues raised but not answered by Baker. The breakthrough in Baker was consolidated in full force in Warren's Reynolds opinion which, not surprisingly, extended his vision of fairness and justice to the mechanics of political representation.

Solicitor General Archibald Cox, Chief Justice Earl Warren, Justice William Brennan, Circuit Court of Appeals Judge David L. Bazelon, the United States Attorney General Robert F. Kennedy, and a few other constitutional scholars understood the far-reaching nature of the decision in *Baker v. Carr*. Without doubt, they understood that the decision opened the opportunity for redress of grievances that had previously been denied. The door to the Court was being pried open by a new Court majority.

Cox was not a strong advocate of the one-person, one-vote principle, but he was deeply concerned with the application of equal protection of the law. Robert Kennedy was a strong advocate of the one-person, one-vote principle, especially in his insistence that the way to overcoming racial strife was the exercise of the franchise by blacks. Chief Justice Warren, Associate Justice Brennan and Judge Bazelon, believed strongly in representative democracy and that the "right to vote freely for the candidate of one's choice is of the essence of a democratic society, and any restrictions on that right strike at the heart of representative government."[13]

Conclusion

It is questionable whether Earl Warren was, in any meaningful sense, a prophet, a philosopher or historian—the three qualities Felix Frankfurter once listed for membership of the High Court.   What Warren did possess was considerable moral character firmly rooted in the rectitude of his heritage and the ability to blend that moral sensibility with political skills. That is an obvious consideration for public life, but one that is all too often absent.

On the equality front Warren was "a dedicated leveller."[14] And it was the active pursuit of that goal which led Eisenhower to proclaim that his selection of Warren was "the biggest damm fool mistake I ever made." Yet is was Warren's outrage at injustice and his commitment to the principle of fairness that provided the motivation for a legal revolution which was long overdo. That judge-led revolution was neither perfect nor problem free, but it struck the chord of justice in compelling fashion.

By definition judicial activism is a two-edged sword.   In Warren's hands, the sword was used to cut away at inequitity and inequality. Others would use the same sword to cut back on the advances made by the Earl of Justice. Such is the non-Hegelian nature of constitutional law.

Through the impact produced by the Court that he led would be of great significance, the exact dimensions of that impact were not always what they first appeared to be. Seventeen years after Warren's death from a heart attack, on the centennial of his birth, schools across the land continued to be marked by racial separation. The monster of de jure segregation had been slain in 1954, yet the courts could not effectively command de facto integration of public education. And on the reapportionment front, the continued population shift from central cities to the suburbs essentially negated that principle as a method of redressing the historical imbalances that had worked against urban America.

These facts, however, do not erase the importance of Warren's 15-year stewardship of the nation's highest court and his willingness to err on the side of too much justice rather than too little.

As Chief Justice, he gave in to requests to head the commission investigating the assassination of President John F. Kennedy which produced the still-debated report that carries Warren's name. While sitting members of the Supreme Court had established precedents for carrying out extra-judicial roles while on the bench, these activities are, at best, a questionable practice. Warren's legacy would have been better served if he had refused the position. His legacy would also have been better served if he had kept politics out of his resignation as Chief Justice. In June 1968 Warren announced his intention to resign for reasons of health to outgoing President Lyndon B. Johnson. The idea was that Johnson would appoint Warren's successor before leaving office. The president's nomination of Justice Abe Fortas however, hit a snag in the Senate where Republicans and Southern Democrats sensed that the upcoming election might send Richard Nixon to the White House. Under a cloud of controversy the Fortas nomination for Chief Justice was withdrawn (and eventually he would leave his seat as an associate justice on the Court). Faced with the Fortas disaster, Warren withdrew his resignation and stayed on the Court until June 1969.

Fortunately greatness does not demand perfection. And Warren was not a perfect man. As attorney general of California he was a willing participant in the internment of Japanese Americans during World War II—an act for which he would later express deep regret. Yet his commitment to justice was anything but shallow. While district attorney of Alameda County, Warren, to us a striking and personal example, refused to sanction improper evidence-gathering techniques even when it came to his father's unsolved murder.

That commitment defined an era that has clearly etched its place in the constitutional law. Changes in politics, policies and personnel have occurred and that era has passed. Its import and impact, however remains living pieces of the fabric of the law and of the search for justice.

Notes

1 Even though the label "strict constructionist" has become part of American political nomenclature, it defies absolute definition. For Richard Nixon, it served as a convenient campaign vehicle to attack American liberalism. He pledged, if elected, to bring the Supreme Court under control. Currently, "strict constructionist" is a colloquialism used by opponents to attack the right of privacy articulated in *Roe v. Wade (1973)*.

2 Jack Bass, *Unlikely Heroes* (New York: Simon and Schuster, 1981) p. 17.

3 The Supreme Court knew that it would take time to implement the changes in public policy called for in its landmark decision in *Brown v. Board of Education I (1954)*. In the final part of that decision the Court asked for amici curiae briefs from the attorneys general of the states affected, from the United States Department of Justice, and others affected, to provide argument "on questions of appropriate decrees." The Court initially set a deadline of October 1, 1954, but felt it necessary to have a full bench to hear argument, so it waited until Justice Harlan was confirmed to succeed Justice Jackson. In the spring of 1955, the Court heard over fourteen hours of arguments. In the decision in *Brown v. Board of Education II (1955)* the Court reversed an envelope of lower court decisions (except that of Delaware) and remanded those cases to the District Courts (again, excepting the Delaware case which was remanded to its state supreme court) "to take such proceedings and enter such orders and decrees consistent with this (Brown) opinion as are necessary and proper to admit to public schools on a racially nondiscriminatory basis with all deliberate speed." The Southern state legislatures and school boards then began a series of actions designed to nullify the effect of school desegregation and they used the language "all deliberate speed" as the legal rationale for continued dual school systems. In the decision *Alexander v. Holmes County Board of Education (1969)* the Supreme Court finally stated that the time for "all deliberate speed" was over and ordered the desegregation of public school to be immediate.

4 Forrest McDonald, *Novus Ordo Seclorum: The Intellectual Origins of the Constitution* (Lawerance, KS: University of Kansas Press, 1985) p. 236.

5 See *The Federalist*, Number 53.

6 Malcolm Feeley and Samuel Krislov, *Constitutional Law* (Glenview, IL: Scott, Foresman, Little and Brown, 1990) p. 34.

7   Earl Warren, *The Memoirs of Chief Justice Earl Warren* (New York: Doubleday and Company, 1977) p. 3.

8   Warren, *The Memoirs*, p. 3

9   Warren, *The Memoirs*, p. 286

10 Warren, *The Memoirs*, p. 286

11 David M. O'Brien, "The Supreme Court: From Warren to Burger to Rehnquist", in *American Politics: Classic and Contemporary Readings*, edited by Allan J. Cigler and Burdett A. Loomis (Boston: Houghton Mifflin Company, 1989) pp. 616-618.

12 Warren, *The Memoirs*, p. 307-308.

13 Quoting from Chief Justice Warren's opinion in *Reynolds v. Sims, 377 U.S. 533 (1964)*.

14 E. Digby Baltzell and Howard Schneiderman: "From Rags to Robes" in *Social Science and Modern Society*, Vol. 28, No. 4 (May/June 1991) p. 527.

Justice William J. Brennan, Jr.

Rodney A. Grunes

By any measure, whether length of service, institutional leadership, or the number and quality of significant opinions, Justice William J. Brennan, Jr. had an enormous impact on constitutional jurisprudence. For thirty-four terms, he was the Supreme Court's most articulate champion of freedom of expression, a strict separation of church and state, the rights of criminal defendants, and expanding equality for racial minorities, women, and the poor. Justice Brennan "so profoundly redefined the framework in which issues are discussed," explains Norman Dorsen, "that he may well be the most influential member of the Court in this century."[1]

Brennan, a Democrat, was appointed to the Supreme Court by Republican President Dwight Eisenhower in 1956. Spanning eight presidencies and three chief justices, Brennan served longer than any brethren except colleagues William O. Douglas and Hugo Black, and, from earlier years, Chief Justice John Marshall, and Justices Stephen J. Field, Joseph Story, and the first John Marshall Harlan. The most productive justice in the history of the United States apart from Douglas, Brennan wrote 425 opinions of the Court, 220 concurring opinions, 492 full or partial dissents, and 16 separate opinions prior to his retirement at the end of the 1989-90 term.[2]

Although always the guardian of liberty, Brennan's leadership on the Court was especially apparent during the 1956-1969 period when Earl Warren served as chief justice. Chief Justice Warren assigned so many significant opinions involving interpretation of the Bill of Rights to his junior colleague that many observers refer to the Warren Court as the Brennan Court.[3]

Justice Brennan's role as the Supreme Court's leading spokesperson for the civil-libertarian creed changed after

Warren's retirement. With the appointment of more conservative justices and the anti-Bill of Rights sentiments of Chief Justices Burger and Rehnquist, Brennan increasingly found himself as the leader of those justices who regularly dissented from the Court's judgment. Nevertheless, because of his exceptional coalition building ability, Brennan continued, on occasion, to marshall majority support for his views in constitutionally significant cases. During his final term, for example, Brennan spoke for the Court in upholding flag-burning[4] and the use of minority preferences by the FCC in awarding broadcast licenses.[5]

Regardless of political ideology, most evaluators have given Justice Brennan high marks for his accomplishments on the Supreme Court. In an assessment of all justices that served on the High Court from its establishment to 1969, for example, Albert P. Blaustein and Roy M. Mersky report that a panel of sixty-five law school deans and professors of law, history, and political science ranked Brennan as a "near great" justice.[6] More recently, commentators have called Brennan the person "who has had more profound and sustained impact upon public policy in the U.S." than any other individual, on or off the Court, over the last quarter century,[7] "the most skillful, most charming, and most intelligent advocate for his activist brand of jurisprudence,"[8] and "the most powerful and influential Supreme Court Justice in the history of the Nation."[9]

Are these evaluations accurate? Based on his record of almost thirty-four years of service, does William J. Brennan, Jr. now qualify as a "great" Supreme Court justice?

In evaluating "greatness," Blaustein and Mersky suggest that a justice's majority and minority positions should be examined for "conspicuous attainments" or contributions to the development of constitutional law. Specifically, exceptional justices should possess the following qualities:

> Scholarship; legal learning and analytical powers; craftsmanship and technique; wide general knowledge and learning; character, moral integrity and impartiality; diligence and industry; the ability to express oneself orally with clarity, logic, and compelling force; openness to change, courage to take unpopular decisions; dedication to the Court as an institution and to the office of Supreme Court justice; ability to carry

a proportionate share of the Court's responsibility in opinion writing; and finally, the quality of statesmanship.[10]

Lacking a contemporary survey of experts, we shall examine Justice Brennan's background, changing roles on the Supreme Court, major opinions, and impact on civil liberties and civil rights law. Finally, attention will be given to evaluations of Brennan's accomplishments by peers and scholars who have studied his contributions to the development of constitutional jurisprudence.

Background

William Joseph Brennan, Jr. was born in 1906 in Newark, New Jersey. The second of eight children of Irish-Catholic immigrant parents, Brennan was raised in a working-class neighborhood. His father, a former boiler stoker and coal heaver, became active in the labor union movement, eventually serving as a member of the Essex County Trades and Labor Council. Later, he served three terms as Director of Public Safety and Police Commissioner.

As a youngster, Brennan attended a parochial grammar school and graduated from a public high school. He worked part-time making change for passengers waiting for trolley cars, delivering milk, and working in a filling station. Although not poor, Brennan was profoundly influenced by the hardships he saw. "What got me interested in people's rights and liberties," Brennan told Nat Hentoff, "was the kind of family and the kind of neighborhood I was brought up in. I saw all kinds of suffering—people had to struggle."[11]

After high school, Brennan earned a degree in economics with honors from the Wharton School of Finance and Commerce of the University of Pennsylvania. Following graduation, he married Marjorie Leonard of East Orange and entered Harvard Law School. A scholarship student, Brennan received his law degree in 1931, graduating in the top 10 per cent of his class. While at Harvard, he nurtured his interest in the rights of the less fortunate by serving as president of the student legal-aid society.

But Brennan did not go into legal aid work. After graduation from Harvard, he joined and later became a partner in
the large establishment firm of Pitney, Hardin & Skinner, spe-
cializing in labor relations from a management perspective.
During World War II, Brennan was an army officer assisting
Secretary of War Robert B. Patterson in procurement and
labor matters. He was discharged as a full colonel.[12]

Following the war, Brennan returned to his law firm and
actively participated in the movement to reform the New Jersey Constitution and its antiquated judicial article. Appearing
before the judiciary committee of the constitutional convention of 1947, Brennan was instrumental in effectuating a completely reorganized court system in the state's new constitution. His work caught the attention of Republican Governor
Alfred E. Driscoll, who, in 1949, appointed Brennan a judge of
the superior court, a state-wide tribunal of original jurisdiction. Upon the recommendation of Chief Justice Arthur T.
Vanderbilt who had been impressed by Brennan's proposals to
relieve congestion and to facilitate speedier trials, Driscoll
elevated Judge Brennan to the appellate division of the Superior Court in 1950 and, two years later, to the New Jersey
Supreme Court.

Given his record as a moderately liberal jurist on an activist
result-oriented state supreme court, Brennan must have been
surprised when, on September 26, 1956, he was called to
Washington, D.C. by Attorney General Brownell and informed
that Republican President Dwight D. Eisenhower wanted to
nominate him, a lifelong Democrat, to replace retiring Justice
Sherman Minton on the U.S. Supreme Court. Yet, his nomination made good political sense.

As Henry J. Abraham has noted, Brennan seemed to meet
Eisenhower's three basic qualifications: relative youth (he was
50 at the time of selection), prior judicial experience (seven
years on New Jersey courts), and strong endorsements by the
American Bar Association and state bar. Equally important,
Brennan's northeast Irish background and Roman Catholicism
were seen as political pluses in a presidential election year
where Republican success required votes from "Eisenhower
Democrats."[13] And, he had the support of Attorney General

Brownell, New Jersey Chief Justice Vanderbilt who said that the nominee "possessed the finest 'judicial mind' that he had known,"[14], and White House Appointments Secretary Bernard Shanley, an old boyhood friend who described Brennan as "extraordinarily brilliant; he has a tremendous personality; and he is genuine from top to toe."[15]

With the exception of Senator Joseph R. McCarthy who accused the nominee of conducting "a guerilla warfare" against legislative committees investigating communism, Brennan's nomination was almost universally applauded. In addition to the New Jersey Bar Association and the A.B.A. which rated the nominee "eminently qualified," enthusiastic support came from the American Judicature Society, the Holy Name Society and other Roman Catholic organizations, the national media, and countless prominent individuals and private groups.

Brennan's response to the nomination was prompt and positive. A recess appointment, the new associate justice began his service on the Supreme Court on October, 16, 1956. Confirmation hearings took place four months later, after Eisenhower's re-election and Congress's return. On March 19, 1957, the United States Senate confirmed Brennan's nomination. Only Senator Joseph McCarthy, the Republican Senator from Wisconsin, voted against confirmation.

Mr. Justice Brennan

Although President Eisenhower and other Republicans may have expected him to adopt a "middle-of-the road" approach, Justice Brennan quickly became a reliable member of the Court's libertarian bloc. This was especially evident in cases involving First Amendment freedoms and procedural fairness. Nevertheless, he avoided the absolutism and doctrinaire liberalism of Justices Black and Douglas and sometimes, as evident in the obscenity area, was willing to limit individual freedom in search of pragmatic solutions to complex constitutional problems.

He also established a special relationship with Chief Justice Earl Warren who Brennan always called "The Chief."

Reflecting their ideological and personal compatibility, Brennan began comparing notes on cases with Warren and, eventually, held weekly meetings, in chambers, prior to Court conferences. Not only did they agree in 89% of the 1400 cases they decided during their thirteen years together on the Court, but the Chief Justice often assigned Brennan the task of speaking for the Court in important cases. "In turning to Brennan," explains Owen Fiss, "Warren could be certain that the task of writing the opinion for the Court was in the hands of someone as thoroughly devoted as he was to the Court as an institution."[16]

Brennan's influence on the Court was greatest during the 1962-1969 period. Here, as the intellectual leader of a liberal activist majority, Brennan authored many of the landmark decisions associated with the Warren Court. He became the chief spokesperson for the values we associate with the Warren Court: freedom of expression, religious liberty, procedural fairness, and equality. "The overall design of the Court's position may have been the work of several minds," notes Fiss, "but it was Brennan who by and large formulated the principle, analyzed the precedents, and chose the words that transformed the ideal into law. Like any master craftsman, he left his distinctive imprint on the finished product."[17]

Justice Brennan's opinions often resulted from great behind-the-scenes skill in building and keeping majority support for his views. "On all the key issues," writes Mark Tushnet, it was Brennan who "put together the coalitions and persuaded the others."[18] A modest man, Brennan has always been uneasy about accepting the title of master coalition builder. As he explained to one interviewer:

> I don't go around cajoling and importuning my colleagues to go along with my point of view. When I have been able to draw a consensus, I have done it by the drafts I circulated among my colleagues. Rather than try to talk something out with another Justice, I sit down and write concrete suggestions. . . . I suggest changes in their drafts, and other Justices will suggest changes in what I've written.[19]

But, as former law clerk Jeffrey Leeds has suggested, Justice Brennan leaves out a crucial detail. While it may true that he didn't personally "buttonhole" his colleagues, Brennan monitored the pulse of the Court by having his law clerks talk regularly with the law clerks of the other Justices.[20]

Perhaps this explains why Brennan's influence on the Supreme Court continued after the retirement of Chief Justice Earl Warren and the appointment of new and more conservative justices by Presidents Nixon and Reagan. Remarkably, few of his major Warren Court opinions were overturned by the Warren Burger and William Rehnquist led Supreme Courts and, at least during the 1970's, Brennan's result oriented "egalitarian activism" often prevailed in gender discrimination, reapportionment, and race-based affirmative action cases.

Increasingly, however, Brennan's views were expressed in dissenting opinions. While he averaged four dissents per term during the Warren Court period, his rate increased to more than 20 per term in cases decided during the Burger and Rehnquist Court periods. In addition to writing 433 full or partial dissenting opinions during the 1970's and 1980's, Brennan issued more than 1500 joint statements with Justice Marshall, dissenting from Court denials of certiorari in death penalty cases. This output has earned Brennan the distinction of being the Supreme Court's greatest dissenter.[21]

In addition to his changing role on the Supreme Court, Brennan broke a long-standing policy and involved himself in three significant extrajudicial activities. First, in 1973, he publicly opposed the creation of a National Court of Appeals, which was proposed by the Freund Committee as a remedy to the Supreme Court's heavy workload. Objecting to the establishment of a new court which would screen cases for Supreme Court review, Brennan argued that this radical proposal would undermine the Supreme Court's "unique mission" of protecting fundamental rights and assuring the uniformity of federal law.[22]

Second, beginning with a 1977 article in the *Harvard Law Review*, Brennan responded to the anti-civil libertarian approach of the Burger Court by suggesting that Warren Court values might be maintained if state and federal courts relied more heavily on state constitutional provisions. In addition, he urged state courts to adopt higher standards than those required by the Constitution in civil liberties cases.[23]

Finally, in what may be an unprecedented exchange, Justice Brennan publicly responded to an attack by Attorney General Edwin Meese on judicial activism and the liberalism of the Warren Court. In what became known as the "Meese-Brennan debate," though neither mentioned the other by name, Brennan denied that liberal activist justices wrote their own policy preferences into the Constitution and rejected the idea of a jurisprudence of "original intent." While conceding that the intent of the framers might be a useful starting point, Brennan emphasized that the Constitution's meaning changes over time and that judges are obligated to interpret the document in a manner that is consistent with the values of the contemporary community. As he explained to the New York City Bar Association in 1987, constitutional interpretation "demands of judges more than proficiency in logical analysis. It requires that we be sensitive to the balance of reason and passion that mark a given age, and the ways in which that balance leaves its mark on the everyday exchanges between government and citizen."[24]

Justice Brennan: Constitutional Rights and Liberties

For more than three decades, Justice Brennan remained faithful to the vision that an expansive interpretation of the Bill of Rights and Civil War amendments was necessary for the creation of a just and humane society. Underlying this vision was his belief in the dignity of all human beings, including the powerless, and the idea that government cannot deny the fundamental rights of any individual. As Chief Justice Earl Warren has explained, these core beliefs "are apparent in the warp and woof of all his opinions."[25]

Having written almost 1200 opinions during more than three decades on the Court, it is only possible to highlight Justice Brennan's most significant contributions to constitutional jurisprudence. Emphasis will be placed on a selection of noteworthy opinions in three areas: the First Amendment freedoms, the rights of the accused, and equality in American life.

The First Amendment Freedoms

Although never an absolutist, Justice Brennan consistently maintained that the power of government to restrict the exercise of First Amendment freedom is extremely narrow. Since freedom of expression is deemed necessary to the development and well-being of our democratic society, "only considerations of the gravest urgency" can be deemed sufficient to justify federal or state intrusion. As Brennan explained in *Roth v. United States* (1957):

> The fundamental freedoms of speech and press have contributed greatly to the development and well-being of our free society and are indispensable to its continued growth. . . . The door barring federal and state intrusion into this area cannot be left ajar; it must be kept tightly closed and opened only the slightest crack necessary to prevent encroachment upon more important interests.[26]

In addition, any governmental regulation touching on the area of freedom of expression must provide procedural safeguards against infringement of constitutionally protected rights.

From Brennan's perspective, his most important majority opinion was the one he wrote in *New York Times v. Sullivan*, the 1964 landmark decision establishing the Court's "actual malice" standard for resolving defamation claims brought by public officials concerning their official conduct. It remains good law today.

Here, L. B. Sullivan, the police commissioner of Montgomery, Alabama, had sued the *Times* for publishing an advertisement, "Heed Their Rising Voices," which contained several factually inaccurate statements. Designed to raise money for the civil rights movement, the advertisement was signed by prominent authors, actors, labor leaders, and black Southern preachers. Although never directly mentioned by name, Sullivan contended that since he was in charge of the police at the time, the advertisement had falsely accused him of conducting "an unprecedented wave of terror" against black student demonstrators by "ringing" the Alabama State College campus with police and trying to starve the students into submission by padlocking their dining room. And it was he who was being charged with trying to intimidate Dr. Martin Luther King, Jr., by assaulting him, bombing his home, and arresting him on false charges. An Alabama jury agreed, awarding $500,000 in damages, the full amount claimed.

Writing for a unanimous Court, Justice Brennan broke new ground when, for the first time, he reversed Alabama's decision and declared that the freedom of speech and press guaranties of the First Amendment limit "a State's power to award damages for libel in actions brought by public officials against critics of their official conduct."[27] Self-government, explained Brennan, requires that "debate on public issues should be uninhibited, robust, and wide-open" and that this could not be assured by leaving libel controversies, as they had in the past, to the common law and procedures of each individual state.

Most important, Brennan articulated a constitutional standard which continues to be used in resolving defamation disputes. Suggesting the need to distinguish between unintentional and malicious misstatements, Brennan stated that a public official is prohibited "from recovering damages for a defamatory falsehood relating to his official conduct unless he proves that the statement was made with 'actual malice' — that is, with knowledge that it was false or with reckless disregard of whether it was false or not."[28]

The "actual malice" standard has become institutionalized. Brennan himself has suggested that it applied to criminal libel actions and to seditious libel, thus rendering unconstitutional the oppressive Alien and Sedition Acts of 1798. In later decisions, the Supreme Court extended the use of Brennan's standard to defamation cases involving public figures in general. And, as Chief Justice Rehnquist's majority opinion in *Flynt v. Falwell* (1988) demonstrates, even today's conservative Supreme Court continues to rely on the arguments and test set forth by Justice Brennan in the *New York Times v. Sullivan*.

Much less successful was Justice Brennan's attempt to find a constitutionally acceptable approach to the problem of obscenity. This was especially evident during the Warren Court period when Justice Brennan was the Court's chief spokesperson on this policy problem. Despite widespread agreement that most sexual expression was entitled to constitutional protection, Brennan was unable to maintain majority support for the approach he developed in his landmark 1957 opinion in *Roth v. United States* and the companion case of *Alberts v. California*.

Samuel Roth had been convicted for mailing obscene circulars and advertising, and an obscene book, in violation of the federal obscenity statute. David Alberts, on the other hand, was convicted for keeping obscene and indecent books for sale, and for writing, composing, and publishing an obscene advertisement of them in violation of California law.

Justice Brennan's *Roth-Alberts* opinion, the first major obscenity decision of the Supreme Court, was ambivalent and confusing, appearing to say one thing while doing another. Using very permissive and libertarian rhetoric, for example, Brennan wrote that "sex and obscenity are not synonymous," and that "all ideas having even the slightest redeeming social importance — unorthodox ideas, controversial ideas, even ideas hateful to the prevailing climate of opinion" are protected under the First Amendment. Yet, the Court affirmed the convictions of Roth and Alberts because obscene ideas are "utterly without redeeming social importance" and not entitled to constitutional protection.

Having accepted a "two-tier" approach to sexual expression, Brennan proposed the following test for distinguishing between constitutionally protected artistic expression and obscenity: "whether to the average person applying contemporary community standards, the dominant theme of the material taken as a whole appeals to prurient interest."[29]

Ironically, this test was intended by Brennan to be more permissive than the popularly used *Hicklin* test, which judged obscenity by the effect of isolated passages upon the minds and morals of young people. But the reliance on such vague and generally undefined terms as "average person" and "contemporary community standards" seemed to lack the precision necessary for the protection of non-obscene and "borderline" sexual expression.

Although Brennan attempted modifications of *Roth*, he never again achieved majority support for his reformulated test for determining obscenity. His only successes occurred when he accepted a "contextual" approach under which the obscenity of material was determined by the particular circumstances surrounding its dissemination or its effect upon children and other special audiences.

Demonstrating honesty and an "openness to change," Brennan abandoned his effort to define obscenity in 1973. While he continued to believe that obscenity was not entitled to constitutional protection, Brennan now conceded that obscenity could never be defined with enough clarity to provide fair notice to those who create and traffic in sexual expression or to prevent the suppression of material that is entitled to First Amendment protection. As he explained dissenting in *Paris Adult Theatre I v. Slaton*: "[A]t least in the absence of distribution to juveniles or obtrusive exposure to unconsenting adults, the First and Fourteenth Amendments prohibit the state and federal governments from attempting wholly to suppress sexually oriented materials on the basis of their allegedly 'obscene' contents."[30]

Although there was no single landmark decision, Justice Brennan was the Supreme Court's most consistent spokesperson for maintaining a high wall of separation between church and state, and during the Burger and Rehnquist Court periods, was its leading supporter of the *Lemon* test for resolving church-state disputes. A devout Roman Catholic, Brennan was the Court's chief antiestablishmentarian.

Brennan's most systematic analysis on the history of the First Amendment's establishment clause and the practice of religion in American life came in what he has described as the "hardest decision" he had to make as a justice, a seventy-five page concurring opinion written in *School District of Abington Township v. Schempp* (1963) striking down state laws mandating the reading each day of at least ten verses from the Bible, without comment, and the recitation of the Lord's Prayer in the public schools.

In what may be his earliest discussion of the limitations of "original intent" jurisprudence, Brennan argued that it was inappropriate to interpret the establishment clause solely on the basis of the eighteenth century ideas. Given the "profound" changes that have taken place since then with respect to religious diversity and educational structure, explained Brennan, practices which might have been acceptable during the time of Madison and Jefferson might be highly offensive to both believers and nonbelievers today. Yet, even the framers, continued Brennan, sincerely believed that " 'members of the Church would be more patriotic, and the citizens of the State more religious, by keeping their respective functions entirely separate.' "[31]

Yet, Brennan was not willing, at least in 1963, to keep church and state entirely separate. By the 1980's, however, he had become a strict separationist. Showing rare judicial courage, Brennan admitted, dissenting in *Marsh v. Chambers* (1983), that he had been "wrong" in *Schempp* when he suggested that invocations before legislative bodies presented no establishment clause problems. Moreover armed with the test established by the Court in *Lemon v. Kurtzman* (1971) to promote separation and neutrality, Brennan voted to strike down aid to parochial schools, the teaching of creationism in the schools, moment of silence legislation, and placing a nativity scene on public property.

Justice Brennan's contribution to First Amendment jurisprudence was also evident in his final years on the bench when, in *Texas v. Johnson* (1989), he spoke for a five member majority in striking down Gregory Lee Johnson's conviction for burning an American flag while protesting outside the Republican National Convention in violation of Texas law.

Although Brennan acknowledged that the flag was a special symbol, he found Johnson's conviction inconsistent with the First Amendment. "If there is a bedrock principle underlying the First Amendment," explained Brennan, "it is that the Government may not prohibit the expression of an idea simply because society finds the idea itself offensive or disagreeable."[32]

The unpopularity of this decision led to Congress adopting the Flag Protection Act of 1989 which made it a federal crime for anyone to knowingly mutilate or deface an American flag. It was quickly challenged by Shawn Eichman who burned an American flag to protest various aspects of American domestic and foreign policy, and by Mark Haggerty who set fire to the flag to protest adoption of the Act itself.

The following year, in *United States v. Eichman* (1990), Brennan again upheld flag burning as a constitutionally protected form of expressive conduct. In one of his last majority opinions, Justice Brennan argued that while flag burning offended many citizens, "[p]unishing desecration of the flag dilutes the very freedom that makes this emblem so revered, and worth revering."[33]

The Rights of the Accused

Although seldom the Court's major spokesperson, Justice Brennan was a loyal member of the liberal Warren Court majority which strengthened the rights of criminal defendants, brought about the *Miranda* revolution, and made virtually all of the provisions of the Bill of Rights pertaining to the criminal justice system applicable to the states through the due process clause of the Fourteenth Amendment. One example was *Malloy v. Hogan* (1964) where Brennan, writing for a five justice majority, held that the Fifth Amendment's privilege against self incrimination was "fundamental" to the concept of ordered liberty and was therefore safeguarded against state action by the Fourteenth Amendment.

However, Justice Brennan's most significant contribution to procedural due process was his numerous dissents in death penalty cases. Believing that even the vilest criminal possessed common human dignity, Brennan spent his last fourteen years arguing that "the evolving standards of decency that mark the progress of a maturing society" would eventually result in the abolition of capital punishment.

According to Justice Thurgood Marshall, a fellow abolitionist, Justice Brennan's greatest contribution to death penalty jurisprudence was his success in imposing procedural limitations in capital punishment cases. His dissent in *McGautha v. California* (1971) is instructive, for there, Brennan disagreed with the Court's majority which had held that neither a bifurcated trial nor statutory guidelines were constitutionally required. Five years later, in *Gregg v. Georgia* (1976), Brennan's dissent became the majority view when five justices held that with proper procedural safeguards, the imposition of the death penalty did not violate the Eighth Amendment's prohibition against "cruel and unusual" punishment.

This offered little satisfaction to Brennan who consistently held that the imposition of the death penalty, for whatever crime and under all circumstances, constituted cruel and unusual punishment. He articulated this view most systematically concurring in *Furman v. Georgia* (1972), the short-lived Burger Court landmark decision striking down the death penalty as "cruel and unusual" punishment when procedural safeguards were absent.

William Henry Furman, a twenty-six year old African-American with a sixth grade education, killed a householder while breaking into the home at night. He shot the deceased through a closed door, Though not psychotic, Furman was diagnosed with "Mental Deficiency, Mild to Moderate."

For Brennan, the Eighth Amendment was designed to protect Furman for it absolutely prohibited the infliction of "uncivilized and inhuman punishments." This conclusion is based on four principles: punishment by death is unusually severe and degrading; there is a strong probability that it is imposed arbitrarily, especially with respect to minorities; contemporary society has totally rejected death as a general punishment; and there is no evidence that the death penalty deters the commission of other capital crimes more effectively than less severe punishment. "The function of these principles," explained Brennan, "is to enable a court to determine whether a punishment comports with human dignity. Death, quite simply, does not."[34]

Equality in American Life

While Justice Brennan was a champion of traditional civil liberties, he will also be remembered for his intellectual leadership and compassion in the area of equal protection analysis.

Whether the issue was political, racial, gender, or economic equality, Brennan forcefully articulated the egalitarian ethic. On all of these issues, Justice Brennan's jurisprudence tended to favor the underdog and powerless in American society and promoted an expansive reading of the equal protection clause of the Fourteenth Amendment.

Apart from *New York Times Co. v. Sullivan*, perhaps Justice Brennan's most significant contribution to our democratic polity was his majority opinion in *Baker v. Carr* (1962). Not only did this decision provide the powerless access to federal courts, but it also led directly to the reapportionment revolution and the establishment of the "one person, one vote" principle.

At issue in *Baker* was the failure of the Tennessee legislature to reapportion its state legislative districts as required by the state's Constitution since 1901. Because of urbanization, this meant that 37 percent of Tennessee voters elected over 60 percent of the State Senate and 40% of the voters elected 64 percent of the House members. In short, rural voters exercised disproportionate voting power at the expense of city dwellers.

Overturning the 1946 Supreme Court decision in *Colegrove v. Green*, Justice Brennan declared that Baker and other urban voters had a constitutionally guaranteed right under the equal protection clause of the Fourteenth Amendment to have the federal courts decide whether they had suffered discrimination because of Tennessee's failure to reapportion its legislature. Legislative reapportionment was not, as the *Colegrove* Court had suggested, a "political question" outside the jurisdiction of federal courts.

In later cases, Brennan insisted on good faith efforts to achieve maximum population equality in legislative apportionment cases. Moreover, as his majority opinion in *Karcher v. Daggett* (1983) indicated, attainment of absolute equality was also required in congressional redistricting under the "equal representation" requirement of Art. I, §2 of the Constitution.

Justice Brennan was also a powerful voice for racial equality, especially in school desegregation and affirmative action cases. Although he came to the Court after *Brown v. Board of*

Education I & II (1954 and 1955), Justice Thurgood Marshall credits Brennan's majority opinion in *Green v. School Board of New Kent County* (1968) as doing the most to restore "Brownian" motion to the Fourteenth Amendment following years of Southern resistance to integration.

In *Green*, the Warren Court unanimously struck down a county's "freedom of choice" plan because it did not lead to the dismantling of the dual school system. In Brennan's view, the *Brown* decisions imposed "an affirmative duty to take whatever steps were necessary to convert to a unitary [public school] system in which racial discrimination would be eliminated root and branch."[35] Noting that the school board had taken eleven years to begin its implementation of *Brown*, Brennan concluded that the burden was on the board to come up with a plan which would disestablish the dual school system "now."

For Brennan, school desegregation extended beyond the southern systems which had been segregated by state law. In *Keyes v. School District #1 Denver* (1973), for example, he argued that when one school board intentionally seeks to segregate students on the basis of race, it can have the effect of establishing a dual school system within an entire district and requiring remedies similar to those used in the South.

The need to eradicate the lingering effects of racial discrimination also marks Justice Brennan's approach to affirmative action cases. Beginning with *Regents of the University of California v. Bakke* (1978), Brennan not only was willing to use race as a "plus" in educational admissions, but sanctioned the use of racial quotas to ameliorate the effects of past societal discrimination.

Bakke, a Caucasian, twice applied for and denied admission at the University of California Medical School at Davis, a state funded and federally supported institution. Applicants with significantly lower grade point averages and standardized test scores were admitted under a separate admissions program that set aside 16 places exclusively for minority students.

Although he did not prevail on whether Bakke should be admitted or the legality of the 16 percent minority quota, Justice Brennan wrote the major defense of preferential admissions. Writing for Justices Marshall, White, and Blackmun, and joined by Justice Powell, Brennan argued that neither Title VI of the Civil Rights Act of 1964 nor the equal protection clause of the Fourteenth Amendment was intended "to bar all race conscious efforts to extend the benefits of federally financed programs to minorities who have been historically excluded from the full benefits of American life."[36]

For Brennan, even racial quotas were permissible as long as they furthered a "benign" or ameliorative purpose and, in addition, did not "stigmatize" the politically powerless in society. He used this reasoning to uphold voluntary employment quotas in *United Steelworkers v. Weber* (1979), and, in *Metro Broadcasting, Inc. v. F.C.C.* (1990), his last majority opinion, to sustain the minority preference policies of the Federal Communications Commission in the awarding of broadcast licenses.

Justice Brennan also sought to promote egalitarianism in another way: through expansion of "suspect" categories for resolution of equal protection claims. Under the Court's "two-tiered" approach, only suspect classifications such as race and alienage required the government to meet a "strict scrutiny" standard in which it had to demonstrate a "compelling" need for the discrimination. Most other claims, especially those involving economic and social policy, were evaluated under the less demanding "ordinary scrutiny" standard which required the state to demonstrate only a "rational" basis for a chosen course of action.

In *Frontiero v. Richardson* (1973), Brennan sought, for the first time, to extend "strict scrutiny" to gender discrimination. At issue here was a federal law under which male members of the uniformed services automatically received extra housing and medical benefits if they had a wife but married servicewomen had to prove that they paid more than half of their husband's living costs to receive similar benefits.

Writing for a four justice plurality, Brennan criticized the attitude of "romantic paternalism" which placed women like Sharron Frontiero "not on a pedestal but in a cage." In his view, classifications based on gender were inherently suspect and that the Air Force had violated equal protection by paying lower benefits to spouses of female military offices than to those of male officers. As Brennan explained:

> what differentiates sex from such nonsuspect statuses as intelligence or physical disability, and aligns with the recognized suspect criteria, is that the sex characteristic frequently bears no relation to ability to perform or contribute to society. As a result, statutory distinctions between the sexes often have the effect of invidiously relegating the entire class of females to inferior legal status without regard to the actual capabilities of its individual members.[37]

Having failed by one vote to have gender discrimination be declared "suspect," Brennan worked to win majority support for a standard that would be more exacting than "ordinary scrutiny." He succeeded in *Craig v. Boren* (1976) when six justices joined him in supporting a "middle-level" approach in which "classifications by gender must serve important governmental objectives and must be substantially related to achievement of those objectives."[38]

Finally, Justice Brennan's egalitarianism is evident in his support for the economically disadvantaged. His majority opinion in *Goldberg v. Kelly* (1970), one of the first cases to recognize the rights of welfare recipients, is representative. Here, writing for a six justice majority, Brennan found that the due process clause of the Fourteenth Amendment required that welfare recipients be afforded the right to an evidentiary hearing prior to termination of benefits. "The opportunity to be heard," explained Brennan. "must be tailored to the capacities and circumstances of those who are to be heard. . . ."[39] Since most welfare recipients lacked sufficient education to write effectively or obtain professional assistance, only a personal appearance with the opportunity to confront and cross-examine government witnesses would protect the rights of poor people.

Justice Brennan: An Assessment

By every standard of measurement, Justice Byron R. White is certainly correct when he observes that William J. Brennan, Jr. "will surely be remembered as among the greatest Justices who have ever sat on the Supreme Court. And well he should be."[40] A prodigious and bright scholar, Brennan participated in more than one-quarter of the cases decided by the Supreme Court in this century and wrote more eloquent and significant opinions than anybody else. Many markedly changed the nation's constitutional and statutory landscape.

While many of Brennan's major contributions have been highlighted above, his overall impact on the law is truly extraordinary. As Nat Hentoff has written, he "greatly expanded and deepened First Amendment rights for the press, for teachers, for students, for book publishers, for moviemakers and for civil rights organizations."[41] In addition, he broadened the rights of the accused, helped assure equal protection for minorities, women, and the less fortunate, and consistently advanced the vision that law is an instrument of "civilizing change." As Court of Appeals Judge Abner J. Mikva has observed, Brennan's "greatest attribute of all was his unshakable belief that one could sit on the highest court, wrestle with the most complex and consequential issues, and still never forget that doing justice was the name of the game."[42]

In doing justice, Brennan wrote exceptionally well-crafted opinions. Whether for the Court, concurring, or dissenting, his opinions have been praised for their clear articulation, reason, logic, meticulous scholarship, choice of language, eloquence, dignity, civility, and passion. As Owen Fiss has observed, successful opinions required "a mastery of legal craft. . . . Everyone on the Court, law clerk and justice alike, admired Brennan's command of vast bodies of learning, ancient and modern. He knew the cases and the statutes, and how they interacted, and understood how the legal system worked and how it might be made to work better."[43]

A master coalition builder, Justice Brennan was both a persuasive advocate and a careful listener. But he also was willing to admit mistakes and change his mind as he did with obscenity and church-state cases. This took some courage since his views on these issues as well as the death penalty and affirmative action were directly contrary to American public opinion. Also, Brennan, a devoutly religious Roman Catholic, was one of the Court's most vigorous supporters of a woman's right to reproductive freedom.

In advocating an expansive Constitution and unpopular opinions, Justice Brennan has been criticized for "over-reaching" and engaging in judicial policy-making. Colleague Byron White disagrees, arguing that Brennan "was absolutely dedicated to the Court as an institution and realized that the Court should not overstep its legitimate role. . . ." But being an honest and caring statesman, suggests White, Brennan often thought, especially during his later years, that the Court's majority "had a far too narrow view of [its] . . . function in this modern world."[44]

What distinguished Justice Brennan's statesmanship was his consistent vision of the proper judicial function. As Thurgood Marshall, another Brennan colleague has explained, "what so distinguished Justice Brennan was his faithfulness to a consistent legal vision of how the Constitution should be interpreted. That vision was based on an unwavering commitment to certain core principles, especially first amendment freedoms and basic principles of civil rights and civil liberties."[45]

But greatness also involves moral integrity. Both supporters and critics of Brennan's jurisprudence acknowledge that he possessed unusual personal qualities. He has been described as loving, caring, warm, generous, good-hearted, honest, kind, and beloved. As Richard A. Posner, a former Brennan law clerk and current judge on the Court of Appeals for the Seventh Circuit, has observed, "[h]is career has been a triumph of character."[46]

Already assessed "near great" in 1969, it seems likely that history will confirm that Justice William J. Brennan, Jr. was one of the Supreme Court's most remarkable and influential justices and entitled to the included among those classified as being "great." As John J. Gibbons, the Seton Hall Law professor from Brennan's home state of New Jersey has concluded: Justice Brennan "'appears far more humane than Holmes, broader in outlook than Brandeis, more practical and flexible than Black, a finer scholar than Warren, more eloquent than Hughes, more painstaking than any of them. He appears, in other words, as the most outstanding justice of the century. . . .'"[47]

Notes

1 Quoted in Nat Henthoff, "Profiles: The Constitutionalist," 66 *The New Yorker*, 45 (March 12, 1990).

2 See Byron W. White, "Tribute to the Honorable William J. Brennan, Jr.," 100 *The Yale Law Journal*, 1113 (1991).

3 Linda Greenhouse, "An Activist's Legacy," *New York Times*, (July 22, 1990), p. 1.

4 *U.S. v. Eichman*, 110 S.Ct. 2404 (1990).

5 *Metro Broadcasting, Inc. v. F.C.C.*, 110 S.Ct. 2997 (1990).

6 Albert P. Blaustein and Roy M. Mersky, "Rating Supreme Court Justices," in Ann M. McLaurin and William D. Pederson (eds.), *The Rating Game in American Politics*. (New York: Irvington Publishers, 1987), pp. 131-147.

7 See Stephen J. Markman and Alfred S. Regnery, "The Mind of Justice Brennan: A 25 Year Tribute," 36 *National Review* 30 (May 18, 1984).

8 See Norman Dorsen, "A Tribute to Justice William J. Brennan, Jr.," 104 *Harvard Law Review* 15 (1990), n. 1, quoting Bruce Fein and William Bradford Reynolds, described as "two Reagan Justice Department officials who had long disagreed with Justice Brennan."

9 Nat Hentoff, "The Justice Breaks His Silence," 38 *Playboy*, 120 (July 1991).

10 Quoted in Henry J. Abraham, *Justices and Presidents*, 2nd edition, (New York: Oxford University Press, 1985), p. 10.

11 Hentoff, *The New Yorker*, p. 46.

12 Elizabeth F. Defeis, "Justice William J. Brennan, Jr.," 16 *Seton Hall Law Review* 429, 430-431 (1986).

13 Abraham, *Justices and Presidents*, pp. 262-263.

14 *Ibid.*, p. 262.

15 Defeis, *Seton Hall Law Review*, p. 432.

16 Owen Fiss, "A Life Lived Twice," 100 *The Yale Law Journal* 1117, 1119 (1991).

17 *Ibid.*

18 Quoted in Greenhouse, *New York Times*, p. 1.

19 Hentoff, *The New Yorker*, p. 59.

20 Jeffrey T. Leeds, "A Life on the Court," *New York Times Magazine*, (October 5, 1986), p. 26.

21 Fiss, *The Yale Law Review*, p. 1125.

22 William J. Brennan, Jr., "The National Court of Appeals: Another Dissent," 40 *University of Chicago Law Review* 473 (1973).

23 William J. Brennan, Jr., "State Constitutions and the Protection of individual Rights," 90 *Harvard Law Review* 489 (1977).

24 Greenhouse, *New York Times*, p. 16.

25 Earl Warren, "Mr. Justice Brennan," 80 *Harvard Law Review* 1, 2 (1966).

26 354 U.S. 476, 488 (1957).

27 *New York Times Co. v. Sullivan*, 376 U.S. 254, 283 (1964).

28 *Ibid.*, pp. 279-280.

29 *Roth v. United States, supra*, at 489.

30 413 U.S. 49, 112-113 (1973).

31 *School District of Abington Township v. Schempp*, 374 U.S. 203, 304 (1963).

32 *Texas v. Johnson*, 109 S.Ct. 2533, 2544 (1989).

33 *U.S. v. Eichman, supra*, at 2410.

34 *Furman v. Georgia*, 408 U.S. 238, 305 (1972).

35 *Green v. School Board of New Kent County*, 391 U.S. 430, 438 (1968).

36 *Regents of the University of California v. Bakke*, 438 U.S. 265, 328 (1978).

37 *Frontiero v. Richardson*, 411 U.S. 677, 686-687 (1973).

38 429 U.S. 190, 197 (1976).

39 *Goldberg v. Kelly*, 397 U.S. 254, 268-269 (1970).

40 White, *The Yale Law Review*, p. 1113.

41   Hentoff, *Playboy*, p. 121.

42   Abner J. Mikva, "A Tribute to Justice William J. Brennan, Jr.," 104 *Harvard Law Review* 9, 12 (1990).

43   Fiss, *The Yale Law Journal*, p. 1120.

44   White, *The Yale Law Journal*, p. 1116.

45   Thurgood Marshall, "A Tribute to Justice William J. Brennan, Jr.," 104 *Harvard Law Review* 1, 1-2 (1990).

46   Richard A. Posner, "A Tribute to Justice William J. Brennan, Jr.," 104 *Harvard Law Review* 13, 14 (1990).

47   John J. Gibbons, "Tribute to Justice Brennan," 74 *Judicature* 242 (February-March 1991).

The Jurisprudence of Justice Lewis Powell, Jr.[*]

William D. Bader

Judicial Greatness

There is impressive evidence that Justice Lewis Powell will be regarded in historical perspective as one of our greatest justices. Supreme Court commentators have often referred to the court on which Justice Powell served as "The Powell Court", despite the nominal stewardship of Chief Justice Warren Burger.[1]   Such was Powell's influence on the course of Supreme Court jurisprudence through his decisive votes and authorship in important cases that he was labelled "the most powerful man in America" by many during his 15½ year tenure.[2]

Judge Richard A. Posner in his pioneering work on the empirical study of judicial reputation counted the number of law review articles published from 1982 until 1989 that mention the names of prominent judges and legal scholars, past and present.[3] In the ranking of these data, both in the "well-known judges" category and in the "judges and scholars" category, Justice Powell places third in number of citations.[4] This is compelling evidence of Justice Powell's important impact on modern legal culture.

In 1978, a poll was taken of prominent legal scholars and practitioners to determine their assessments of the sitting Supreme Court justices. Significantly, Lewis Powell was rated as "the best justice" in this survey.[5]

In the middle of Justice Powell's Supreme Court tenure, an elite group of lawyers from the Solicitor General's Office, who argue cases before the Supreme Court, took an informal vote as to which justice they would choose to hear all cases if the

Court were to be a court of one.[6] Justice Powell won that vote easily.[7]

Finally, Gerald Gunther of Stanford Law School has analysed Justice Powell's opinions using Judge Learned Hand's criteria for judicial quality.[8] Specifically, Hand most valued detachment from personal prejudices and ideologies and the ability and will to deal with the complexities of a case.[9] On the basis of these factors, Gunther concludes that Justice Powell has been the model judge of his judicial generation.[10]

Background[11]

Lewis F. Powell, Jr. was born in 1907 in Suffolk, Virginia and spent his formative years in Richmond. In 1929, he graduated from Washington and Lee University in Lexington, Virginia where he was elected to Phi Beta Kappa and was chosen president of his class.[12] Powell graduated first in his class from the Law School of Washington and Lee in 1931 and spent the following year at Harvard University pursuing legal graduate study with Felix Frankfurter and Roscoe Pound, among others.

After Harvard, Powell commenced the private practice of law in Richmond, a practice which would lead to his standing as the top corporate litigator in Virginia. Justice Powell has described the partners at Hunton and Williams, the great Richmond law firm he helped build, revealing as much about himself as about them:

> They had a perception of the practice of law that I admired. Law was one of the ancient professions. The primary purpose of practicing was not to make money.

During World War II, Powell served with high distinction in North Africa and Europe as an Army-Air Force intelligence officer. In this capacity, he also saw a considerable amount of combat.

Lewis Powell always maintained an active interest in the civic affairs of Richmond as well as the State of Virginia in general. Significantly, he served as chairman of the Richmond City School Board during the controversy over desegregation, and was able to keep the public schools from closing as they had in other cities. Of equal importance, Powell played a role as a co-drafter of the revised Virginia Constitution in 1969.

Early in his career, Powell assumed a position of leadership in the organized bar. His activities culminated in the presidency of the American Bar Association, the American College of Trial Lawyers and the American Bar Foundation, respectively.

In 1971, President Nixon wished to nominate Powell to be an Associate Justice of the United States Supreme Court. He was initially reluctant to accept because he had developed a zest for private practice and had also thought himself too old for such a position. His sense of patriotic duty prevailed, however, and Powell consented to the nomination.

Similarly, in 1987, after 15½ years of service, he stepped down as Associate Justice out of a sense of duty, not only to the nation, but to the Court, which he had grown to love. He was concerned that illness had the potential of seriously and unpredictably disrupting his work, thereby affecting the entire Court.[13]

Since that time, Justice Powell has maintained Chambers at the U.S. Supreme Court. In addition, he regularly sits on various U.S. Courts of Appeal.[14] The appeals briefs which are lined along or piled upon virtually every piece of furniture in his chambers indicate that "retired" is merely a legal fiction when applied to Lewis Powell.

Justice Powell's Balancing Jurisprudence

Justice Powell has been the Supreme Court's most articulate spokesman for a case-by-case judicial decision making process that applies a balancing approach to competing legal interests. In his judicial balancing, he carefully focuses on the facts of each case and the disparate values involved. Justice Powell gleans the meaning and import of competing legal values from Supreme Court precedent, Constitutional or statutory language, and, occasionally and more broadly, from "this Nation's history and tradition".[15] Justice Powell's balancing method leads to the fact-specific result in a case rather than serving as the rationalization for a pre-determined theoretical outcome. Theoretical constructs develop in an incremental fashion after many case-by-case resolutions of specific legal conflicts in a manner which is consistent with the Aristotelian model of political philosophy where argument is "to", not "from", first principles.[16]

A good example of Justice Powell's balancing is provided in his concurring opinion in *Branzburg* v. *Hayes* where a journalist's claims of absolute privilege not to disclose sources were countered by his absolute duty to provide relevant testimony in criminal matters.[17] He carefully examined precedent and history, then rejected the two theoretical extremes for a case-by-case weighing of the relevant constitutional values.[18] One must analyse the facts in each case, Justice Powell concluded, to determine whether a journalist's compelled testimony would significantly damage his ability to obtain information from confidential sources, and if so, whether the administration of criminal justice would, under the circumstances, necessitate such impairment.

In *Gertz* v. *Robert Welch, Inc.*, the question for the Court was one of extending the public figure defamation privilege of the press to a public issues privilege. Justice Powell, writing for the Court, characteristically framed the issue in terms of striking a balance.[19] Specifically, he wrote that ". . . some tension necessarily exists between the need for a vigorous and uninhibited press and the legitimate interest in redressing wrongful injury . . .",[20] requiring a proper accommodation of the competing concerns.[21] He noted that private persons, unlike public officials or public figures, have not "voluntarily exposed themselves to increased risk of injury from defamatory falsehood." Furthermore, private persons, he observed, lack access to the channels of communication and "are therefore more vulnerable to injury, and the state interest in protecting them is correspondingly greater."[22] Justice Powell then reached an accommodation among the competing legal values whereby private individuals, as distinguished from public officials or public figures, may be permitted to sue the media for libel under state law in cases involving public issues, using a liability standard which is lower than "actual malice", as long as the liability is fault-based; punitive damages are restricted to instances where the media is shown to have had knowledge of falsity or to have displayed reckless disregard for the truth.[23]

With respect to the Fourth Amendment, Justice Powell has noted that since it ". . . is not absolute in its terms, our task is to examine and balance the basic values at stake".[24] In *U.S.* v. *U.S. District Court for the Eastern District of Michigan*, he confronted the question of whether the President had constitutional or statutory authority to order electronic surveillance without prior judicial permission in cases involving internal security.[25] Powell wrote for the Court:

> Resolution [requires] sensitivity both to the Government's right to protect itself from unlawful subversion and attack and to the citizen's right to be secure in his privacy against unreasonable Government intrusion.[26]

Justice Powell, after balancing these conflicting constitutional values, found such surveillance to be a violation of the Fourth Amendment.[27]

Justice Powell has successfully applied his case-by-case balancing process to the question of the applicability of the Bill of Rights to the states through the Fourteenth Amendment. In developing his position, he rejected selective incorporation of superior rights as established by Justice Cardozo in *Palko* v. *Connecticut*,[28] as well as total incorporation, the position long espoused by Justice Black.[29] Instead, Justice Powell has advocated a careful examination of each alleged violation of due process of law, weighing the conflicting interests to determine whether the petitioner obtained an essentially fair trial.[30] His concurring opinion in *Argersinger* v. *Hamlin* is an exemplification of this approach. Here the Court extended the incorporation of the Sixth Amendment right to appointed counsel for indigents to include all state cases where incarceration was a possible punishment. Justice Powell opposed incorporation and propounded a case-by-case determination balancing such factors as the length of possible sentence, the defendant's competence, and the community's attitude toward the defendant.[31]

Implicit in a case-by-case balancing approach is a rejection of broad iron-clad rules. Justice Powell acknowledges that simplistic formulas may "achieve greater analytical tidiness", but usually at high cost to life and law.[32] He has therefore rigorously avoided, in his words, "mechanically applied" doctrines.[33] He truly deals with the conflicting constitutional values which underlie many cases rather than ignoring them because they cannot be accommodated within the sweep of some Grand Theory. His jurisprudence represents the most faithful embodiment of Holmes' admonishment that "To rest upon a formula is a slumber that, prolonged, means death". Most importantly, Justice Powell's case-by-case balancing methodology clearly reflects the underlying approach demanded of Article III judges by our Constitutional tradition. This approach requires a narrow focus on individual litigants and their particular case or controversy at bar. Sweeping rules, be they "liberal" or "conservative" in substance, amount to legislation by any other name, and must be left to the democratically elected legislative branch.

Stare Decisis

Another cornerstone of Justice Powell's jurisprudence that has been traditional among judges in our constitutional culture, as distinguished from legislators, is the doctrine of stare decisis or institutional respect for precedent. Justice Powell has indicated that he believes adherence to stare decisis is essential to a stable and predictable set of rules on which Americans might rely in forming their behavior.[34] He has also written about an even more important rationale for stare decisis:

> Perhaps the most important and familiar argument for stare decisis is one of public legitimacy. The respect given the Court by the public and by the other branches of government rests in large part on the knowledge that the Court is not composed of unelected judges free to write their policy views into law. Rather, the Court is a body vested with the duty to exercise the judicial power prescribed by the Constitution. An important aspect of this is the respect that the Court shows for its own previous opinions.[35]

It is an illustrative example that Justice Powell dissented in *Bates* v. *State Bar*[36] and remarked in conference that the Court's opinion which held that lawyers have a right to advertise ". . . destroyed the essential character of our profession".[37] Nevertheless, in *In re R.M.J.*, the next case on lawyer advertising, Justice Powell wrote for the Court striking down regulations which impeded such advertising.[38] He explained to the conference that despite his strongly held negative views of the Court's opinion in *Bates* v. *State Bar*, stare decisis required that *Bates* be the controlling precedent in *R.M.J.*.[39] In his respect for stare decisis, we once again view Lewis Powell as an exemplar of the great Article III tradition rather than a legislator in judicial robes.

Federalism

The important substantive value which serves as a uniting theme for the corpus of Justice Powell's case-by-case jurisprudence is federalism. He acknowledges that his deep respect for the constitutional requirement of states' rights, indeed a dual federalism in American constitutional law and history, might be understood in terms of his formative Virginia experiences.[40]

As a result of his chairmanship of the Richmond City School Board during turbulent racial conflict of the 1950s and 1960s and his role in redrafting the Virginia State Constitution, Justice Powell relates that he "experienced firsthand the crucial importance of a state's citizenry exercising its rightful control over local institutions and the solution of local problems".[41] Justice Powell also thinks that "the social and cultural richness of a Virginia upbringing makes for deep attachments to one's state, tends to inhibit migration to other states, and generally facilitates a deep appreciation for the integrity of the state as a political entity".[42] In his own case, he believes that appreciation for such integrity was heightened by his awareness of and pride in the long and distinguished history of his family in the affairs of Virginia.[43]

Justice Powell strongly feels that "Constitutional provisions providing for state sovereignty are now out of fashion for many ideologues, and are often reduced to virtual dead letters".[44] He points out this disturbing trend by noting that "In the 1950s, the burden of proof was always on the proponents of state intervention, but today it is on the opponents, virtually every time".[45]   Justice Powell also indicates that his only Supreme Court colleague to evidence an impressive degree of respect for federalism as a value has been Justice Sandra Day O'Connor.[46] He speculates that "Her many activities in state affairs prior to acceding to the high court probably provided her, as they did me, with a better understanding of federalism in constitutional perspective".[47]

Justice Powell is especially concerned about the integrity and, indeed, the essential independence of state courts today.[48] "The Supreme Court of Virginia is one of the finest tribunals anywhere, and is composed of Virginians who possess the highest erudition and character. Why should their decisions be subject to reversal by one federal judge?", he asks with a trace of indignation.[49]

Justice Powell's opinions abound with the boldest expressions propounding federalism that can be found in modern jurisprudence. Particularly important are his Tenth Amendment opinions. The Tenth Amendment states:

> The powers not delegated to the United States by the Constitution, nor prohibited by it to the States are reserved to the States, respectively, or to the people.

In *FERC* v. *Mississippi*, for example, Congress had enacted a law, using the Commerce Clause as authority, to impose federal procedural requirements on state administrative bodies regulating utilities.[50]   The state regulatory bodies were to remain, but, through selective pre-emption, Congress imposed its authority in certain areas. Powell wrote that Congress was not displaying proper deference for federalism.[51]   He disagreed with the majority reasoning that Congress has the power to completely pre-empt all state utility regulatory activities: "Under this 'threat of pre-emption' reasoning, Congress . . . could reduce the States to federal provinces".[52]   Justice Powell then concluded:

. . . 'the general rule, bottomed deeply in the belief in the importance of State control of state judicial procedure, is that the federal law takes the state courts as it finds them. I believe the same principle must apply to other organs of state government'.[53]

In *EEOC* v. *Wyoming*, another Commerce Clause case, Justice Powell again championed federalism by way of Tenth Amendment precedent as well as the Amendment's intellectual and historical underpinnings.[54] He strongly dissented from the Court's opinion which, ignoring the Tenth Amendment, held that state and local government agencies are subject to federal age discrimination law based on the Commerce Clause. He concluded:

Although its contours have changed over two centuries, state sovereignty remains a fundamental component of our system that this court has recognized again and again . . . In sum, all of the evidence reminds us of the importance of the principles of federalism in our constitutional system. The Founding Fathers, and those who participated in the earliest phase of constitutional development, understood the States' reserved powers to be a limitation on the power of Congress — including its power under the Commerce Clause.[55]

Justice Powell's consistent opposition to the ease with which state court criminal convictions are reviewed under the federal habeas corpus statute can really be understood in terms of his federalism jurisprudence. In his dissenting *Rose* v. *Mitchell* opinion, for example, he passionately urged restraint in granting such review because "contrary to principles of federalism, a lower federal court is asked to review not only a state trial court's judgment, but almost invariably the judgment of the highest court of the state as well".[56]

The Fourteenth Amendment has been a favorite vehicle for those who have wished to abridge states' rights. Justice Powell is the leading spokesman for a Fourteenth Amendment jurisprudence which is true to the amendment's spirit while respecting the requirements of federalism.

In the late nineteenth and early twentieth centuries, the justices gave primacy to economic rights and prevented states, through substantive use of the Fourteenth Amendment's Due Process Clause, from implementing social welfare legislation that affected business relations.[57] By the Warren era, the justices' personal philosophies had changed, and the Court accorded selected personal rights a preferential Constitutional status, striking down state laws of a limiting nature, by using the Fourteenth Amendment's Equal Protection Clause as the functional equivalent of substantive due process.[58] With this technique, they implemented a policy whereby a panoply of actions by state legislatures and state courts were negated in the name of a special solicitude for the societal groups it felt deserving and new rights it considered fundamental. The Warren Court's foray into equal protection as the functional equivalent of substantive due process, combined with their wholesale incorporation of preferred rights from the Bill of Rights into the Due Process Clause (see above), dramatically altered the traditional relationship between the federal and state governments.

Justice Powell's case-by-case balancing jurisprudence provided an excellent method for countering the political subversion of the Fourteenth Amendment and the consequent abridgement of the federalism he has so prized. As mentioned above, he rejected the selective incorporation of preferred rights from the Bill of Rights into the Due Process Clause for a case-by-case weighing of the facts to determine whether fundamental fairness was provided. This approach left the political and judicial institutions of the states intact while discerning whether due process was accorded the litigants in each case.

Similarly, Justice Powell recognized the danger posed to federalism by using the Equal Protection Clause as the functional equivalent of substantive due process in order to create new Constitutional rights for particular groups or classes. His opinion for the Court in *San Antonio Independent School District v. Rodriguez* was a landmark decision that signaled the demise of such Equal Protection policy-making.[59] In *Rodriguez*, Mexican-American parents attacked the Texas system of financing public schools on Equal Protection grounds. Since state funds were divided among school districts on the basis of each district's assessed property, the parents alleged that discrepancies among districts represented unconstitutional discrimination based on the "suspect" classification of wealth, with respect to the fundamental right of education. Justice Powell, in rejecting the Equal Protection claim, wrote that a fundamental right must have an explicit or implicit basis in the Constitution. There is no such Constitutional basis for education, he held.[60] Furthermore, he held that the poor, as a class, have not been subjected to a history of purposeful unequal treatment nor relegated to political powerlessness and should not be considered a "suspect class".[61] Justice Powell therefore held that the state action in question should not be reviewed under the "strict scrutiny" standard, but, rather, under the traditional and deferential "rational relationship to legitimate state interests" standard.[62] Such a "rational relationship" exists in this case, to be sure.

Justice Powell's deep respect for federalism is key to understanding his approach to *Rodriguez*. Significantly, he wrote:

> It must be remembered, also, that every claim arising under the Equal Protection Clause has implications for the relationship between national and state power under our federal system. Questions of federalism are always inherent in the process of determining whether a State's laws are to be accorded the traditional presumption of constitutionality, or are to be subjected instead to rigorous judicial scrutiny. While "the maintenance of the principles of federalism is a foremost consideration in interpreting any of the pertinent constitutional provisions under which this Court examines state action," it would be difficult to imagine a case having a greater potential impact on our federal system than the one now before us, in which we are urged to abrogate systems of financing public education presently in existence in virtually every State.[63]

Conclusion

In conclusion, given historical perspective, it is likely that Justice Lewis Powell will rank among our greatest Supreme Court Justices. His case-by-case balancing jurisprudence which respects stare decisis exemplifies judging as understood in our Constitutional tradition. As such, his work stands in favorable contrast to much of the legislation which masquerades as judicial opinion and fills the pages of the United States Reports. Justice Powell's singular sensitivity to the forgotten rights of states in our Constitutional ethic and his bold and articulate espousal of a dual federalism counter a centralized, uniform and bureaucratic vision of government with grass roots democracy itself.

Notes

* I wish to express respectful appreciation to Justice Lewis Powell who has generously shared his thoughts with me on various aspects of his jurisprudence. I am grateful to the library staff of the City University of New York School of Law for their kind assistance. Finally, I wish to thank my wife, Pearl Gong, M.D., for her wise assistance, moral support and beef chow fun.

1 Ethan Bronner, *Battle for Justice: How the Bork Nomination Shook America* (New York: Anchor Books, 1989), p. 17.

2 Id.

3 Richard A. Posner, *Cardozo: A Study in Reputation* (Chicago: The University of Chicago Press, 1990), pp. 74-77.

4 Id. at pp. 77-78.

5 Alpheus Thomas Mason, *The Supreme Court from Taft to Burger*, (Baton Rouge: Louisiana State University Press, 1979), p. 300.

6 David Westin, "Justice Powell and His Law Clerks", *Supreme Court Historical Society Yearbook 1987*, p. 17.

7 Id.

8 Gerald Gunther, "A Tribute to Justice Lewis F. Powell, Jr.", 101 Harv L. Rev. 409, 413 (1987).

9 Id. at pp. 413-414.

10 Id. at pp. 410-414.

11 Unless otherwise specified, the source of information in this section is Anne Hobson Freeman, *The Style of a Law Firm: Eight Gentlemen from Virginia* (Chapel Hill: Algonquin Books of Chapel Hill, 1989), pp. 147-169.

12 Leon Friedman, ed., *The Justices of the United States Supreme Court: Their Lives and Major Opinions*, vol. 5 (New York: Chelsea House Publishers, 1980).

13 Interview conducted by author with Justice Lewis F. Powell, Jr. at the U.S. Supreme Court on October 3, 1990.

14 Id.

15 *Moore* v. *City of East Cleveland*, 431 U.S. 494, 503 (1977) (plurality opinion).

16 Aristotle, *Nichomachaen Ethics*, reprinted in *The Complete Works of Aristotle* (J. Barnes ed., 1984), p. 1731.

17 *Branzburg* v. *Hayes*, 408 U.S. 665, 709 (1972)

18 Id.

19 *Gertz* v. *Robert Welch, Inc.*, 418 U.S. 323, 342 (1974).

20 Id.

21 Id.

22 Id. at pp. 344-345.

23 Id. at pp. 347-349.

24 *U.S.* v. *U.S. Dist. Court for the E. Dist. of Mich.*, 407 U.S. 297, 314 (1972).

25 Id.

26 Id. at p. 299.

27 Id. at pp. 302-303.

28 *Palko* v. *Connecticut*, 302 U.S. 319 (1937).

29 Hugo L. Black, *A Constitutional Faith* (New York: Alfred A. Knopf, 1968).

30 *Argersinger* v. *Hamlin*, 407 U.S. 25 (1972) (Concurring opinion); *Crist* v. *Bretz*, 437 U.S. 28 (1978) (Dissenting opinion).

31 *Argersinger* v. *Hamlin*, 407 U.S. 25, 65 (1972).

32 *Wolman* v. *Walter*, 433 U.S. 229, 263 (1977) (Concurring in part and dissenting in part).

33 *Young* v. *American Mini-Theaters, Inc.*, 427 U.S. 50, 76 (1976) (Concurring opinion).

34 Lewis Powell, "Stare Decisis and Judicial Restraint", *Journal of Supreme Court History 1991*, p. 16.

35 Id.

36 *Bates* v. *State Bar*, 433 U.S. 350 (1977).

37 Bernard Schwartz, *The Ascent of Pragmatism: The Burger Court in Action*, (Reading, MA: Addison-Wesley Publishing Co., Inc., 1990), p. 135.

38 *In re R.M.J.*, 455 U.S. 191 (1982).

39 Supra note 37.

40 Interview conducted by author with Justice Lewis F. Powell, Jr. at the U.S. Supreme Court on October 3, 1990.

41 Id.

42 Id.

43 Id.

44 Id.

45 Id.

46 Id.

47 Id.

48 Id.

49 Id.

50 *FERC* v. *Mississippi*, 456 U.S. 742, 771 (1982) (Concurring in part and dissenting in part).

51 Id. at p. 772.

52 Id. at p. 773.

53 Id. at p. 774 (quoting Hart, *The Relations Between State and Federal Law*, 54 Colum. L. Rev. 489, 508 (1954).

54 *EEOC* v. *Wyoming*, 460 U.S. 226 (1983) (Dissenting opinion).

55 Id. at pp. 273-275.

56 *Rose* v. *Mitchell*, 443 U.S. 545, 579 (1979).

57 Raoul Berger, *Government by Judiciary: The Transformation of the Fourteenth Amendment* (Cambridge: Harvard University Press, 1977), pp. 265-282.

58 Id.

59 *San Antonio Independent School District* v. *Rodriguez*, 411 U.S. 1 (1973).

60 Id. at pp. 33-35.

61 Id. at p. 27.

62 Id. at p. 39.

63 Id. at p. 44.

The Reagan Supreme Court Appointees

Barbara A. Perry
Henry J. Abraham

I

Ronald Wilson Reagan twice attained the presidency with overwhelming margins. In 1980 he garnered forty-four states; in 1984 only Minnesota (the home state of his opponent, President Jimmy Carter's Vice President, Walter Mondale) and the District of Columbia denied him their electoral votes. Notwithstanding persistent and pronounced opposition to him in the academic world and among the most influential segments of the media, President Reagan enjoyed a consistent popularity that rivaled, if indeed it did not exceed, that of the century's two other enormously popular-in-the-public-eye chief executives, Frankling D. Roosevelt and Dwight D. Eisenhower. However controversial Reagan's clearly stated governmental agenda may have been, he possessed, as did "F.D.R." and "Ike," a personality that, in the words of his Secretary of Defense, Caspar W. Weinberger, "was so open and friendly, and . . . so funny, that he always succeeded in making people around him laugh and feel comfortable and happy at the same time he was inspiring great loyalty."[1]

The agenda demonstrably included an attempt to alter the contemporary jurisprudential approach of the federal judiciary. Although his immediate predecessor, Carter, did not have any opportunity to appoint a member of the Supreme Court of the United States, he had been able to nominate and see Senate-confirmed more members of the federal judiciary in absolute numbers than any other president in the country's history (although in percentage terms he was exceeded by Presidents Franklin Roosevelt, Eisenhower, Truman, and

Nixon, and would be by Reagan in absolute numbers as well as percentage terms). Thus, while there was no Carter Supreme Court appointee, the president from Georgia's judicial selections left a considerable mark on the judicial process: Jimmy Carter's commitment to the burgeoning egalitarianism of the second half of the twentieth century resulted in the appointment of almost one hundred women and non-whites, whose numbers in the federal judiciary had theretofore been indeed small. In short, he embraced a sociopolitical obligation of "representativeness" based on gender, race, and ethnicity. As his first Attorney General, ex-Federal Judge Griffin Bell, testified to both critical and approbative members of the Senate Committee on the Judiciary in 1979: "Mr. Carter was prepared to appoint to the Federal bench a black, Hispanic, or woman lawyer who was found to be less qualified than a white male as long as the appointee was found qualified."[2] President Carter had candidly admitted to a December 1978 press conference: "If I didn't have to get Senate confirmation of appointees, I could tell you flatly that twelve per cent of my judicial appointments would be black and three per cent would be Spanish-speaking, and forty per cent would be women and so forth."[3]

As a candidate in his successful run for the presidency in 1980, Reagan had made crystal clear his opposition to any type of racial or other quotas (as indeed he had done in his successful quest for the Republican nomination in 1976), and early in 1981 the new Attorney General, Mr. Reagan's friend and counsel from California, Williamm French Smith, issued a "Memorandum on Judicial Selection Procedures" that emphasized the new Administration's determination to return to "traditional criteria" in selecting jurists, promising that "federal judges would be chosen on the basis of merit and quality."[4] The overall guideline was the principle of a commitment to "strict construction" of the Constitution rather than a liberal agenda based upon a concept of "judicial activism," characterized by some as judicial lawmaking and/or social engineering by non-elected jurists. The Administration's policy was quickly attacked as requiring conservative "litmus tests" as a prolegomenum for nomination. Whatever the merits of these consistently denied charges may be, comparative ratings of the American Bar Association on the qualification of all appointed federal judges during the Carter and Reagan Administrations were: "Exceptionally Well Qualified" (Carter, 6.1 and Reagan, 7.1%); "Well Qualified" (Carter 49.6 and Reagain, 48.1%); "Qualified" (Carter, 43.1 and Reagan, 44.8%); and "Unqualified (Carter, 1.5 and Reagan, 0.0%).[5]

It has been the practice by all of America's presidents, barring none, that the plums that comprise federal judicial appointments go overwhelmingly to members of the incumbent president's political party.[6] Ronald Reagan's Administration was no exception with his 94.4 per cent Republican appointees, a figure somewhat below his predecessors' averages.[7] In a country that now (mid-1990) boasts of, or laments, the presence of 800,000 lawyers, surely the vacancies that regularly occur in the relatively small federal judiciary (*circa* 1,300, including bankruptcy judges) are fillable qualitatively by members of the president's political party.

Beyond the obvious requirement of Republican identifiability, the Reagan Administration, presumably with the president's imprimatur and his Department of Justice's procedure and substantive application, opted for candidates who (1) were relatively youthful (under fifty for the lower federal benches); (2) had judicial or law school teaching experience (for the appellate levels); (3) voiced "judicial restraint" in their role conceptualization; and (4), to the extent decently ascertainable, were in general sympathy with the philosophical thrust of the Administration.

Fate would permit President Reagan to nominate almost fifty percent of the federal judiciary during his eight years in office; and, had the Senate not become majoritarianly Democratic in 1986, he would have attained an even higher percentage. Among the 374 federal constitutional court slots he filled were four to the highest tribunal in the land, the Supreme Court of the United States: Associate Justices Sandra Day O'Connor (1981), Antonin Scalia (1986), and Anthony M. Kennedy (1988), and the promotion of Associate Justice William H. Rehnquist to chief justice (1986). As the following discussion will manifest, although the president saw the above-indicated quartet confirmed by the Senate, Justice Kennedy took the seat originally intended for Judge Robert H. Bork of the United States Court of Appeals for the District of Columbia, whose dramatic rejection by the Senate followed what was arguable the most bitterly contested nomination battle in the Court's now 200-year-plus history.

II

Despite Reagan's repudiation of his predecessor's policy of gender and race representation on the federal judiciary, he promised in the 1980 campaign: "One of the first Supreme Court vacancies in my administration will be filled by the most qualified woman I can find, one who meets the high standards I will demand for all my appointments."[8] The opportunity to fulfill his campaign pledge and nominate the first woman member of the Court came within the initial six months of his presidency. On June 18, 1981, in what constituted a major surprise in many normally knowledgeable circles, Justice Potter Stewart publicly announced his retirement from the Supreme Court. Members of the Reagan Administration, however, had known of Stewart's intention to step down since March and had informed the president on April 21, while the latter was still recovering from the assassination attempt one month earlier. Significantly, this advance notice of Stewart's departure gave the Administration three months to search quietly for a nominee without political pressure from outside and without media speculation.[9]

On July 23, Attorney General William French Smith provided the president with an initial list of *circa* twenty-five candidates, approximately half of whom were women—clearly a record to that date. Among the women in contention were: Arizona Court of Appeals Judge Sandra Day O'Connor; U.S. Court of Appeals Judge for the Sixth Circuit, Cornelia Kennedy; Chief Justice of the Michigan Supreme Court, Mary Coleman; and U.S. Court of Appeals Judge for the Second Circuit, Amalya L. Kearse, a youthful liberal black Carter appointee to that tribunal.[10]

By the end of June, the Attorney General had winnowed the "long list" of twenty-five to a "short list" of about five putative candidates. Judge O'Connor was among the names on that final roster, which also included Judge Kennedy and three men: Utah Supreme Court Judge and ex-President of Brigham Young University, Dallin H. Oaks; U.S. Court of Appeals Judge for the Ninth Circuit, J. Clifford Wallace; and Yale law professor and former U.S. Solicitor General, Robert H. Bork.[11]

On June 27, Attorney General Smith sent his chief counselor, Kenneth W. Starr, and Assistant Attorney General Jonathan Rose to Phoenix to interview Judge O'Connor as well as several Arizonans who were familiar with her personal and professional background. The Attorney General received a highly favorable report, and Judge O'Connor flew to Washington two days later for a secret meeting with Smith. On July 1, Judge O'Connor and the president met in the Oval Office, and she quickly reminded him that they had first met ten years earlier when he was governor of California and she was a member of the Arizona State Senate. The president and Judge O'Connor reportedly had a productive hour-long chat.[12] The Arizona jurist would be the only candidate to be interviewed directly by the president and his top aides for the Stewart vacancy.

Backed by leading political and professional public figures, O'Connor gained the inside track. On July 7, three weeks after Justice Stewart's retirement, President Reagan made his historic announcement that he would nominate the fifty-one-year-old Arizona judge to the Supreme Court. In his statement, the president pronounced O'Connor "truly a 'person for all seasons,' possessing those unique qualities of temperament, fairness, intellectual capacity and devotion to the public good which have characterized the 101 'brethren' who have preceded her."[13]

Women's rights groups and prominent liberals, such as Senator Edward M. Kennedy (D.-Mass.) and Congressman Morris K. Udall (D.-Ariz.), were quick to announce their support for the first woman to be nominated to the highest court in the land. Udall commented of his fellow Arizonan,

"She's about as moderate a Republican you'll ever find being appointed by Reagan."[14]   Although members of the "Old Right" (most significantly its guru, Senator Barry Goldwater) professed their support for Judge O'Connor, leaders of the "New Right," who had backed President Reagan so fervently in his 1980 campaign, unleashed a wave of protest against his first Supreme Court nominee. The Reverend Jerry Falwell, head of the fundamentalist Moral Majority, encouraged all "good Christians" to express concern over O'Connor's nomination. Falwell's opposition prompted a characteristically frank comment from Goldwater: "Every good Christian ought to kick Falwell right in the ass."[15] Antiabortion groups also criticized O'Connor for several proabortion votes during her career as a state legislator.

As the abortion issue threatened a smooth confirmation, the White House announced that O'Connor had assured the president that she is "personally opposed" to abortions, but that she believes abortion to be a legitimate matter for legislative regulation. During her Senate confirmation hearings, O'Connor called her vote in the Arizona legislature to decriminalize abortion a mistake. She quite properly refused, however, to state how she would vote on the abortion matter or any other issues that might come before the Supreme Court. Nevertheless, she expressed her personal feelings in favor of the death penalty and preventive detention and in opposition to busing to achieve racial integration. More generally, O'Connor explained her belief in a restrained role for the federal judiciary. She declared to the Senate Judiciary Committee: "I do not believe it is the function of the judiciary to step in and change the law because the times have changed. I do well understand the difference between legislating and judging." She continued: "As a judge, it is not my function to develop public policy."[16]

On September 15, 1981, the Senate Judiciary Committee approved Judge O'Connor's nomination by the unanimous vote of 17:0, with Senator Jeremiah Denton (D.-Ala.) voting "present" because O'Connor refused to criticize the 1973 *Roe* decision.[17] Six days later the full Senate voted 99:0 to confirm

Sandra Day O'Connor as an associate justice of the U.S. Supreme Court. History had indeed been made!

Although Reagan had hoped to fulfill his campaign pledge to appoint a woman to the Supreme Court, he had insisted that his nominee meet his political ideological criteria. Thus, the Reagan team had searched for a woman with demonstrable conservative political and judicial views. White House aides conducted an extensive examination of O'Connor's record as a legislator and judge. That research on O'Connor revealed a record of "mainstream pragmatic Republicanism" while a member of the Arizona State Senate from 1969 to 1974. After the president's announcement of her nomination, Attorney General Smith stated that Judge O'Connor shared Reagan's "overall judicial philosophy" of "restraint" and deference to the legislative branch in law making. In an issue of the *William and Mary Law Review*, published just prior to O'Connor's nomination, the Arizona judge had referred with warm approbation to Supreme Court decisions that required federal judges to defer to some initial findings of fact by state courts.[18] Yet Judge O'Connor was by no means considered an extremist. One of her Democratic colleagues in the Arizona Senate described her as "a conservative in a conventional sense but beyond that she's extremely fair. She is not an ideologue. She is a perfectionist rooted in the law."[19]

In announcing O'Connor's nomination, the president had stressed that he would not "appoint a woman merely to do so" and that he was convinced that she possessed those qualities necessary to serve on the Supreme Court.[20] Nevertheless, the A.B.A. Committee on Judiciary gave Judge O'Connor a qualified endorsement. Although declaring that she met "the highest standards of judicial temperament and integrity," the Committee expressed its concern over her limited experience as a judge and practicing attorney. The A.B.A. panel told the Senate Judiciary Committee that O'Connor's experience "has not been as extensive or challenging as that of some other persons who might be available for appointment."[21] Indeed, as University of Virginia Law Professor G. Edward White, among others, commented, a man with O'Connor's background would probably not be nominated to the Supreme Court.[22]

Nonetheless, although she lacked experience at the federal level before her nomination to the nation's highest tribunal, Judge O'Connor possessed impressive academic credentials. After a childhood on the family ranch on the Arizona-New Mexico border, Sandra Day was graduated from high school at the age of sixteen and enrolled at Standard University. She completed her undergraduate work and her law degree in just five years, was graduated *magna cum laude,* and was accepted into the Society of the Coif, *the* honorary society for outstanding law students. She ranked near the top of her class (as did her future colleague William H. Rehnquist) and won a position on the *Stanford Law Review.*

Despite that outstanding record, Sandra Day was unsuccessful in finding a law firm that would hire a woman attorney. Her only job offer was for a legal secretary's position. She persisted, however, and began her legal career as deputy county attorney in San Mateo, California, a post she held for two years. In 1952 she married John O'Connor. For three years she worked as a civilian lawyer for the Quartermaster Corps in Frankfurt, West Germany, while her husband served in the Army's Judge Advocate General's Corps. When they returned to the United States, she began raising their three sons, entered private practice, and subsequently became an assistant attorney general in Arizona. In 1969 she took a seat in the State Senate; three years later her Republican colleagues elected her majority leader—the first woman in the nation to hold such a position. She decided to pursue a judicial career in 1974 and won a seat on the Maricopa Superior Court. In 1980, Democratic Governor Bruce Babbitt nominated her to the Arizona Court of Appeals, one step below the state's Supreme Court. She had served on the Appeals Court for eighteen months when she received President Reagan's historic nomination to the U.S. Supreme Court.

In an appealingly frank statement reflective of her selection as the first woman to serve on the highest tribunal in the land, O'Connor told the American Law Institute in May 1983 why she thought lightning had struck her when it did: "While there are many supposed criteria for the selection of a Justice, when the eventual decision is made as to who the nominee will be, that decision from the nominee's viewpoint is probably a classic example of being the right person in the right spot at the right time. Stated simply, you must be lucky. That certainly is how I view my nomination. . . ."[23]

Now (mid-1990), at the end of her ninth year on the Court, Justice O'Connor has generally met her nominator's expectations. In particular her jurisprudence has manifested a faithful, if not inevitably predictive, adherence to the gravamen of her testimony during her nomination hearings: the role of state courts and the attendant desirability as well as necessity for federal courts to respect that role by deferring to it, absent constitutional errors so blatant that they necessitate federal interference. Similar (if not the same) respect has informed her posture vis-à-vis actions by state legislatures, evincing a commitment to the propositions that, as a matter of basic democratic policy, the people's representatives must be granted the benefit of the doubt in setting and executing public policy and that judicial interference is justified only *in extremis*. Thus, she has been echoing the famed Holmesian creed that courts have not justifiable concern with legislative *wisdom*, only with its constitutionality; that a legislative enactment, or an executive action, may well be unwise, unjust, unfair, undemocratic, injudicious, or just plain stupid—yet still be constitutional.[24] It is a creed that Justice O'Connor has applied with particular fealty to the role of the states in our federal system. But that has by no means signaled either blind or Pavlovian support of state authority *versus* federal authority.

Whereas she spent much of her first term (1981-82) roundly denouncing encroachments on states' rights, O'Connor proved herself eminently capable of voting to invalidate state laws, even providing the decisive vote, as she did in the Court's 5:4 vote sustaining one Joe Hogan's equal-protection challenge to Mississippi's policy of excluding men from the Mississipp University for Women School of Nursing.[25] Moreover, she left the "conservative" reservation three times during that term to enable a "liberal" 5:4 holding in a New Jersey redistricting case,[26] in a ruling holding a union liable to a member it failed to represent,[27] and in the seminal sex-discrimination case of *Arizona v. Norris*.[28] In the last she cast the decisive vote that henceforth required equal treatment of men and women in montly annuity-benefit payments under insurance pension plans, such as those in her home state of Arizona.

Justice Powell's departure from the Court at the end of its 1986-87 term not only enhanced Justice O'Connor's role as an independent, moderately conservative centrist, it cast her into a position of being the "swing" vote in a number of highly topical and controversial public law issues that have reached the Court. Closer on many issues than Justice Powell had been to the emerging conservative wing on the Court, led by the now Chief Justice Rehnquist and the two most recent additions to the Court, Justices Scalia and Kennedy, O'Connor has nonetheless been cast as a key player in such continuously volatile and contentious areas as abortion, affirmative action/ reverse discrimination, and separation of church and state. Because her innate conservatism is neither doctrinaire nor ideological, her vote has indeed become central in the Rehnquist Court's ongoing—if not inevitably successful— dedication to a more conservative, less libertarian stance. Cautious, deliberate, deferential to the legislative process and the federal principle, she is dedicated to the embrace of legal principles rather than *ad hoc, ad hominem* value-prone decisions.

Thus while continuing to vote to uphold certain emerging state legislation restrictive of abortion,[29] significantly encouraged by the Court's dramatic 1989 holding in *Webster v. Reproductive Health Services*,[30] Justice O'Connor would have no truck—at least not as of this writing—with re-examining the constitutional validity of *Roe*, causing Justice Scalia to characterize her remarks to that effect in *Webster* as "irresponsible," "irrational", and "not to be taken seriously." But her position prevented, at least temporarily, the desired re-examination by her three or four customary allies on the right.

Clearly uncomfortable with many aspects of affirmative action programs, in particular those involving the utilization of racial—but also gender—quotas, she has been particularly attentive lest they involve patent violation of due process and/or equal protection safeguards under Amendments Five and Fourteen. Thus, while she has cast her vote, albeit often clearly uncomfortably, to uphold a number of the programs,[31] she used the opportunity of the "Richmond-30%-Set-Aside" program for minority enterprises to author the Court's opinion declaring it unconstitutional as a crass violation of the equal protection of the laws, as being "overinclusive," not "narrowly tailored," not of a "compelling state interest," and as constituting "reverse discrimination."[32] She also sided with the controlling votes in the series of five other 1989 Supreme Court rulings that narrowed prevailing affirmative action measures.[33] She dissented vigorously in the Court's 1990 ruling upholding 5:4 the FCC's minority-preferential policies.[34]

Justice O'Connor has also demonstrably been a key vote on the church-state front, the live issue of "separation" or "establishment" being a constant on the Court's menu — with few "bright" lines ascertainable. Thus, although she has manifested a considerable degree of accommodationist sentiment, here, too, her limits have been as visible as they have been carefully pondered, and they have often been decisive. Hence, although supporting the 5:4 majority in sanctioning the Pawtucket, Rhode Island Christmas display in 1984,[35] she would have no part of Louisiana's attempt to mandate the outlawing of the teaching of the theory of evolution unless it was accompanied by instruction in the theory of "creation science," joining her six colleagues in striking the law down in 1987 as a violation of the separation of church and state.[36] In the criminal justice realm, she provided the fifth vote for her divided colleagues in two controversial 5:4 rulings that upheld the power of states to impose capital punishment on murderers who are retarded or who were juveniles when the crimes were committed, but she did so only hesitantly in a pained concurring opinion.[37]

Whatever else may lie ahead in Justice O'Connor's voting profile, it would seem highly unlikely that she would depart dramatically from what is an ably articulated, warmly embraced commitment to and recognition of the role of the states and their institutions, especially that of the state judiciary, in the American federal system. However Justice O'Connor's jurisprudence evolves in the years ahead, her ascendancy to the Court as its first nonmale member has been a remarkably smooth one. Poised, intelligent, literate, an assiduous worker (even after an emergency appendectomy, surgery for breast cancer, and chemotherapy treatments in 1989), she quickly became and remains a respected and admired member of the high court.

III

On June 17, 1986, to the surprise not only of the public at large but also to his colleagues on the bench, Chief Justice Warren E. Burger, within months of this 79th birthday, submitted his resignation to President Reagan after seventeen years in the center chair, saying that he wanted to devote his entire time to organizing ceremonies surrounding the Bicentennial of the United States Constitution in 1987. The president immediately announced his choice as Burger's successor: sitting Associate Justice William H. Rehnquist, along with that of Judge Antonin Scalia of the United States Court of Appeals for the District of Columbia to fill the vacancy created by the former's proposed elevation. The Burger Court, far from reversing or otherwise undoing its predecessor Warren Court, was marked by a generally surprising penchant for judicial activism, even in such unexpected areas as civil rights and liberties. In fact, the dominant figure during its span had been the Court's most effective liberal, William J. Brennan, Jr. It was undoubtedly with that history in mind that President Reagan resolved to endeavor to fill the two vacancies with replacements of whose conservative, "strict constitutional constructionist," jurisprudence he could be relatively comfortably secure. The established record of his two nominees assuredly lent themselves to that prognosis. With some exceptions on the part of Justice Scalia (and later, of his last appointee, Justice Anthony M. Kennedy) in the freedom of speech and, less so, in the criminal justice realms — and perhaps less than a handful in the instance of the new chief justice, Ronald Reagan has had no cause to regret the selection of the highly qualified, articulate, intellectual lawyers he succeeded in elevating to, or promoting on, the highest court in the land.

Chief Justice-designate Rehnquist, of course, had an established on-Court record, amassed during a fourteen-and-a-half-year tenure as an associate justice. It was a record that those who opposed his selection for that post by President Nixon in 1971 (together with Lewis F. Powell, Jr., for another existing position) accurately gauged as part-and-parcel of Rehnquist's fundamental jurisprudential commitment, one to which he predictably adhered as associate justice and now as chief justice. An intensively hard worker, always thoroughly prepared for oral argument; intellectual, literate, and scholarly; ever ready with precise, quick, often difficult and trying questions for fellow justices, Rehnquist is a formidable and predictable advocate for his ideological view of the Constitution and the role of government thereunder. Blackstonian in commitment to popular rule, he not only embraces, but exceeds the Holmes-Frankfurter creed of permitting legislatures, the people's representatives, wide discretion in forging public policy and public law, so long as the latter is not unconstitutional. And for him — grounded in legal positivism founded upon moral skepticism — that line, of course is not reached nearly as soon as it is for the obvious contrary examples of Justices Brennan, Marshall, and almost, but not always, as quickly, for Justices Blackmun and Stevens.

A committed and consistent adherent to federalism, Rehnquist — here most frequently in accord with Justices O'Connor and White, and often with Justices Scalia and Kennedy — will ride close and frequent herd on what he views as the intrusion of the national government on states' rights. Devoted to the principle of deference to the other two branches of the government, especially the legislative, he is probably the Court's most consistent and most articulate exponent and defender of judicial restraint, here following what he views as the similar commitment of Justices Frankfurter and Harlan II. Unlike Holmes, for example, he does not adhere to a rule of less deference in the civil rights and liberties realm: to him, there are no such things as "preferred freedoms" and double standards between the judicial stance on "economic-proprietarian" and "fundamental" rights or freedoms.[38]

Rehnquist, a connoisseur of language and literature, has an ideology and commitment to the judicial role and its obligations to the other institutions of government as well as to the body politic that is perhaps best encompassed in his now famed, passionate, eminently *a priori* logical, dramatic, sarcastic, powerful dissenting opinion in the major 1979 affirmative action/reverse discrimination *Weber* case,[39] which the Court decided one year after *Bakke*.[40] In what may well constitute one of the angriest dissenting opinions in recent times, Justice Rehnquist, joined by Chief Justice Burger, alliteratively accused the Court majority of acting like Harry Houdini, the escape artist: "Thus, by a tour de force reminiscent not of jurists such as Hale, Holmes, and Hughes, but of escape artists such as Houdini, the Court eludes clear statutory language, 'uncontradicted' legislative history, and uniform precedent in concluding that employers are, after all, permitted to consider race in making employment decisions."[41] Congress sought to require racial equality in government, Rehnquist contended: "[T]here is perhaps no device more destructive to the notion of equality than . . . the quota. Whether described as 'benign discrimination' or 'affirmative action,' the racial quota is nonetheless a creator of castes, a two-edged sword that must demean one in order to prefer the other." He concluded: "With today's holding, the Court introduces . . . a tolerance for the very evil that the law was intended to eradicate, without offering even a clue as to what the limits on that tolerance may be. . . . The Court has sown the wind. Later courts will face the impossible task of reaping the whirlwind."[42]

That dissent is vintage Rehnquist. Whatever one's personal views on the underlying issue, whatever one's sympathies, "it is simply unanswerable in terms of statutory construction and congressional intent," in the words of Philip B. Kurland, distinguished Professor of Constitutional Law at the University of Chicago.[43] It speaks to Rehnquist's manifold talents and to his ideological commitments, to his views of government under law and institutional obligations, in fine, to his perception of the nature and function of a judge under our written Constitution. A good many members of the Supreme Court have undergone demonstrable major ideological and process changes during their careers on the Court—contemporarily most obviously Justice Blackmun. But it would be a veritable revolutionary development were Chief Justice Rehnquist to alter his basic jurisprudential stance! His principles, his commitments, and his consistency are *res judicata*.

He had made resolutely clear during his confirmation hearings which opened July 30, 1986, that his questioners could not, and should not, expect any change in his jurisprudence; that his years as associate justice were on the record. Stipulating that fact, Rehnquist's chief opponent, Senator Edward M. Kennedy assailed the nominee-promotee in harsh terms within moments after the hearings commenced. Cataloguing his objections—many of which were framed with the aid of Harvard's well-known Professor of Constitutional Law, Laurence H. Tribe—Kennedy thundered that "by his own record of massive isolated dissent" he demonstrates that "he is too extreme on race, too extreme on women's rights, too extreme on freedom of speech, too extreme on separation of church and state, too extreme to be chief justice."[44] Kennedy's charges set the tone for two weeks of stormy testimony. None of his detractors disputed the nominee's powerful intellect or his keen knowledge or understanding of the law. Their central thrust was directed to the allegation that Rehnquist was "out of the mainstream"—a charge that would be echoed multiply, and with far more success, during the Bork hearings one year later.

On August 14, the full Judiciary Committee voted 13:5 to recommend confirmation.[45] After an additional month of divisive, acrimonious debate, the Senate confirmed him 65:33, to become the 16th chief justice of the United States. The thirty-three "nays" constituted the largest number of votes ever cast against a nominee who won confirmation. Yet, Rehnquist could take comfort in the fact that he was not the first chief justice to gain the office from a divided Senate after vehement verbal combat: Charles Evans Hughes prevailed in 1930 only after bitter, protracted debate, by a similar 2:1 margin, 52:26.[46] And one of their predecessor-nominees, John Rutledge, although confirmed as associate justice in 1789, was rejected for the center chair by a vote of 10:14 late in 1795.

There were those commentators who suggested that, because of his new status as *primus inter pares*, Chief Justice Rehnquist would adopt an amended jurisprudence in order to "marshal" his Court. There is no convincing evidence that he has done so, notwithstanding a number of perhaps surprising votes, among them his authorship in *Meritor Savings Bank v. Vinson*, a significant sex discrimination claim resolved in the plaintiff's favor; in *Hustler Magazine v. Falwell*, the Rev. Jerry Falwell's unsuccessful libel and emotional distress suit against *Hustler's* publisher, Larry Flynt; and in *Morrison v. Olson*, the upholding of the office of federal "independent counsel"/"special prosecutor."[47]   He had demonstrated an abiding capacity for effective, efficient, considerate leadership, coupled with a concern and regard for his colleagues that has served to render him as a genuinely respected and popular "chief," and caused his leading jurisprudential adversary, Associate Justice Brennan, to praise him as "the most all-around successful" of the three under whom he had served.[48]

IV

Antonin Scalia's nomination to fill Rehnquist's associate justice's seat came as no surprise to Court observers. One year before, *The New Republic* had written: "A Scalia nomination makes political sense." The prognostication continued with a quotation from an unnamed "White House official," who had exclaimed about Scalia: "What a political symbol. Nino would be the first Italian-Catholic on the Court. He's got nine kids. He's warm and friendly. Everybody likes him. He's a brilliant conservative. What more could you want?" Moreover, the fifty-year-old Scalia was ten years younger than Judge Robert H. Bork, who also was rumored to be on Reagan's list of potential Supreme Court appointees[49] — as indeed he had been on the occasion of every vacancy since the late 1960s. In light of the firestorm over Bork's ideology when he was nominated in 1987, it is indeed ironic that *Time* magazine reported in the summer of 1986 that Bork had lost out to Scalia because the latter "was a more energetic true believer" in the conservative cause.[50]   Attorney General Edwin Meese III, a member of the three-man panel that made recommendations to Reagan on Court appointments, listed three basic criteria followed by the president in his decision to promote Associate Justice Rehnquist and name Scalia as his replacement: intellectual and lawyerly capability, "integrity," and "a commitment to the interpretation of the law rather than making it from the bench."[51] The president's announcement of his intention to nominate Scalia cited his "great personal energy, the force of his intellect and the depth of his understanding of our constitutional jurisprudence [which] uniquely qualify him for elevation to our highest court."[52]

Even ideological foes were hard pressed to challenge Scalia's demonstrably meritorious credentials. By all accounts, devotion to his religious faith and academic pursuits had guided the future justice's youth. A product of New York public schools at the primary level,[53] Scalia was graduated from Xavier High School, a Jesuit institution in Manhattan. A former classmate offered the following description of the young Scalia: "This kid was a conservative when he was 17 years old. An archconservative Catholic. He could have been a member of the Curia. He was the top student in his class. He was brilliant, way above everybody else."[54]

Scalia continued his pattern of academic excellence at Georgetown University, from which he was graduated as valedictorian and *summa cum laude*. He earned his law degree at Harvard, where he served as an editor of the law review and a post-graduate fellow. Upon leaving Harvard, Scalia began a six-year stint as an associate at Jones, Day, Reavis & Pogue, a Cleveland law firm. He left the firm to join the law faculty at the University of Virginia and never returned to private practice. Instead, he alternated between government positions (1971-72, General Counsel, White House Office of Telecommunications Policy; 1974-77, Assistant Attorney General) and academic appointments at the Georgetown Law Center, the American Enterprise Institute, Stanford Law School, and the University of Chicago Law School. He had been a Chicago law professor for five years when in 1982 President Reagan nominated him for a seat on the United States Court of Appeals for the District of Columbia.

Scalia's impeccable professional and personal attributes, his well-articulated conservative ideology, and his restraintist jurisprudence provided a perfect fit with the Meese committee's and Reagan's expressed selection criteria. Moreover, Scalia's age (the same as Brennan's at his nomination in 1956) assured that, barring ill-health or ideological conversion, the new justice could carry the tenets of Reagan judicial philosophy well into the twenty-first century. Finally, the Reagan administration was assuredly not blind to ethnic realities and the potential political capital generated by naming the first Italian-American to the Court. Indeed, virtually every press account of Scalia's nomination cited the truism that he would be the first Italian-American to serve on the nation's highest bench.[55]   Not surprisingly, politicians of Italian descent responded warmly and enthusiastically to Scalia's nomination. Republican Senator Pete V. Domenici of new Mexico hailed Reagan's decision to name Scalia as a "magnificent tribute" to Italian-Americans. Congressman Mario Biaggi, a Democratic U.S. Representative from the Bronx, added his praise: "Of course, there is a special pride I feel as an Italian-American. Our community has always asked for consideration based on merit."[56]

Scalia's smooth sailing through the Senate, with unanimous approval from both the Judiciary Committee (18:0) and the full chamber (98:0), may have been facilitated by the symbolism of the nominee's Italian heritage, which was certainly not lost on Democrats with ethnic constituencies.[57] Perhaps the overriding element in Scalia's favor, however, was the fact that the Republicans controlled the Senate with a 53:47 margin over the Democrats.   Nevertheless the Democrats had mounted a vociferous if unfocused and ultimately unsuccessful, campaign against Rehnquist's promotion. In fact, the Rehnquist battle may have drawn some of the fire away from Scalia, leaving the Senate too fatigued to take up another political crusade against him. In addition, Reagan drew political strength from his unquestionable popularity, which bolstered his administration well into its second term. Furthermore, Scalia employed an astute and effective strategy at his hearings by avoiding expansive answers to questions on controversial issues.[58]   Yet even if he had foreshadowed his future conservative votes, the seat he was to fill—promotee Rehnquist's—was not a crucial one for changing the configuration of the Court; in that sense, he represented an even trade for the Rehnquist vote, as Rehnquist did more or less for Burger's.

After four terms on the Court, Scalia has, by and large, lived up to the restraintist credentials which propelled him to the high bench. In general, his votes have been guided and circumscribed by a deference to the federal structure and to the democratically elected branches of government, faithfulness to clear constitutional and statutory commands, and adherence to judicial precedents. An inveterate critic of the "imperial judiciary," Scalia has never hesitated to aim his rapier-like intellect against his activist colleagues, whom he views as creating extra-constitutional rights on which there is no national consensus. Some of his most bitter and emotive, yet articulate, assaults on judicial imperialism have been volleyed in affirmative action, abortion, and church-state cases.

In the Court's first gender-based affirmative action case,[59] Scalia excoriated the six-person majority for approving a local transportation agency's promotion of a female employee over a more qualified male colleague. In harsh, blistering, forceful language he contended that the decision now "effectively requires employers, public as well as private, to engage in intentional discrimination on the basis of race or sex," in clear violation of Title VII of the Civil Rights Act. With deep feeling and thinly veiled sarcasm, he concluded his dissent with a sympathetic reference to the male petitioner in the case, one Paul Johnson, and all victims of reverse discrimination: "The only losers in the process are the Johnsons of the country, for whom Title VII has been not merely repealed [by the Court] but actually inverted. The irony is that these individuals— predominantly unknown, unaffluent, unorganized—suffer this injustice at the hands of a court fond of thinking itself the champion of the politically impotent."

His first opportunity to vote on the abortion issue came in the 1988-89 Term's highly charged *Webster* case,[60] in which he willingly sided with the narrow majority in upholding substantial state restrictions on abortions. He went a step farther in his scathing concurring opinion, however, chastising Justice O'Connor for her refusal to overturn *Roe* and attacking the rest of the majority for "needlessly . . . prolong[ing] the Court's self-awarded sovereignty over a field where it has little proper business since the answers to most of the cruel questions posed are political and not juridical. . . ."

Scalia's deference to state policy and the legislative process were also evident in his 1987 dissent from the Court's 7:2 church-state decision striking down Louisiana's "creationism" statute.[61] Joined by Chief Justice Rehnquist, he denounced the ruling as a "repressive" and "illiberal" action that prevented the people of Louisiana from having "whatever scientific evidence there may be against evolution presented in their schools."

In another demonstration of his firm faith in the constitutionally mandated separation of powers, Scalia authored a staunch defense of executive power in his dissent from the Court's upholding of the Congress-created "independent counsel" to investigate high-ranking officials in the executive branch.[62] Again criticizing the seven-person majority for its ad hoc, result-oriented constitutional adjudication, he offered an alternative governed by language, intent, and tradition: "I prefer to rely upon the judgment of the wise men who constructed our system, and of the people who approved it, and of two centures of history that have shown it to be sound. Like it or not, that judgment says, quite plainly, that '[t]he executive Power shall be vested in a President of the United States.'"

Yet Scalia has occasionally arrived at some surprising judicial results that seemingly mitigate his usually reliable conservatism. In a 1987 Fourth Amendment case,[63] Scalia was the unexpected author of the majority opinion for a 6:3 Court that refused to extend the "plain view" exception to a warrantless search that had discovered stolen stereo equipment. A police officer had moved the stereo components to reveal their serial numbers and to the Scalia-led majority that fact was determinative because "the distinction between looking at a suspicious object in plain view and moving it even a few inches is much more than trivial for purposes of the Fourth Amendment."[64]

Scalia's votes with the Court's majority in the two contentious decisions[65] upholding flag-burning as a form of political expression protected under the First Amendment seemed even more incongruous, for they required him to abandon his usual deference to national and state legislative bodies that had statutorily banned flag desecration and embrace an expansive interpretation of free speech rights that includes symbolic expression bordering on conduct.

Yet Scalia's occasional unpredictability has only enhanced his image as one of the Court's most intellectually interesting and personally colorful members. His frequent questions during oral argument are penetrating, yet, to the delight of the audience, often laced with impish humor. On one occasion he told a rather flustered counsel, who was frantically searching his brief for the Scalia-requested information, to "just shout 'bingo!' when you find it." But as the above-quoted passages from both his majority and dissenting opinions illustrate, his quick-wittedness can just as easily turn acerbic in defense of those jurisprudential tenets that he holds most dear and will likely continue to espouse.

V

When Associate Justice Lewis F. Powell, Jr., unexpectedly announced his retirement from the Supreme Court in June 1987, no commentator failed to report the ramifications for the tribunal's future direction. Calling Powell "the determined moderate" who had provided the "critical fifth votes in key Supreme Court rulings," the *New York Times* stated the obvious fact that "[h]is resignation gave President Reagan a historic opportunity to shape the future of the court."[66] Indeed Powell had played a pivotal role as the tie-breaking vote in cases determining the Court's interpretation of constitutional law on abortion, affirmative action, and separation of church and state.[67] Yet Powell was not merely a tie-breaker. Because he was not consistently conservative or liberal across the broad range of issues, he could sway the Court's decisional outcomes from one ideological camp to another by virtue of his "swing" vote.

Despite U.S. Court of Appeals Judge Robert Bork's judicial and scholarly record, which identified him as a solid conservative, President Reagan described his nominee for the Court's swing seat, announced in July 1987, as neither a conservative nor a liberal. Attempting to cast Bork in the Powell mold, the president stressed that the former was "evenhanded and openminded." Reagan also highlighted his nominee's unquestionably strong qualifications as a means of placing him above the political fray,[68] but the president's lack of success in doing so was immediately evident when Senator Edward M. Kennedy, in his now famous (or infamous) harangue on the floor of the Senate—45 minutes after the formal announcement of Bork's selection—fired the opening salvo in the battle against Bork's record on abortion and civil and criminal rights. In a fit of exaggeration, Senator Kennedy declared: "Robert Bork's America is a land in which women would be forced into back alley abortions, blacks would sit at segregated lunch counters, and rogue policemen could break down citizen's doors in midnight raids."[69]

Once Kennedy had unleashed the politics of the swing seat, there was no turning back. Moreover, such distortions were amplified by other political variables like the outcome of the 1986 congressional elections, which had returned control of the Senate to the Democrats by a 55-45 majority.[70] Southern Democrats in the Senate, whom the Reagan Administration hoped to woo to Bork's side, found themselves in the especially difficult situation of fearing a loss of black ballots if they voted for a nominee portrayed as anti-civil rights.[71] Besides senatorial politics, President Reagan's political fortunes were waning as he approached the end of his second term. Weakened by the Iran-Contra scandal and economic concerns prompted by the Wall Street crash in the fall of 1987, Reagan's leadership was under fire at home and abroad; and that turn of events arguably contributed to Bork's defeat.[72] Moreover, liberals in the Senate and in political interest groups, like the well-organized, heavily financed People for the American Way, were gunning for a fight after nearly eight years of frustrating losses to the conservatives.[73]

Stepping into this hornet's nest, Bork typified the very opposite of Sandra Day O'Connor's explanation of her own successful appointment in 1981: Bork was the wrong person in the wrong spot at the wrong time. His copious scholarly writings, which would have been an enviable asset in any academic setting, and his opinions on the appellate bench contained attacks on Warren and Burger Court precedents that played directly into the hands of interest group and Senate opponents.[74] His intellectual commitment to a jurisprudence of original intent appeared rigid and was fair game for being portrayed as beyond the mainstream of contemporary judicial philosophy.[75] Moreover, Bork's personal appearance and demeanor seemed as suspect as his ideology. His devilish beard and sometimes turgid academic discourse did not endear him to wavering Senators or the public. Nor did his detailed, lecture-like answers to every conceivable question posed to him by the Senate Judiciary Committee.[76] Reagan's eleventh-hour attempts to sell Bork as the logical heir to the Powell legacy could not overcome the simple truth that neither his judicial nor personal style qualified him as a Powell clone. No careful observer of the drama over filling the swing seat could have been surprised by the ultimate denouement that saw Bork's nomination go down to a resounding 42:58 defeat in the Senate.

Although Reagan's next nominee, Douglas Ginsburg, will merit no more than a footnote in the long history of Supreme Court appointments, a brief look at his selection does set the stage for Anthony Kennedy's eventual appointment. A vindictive gesture by the more extreme Administration faction, led by Attorney General Edwin Meese, the selection of Ginsburg seemed to fulfill Reagan's threat after Bork's defeat that he would give the Senate a "nominee that they would object to just as much as Judge Bork."[77] Indeed, as a young devotee of the "Law and Economics Movement," Ginsburg was once described as "dancing along this periphery of what can be called conservative economic extremism."[78] Yet Ginsburg had virtually no academic or judicial trail on which opponents could have seized. To add insult to injury, Reagan's second nominee was also bearded! Only the startling disclosure of his past marijuana use, both as a student and as a law professor, saved the country from another wrangle over the nomination of a perceived extremist for the swing seat.

VI

The Reagan Administration finally took the lessons of swing seat politics to heart and in November 1987 selected a nominee, Ninth Circuit Court of Appeals Judge Anthony M. Kennedy, who was simply less controversial and far less well-known than Bork. By virtue of his moderately conservative judicial record, his moral propriety, and his pleasant appearance and personality, he was perceived as being closer to the Powell model than Bork or Ginsburg could have been. There was no doubt that Kennedy's decisions during his twelve-year tenure on the Ninth Circuit produced conservative results, but his opinions seemed more narrowly crafted than Bork's.[79] Thus Kennedy could plausibly argue in his written responses to a standard Judiciary Committee questionnaire that "[l]ife tenure is in part a constitutional mandate to the federal judiciary to proceed with caution, to avoid reaching issues not necessary to the resolution of the suit at hand, and to defer to the political process."[80]

Kennedy's propriety also matched that of the justice he was to replace. He reportedly had experienced a remarkably trouble-free boyhood that apparently included regular service as an altar boy at his Roman Catholic parish church. In fact, the future justice used to joke with his young friends that his father in a fit of affectionate despair had offered to pay him $100 if just once he would do something requiring his parents to come pick him up at the local police station. The youngster never collected on the dare.[81]

Instead the young Kennedy devoted himself to his studies. An honor roll student at a public school in Sacramento, California, where he was born and raised, Kennedy always assumed that he would attend Stanford University as his mother had.[82] As an undergraduate, the future justice continued his outstanding academic career, completing his graduation requirements in just three years. His father apparently thought his son was too young to enroll immediately in law school, so Kennedy spent a year at the London School of Economics. Upon his return to the states, he received his B.A. degree from Stanford, where he was elected to Phi Beta Kappa. He then attended Harvard Law School, from which he attained his LL.B., *cum laude.*

He returned to California to practice law in the prestigious San Francisco law firm of Thelen, Marrin, John & Bridges, but within two years was back in Sacramento to assume the law practice of his father who had died suddenly of a heart attack in 1963. Described by associates as "intellectual," Kennedy apparently disliked the flesh-pressing required of lobbying work in the state capital. Nevertheless, he was involved in California politics behind the scenes. Notably, he drafted Governor Ronald Reagan's tax-limitation initiative known as Proposition 1. Kennedy's expertise prompted Reagan to recommend him to President Gerald Ford, who appointed Kennedy to the U.S. Court of Appeals in 1975.

Yet despite such numerous positive qualifications for following in Powell's footsteps, Kennedy's most salable quality was a negative one: he wasn't Bork. Thus, Judiciary Committee Chairman Joseph Biden, who had led the fight against Bork, happily characterized Kennedy as "open-minded" and as a judge who "does not have an ideological brief in [his] back pocket."[83] Although Kennedy may not have led a life devoted to the intellectual pursuit of an overarching jurisprudence, he did acknowledge a clear preference for a judicial philosophy of restraint. He argued in his written responses to the Judiciary Committee: "It is a fact . . . not a perception, that courts have become more active in the public dialogue and in policy making than at any other time in our constitutional history. This expanded role of the courts tends to erode the boundaries of judicial power and also threatens to permit the individual biases of the judge to operate."[84] In unanimously approving Kennedy's nomination, the Judiciary Committee noted that he "seems to possess the truly judicious qualities that Justice Lewis Powell embodied. . . . [H]e his open-minded, fair and independent."[85] Likewise, the full Senate voted unanimously (97:0) to confirm Kennedy's nomination on February 3, 1988.

Kennedy's first terms on the high court may not offer a definitive portrait of his Supreme Court jurisprudence, but his initial votes and opinions have begun to reveal identifiable trends. As occupied by Justice Kennedy, the Court's swing seat no longer functions as a vote that balances the liberal and conservative blocs by siding with one or the other from case to case. Instead, Kennedy's vote most often serves as a tie-breaker that can tip the balance in favor of the conservatives.

In the abortion realm, for example, Kennedy voted with the 5:4 majority in *Webster*;[86] and at the end of the 1989-90 Term authored the majority opinion in a 6:3 decision upholding an Ohio statute requiring a physician to notify *one* parent of a pregnant minor of her intent to have an abortion, provided that a judicial bypass procedure is available to the minor.[87] Kennedy also arrived at a conservative result on the matter of the right to privacy vis-à-vis the drug-testing issue when he wrote the majority opinions in two 1989 cases in which the Court constitutionally sanctioned the federal government's mandatory drug tests for railroad workers after accidents and for armed Customs Service employees involved in drug interdiction programs.[88]

It is in the area of affirmative action, however, that Justice Kennedy's vote has begun to distinguish him most fundamentally from Justice Powell. He voted with the majority in all of the 1989 cases narrowing the use of affirmative action programs.[89] Kennedy's most notable contribution to the Court's more conservative tack in employment discrimination cases was his majority opinion in *Patterson v. McClean Credit Union*,[90] which upheld the use of the 1866 Civil Rights Act for claims of discrimination at the initial hiring stage, but barred use of the statute for claims of on-the-job bias. But the intensity and emotion of the newest justice's views were most evident on the last day of the Court's 1989-90 Term when he issued an angry dissent, joined by Scalia, from the five-person majority ruling upholding federal minority preference plans for boosting minority ownership of radio and television stations in order to increase diversity of programming.[91] Kennedy decried the

Court's approval of such an affirmative action plan, the justifications for which he pointedly compared to those underlying the South African system of apartheid: "Perhaps the Court can succeed in its assumed role of case-by-case arbiter of when it is desirable and benign for the government to disfavor some citizens and favor others based on the color of their skin." Accusing the Court of returning to the days of *Plessy v. Ferguson*,[92] he continued: "But history suggests much peril in this enterprise, and so the Constitution forbids us to undertake it. I regret that after a century of judicial opinion we interpret the Constitution to do no more than move from 'separate but equal' to 'unequal but benign.'"

In church-state matters, Kennedy tipped his hand during his first half-term on the Court in 1988. He joined the 5:4 majority in upholding a federal law providing money to religious groups to counsel teen-age girls to abstain from sexual relations and to avoid abortion.[93] In a particularly accommodationist concurrence, seconded by Justice Scalia, Kennedy wrote that government aid even to "pervasively sectarian" groups would be constitutional, absent proof that "the funds are in fact being used to further religion."

Kennedy maintained his accommodationist stance in the Court's simultaneous rulings at the end of the 1988-89 Term on Christmas season displays sponsored by city and county governments in Pittsburgh.[94] He dissented from a decision declaring that a Nativity scene, unaccompanied by any more secular symbols of the season, amounted to an unconstitutional endorsement of the Christian faith. He found himself in the majority, however, when the Court permitted a Hanukkah menorah to be displayed next to a Christmas tree. In declaring both the menorah and creche displays to be constitutional, Kennedy called for "substantial revision of our establishment clause doctrine. . . ." His proposed two-pronged test would ask whether anyone was "coerced" into supporting religion or participating in a religious observance and whether the government program gives "direct benefits to religion in such a degree that it in fact establishes a state religion or religious faith."

In the 1989/1990 flag-burning cases, Kennedy joined with Scalia in a rare alignment with Justices Brennan, Marshall, and Blackmun to create the five-person majority that overturned flag-desecration statutes.[95] Kennedy's concurrence in *Johnson v. Texas* expressed unqualified support for Brennan's majority opinion but cited the "personal toll" exacted by such agonizing decisions. Referring indirectly to his belief in judicial restraint, he noted that this case illustrated "that the judicial power is often difficult in its exercise" and that in instances of statutory construction the courts can "ask another branch to share responsibility." But when a statute must be "judged against a pure command of the Constitution," Kennedy argued, "[t]he outcome can be laid at no door but ours. The hard fact is that sometimes we must make decisions we do not like. We make them because they are right, right in the sense that the law and the Constitution, as we see them, compel the result."

Despite his vote in the flag-burning cases, Kennedy seems to be clinging to a pronounced conservatism bolstered by a professed adherence to judicial restraint. In general, he has chartered a course guided by deference to precedent and legislative intent. It is indeed ironic that although Kennedy may not have an overarching theory of constitutional interpretation, his case-by-case approach has produced outcomes more similar to those predicted of Bork than displayed by Powell.

VII

With the possible exception of some of Justice O'Connor's votes in crucial gender-related cases and some First Amendment freedom of expression stances by Justice Scalia and Kennedy, the Reagan-appointed quartet has broadly lived up to the former president's expectations, although, other than in the criminal justice realm and certain aspects of racial quota decisions, they had not succeeded to date (the end of the Court's 1989-90 term in June 1990) in forming a predictable "pro-Reagan philosophy" majority. For the John F. Kennedy-appointed Associate Justice Byron R. White, although more often than not an ally in "law-and-order" issues, has been mercurial in many other segments of public law and has on numerous key occasions joined the almost always solid "pro-civil libertarian" bloc of the three senior members of the Court in terms of age, Associate Justices Brennan (Eisenhower), Marshall (Johnson), and Blackmun (Nixon) and their customary, although not inevitable ally, Associate Justice Stevens (Ford). White's penchant for unpredictable departures from the Court's conservative wing was highlighted by his decisive votes—although in terms of his recent record quite inconsistent ones—in two crucial race issue cases, in which he supplied the Brennan-led group with the unexpected fifth vote and victory: the Kansas City, Missouri, federal judge-ordered taxation-for-school desegregation ruling,[96] and the aforementioned preferential television channels assignment holding.[97] Moreover, the post-1986, heavily Democratic Congress has severally seen fit to overturn "pro-Reagan" Supreme Court rulings by remedial legislation and, at this writing (August 1990) was poised to do so again to modify, or even totally to reverse, seminal aspects of the effects of the Court's 1989 quintet of "anti"-affirmative action holdings.[98] The developmental governmental process, including the realm of constitutional interpretation, is, in the words of the late Alexander M. Bickel's daunting characterization, "common property," a joint enterprise.[99]   And the individual chosen to take the retired Justice Brennan's seat on the high bench, Judge David H. Souter, will of course play a major role in that process.

Notes

1 *Fighting for Peace: Seven Critical Years in the Pentagon* (New York: Warner Books, 1990), p. 13.

2 *The New York Times*, February 17, 1979, p. 16.

3 White House Press Conference, February 7, 1978.

4 Reprinted in 64 *Judicature* 9 (April 1981): 428.

5 Compiled from statistics supplied by the *Congressional Quarterly*, the American Bar Association's Committee on Judiciary, and *Judicature*, 1980-90. For a more detailed statistical analysis, see Sheldon Goldman's "Reagan's Judicial Legacy: Completing the Puzzle and Summing Up," 72 *Judicature* 6 (April-May 1989): 318-30.

6 See Henry J. Abraham, *Justices and Presidents: A Political History of Appointments to the Supreme Court*, 2d ed. (New York: Oxford University Press, 1985), especially Ch. 4, Tables 6 and 7 and accompanying text, pp. 65ff.

7 Ibid., p. 67 (adjusted post-second edition, to appear in forthcoming revised and extended version of Abraham's *Justices and Presidents*, to be published by Oxford University Press in 1991).

8 *The New York Times*, October 15, 1980, p. 24.

9 *The Washington Post*, July 8, 1981, p. 1.

10 *Time,* July 20, 1981, p. 11.

11 *The New York Times*, July 8, 1981, p. 12.

12 *Time*, pp. 11-12.

13 As quoted in *The New York Times*, July 8, 1981, pp. 1, 12.

14 As quoted in *The Washington Post*, July 8, 1981, p. 7.

15 As quoted in *Time*, p. 10.

16 As quoted in *The Washington Post*, July 8, 1981, p. 1.

17 *The New York Times*, September 16, 1981, p. 16.

18 Summer 1981, Vol. 22, pp. 801-815.

19 As quoted in *The New York Times*, July 8, 1981, p. 13.

20 *The New York Times*, July 8, 1981, p. 12.

21 As quoted in *The Washington Post*, September 9, 1981, p. 1.

22 *The* [Charlottesville, Virginia] *Daily Progress*, July 8, 1981, p. 8.

23 As quoted in Abraham, *Justices and Presidents*, p. 336.

24 See Abraham, *The Judicial Process: An Introductory Analysis of the Courts of the United States, England, and France*, 5th ed. (New York: Oxford University Press, 1986), fns. 105-14, pp. 390-91.

25 *Mississippi University for Women v. Hogan*, 458 U.S. 718 (1982).

26 *Karcher v. Daggett*, 462 U.S. 725 (1983).

27 *Bower v. U.S. Postal Service*, U.S. (1983).

28 464 U.S. 808 (1983).

29 In *Akron v. Akron Center for Reproductive Health, Inc.*, 462 U.S. 416 (1983), the Court declared various local regulations on the performance of abortions to be unconstitutional as a violation of a woman's right to privacy and the resultant right to decide whether to terminate her pregnancy as established in *Roe v. Wade*, 410 U.S. 113 (1973). Joined in a vigorous dissent by Justices White and Rehnquist, O'Connor attacked the majority opinion on the grounds that "neither sound constitutional theory nor our need to decide cases based on the application of neutral principles can accommodate . . . [*Roe's*] analytical framework that varies according to the 'stages' of pregnancy, where those stages, and their concomitant standards of review, differ according to the level of medical technology available when a particular challenge to state regulation occurs." Also see her votes and opinions in *Ohio v. Akron Center for Reproductive Health*, 58 LW 4979 (1990) and *Hodgson v. Minnesota*, 58 LW 4957 (1990).

30 109 S.Ct. 3040 (1989).

31 *Firefighters v. Cleveland*, 478 U.S. 501 (1986); *United States v. Paradise*, 480 U.S. 149 (1987); and *Johnson v. Transportation Agency, Santa Clara County*, 480 U.S. 616 (1987).

32 *City of Richmond v. J. A. Croson Co.*, 109 S.Ct. 706 (1989).

33 *Wards Cove Packing v. Atonia*, 109 S.Ct. 2115; *Martin v. Wilks*, 109 S.Ct. 2180; *Lorance v. A. T. & T. Technologies*, 109 S.Ct. 2261; *Jett v. Dallas Independent School Dist.*, 109 S.Ct. 2702; and *Patterson v. McClean Credit Union*, 109 S.Ct. 2363.

34　*Metro Broadcasting v. FCC*, 58 LW 5053 (1990).

35　*Lynch v. Donnelly*, 465 U.S. 668.

36　*Edwards v. Aguillard*, 482 U.S. 578.

37　*Wilkins v. Missouri, Stanford v. Kentucky*, and *Penry v. Lynaugh*, 57 LW 4958. The first two cases dealt with convicted murderers who were 16 and 17, respectively, when they committed their crimes. The last case involved a convicted murderer who had an IQ of 54 and the mental age of a six-and-a-half-year-old child.

38　See Abraham's *Freedom and the Court: Civil Rights and Liberties in the United States*, 5th ed. (New York: Oxford University Press, 1988), Ch. II, "The 'Double Standard.' "

39　*United Steelworkers v. Weber*, 443 U.S. 193 (1979).

40　*Regents of the University of California v. Bakke*, 438 U.S. 265 (1978).

41　*Weber*, at 222.

42　Ibid., at 255.

43　Letter to Abraham, July 7, 1979.

44　As quoted in *The Washington Post*, July 30, 1986, p. 1.

45　The five "no" votes were cast by Democrats Joseph Biden (Del.), Edward Kennedy (Mass.), Howard Metzenbaum (Ohio), Patrick Leahy (Vt.), and Paul Simon (Ill.).

46　See *The New York Times*, September 27, 1986, p. Y19. Among the 26 negative votes was that of a future Supreme Court justice, Hugo L. Black (D.-Ala.).

47　477 U.S. 57 (1986); 108 S.Ct. 876 (1987); and 108 S.Ct. 2597 (1988), respectively.

48　Responding to a student's question, East Conference Room of the Supreme Court of the United States, Washington, D.C., November 27, 1989. (The other two chief justices were Earl Warren and Warren Burger.)

49　*The New Republic*, June 10, 1985, p. 16. Academic observers had commented similarly about Scalia's positive attributes. See generally Jeffrey Segal and Harold Spaeth, "If a Supreme Court Vacancy Occurs, Will the Senate Confirm a Reagan Nominee?" 69 *Judicature* 4 (1986): 186-90.

50　June 30, 1986, p. 28.

51 *The New York Times,* June 18, 1986, p. 32.

52 Ibid., p. 30.

53 Interview with Justice Antonin Scalia, Supreme Court of the United States, Washington, D.C., March 18, 1987.

54 *The New York Times,* June 1986, p. 31.

55 See, e.g., *The New York Times,* June 18, 1986, p. 31; *The Washington Post,* June 18, 1986, p. 15; *The Chicago Tribune,* June 18, 1986, p. 1; and *Time,* June 30, 1986, p. 24.

56 *The New York Times,* June 18, 1986, p. 32.

57 See Perry, "The Life and Death of the 'Catholic Seat' on the United States Supreme Court," VI *The Journal of Law and Politics* 55 (Fall 1989), for an analysis of other "representative" factors affecting the Scalia nomination.

58 Stephen M. Griffin, "Politics and the Supreme Court: The Case of the Bork Nomination," V *The Journal of Law and Politics* 551 (Spring 1989): at 554.

59 *Johnson v. Transportation Agency, Santa Clara County,* 480 U.S. 616 (1987).

60 See fn. 30, supra.

61 See fn. 36, supra.

62 See fn. 47, supra.

63 *Arizona v. Hicks,* 480 U.S. 321 (1987).

64 As quoted in James E. Wyzanski, "In Praise of Judicial Restraint: The Jurisprudence of Justice Antonin Scalia," 1 *Detroit College of Law Review* 117 (1989): at 143.

65 *Johnson v. Texas,* 57 LW 3679 (1989) and *U.S. v. Eichman* and *U.S. v. Haggerty,* 58 LW 4744 (1990).

66 June 27, 1987, p. 1.

67 See, e.g., *Thornburgh v. American College of Obstetricians and Gynecologists,* 476 U.S. 747 (1986) and *Planned Parenthood v. Ashcraft,* 462 U.S. 476 (1983), in the abortion realm. Affirmative action cases in which Powell cast the deciding vote include *United States v. Paradise,* 480 U.S. 149 (1987); *Wygant v. Jackson Bd. of Educ.,* 476 U.S. 267 (1986); and *Regents of the University of California v. Bakke,* 438 U.S. 265 (1978). In the area of church-state separation, see, e. g., *Lynch v. Donnelly,* 465 U.S. 668 and *Mueller v. Allen,* 463 U.S. 388 (1983).

68 For a complete bibliographical listing of Bork's judicial opinions and scholarly articles, see 9 *Cardozo Law Review* (1987), which devoted the entire issue to an analysis of the Bork nomination. See also *The New York Times*, July 2, 1987, p. 1 and *The Washington Post*, October 1, 1987, p. 3.

69 As quoted in Ethan Bronner, *Battle for Justice: How the Bork Nomination Shook America* (New York: W. W. Norton & Co., 1989), p. 98.

70 Griffin, "Politics and the Supreme Court," p. 556.

71 Nadine Cohodas, "Kennedy Finds Bork an Easy Act to Follow," 45 *Congressional Quarterly Weekly Report* 2989 (1987).

72 See *The Washington Post*, November 8, 1987, p. 1 and November 9, 1987, p. 1; *The New York Times*, November 8, 1987, p. 1.

73 Bronner, *Battle for Justice*.

74 Cohodas, "Kennedy Finds Bork an Easy Act to Follow," p. 2989. The Bork bibliography cited in fn. 66, supra, specifically lists publications in which Bork attacked Supreme Court precedents.

75 Ibid., p. 2989.

76 Ibid., p. 2990.

77 As quoted in *The Washington Post*, November 12, 1987, p. 38.

78 Kevin Phillips, "Bork/Ginsburg foul ups expose conservative disarray," *The* (Louisville) *Courier Journal*, November 29, 1987, p. D5.

79 See Charles F. Williams, "The Opinions of Anthony Kennedy: No Time for Ideology," *American Bar Association Journal* 56 (March 1, 1988).

80 As quoted in Cohodas, "Kennedy Finds Bork an Easy Act to Follow," p. 1989.

81 *The Washington Post*, December 14, 1987, p. 20 and Cohodas, "Kennedy Hearings Indicate Easy Confirmation," 45 *Congressional Quarterly Weekly Report* 3129 (1987).

82 Biographical material on Justice Kennedy is taken from Perry's entry in *Encyclopedia of World Biography* Volume 17 (forthcoming).

83 As quoted by Cohodas, "Kennedy Hearings Indicate Easy Confirmation," p. 3129.

84 As quoted in *The Washington Post*, December 2, 1987, p. 3.

85 U.S. Congress, Senate, Committee on the Judiciary, *Report on the Nomination of Anthony M. Kennedy to Be an Associate Justice of the United States Supreme Court*, 100th Cong., 2d sess., 1988, p. 2.

86 See fn. 30, supra.

87 See fn. 29, supra.

88 *Skinner v. Railway Labor Executives*, 109 S.Ct. 1384 (1989) and *National Treasury Employees v. Von Raab*, 109 S.Ct. 1384 (1989).

89 See fn. 33, supra.

90 109 S.Ct. 2363 (1989).

91 See fn. 34, supra.

92 163 U.S. 537 (1896).

93 *Bowen v. Kendrick*, 108 S.Ct. 2562 (1988).

94 *Allegheny County v. Greater Pittsburgh ACLU*, 109 S.Ct. 3086 (1989).

95 See fn. 65, supra.

96 *Missouri v. Jenkins*, 58 LW 4480 (1990).

97 See fn. 34, supra.

98 See fn. 33, supra, for the five 1989 cases.

99 *The Supreme Court and the Idea of Progress* (New York: Harper & Row, 1970), p. 181.

References

Abraham, Henry J. *Freedom and the Court: Civil Rights and Liberties in the United States*, 5th ed. New York: Oxford University Press, 1988.

_____. *The Judicial Process: An Introductory Analysis of the Courts of the United States, England, and France*, 5th ed. New York: Oxford University Press, 1986.

_____. *Justices and Presidents: A Political History of Appointments to the Supreme Court*, 2d ed. New York: Oxford University Press, 1985.

"The Bork Nomination" Issue. 9 *Cardozo Law Review* 1 (1987-88).

Bork, Robert H. *The Tempting of America: The Political Seduction of the Law*. New York: Free Press, 1989.

Bronner, Ethan. *Battle for Justice: How the Bork Nomination Shook America*. New York: Norton, 1989.

Bryden, David P. "How to Select a Supreme Court Justice: The Case of Robert Bork." 57 *The American Scholar* 201 (1988).

Congressional Quarterly Weekly Report (1987-89).

Davis, Sue. *Justice Rehnquist and the Constitution*. Princeton: Princeton University Press, 1989.

Fallon, Richard H., Jr. "A Tribute to Lewis F. Powell, Jr." 101 *Harvard Law Review* 401 (1987-88).

Goldman, Sheldon. "Reagan's Judicial Legacy: Completing the Puzzle and Summing Up." 72 *Judicature* 318 (April-May 1989).

Griffin, Stephen M. "Politics and the Supreme Court: The Case of the Bork Nomination." V *The Journal of Law and Politics* 551 (Spring 1989).

McGuigan, P. B. and D. W. Weyrich. *Ninth Justice: The Fight for Bork.* Washington: Washington Legal Foundation, 1989.

Perry, Barbara A. "From Swing Vote to Tie-Breaker: Justice Anthony M. Kennedy's Initial Supreme Court Record." Paper presented at the Annual Meeting of the Southern Political Science Association, November 2-4, 1989, Memphis, Tennessee.

_____. "The Life and Death of the 'Catholic Seat' on the United States Supreme Court." VI *Journal of Law and Politics* 55 (Fall 1989).

Phillips, Kevin. "Bork/Ginsburg Foul-ups Expose Conservative Disarray." *The* (Louisville) *Courier-Journal.* November 29, 1987.

Scheb, John M. II and Lee W. Ailshie. "Justice Sandra Day O'Connor and the 'Freshman Effect.'" 69 *Judicature* 9 (June-July 1985).

U.S. Congress. Senate. Committee on the Judiciary. *Hearings on the Nomination of Anthony M. Kennedy to Be Associate Justice of the Supreme Court of the United States.* 100th Cong., 1st sess. 1987.

_____. Senate. Committee on the Judiciary. *Report on the Nomination of Anthony M. Kennedy to Be Associated Justice of the United States Supreme Court.* 100th Cong., 2d sess. 1988.

Williams, Charles F. "The Opinions of Anthony Kennedy: No Time for Ideology." *American Bar Association Journal* 56 (March 1988).

Williams, Marjorie and Al Kamen. "Sandra Day O'Connor, In Control." *The Washington Post Magazine* 22 (June 11, 1989).

Witt, Elder. *A Different Justice: Reagan and the Supreme Court.* Washington: Congressional Quarterly, 1986.

Wyszynski, James Edward, Jr. "In Praise of Judicial Restraint: The Jurisprudence of Justice Antonin Scalia," 1 *Detroit College Law Review* 117 (1989).

Leadership on the United States Supreme Court: Justices Who Have Made A Difference*

Sherman G. Finesilver

Leadership is not necessarily equated with greatness in our evaluation of Supreme Court Justices. As we will see, leadership is a quality that is gauged by different criteria in different fields. In science and medicine, diligence in research and success in making significant new discoveries often become badges of leadership. Dr. Albert Einstein and Dr. Jonas Salk illustrate scientific and medical leadership. In politics, it is often the great orator, the person who initiates needed legislation or shapes opinion, or the person who instigates profound change that history holds up to be a leader. Such persons include Sir Winston Churchill, President Abraham Lincoln, President Franklin Delano Roosevelt, President Harry S. Truman, and President John F. Kennedy. Leadership is generally considered to be the ability to move or direct a person or group in a positive way.[1] With Supreme Court Justices, our criteria are slightly different than in other fields.

In the legal profession, justices of the United States Supreme Court hold the preeminent positions in terms of status, prestige, and influence. These persons are leaders, celebrities, and clarifiers. Attorneys and lower court judges look to the Supreme Court for guidance. The opinions and other pronouncements issued by the Supreme Court shape the development of law. A seemingly inconsequential comment, sentence, or footnote can have profound impact when pronounced by one of the justices. By reason of their positions, justices have a rare opportunity to exercise leadership and achieve greatness through their judicial and quasi-judicial work. The nine justices have profound impact on how Americans live, work, transact business, and are educated, in addition to how Americans die as reflected in *Cruzan v. Mississippi*,[2] a case involving parental rights in the comatose fate of their daughter.

Certain characteristics serve as earmarks of determining leadership qualities of the justices. The important characteristics include clarity of writings, consistency of principles, the ability to shape public opinion, the ability to form a consensus on the Court, assistance rendered to the legal profession, and the lasting effect of the principles espoused by the justice.[3]

1. Clarity of Writings

The clarity of a justice's writings is a key element of leadership. Lower courts and practitioners carefully study the opinions of the Supreme Court. Every sentence, phrase, and footnote in Court opinions carries significant weight in the legal community. Wordy or sloppy opinions that fail to enunciate clearly the rule and rationale of the case tend to cause confusion and generate further litigation. By contrast, reasoned and clearly worded opinions guide the lower courts and practitioners, define the parameters of the holding, and anticipate problems and possible exceptions to the rule.

The writings of Justice Oliver Wendell Holmes exemplify the finest in judicial craftsmanship. Holmes' opinions are characterized by their brevity, originality, and freshness of style.[4] It was Justice Holmes who coined many of the standard quotations in legal literature, for example, "clear and present danger".[5] Moreover, Justice Holmes' opinions frequently place legal principles in the context of history.[6] By placing law in an historical context, Justice Holmes made his opinions informative and insightful beyond the mere enunciation of legal principles.

Named to the Supreme Court in 1902, Justice Holmes served until 1932, when he was 91 years old. He made lasting doctrine in his defense of the right of every citizen under the First Amendment to free speech, up to but not including "falsely shouting fire in a theater and causing a panic."

Clarity of style and brevity also characterize the work of Justice Louis D. Brandeis.[7] In his precisely crafted opinions, Justice Brandeis sought not only to enunciate the law, but also to instruct and teach. There is little dout as to the ruling in a Brandeis opinion.[8]

Any discussion of clarity and quality in Supreme Court opinions inevitably brings up the name of Justice William J. Brennan, Jr. Chief Justice Earl Warren wrote in 1966: "In the entire history of the Court, it would be difficult to name another Justice who wrote more important opinions in his first ten years than has [Justice Brennan]."[9] Scholars commend Justice Brennan's opinions for "regularly reveal[ing] the skill of a craftsman."[10] Although style is important, style only complements the substantive import of a justice's writings.[11]

2. Consistency of Principles

Leadership in a justice often manifests itself through the justice's consistent adherence to and advocacy of certain principles. By holding and applying consistent principles, a justice develops a judicial philosophy and retains a sense of humanity and compassion. Of course, by holding consistent principles, a Justice must not be reluctant to reevaluate *stare decisis* in order to correct past injustices, make the law responsive to contemporary mores and values, and promote respect for the law by rethinking antiquated ideas.

Chief Justice John Marshall expounded the most fundamental constitutional principles regarding the relationship between the federal and state governments and between the branches of the federal government. Indeed, he framed the initial contours of judicial activities under the constitutional boundaries frequently referred to today. His vision as to the judicial function is masterful. The decisions of Justice Marshall and the Marshall Court reflect three concerns: first, the need for a strong federal government; second, the need to control federal abuses through a system of checks and balances; and third, the need to have a strong and independent federal judiciary.

Chief Justice Marshall addressed the second and third concerns in *Marbury v. Madison*.[12]   In *Marbury*, Chief Justice Marshall established the concept of judicial review, with the Court serving as the ultimate arbiter of the Constitution. Although the impeachment of judges was common at the time and the executive and legislative branches opposed judicial review, Marshall skillfully used this first foray into the realm of judicial review to reach a result in harmony with the Jefferson administration's position.[13]

Justice Marshall's opinions relating to federal-state relations profoundly and permanently reshaped our political landscape. In *McCulloch v. Maryland*,[14] Chief Justice Marshall invalidated a state tax against a federally-chartered national bank, holding that the necessary and proper clause gave Congress wide latitude to implement the enumerated powers and State laws that interfered with the exercise of those powers were invalid. In *Cohens v. Virginia*,[15] Justice Marshall repeated the technique used in *Marbury* to establish the authority of the Supreme Court to review state criminal proceedings while upholding the state's prosecution.[16] Likewise, in *Gibbons v. Ogden*,[17] Chief Justice Marshall examined the scope of federal and state powers under the commerce clause. Justice Marshall held that federal power to regulate commerce superseded the power of states to regulate commerce when the commerce concerned more than one case. In each of these decisions, Chief Justice Marshall worked to create a strong and independent federal judiciary and to define the federal-state relationship in such a way that the federal government would be able to unite the states in the experiment of government by constitution. Recognizing the unique historical role of John Marshall, the principles of later justices take shape within the framework crafted by Justice Marshall.

Justice Louis D. Brandeis stands as a one of the Court's most principled jurists.   The principles that defined Justice Brandeis were his unwavering belief in the individual, his support for the weak and less fortunate, and his fervent opposition to the aggrandizement and abuse of power.[18]

Chief Justice Earl Warren also exemplifies this commitment to principle. Every citizen mattered to this exemplary judicial leader, regardless of race, creed, color, national origin, religion, gender, or other attributes. To Chief Justice Warren, legal doctrine, precedent, and institutional concepts must be balanced against considerations of fairness, justice, and ideals of liberty.[19] As one commentator has noted, Chief Justice Warren's leadership "brought the law more nearly into accord with the best and truest aspirations of the American people."[20]

Few decisions in American legal history underscore this commitment to principle better than *Brown v. Board of Education*.[21] In *Brown*, the Court rejected *Plessy v. Ferguson*,[22] the case that gave constitutional approval to the "separate, but equal" doctrine. Indirectly, the Court also rejected the rationale of the Court's regrettable decisions upholding the internment of Japanese-Americans during World War II.[23] These decisions marked a low point in judicial interpretation. All justices on the Court must share the blame for the insensibility and lack of fairness extended to fellow Americans who happened to have certain ethnic and racial origins.

The position that Chief Justice Warren took in *Brown v. Board of Education* set the tenor of judicial activities for the 16 years he served as Chief Justice. He was the catalyst on the Court in a unanimous decision to outlaw racial segregation in public schools. Likewise, Chief Justice Warren's opinion in *Miranda v. Arizona*[24] fortified the rights of criminal suspects. The *Miranda* decision remains a cornerstone of the rights of persons accused of crimes. Chief Justice Warren and Holmes are listed among the 100 most important Americans of the 20th Century.[25]

Any discussion of principles as a basis for Supreme Court leadership would be incomplete without mention of Justice William Brennan. In tribute to his colleague, Justice Thurgood Marshall commended Justice Brennan's "consistent legal vision . . . based on an unwavering commitment to certain core principles, especially first amendment freedoms and basic principles of civil rights and civil liberties."[26] Justice Brennan had the rare ability to craft an opinion that laid a logical foundation for later decisions.[27] He contributed a unique and substantive vision of the role that speech plays in our country. To many, he is perhaps the most singular architect of the Bill of Rights in modern times. The principles attributed to Justice Brennan are reflected in his persistent opposition to capital punishment,[28] his regard for voting rights,[29] and his interest in the special problems of women in society.[30]

3. Shaping Public Opinion

Justices also exercise leadership by taking the initiative to shape and lead public opinion. Justices may use several methods to change public opinion. First, the opinions issued by the Court may change unjust or offensive laws in advance of a change in public opinion. Second, by participating in extrajudicial activities, such as lecturing at bar association meetings, law schools, and other forums, justices can propose new approaches to legal problems, advocate reforms, and persuade attorneys, judges, and laypersons to experiment with solutions.

Chief Justice Warren is among the justices whose vision served to change the law in advance of public opinion. *Brown v. Board of Education*[31] and its progeny inaugurated the beginning of the end of segregation in America. Despite the anger aimed at the Chief Justice over his opinions in *Brown*, the Chief Justice and the Warren Court remained faithful to the principle of equality for all citizens.

During his tenure, Chief Justice Warren E. Burger adroitly used the second method of shaping public opinion. Through his active participation in the Judicial Conference of the United States, the Federal Judicial Center, and other legal forums, Chief Justice Burger played a critical leadership role by focusing the attention of the legal profession on issues sorely in need of reform, such as judicial administration and alternative dispute resolution.[32] His leadership improved professionalism of lawyers, and his discouragement of frivolous lawsuits set in motion routine debate and action.

4. Consensus Building on the Court

Justices also exercise leadership through consensus building on the Court. Controversial and innovative decisions carry more weight and better stand the test of time when a unanimous or near-unanimous Court joins in the decision. Consensus building also permits the creation of coalitions of justices united by common principles that direct the evolution of the law toward certain shared goals. The expectation that certain justices will form a voting bloc on the Court or serve as consensus builders frequently fails.[33]

Consensus building was a trait critical to the success of Chief Justice John Marshall. Justice Marshall pioneered the single opinion written on behalf of the entire Court.[34] The ability to achieve unanimity gave creditbility and legitimacy to the Court during its formative years when the allocation of power among the three branches of government remained largely unsettled.[35] Justice Lewis Powell has commented on the negative effect of splintered opinions, noting that:

> Splintered decisions provide insufficient guidance for lower courts. They may promote disrespect for the Court as a whole and more emphasis on "vote counting." Failure of the Court to settle on a rationale for a decision invites perpetual attack and reexamination.[36]

Perhaps the most remarkable trait of Chief Justice Warren was his ability to forge coalitions on difficult and divisive issues. Although the "with all deliberate speed" language of the second *Brown* opinion[37] may be criticized for vagueness and for affording states and municipalities an escape clause, the unanimity of the *Brown* decisions, which resulted from Chief Justice Warren's careful compromise and consensus building, has contributed immeasurably to the lasting impact of those decisions on the American legal landscape.

5. Assistance to the Legal Profession

Justices demonstrate extra-judicial leadership by taking initiatives to assist the legal profession. Lectures and participation in other bar-oriented events create a rapport between the bench and bar. Furthermore, justices, particularly the Chief Justice, have the opportunity to create and participate in committees to address specific problems in the legal profession. As the law becomes more complex and specialized, such endeavors provide invaluable assistance to the bar.

Chief Justice Warren Burger stands out as the finest example of a justice committed to active interaction with the bar. Chief Justice Rehnquist wrote that "[Chief Justice Burger] felt a responsibility not merely for federal judges, . . . but for the entire legal profession in the United States."[38]   Chief Justice Burger believed that a competent and well-trained bench and bar were required to give effect to the Court's pronouncements.[39]   As Chief Justice Rehnquist noted, "[p]erhaps no Chief Justice before him carried on such a dialogue with the bar about the current condition of the legal profession."[40]

Specifically, Chief Justice Burger devoted himself tirelessly to the improvement of judicial administration.[41]   Chief Justice Burger fought to modernize court management, promote arbitration as an alternative to litigation, to increase legal education in lawyering skills, and to expand prison employment for inmates.[42]   The Chief Justice chaired the Judicial Conference of the United States and actively promoted both the Federal Judicial Center and the American Inns of Court program.[43] Through his example, Chief Justice Burger demonstrated how a contemporary justice can promote change and reform by interacting with the legal profession and assisting the bar. Chief Justice Burger also enjoyed unparalleled popularity among the nation's federal and state judges and maintained frequent correspondence with members of the federal judiciary.

6. Lasting Effect of Principles

Finally, leadership in justices can be measured by the lasting effect of the principles that they espouse. A justice whose principles remain a potent force long after the justice's passing is a person whose foresight and vision command respect.

To this day, Chief Justice Marshall's views on judicial review, a strong and independent judiciary, and federal-state relations remain cornerstones of American legal thought and constitutional jurisprudence. The power and prestige of the judiciary and the ability of judges and justices to exercise leadership derive from the vision expounded by Chief Justice Marshall and the Marshall Court.

The jurisprudence of Justice Holmes continues to exercise considerable influence on contemporary legal thought.[44] Holmes' tripartite theory of tort law based on damage, foreseeability, and just cause or excuse is embedded in contemporary tort law.[45]   In his opinions, Justice Holmes frequently deferred to the viewpoints of others, including the legislature and private individuals.[46] This predisposition toward deference makes Holmes a model for proponents of judicial restraint. Finally, Justice Holmes' emphasis on judicial pragmatism led him to write his famous dissent in *Lochner v. New York*,[47] a dissent that laid the cornerstone for undermining natural law as a judicial consideration.[48] Through his work, Justice Holmes educated the profession.   Justice Holmes' commitment to the legal profession was summarized by the Justice himself when he said:

> Law is a business to which my life is devoted, and I should show less than devotion if I did not do what in me lies to improve it, and when I perceive what seems to me to be the ideal of its future, if I hesitated to point it out and press toward it with all my heart.[49]

Although his voice increasingly became the voice of dissent in his later years on the Court, Justice Brennan's concern for the individual and respect for human dignity promises to leave a lasting mark on American jurisprudence.[50] Even Justice Brennan's conservative critics recognized that "there is no individual in this country, on or off the Court, who has had a more profound and sustained impact upon public policy in the United States" over the past twenty-five years.[51]

7. Leadership by Lower-Court Judges:
The Example of Learned Hand

It is important to recognize that leadership in the judiciary may be exercised not only by Justices of the United States Supreme Court, but also by lower federal court judges and state court judges. Despite the fact that he never received an appointment to the Supreme Court, Judge Learned Hand demonstrates that lower court judges may exercise leadership. Judge Hand's scholarship, clarity of writings, principles, and keen insight into the role of judges make him one of the pillars of the legal profession.

Judge Hand succinctly expressed his judicial philosophy when he wrote:

> The judge must . . . find out the will of the government from words which are chosen from common speech and which had better not attempt to provide for every possible contingency . . . [W]hat he really does is to take the language before him, whether it be from a statute or from the decision of a former judge, and try to find out what the government, or his predecessor, would have done, if the case before him had been before them . . . [I]t is not enough for the judge just to use a dictionary . . . [O]n the one hand, he cannot go beyond what has been said, because he is bound to enforce existing commands and only those; on the other, he cannot suppose that what has been said should clearly frustrate or leave unexecutive its own purpose.[52]

Judge Hand, recognizing the limits and the dangers inherent in his approach to judging, cautioned judges against excessive activism when he wrote:

> When a judge tries to find out what the government would have intended which it did not say, he puts into its mouth things which he thinks it ought to have said, and that is very close to substituting what he himself thinks right. Let him beware, however, or he will usurp the office of government, even though in a small way he must do so in order to execute its real commands at all . . . [T]he judge must always remember that he should go no further than he is sure the government would have gone, had it been faced with the case before him. If he is in doubt, he must stop, for he cannot tell that the conflicting interests in the society for which he speaks would have come to a just result, even though he is sure that he knows what the just result should be. He is not to substitute even his just will for theirs; otherwise it would not be the common will which prevails, and to that extent the people would not govern.[53]

Judge Hand enunciated certain principles that all judges would do well to follow. To Judge Hand, the courts should speak clearly and persuasively to laypersons. Judges should make the law an effective instrument of justice without becoming crusaders. Finally, judges should be fair and reflective when subjected to various contradictory pressures and should never take themselves too seriously. Judge Hand summarized his philosophy in the context of discussing the spirit of liberty:

What then is the spirit of liberty? I cannot define it; I can only tell you my own faith. The spirit of liberty is the spirit which is not too sure that it is right; the spirit of liberty is the spirit which seeks to understand the minds of other men and women; the spirit of liberty is the spirit which weighs their interests alongside its own without bias; the spirit of liberty remembers that not even a sparrow falls to earth unheeded; the spirit of libery is the spirit of Him who, near two thousand years ago, taught mankind that lesson it has never learned, but has never quite forgotten; that there may be a kingdom where the least shall be heard and considered side by side with the greatest.[54]

The words of Judge Hand should inspire every judge on the federal and state benches to approach his or her job with the diligence and humility that will earn respect for the courts and the legal profession.

Conclusion

This essay has explored various characteristics of judicial leadership and greatness and the justices who best reflect those attributes. How we identify leadership characteristics and determine greatness in Supreme Court justices is important, because the role that justices play are examples for the entire legal profession. A justice who aspires to distinction in each of the categories discussed above will earn the respect of colleagues, assist in the positive development of the law, and become a model for other judges and attorneys. Furthermore, the legal profession is improved when judges and justices alike write with clarity and precision, enunciate consistent principles, demonstrate courage to defend their principles, and work to build consensus, shape public opinion, and assist the legal profession. Their potential for strengthening judicial and decision making bodies is immeasurable and is often overlooked by the personalities involved.

Notes

* The author acknowledges with appreciation the excellent support of David A. Stein, Esq., in the preparation of this essay.

1 A noted author on leadership states: "Leadership is the process of persuasion or example by which an individual (or leadership team) induces a group to pursue objectives held by the leader or shared by the leader and his or her followers." John W. Gardner, On Leadership 1 (1990).

2 110 S. Ct. 2841 (1990).

3 There are other attributes of significance that also are considerations, but not discussed here, such as analytical powers, judicial temperament, professional integrity, an agile and keen mind, educational background, fairness and impartiality, a principled understanding of the proper judicial role of judges under our Constitution, diligence, and industry.

4 McKinnon, *The Secret of Mr. Justice Holmes*, in the Supreme Court and its Justices 72, 85 (Jesse H. Choper ed., 1987).

5 *Id.*

6 Wigmore, *Justice Holmes and the Law of Torts*, 29 Harv. L. Rev. 601, 604-5 (1916).

7 Resolution, *Mr. Justice Brandeis*, 317 U.S. xi (1942), *reprinted in* 1 Memorials of the Justices of the Supreme Court of the United States 167, 173 (R. Jacobs compiler 1981).

8 reund, *Mr. Justice Brandeis*, 317 U.S. xi (1942), *reprinted in* 1 Memorials of the Justices of the Supreme Court of the United States 185, 187 (R. Jacobs compiler 1981).

9 Warren, *Mr. Justice Brennan*, 80 Harv. L. Rev. 1, 2 (1966).

10 Dorsen, *A Tribute to Justice William J. Brennan, Jr.*, 104 Harv. L. Rev. 15, 20-21 (1990).

11 Justice Brennan's seminal opinions include *New York Times Co. v. Sullivan*, 376 U.S. 254 (1964), and *Baker v. Carr*, 369 U.S. 186 (1962).

12 5 U.S. (1 Cranch) 137 (1803).

13 Gordon, *John Marshall: A Judicial Pioneer, contained in* The Supreme Court and its Justices at 30, 36-37 (Jesse H. Choper, ed. 1987); Nowak, Rotunda & Young, Constitutional Law at 2-7 (West 1978).

14 17 U.S. (4 Wheat.) 316 (1819).

15 19 U.S. (6 Wheat.) 264 (1821).

16 Gordon, *John Marshall: A Judicial Pioneer, contained in* The Supreme Court and its Justices at 30, 45 (Jesse H. Choper, ed. 1987); Nowak, Rotunda & Young, Constitutional Law at 18 (West 1978).

17 22 U.S. (9 Wheat.) 1 (1824).

18 Hand, *Mr. Justice Brandeis*, 317 U.S. xi (1942), *reprinted in* 1 Memorials of the Justices of the Supreme Court of the United States 177, 178-80 (R. Jacobs compiler 1981); Freund, *Mr. Justice Brandeis*, 317 U.S. xi (1942), *reprinted in* 1 Memorials of the Justices of the Supreme Court of the United States 185, 185-86 (R. Jacobs compiler 1981); Norris, *Mr. Justice Brandeis*, 317 U.S. xi (1942), *reprinted in* 1 Memorials of the Justices of the Supreme Court of the United States 191, 191-93 (R. Jacobs compiler 1981).

19 Cox, *Chief Justice Earl Warren*, 83 Harv. L. Rev. 1, 2 (1969).

20 *Id*. at 3.

21 347 U.S. 483 (1954), and 349 U.S. 294 (1955).

22 163 U.S. 537 (1896).

23 *Ex parte Endo*, 323 U.S. 283 (1944); *Korematsu v. United States*, 323 U.S. 214 (1944); *Hirabiyashi v. United States*, 320 U.S. 81 (1943).

24 384 U.S. 436 (1966).

25 *Life*, Fall 1990, at 87.

26 Marshall, *A Tribute to Justice William J. Brennan, Jr.*, 104 Harv. L. Rev. 1, 1-2 (1990).

27 Laurence H. Tribe, *Justice William J. Brennan Jr.: Architect of the Bill of Rights*, 77 A.B.A. 47, 48 (February 1991).

28 *See McGautha v. California*, 402 U.S. 183 (1971); *Furman v. Georgia*, 408 U.S. 238 (1972) (Brennan, J., concurring).

29 *See Baker v. Carr*, 369 U.S. 186 (1962).

30 *See Frontiero v. Richardson*, 411 U.S. 677 (1973); *Craig v. Boren*, 429 U.S. 190 (1976).

31   347 U.S. 483 (1954), and 349 U.S. 294 (1955).

32   Rehnquist, *A Tribute to Chief Justice Warren E. Burger*, 100 Harv L. Rev. 969, 969-70 (1987).

33   Paul M. Barrett, *Despite Expectations, Scalia Fails to Unify Conservatives on Court*, Wall St. J., April 28, 1992, at A1, A6.

34   Gordon, *John Marshall: A Judicial Pioneer, contained in* The Supreme Court and its Justices at 30, 36 (Jesse H. Choper, ed. 1987).

35   *Id.*

36   Justice Lewis F. Powell, Jr., Stare Decisis and Judicial Restraint, Speech Before the Association of the Bar of the City of New York (October 17, 1989), *in* Vital Speeches of the Day, November 15, 1989, at 70, 73.

37   349 U.S. at 301.

38   Rehnquist, *A Tribute to Chief Justice Warren E. Burger*, 100 Harv. L. Rev. 969, 969 (1987).

39   *Id.*

40   *Id.* at 970.

41   *Id.* at 969-970.

42   Cannon, *A Tribute to Chief Justice Warren E. Burger*, 100 Harv. L. Rev. 984, 985 (1987).

43   Rehnquist, *A Tribute to Chief Justice Warren E. Burger*, 100 Harv. L. Rev. 969, 969-70 (1987).

44   *See, e.g.,* Hantzis, *Legal Innovation Within the Wider Intellectual Tradition: The Pragmatism of Oliver Wendell Holmes, Jr.*, 82 N.W.U.L. Rev. 541, 543 (1988) ("Hantzis").

45   *See* Wigmore, *Justice Holmes and the Law of Torts*, 29 Harv. L. Rev. 601, 608 (1916).

46   Hantzis, 82 N.W.U.L. Rev. at 590-91.

47   198 U.S. 45, 74 (1904).

48   McKinnon, *The Secret of Mr. Justice Holmes*, in the Supreme Court and its Justices 72, 80-84 (Jesse H. Choper ed., 1987).

49   Vanderbilt, *The Five Functions of the Lawyer, reprinted in* The Lawyer's Treasury 211, 222 (Eugene C. Gerhart ed. 1956).

50 *See* Dorsen, *A Tribute to Justice William J. Brennan, Jr.*, 104 Harv. L. Rev. 15, 21-22 (1990).

51 Markman & Regnery, *The Mind of Justice Brennan: A 25-Year Tribute*, Nat'l Rev. at 30, May 15, 1984.

52 *The Spirit of Liberty*, Papers and Addresses of Learned Hand at 106-07 (Dillard ed., 1974).

53 *Id*. at 108-09.

54 *Id*. at 190.

Select Bibliography

Brenda J. Cox

Great Justices

(1) John Marshall (1755-1835)

Provizer, Norman W. "Principles and Practice: John Marshall and the Foundations of Judicial Power in America," in William D. Pederson and Ann McLaurin, eds. *The Rating Game in America*. (NY: Irvington Publishers, 1987), pp. 247-261.

Stites, Francis N. *John Marshall: Defender of the Court*. Glenview, IL: Scott Foresman, 1981.

White, Edward G. *The Marshall Court and Cultural Change, 1815-1835*. N.Y.: Oxford University Press, 1991.

Baker, Leonard. *John Marshall: A Life in Law*. N.Y.: MacMillan, 1974.

(2) Roger Brooke Taney (1777-1864)

Holland, Kenneth M. "Roger Taney," in Morton J. Frisch and Richard G. Stevens, eds. *American Political Thought*, 2nd ed. (Itasca, IL: Peacock Publishers, 1983), pp. 170-184.

(3) Joseph Story (1779-1845)

McClellan, James. *Joseph Story and the American Constitution: A Study in Political and Legal Thought*. Norman: University of Oklahoma Press, 1990.

Newmyer, R. Kent. *Supreme Court Justice Joseph Story: Statesman of the Old Republic.* Chapel Hill: University of North Carolina Press, 1986.

(4) John Marshall Harlan, I. (1833-1911)

Beth, Loren. *John Marshall Harlan. The Last Whig.* Lexington: University of Kentucky Press, 1992.

Clark, Floyd B. *Constitutional Doctrines of Justice Harlan.* Baltimore: Johns Hopkins University, 1915.

Przybyszewski, Linda C. A. "Evolution of a Supreme Court Justice," *The Times* (Shrevesport, LA), November 14, 1990, p. 6A.

White, G. Edward. "John Marshall Harlan, I: The Precursor." *American Journal of Legal History.* vol. 19, no. 1 (January, 1975).

(5) Oliver Wendell Holmes, Jr. (1841-1935)

Aichele, Gary J. *Oliver Wendell Holmes, Jr.: Soldier, Scholar, Judge.* Boston: G. K. Hall, 1989.

Baker, Liva. *The Justice from Beacon Hill: The Life and Times of Oliver Wendell Holmes.* New York: Harper Collins, 1991.

Cohen, Jeremy. *Congress Shall Make No Law: Oliver Wendell Holmes, the First Amendment and Judicial Decision-Making.* Ames, IA: Iowa State University Press, 1989.

Novick, Sheldon M. *Honorable Justice: The Life of Oliver Wendell Holmes.* Boston: Little, Brown, 1989.

Pohlman, H. L. *Justice Oliver Wendell Holmes & Utilitarian Jurisprudence.* Cambridge: Harvard University Press, 1984.

Shriver, Harry C. *What Holmes Wrote, and What Has Been Written About Him, a Bibliography 1866-1976.* Annapolis, MD: Fox Hills Press, 1978.

White, G. Edward. *Justice Oliver Wendell Holmes: Law and the Inner Self*. New York: Oxford University Press, 1993.

(6) Louis D. Brandeis. (1856-1941)

Allon, Gal. *Brandeis of Boston*. Cambridge: Harvard University Press, 1980.

Baker, Leonard. *Brandeis and Frankfurter: A Dual Biography*. N.Y.: Harper & Row, 1984.

Baskerville, Stephen W. *Of Laws and Limitations: An Intellectual Portrait of Louis Dembitz Brandeis*. New Jersey: Fairleigh Dickenson University Press, 1994.

Burt, Robert A. *Two Jewish Justices: Outcasts in the Promised Land*. Berkeley: University of California Press, 1988.

Mersky, Roy M., ed. *Louis Dembitz Brandeis 1856-1941, a Bibliography*. Littleton, CO: Rothman, 1987.

Strum, Philippa. *Louis D. Brandeis: Justice for the People*. Cambridge: Harvard University Press, 1984.

Urofsky, Melvin I. *Louis D. Brandeis and the Progressive Tradition in America*. Boston: Little, Brown and Co., 1981.

(7) Benjamin Cardozo (1870-1938)

Pollard, Joseph P. *Mr. Justice Cardozo: A Liberal Mind in Action*. Westport, CT: Greenwood Press, 1970.

Posner, Richard A. *Cardozo: A Study in Reputation*. Chicago: University of Chicago Press, 1990.

(8) Charles Evans Hughes. (1862-1948)

Perkins, Dexter. *Charles Evans Hughes and American Democratic Statesmanship*. Westport, CT: Greenwood Press, 1978.

(9) Hugo L. Black (1886-1971)

Ball, Howard and Phillip J. Cooper. *Of Power and Right: Hugo Black, William O. Douglas, and America's Constitutional Revolution.* N.Y.: Oxford University Press, 1991.

Simon, James F. *The Antagonists: Hugo Black, Felix Frankfurter and Civil Liberties in Modern America.* N.Y.: Simon & Shuster, 1989.

(10) Felix Frankfurter (1882-1965)

Parrish, Michael E. *The Enigma of Felix Frankfurter.* N.Y.: Basic Books, 1981.

Silverstein, Mark. *Constitutional Faiths: Felix Frankfurter, Hugo Black and the Process of Judicial Decision-Making.* Ithaca, N.Y.: Cornell University Press, 1984.

Urofsky, Melvin I. *Felix Frankfurter: Judicial Restraint and Individual Liberties.* Boston: Twayne Publishers, 1991.

(11) Harlan F. Stone (1872-1946)

Mason, Alpheus T. *Harlan Fiske Stone: Pillar of the Law.* N.Y.: Viking Press, 1956.

(12) Earl Warren (1891-1974)

White, G. Edward. *Earl Warren: A Public Life.* N.Y.: Viking Press, 1956.

(13) Other Justices

Boles, Donald. *Mr. Justice Rehnquist: Judicial Activist.* Ames, IA: Iowa State University Press, 1980.

Brisbin, Richard A., Jr. "Justice Antonin Scalia, Constitutional Discourse, and the Legalistic State." *Western Political Quarterly.* vol. 44, no. 4 (December 1991), pp. 1005-1038.

Bosmajian, Haig. *Justice Douglas and Freedom of Speech.* N.Y.: Scarecrow Press, 1980.

Davis, Sue. *Justice Rehnquist and the Constitution*. Princeton, NJ: Princeton University Press, 1989.

Eisler, Kim I. *A Justice for All. William J. Brennan*. N.Y.: Simon and Schuster, 1993.

Hopkins, W. Wat. *Mr. Justice Brennan and Freedom of Expression*. N.Y.: Praeger Publications, 1991.

Jefferies, Jr., John C. *Justice Lewis F. Powell, Jr. and the Era of Judicial Balance*. N.Y.: Scribner, 1994.

Pederson, William D. "U.S. Chief Justice Edward Douglass White and the Path to Individual Power," in Norman W. Provizer and William D. Pederson, eds., *Grassroots Constitutionalism*. (Lanham, MD: University Press of America, 1988), pp. 69-76.

Steamer, Robert J. *Chief Justice*. Columbia: University of South Carolina Press, 1986.

White, G. Edward. *The American Judicial Tradition: Profiles of Leading American Judges*. N.Y.: Oxford University Press, 1988.

Great Cases

Clinton, Robert L. *Marbury v. Madison and Judicial Review*. Lawrence: University Press of Kansas, 1989.

Garrow, David J. *Liberty and Sexuality: The Right to Privacy and the Making of Roe v. Wade*. N.Y.: Macmillan, 1994.

Irons, Peter. *The Courage of Their Convictions*. N.Y.: Penguin Books, 1988.

Kens, Paul. *Judicial Power and Reform Politics: The Anatomy of Lochner v. NY*. Lawrence: University Press of Kansas, 1990.

Lewis, Anthony. *Gideon's Trumpet*. N.Y.: Vintage Books, 1964.

_____. *Make No Law: The Sullivan Case and the First Amendment.* N.Y.: Random House, 1991.

Lofgren, Charles A. *The Plessy Case.* N.Y.: Oxford University Press, 1987.

Polenberg, Richard. *Fighting Faiths: The Abrams Case, the Supreme Court and Free Speech.* N.Y.: Penguin Books, 1987.

Sindler, Allan P. *Bakke, DeFunis, and Minority Admissions: The Quest for Equal Opportunity.* N.Y.: Longman, 1978.

Superlawyers

Clifford, Clark and Richard Holbrooke. *Counsel to the President: A Memoir.* N.Y.: Random House, 1991.

Hoffman, Nicholas von. *Citizen Cohn.* N.Y.: Doubleday, 1988.

Thomas, Evan. *The Man to See: Edward Bennett Williams, Ultimate Insider, Legendary Trial Lawyer.* N.Y.: Simon & Shuster, 1991.

Tierney, Kevin. *Darrow: A Biography.* N.Y.: Thomas Y. Crowell, 1979.

Weinberg, Arthur and Lila. *Clarence Darrow: A Sentimental Rebel.* N.Y.: Atheneum, 1987.

Lawyer-Presidents

Abraham, Henry W. *Justices and Presidents: A Political History of Appointments to the Supreme Court.* N.Y.: Oxford University Press, 1974.

Burton, David H. *William Howard Taft: In the Public Service.* Melbourne, FLA: Krieger, 1985.

Dewey, Frank L. *Thomas Jefferson, Lawyer.* Charlottesville: University of Virginia Press, 1986.

Dumbauld, Edward. *Thomas Jefferson and the Law.* Norman OK: University of Oklahoma Press, 1978.

Green, Thomas M. and William D. Pederson. "Behavior of Lawyer-Presidents: A 'Barberian' Link," *The Barberian Presidency.* (N.Y.: Peter Lang, 1989.), pp. 153-167.

Mason, Alpheus T. *William Howard Taft: Chief Justice.* Lanham, MD: University Press of America, 1983.

Matthews, Elizabeth W. *Lincoln as a Lawyer: An Annotated Bibliography.* Carbondale, IL: Southern Illinois University Press, 1991.

Ross, William G. "The Legal Career of John Q. Adams," *Akron Law Review,* vol. 23, no. 3 (Spring, 1990), pp. 415-453.

Reference Works

Blaustein, Albert P. and Roy M. Mersky. *The First 100 Justices: Statistical Studies on the Supreme Court of the United States.* Hamden, CT: Archon Books, 1978.

Congressional Quarterly, Inc. *Congressional Quarterly's Guide to the U.S. Supreme Court.* Washington, D.C.: Congressional Quarterly, 1979.

Cushman, Clare, ed. *The Supreme Court Justices. Illustrated Biographies, 1789-1993.* Washington, D.C.: Congressional Quarterly, 1993.

Epstein, Lee, Jeffrey A. Segal, Harold J. Spaeth, and Thomas G. Walker. *The Supreme Court Compendium. Data, Decisions, and Development.* Washington, D.C.: Congressional Quarterly, 1994.

Hall, Kermit L., ed. *The Oxford Companion to the Supreme Court of the United States*. New York: Oxford University Press, 1992.

Martin, Fenton S. and Robert U. Goehlert. *The U.S. Supreme Court: A Bibliography*. Washington, D.C.: Congressional Quarterly, 1990.

Shayerson, Robert. *The Illustrated History of the Supreme Court of the United States*. N.Y.: Harry N. Abrams, 1986.

Urofsky, Melvin I. *The Supreme Court Justices. A Biographical Dictionary*. Hamden, CT: Garland Publishing, 1994.

Index